ARDUOUS JOURNEY

ARDUOUS JOURNEY

canadian indians and decolonization

edited by

J. RICK PONTING

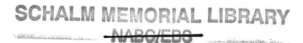
McClelland and Stewart

McClelland and Stewart Limited
The Canadian Publishers
481 University Avenue
Toronto, Ontario
M5G 2E9

Canadian Cataloguing in Publication Data
Main entry under title:
Arduous journey: Canadian Indians and decolonization

Includes bibliographical references.
ISBN 0-7710-7037-3

1. Indians of North America – Canada – Government relations – Addresses, essays, lectures.   2. Indians of North America – Canada – Economic conditions – Addresses, essays, lectures.   3. Indians of North America – Canada – Social conditions – Addresses, essays, lectures.   I. Ponting, J. Rick.

E92.A73 1986   971 '.00497   C86-093427-6

Maps 1 and 2: James Loates Illustrating

Printed and bound in Canada by T.H. Best Ltd.

Contents

Part One   Introduction

Part Two   Economic and Community Development

List of Maps

List of Tables

List of Figures

Contributors

THOMAS BERGER is a former Justice of the Supreme Court of British Columbia and former leader of the New Democratic Party of British Columbia. As a lawyer he represented the Nishga Indians in a land claims case before the Supreme Court of Canada, the outcome of which led the government of Canada to recognize aboriginal rights. As Commissioner of the Mackenzie Valley Pipeline Inquiry he established procedural precedents of fairness and openness that have won him international acclaim.

HAROLD DYCK received his Ph.D. in management studies from Stanford University in California. In the 1960s he held academic appointments at the University of California at Berkeley and at the University of British Columbia. In 1971 he joined the federal public service as director of policy planning in a Crown corporation. He later served as a deputy minister in the government of Saskatchewan. Since 1978 he has conducted his own management and policy consulting business from his base in Ottawa. He has been deeply involved with Indian groups at all levels.

JAMES FRIDERES is a sociology professor at the University of Calgary. He is author of one of the first textbooks in contemporary native studies and co-editor of the journal *Canadian Ethnic Studies*. He has taught and published widely on various aspects of Canadian ethnic relations, especially native peoples. He teaches a course on the Canadian North.

ROGER GIBBINS is one of the few political scientists in Canada who has done research and writing on the topic of Indians in the Canadian political system. He has published numerous articles and books on Canadian politics and was joint author of an earlier book on Indian affairs in Canada. He has served frequently as a government consultant and political commentator on radio and television. He teaches courses on radical politics, native politics, and Canadian politics at the University of Calgary, where he is director of the Research Unit for Public Policy Studies.

KATHLEEN JAMIESON was born and raised in the Hebrides. She has lived for long periods in different cultures, including six years in

Chile, where her interest in aboriginal peoples was first triggered. She holds an M.A. degree in history and philosophy from the University of Edinburgh, a Diploma of Art from Edinburgh College of Art, and has returned to school to pursue a Master's degree in social anthropology from Carleton and Simon Fraser universities. Since 1977 she has worked extensively as an independent researcher with several native women's groups and associations in community-based research projects concerning socio-economic conditions, employment development, and alcohol and drug abuse.

Sister DEIRDRE JORDAN is presently chair of the Department of Education at the University of Adelaide in Australia. She has an extensive record as an author and consultant on aboriginal education in Australia. In 1985 she conducted a study tour through Canada, Alaska, and Fennoscandia to research the status of aboriginal education in these various countries.

LEROY LITTLE BEAR, a member of the Blood tribe of southern Alberta, was founding chairman of the Department of Native American Studies at the University of Lethbridge in Alberta. A lawyer and member of the Canadian Native Lawyers Association, he is consulted frequently by indigenous peoples organizations, government, and international organizations on aboriginal matters. On his own or with colleagues he has authored or edited various works on aboriginal peoples in Canada.

CAM MACKIE is presently co-ordinator of the federal government's Native Economic Development Program and was a senior executive (assistant deputy minister) in the federal Department of Indian Affairs in the late 1970s. Trained in community development at the University of Manitoba, he has studied at the London Graduate School of Business Studies and at the International Management Institute in Geneva.

J. RICK PONTING teaches courses on Canadian society and public policy in the Department of Sociology at the University of Calgary, where he was founding director of the Research Unit for Public Policy Studies. He has authored or co-authored a book and various articles on Indians in Canada, including articles issuing from his national survey (with R. Gibbins) of nonIndians' attitudes and opinions toward Indians and Indian issues. In addition to editing this book he is presently working on updating that national survey.

WILLAM REEVES is a specialist in the sociology of organizations at the University of Calgary. His prior work in the field of inter-group relations includes a study of urban organizations serving a native clientele and a study of the processing of discrimination complaints in the Canadian Human Rights Commission (with J. Frideres).

WALTER RUDNICKI is director of policy development (Indian affairs) in the federal Department of Indian Affairs and Northern Development. As a senior official in the department in the mid-1960s he was instrumental both in bringing Indian poverty to public attention and in launching the department's controversial community development program. He subsequently served in the Privy Council Office where he played a major role in shaping the course of Indian policy. Between 1973 and 1983 he operated his own consulting firm specializing in native affairs and has been doing similar work with the federal government for the past two years.

ANDREW J. SIGGNER, as former senior demographer in the Department of Indian Affairs and Northern Development, is one of Canada's foremost demographers specializing in native peoples. At Indian Affairs he was the prime mover behind the compilation of various regional demographic profiles that serve as an important resource to policy planners in government and Indian organizations. He has recently served with the National Energy Board, where he was involved with preparations for monitoring the social impact of the Norman Wells pipeline on native communities in the Mackenzie Valley. He is presently with the Population Studies Branch of Statistics Canada.

THE SPECIAL PARLIAMENTARY COMMITTEE ON INDIAN SELF-GOVERNMENT was a subcommittee of the House of Commons Standing Committee on Indian Affairs and Northern Development. Under the chairmanship of Liberal MP Keith Penner the committee produced a path-breaking report with recommendations for sweeping reforms that were unanimously endorsed by all members of the committee, regardless of their party affiliation. The other members of the committee were: Stan Schellenberger (PC), Hon. Warren Allmand (Lib.), Jim Manly (NDP), Frank Oberle (PC), Raymond Chenier (Lib.), Henri Tousignant (Lib.), and Roberta Jamieson (ex officio, representing the Assembly of First Nations). Bill Wilson and Sandra Isaac served as liaison members for the National Council of Canada and the Native Women's Association of Canada, respectively.

This book is dedicated to
George Manuel, a past president of the former National
Indian Brotherhood, founding president of the World
Council of Indigenous People, a wise, dedicated, and
visionary leader whom I have come to admire and
respect greatly.

Preface

For Indians the 1970s and first half of the 1980s was a period of enormous social change. Borrowing a phrase from Indian leader Harold Cardinal and from Quebec Francophones' experience, I have described this elsewhere as "an Indian Quiet Revolution."[1] This social, political, cultural, and to a lesser extent economic revolution was triggered by events surrounding the federal government's 1969 white paper on Indian policy. The revolution has been sustained by the political and humanitarian energies within the Indian population, and has continued – albeit at a slower pace and in a less sensational manner – into the last half of the 1980s. Thus, this book deals with Indians in a period of transition, as Indians and governments move, sometimes in unison but usually out of step with each other, through a process of decolonization for which no readily applicable and jointly acceptable models exist.

Some of the chapters in this book deal with issues from the early stage of this process of decolonization or focus on the historical background to that process; most, though, deal with the issues of the 1980s, many of which will carry over into the 1990s. Throughout it will be evident that although Indians do not enjoy large amounts of power, prestige, and wealth, Indians will no longer accept being relegated to the margins of Canadian society. Indians have moved out of a position of virtual irrelevance to Canadian society, to which they were relegated with the influx of nonIndian immigrants. Indians have moved out of the wings, much closer to centre stage, to the point of being involved in renegotiating the very constitution of Canadian society. Despite the paucity of their political and economic resources, Indians have become a "force to be reckoned with," for they possess the ability to command the attention of the mass media and to embarrass publicly those who would do them injustice.

Particular attention will be devoted in this book to Indian attempts to generate more power and more self-sufficiency at the grassroots level of Indian communities. Indeed, this is an underlying thrust not only of Indian economic development projects and the quest for self-determination, but also of many Indian demands and claims (particularly the so-called "comprehensive claims"). In focusing on Indian government, the last section of the book approaches this issue of community empowerment from a variety of perspectives, the utility of which is perhaps best assessed as this issue continues to evolve into the 1990s.

The interest in community empowerment (broadly defined) and community-level impacts of developments in Indian affairs marks a significant departure from my past concentration on national-level developments in Ottawa. That widening of intellectual horizons derives in part from the flow of events themselves and in part from a concern with issues of social class in the Indian population itself. With regard to national-level developments, an observer writing in 1985 cannot help but be struck by the various impediments (e.g., Indian factionalism, fiscal restraint and economic recession, timid or re-calcitrant premiers, etc.) that have slowed progress to a snail's pace. Yet, at the same time, much is changing on Indian reserves across the country; indeed, the pace of change in local communities may have quickened as it slowed at the national level. However, experience with decolonization elsewhere around the globe, reinforced by the Quebec case and by the theoretical writings of the academic school of thought known as political economy, suggests that at the local level the benefits of the Indian ''quiet revolution'' will be disproportionately reaped by the Indian elite and middle class.

It is not at all clear how widespread and how deep is the support for the national Indian political elite among the grassroots residents of Indian communities. Indeed, the grassroots repudiation of agreements-in-principle that some Inuit and Indian negotiators have reached with federal government negotiators and the difficulties some chiefs encounter in sustaining their constituents' interest in self-government in the face of pressing socio-economic problems both suggest that at times leaders and followers may be fundamentally out of step with each other.[2] Hence, the grassroots level warrants close scrutiny by social scientists seeking to understand developments among Indians.

As an edited volume, this book is somewhat unorthodox in its contents. This reflects the fact that the book is in part intended to replace my earlier book with Roger Gibbins, *Out Of Irrelevance*, which is now out of print. The passages and authors selected also reflect the fact that, in its scope, the present book is intended to go beyond *Out Of Irrelevance* into some areas that Gibbins and I have explored together as well as into other areas in which I have little or no experience. In pursuing the latter I have called upon a diversity of contacts and colleagues, including some from a growing and intellectually stimulating informal group of scholars interested in native studies at the University of Calgary. The final product contains eighteen chapters, of which eleven were written especially for this volume. One other contains a lengthy new section not previously published, while two others contain epilogues that their authors have written for this book. Chapters published here with the permission of another publisher have usually been condensed and rewritten by me and then submitted to the original authors for approval or modification.

A book such as this would not be possible without the assistance of a large number of people. To the authors who have contributed chapters I extend a special word of thanks for your participation, for your efforts to meet deadlines, and for your graciousness in response to my heavy editorial hand. I am also grateful for the major contributions of time made by respondents in field studies reported herein.

My task as editor and researcher was greatly facilitated by Liz Fraikin, then Director, Research Branch, Department of Indian Affairs and Northern Development. The unfailing co-operation of Ms. Fraikin and her able staff in locating and providing data and phone numbers was an exemplary model of the service ethic in Canada's civil service. Stella Etherington was equally helpful in her capacity as senior librarian at the Assembly of First Nations in Ottawa. The collegiality, considered opinions, and continuing support of Michael Harrison, college acquisitions editor at McClelland and Stewart, played an important role in bringing the project to a successful conclusion.

Few authors have enjoyed such an abundance of support from their university as I have from mine. The Killam Resident Fellowship that relieved me of teaching and committee responsibilities during the fall of 1985 was an invaluable resource without which the book would never have been finished. University of Calgary sociology department heads Harry Hiller and Joseph DiSanto and administrative assistant Carol Yopp were prompt and generous in mobilizing university resources on my behalf. Many an eye-straining hour was contributed by typists Adina Lyon, Jan Davis, Maryanne Nielson, Verna Hellmer, Sue Henderson, and others who proficiently translated thousands of pages of handwritten mess into typed manuscript. Isabel Gibbins provided attractive graphics for Chapter 2.

I also wish to thank the various publishers who granted permission for me to include material to which they hold copyrights. They are formally acknowledged at the beginning of the respective chapters.

The assistance of Drs. Roger Gibbins, James Frideres, Tullio Caputo, and other colleagues who reviewed earlier drafts of particular chapters is gratefully acknowledged, as is that of Drs. Jean Burnet and Carl Grindstaff and Mr. Nelson Gutnick.

Finally, to Pat, Susan, and Michael I am grateful for the understanding shown in allowing me to immerse myself in a very demanding project.

J.R.P. December, 1985

Notes

1. J. Rick Ponting and Roger Gibbins, *Out Of Irrelevance: A Socio-political Introduction to Indian Affairs in Canada* (Scarborough, Ont.: Butterworths, 1980), pp. 321-23.
2. To say that leaders and followers may be fundamentally out of step is not to make invidious, implicit comparisons with nonIndians, for nonIndian political leaders often give ample evidence of being at odds with their constituents. Some would submit that such is the essence of leadership.

Part One

Introduction

Chapter One

Historical Overview and Background

by Roger Gibbins and J. Rick Ponting

A proper understanding of the contemporary situation of Indians in Canada is impossible without some understanding of the diversity of the Indian population and some flavour of the history of Indian-nonIndian relations since at least the mid-nineteenth century. This chapter provides that contextual information.[1]

From the outset, the difference between status (registered) Indians and non-status Indians must be noted. Status Indians, who are the focal concern of this book and of whom there were about 350,000 in 1985, are persons who fall under the legal jurisdiction of the federal Indian Act and therefore have their names included on a register kept by the Department of Indian Affairs and Northern Development (DIAND). Non-status Indians are either (1) former registered Indians who have lost their registered status by marriage to a nonIndian or by a process (discussed later) known as enfranchisement, or (2) the off-spring of such persons. Métis are the offspring of a mixed (Indian and white) marriage. Métis are sometimes known as "half-breeds" and sometimes identify themselves as non-status Indians. However, as Sealey and Lussier[2] have demonstrated, many Métis have a distinct Métis self-identity that contrasts sharply with an Indian identity and is sometimes based in part on the larger society's denial to Métis of rights and privileges that are extended to status Indians.

In addition to Métis, status Indians, and non-status Indians, there is the Inuit population in Canada who, at the time of the 1981 census, numbered about 25,400, including about 5,000 (mainly in northern Quebec) who have been served by the Indian and Inuit Affairs program of DIAND rather than by DIAND's Northern Development Program or by the governments of the Northwest Territories and Yukon.

Although all of the foregoing may be described as "native people," and although any given pair of status and non-status Indians may be indistinguishable in terms of the cultural and physical attributes of

"Indianness," the term "native people" is not one they prefer. Status Indians have been particularly vocal in their objections to being called "Natives," for it is felt that policies based on such a term will seriously erode their special rights and privileges.

Almost all registered Indians are members of a band, which is a political-administrative unit created by the federal government. However, contrary to the frequent usage of the term in the popular media, not all registered Indians are treaty Indians. Indeed, in many parts of Canada, treaties were never signed (or offered), so that today only about 57 per cent of all status Indians are also treaty Indians. Map 1 shows those parts of the country which are covered by treaty.

The Indian population is incredibly diverse ethnically. Indeed, different peoples whom Canadians of European ancestry lump together under the term "Indian" have long thought of themselves as quite different peoples (e.g., Micmacs, Haudenosaunee, Cree, Haida, Dogrib). This self-definition of separateness is reinforced by different ecological adaptations to quite different physical environments (for instance, Plains Cree versus Woodland Cree versus West Coast), with resultant vast differences in symbolic and material culture and in economies in earlier times (as illustrated by the sedentary agricultural way of life in southern Ontario compared to the migratory buffalo-oriented life on the Prairies). Geographical and linguistic barriers once reinforced these differences. Thus, it is not very realistic for other Canadians to expect "Indians" to be able to develop Indian unity and sustain it for a lengthy period of time. However, notwithstanding the ethnic diversity within the Indian population, all Indian nations in Canada have held one thing in common at least since the middle of the nineteenth century. This factor, one of the central features in the daily lives of Indians, is Indians' relationship with the government of Canada, especially as that relationship has been mediated through the Indian Act and earlier statutes. It is to a consideration of these that we now turn.

The Indian Act of 1876 and Its Evolution

The Indian Act is of great importance because it touches, and not lightly, virtually every aspect of Indians' lives. As Dr. Munro, former assistant deputy minister of the Indian Affairs Branch, describes it:

> The Indian Act is a Lands Act. It is a Municipal Act, an Education Act and a Societies Act. It is primarily social legislation, but is has a very broad scope: there are provisions about liquor, agriculture and mining as well as Indian lands, band membership and so forth. It has elements that

Map 1
Treaty Areas of Canada

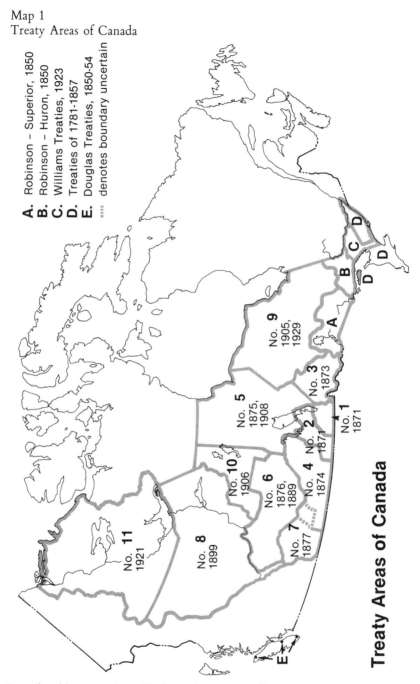

A. Robinson – Superior, 1850
B. Robinson – Huron, 1850
C. Williams Treaties, 1923
D. Treaties of 1781-1857
E. Douglas Treaties, 1850-54
▬▬ denotes boundary uncertain

No. 9
1905,
1929

No. 3
1873

No. 5
1875,
1908

No. 1
1871

No. 2
1871

No. 10
1906

No. 6
1876,
1889

No. 4
1874

No. 11
1921

No. 8
1899

No. 7
1877

Treaty Areas of Canada

Reproduced by permission of Indian and Northern Affairs Canada (revised October, 1977). Reproduced with permission of the Minister of Supply and Services Canada.

are embodied in perhaps two dozen different acts of any of the provinces and overrides some federal legislation in some respects. . . . It has the force of the Criminal Code and the impact of a constitution on those people and communities that come within its purview.[3]

Thus, in the scope of its impact on the lives of individuals, the Indian Act approximates what sociologists call a "total institution." Furthermore, in many respects the Indian Act, not the treaties, defines the relationship between Indians and the broader Canadian society. Yet, the treaties rather than the Act protect land, hunting, fishing, and trapping rights, to the extent that this is done at all. The treaties and the Act are not two sides of the same coin – while the former provide a limited form of protection, the latter provides a comprehensive mechanism of social control.

Definition of Indian
Under the Indian Act of 1876, an "Indian" became any male person of Indian blood reputed to belong to a particular band, any child of such person, and any woman who is or was lawfully married to such a person. Excluded from Indian status were persons living continuously five years or more in another country, Indian women marrying non-Indian men, and, in some cases, illegitimate children. Through this definitional exercise the Indian Act fragmented the native population in Canada into legally and legislatively distinct blocs experiencing quite different rights, restrictions, and obligations. The contemporary conflicts among status Indians, non-status Indians, and Indian women married to nonIndian men are today's legacy of this definitional approach. However, it should be kept in mind here that while the Indian Act applies only to Indians as defined by the Act, the responsibilities and legislative prerogatives of the federal government are not so limited. In contrast to our usage in this book, the term "Indian" has been more broadly interpreted with respect to the British North America Act (now known as the Constitution Act, 1867) than it has been within the Indian Act. Thus, while Parliament has the power to legislate for all Natives, under the Indian Act Parliament chooses to make laws only for some.

The Indian Act set forth a process of enfranchisement whereby Indians could acquire full Canadian citizenship by severing their ties to the native community. The Act also laid down the framework for a limited form of local government and for the election of chiefs and councils: "the Government no doubt assumed that substitution of limited local administration for existing tribal organizations would accelerate the assimilation process."[4]

Indian Lands

Clause 25 of the Act retained the government's guardianship of Indian lands. Procedures for surrender of lands were put in place by the Act to protect Indian interests in the conveyance process. In this and related sections, the Act establishes what might be termed "boundary-maintenance" mechanisms for the Indian societies, mechanisms that Indians were unable to provide internally.[5] These mechanisms protected Indian societies by inhibiting assimilation.

Indian land was also protected in part through clauses that "excluded Indian people from taxes, liens, mortgages or other charges on their lands and from loss of possessions through debt or through pawns for intoxicants."[6] However, while protecting Indian land these provisions have often made it next to impossible for Indians to raise outside investment capital, for potentially valuable Indian land cannot be mortgaged. Thus, Indians usually must rely on the federal government for the capital needed to promote economic development. These provisions of the Act, necessary as they may once have been, now serve as a shackle on Indian self-reliance.

Concentration of Authority

Over the long run the most contentious aspect of the Indian Act was the sweeping power it gave to administrators and to the federal government. The Indian Act extended the regulatory reach of the government into virtually every nook and cranny of Indian life. Unlike other Canadians, Indians were not faced with a plurality of governments and government departments but rather with a single government and single department. Although the Act presented a veneer of self-government and Indian participation in the control of their lives, even the veneer was an illusion.

The Indian Act was administered in the Indian communities by the Indian agent. In the words of Manuel and Posluns, "it was the job of these new white chiefs to displace our traditional leaders in their care over our day-to-day lives in order to bring our way of life into line with the policies that had been decreed in Ottawa."[7] To assist him in this task the agent, like the heads of other total institutions (e.g., prison wardens), had an extraordinary range of administrative and discretionary powers; he was an instrument of social control par excellence. Because of his sweeping powers the agent inevitably generated a state of dependency among his Indian clientele. Also, because the agent personified the Indian Act and the character of the relationship between Indians and the government, he became the focal point for Indian hostility and anger, no matter how repressed. Despite the admirable personal qualities of some agents, few Indian leaders today would contest Manuel and Posluns' description of the Indian agent as a destructive force within the Indian community.

In large part it has been the social control features of the Indian Act that have placed Indians in the position of a colonized people. In this respect Indian leader Harold Cardinal asserts that "instead of implementing the treaties and offering much-needed protection to Indian rights, [the Indian Act] subjugated to colonial rule the very people whose rights it was supposed to protect."[8] He goes on to argue that the Indian Act "enslaved and bound the Indian to a life under a tyranny often as cruel and harsh as that of any totalitarian state."[9] Paradoxically, however, the Act is also perceived by some Indians today as one of the major protections for Indian rights (as discussed later in this chapter), and plans for its abolition in 1969 met with vociferous Indian opposition.

Amendments to the Act

The Indian Act was subjected to frequent legislative fine-tuning and amendment. Throughout, however, its basic features were not altered and the legislation governing Indian affairs in the 1980s bears a close resemblance to the Act passed in 1876.

The passage of amendments to the Indian Act in 1889 demonstrated a move to greater government control over Indian education, morality, local government, and land. For example, the government was given the power to override a band's reluctance to lease reserve land. In 1920 the Conservative government, led by Arthur Meighen and displaying the same insensitivity to minority views that had already won him the lasting antipathy of French Canadians, passed legislation empowering the government to order the enfranchisement of qualified Indians without any such request from individuals concerned. The Indian Act was also amended in 1924 to give the Superintendent-General of Indian Affairs responsibility for Canada's Eskimo (Inuit) population. Interestingly, though, the Indian Act itself was not applied to Eskimos, in part due to the feeling that the Act was doing little to help Indians and that the problem should not be compounded by extending its coverage to other groups.

The 1951 Indian Act, like its predecessors, was framed to promote the integration of Indians into Canadian society. The main features of the 1876 legislation had not been altered, although the revised Act reduced the degree of government intrusion into the cultural affairs of Indians. The prohibition on the potlach was repealed, Indians were now allowed to consume liquor in public places, and the provision that allowed an Indian to be enfranchised without his consent was dropped, as was a 1927 ban on political organizing. In general the powers of the minister were curtailed, although they remained formidable.

A change of at least major symbolic significance occurred in 1960 when legislation prohibiting residents of reserves from voting in federal elections was repealed. Enfranchisement ceased to be held out as an enticement for assimilation. Citizenship and assimilation were no longer equated – one could be both an Indian and a full-fledged Canadian citizen, a combination that had been largely prevented by previous federal legislation.

In the 1960s the Indian Act still dominated Indian affairs in Canada. However, it should be noted that with the general expansion of government activity since the end of the Second World War, Indians came to be affected by an array of federal and provincial legislation from which the Indian Act and the treaties offered little shelter. As Cardinal has written, "it is difficult for Indian people to understand that many decisions that vitally affect them are made for reasons totally unrelated to the Indian scene and without regard to their effect on the Indians."[10] Thus, as Indians today try to redefine their relationship with the government and with the nonIndian society, more than the Indian Act and the constitution is at issue. To mention but a few illustrations, the Fisheries Act, the Migratory Birds Convention Act, and provincial fish and game regulations all come into play.

The Evolution of Indian Policy

The confinement of legislative activity in Indian affairs to the national government and the legislative dominance of the Indian Act – compared to over 4,000 separate and unsystematized statutory enactments in the United States[11] – make the evolution of Indian policy relatively easy to follow. There are, of course, some complications. For example, the policies of the national government, particularly in the early decades after Confederation, were often different in eastern Canada than they were in the West. Prime Minister Macdonald, for instance, in discussing 1880 legislation that restricted the sale of agricultural products by the Indians of western Canada, commented that the "wild nomads of the North-West" could not be judged on the same basis as the Indians of Ontario. Nevertheless, the major threads of public policy can be readily followed. Several major goals or policy motifs can be isolated.

Protection

The officials who forged Canadian Indian policy were not imbued with an overly noble view of white society. While they may have believed that European civilization was unsurpassed in the advantages it had to offer, they were acutely aware of the evils of drink, greed, dishonesty, and prostitution that flourished in great abundance, particularly on the edge of the frontier. Thus, one of the earliest and most humanitarian goals of Indian policy was the protection of Indians from the manifest evils of the white society. This goal led to laws prohibiting the private sale of Indian land, Indian consumption of alcohol, and the prostitution of Indian women. The reserve system itself was in part a device to isolate and protect Indians, while at the same time becoming "the cradle of the Indian civilizing effort and the means of securing the white man's freedom to exploit the vast riches of a growing dominion."[12] The prominence of protection as a policy goal, however, faded over time, although as late as 1930 there was an amendment to the Indian Act restricting the use of poolrooms by Indians, and it was not until the sixties that all prohibitions on Indians' use of liquor were removed.

The policy of protection, guardianship, or wardship fostered in the administration of Indian affairs an air of paternalism that has been difficult to dispel. The development of paternalistic attitudes was understandable given the early history of Indian-nonIndian contact in North America. Indians had not been successful in defending themselves or their land in the face of advancing nonIndian settlement and the government had become a buffer between the Indians and the crush of settlement. However, rather than acting as an impregnable wall, the government pursued the more limited goal of temporarily protecting Indians until they could be assimilated into the white society. This protective stance led in turn to the attitude that Indians' views on their own welfare were not to be given much weight, that the government knew the best interest of the Indian people in the long run. This outlook, coupled with the sweeping powers of the Indian Act and the high proportion of former military men and clergymen attached to Indian Affairs, entrenched paternalism within the department. As a target for Indian protest it has persisted to this day.

Assimilation

If there has been a central pillar to Canadian Indian policy, it has been the goal of assimilation. While the terminology has varied among "assimilation," "integration," "civilization," and "moving into the mainstream," the policy has remained virtually unaltered; Indians

25

were to be prepared for absorption into the broader Canadian society. It was expected that eventually Indians would shed their native languages, customs, and religious beliefs and become self-sufficient members of the modern Canadian society and labour force. In 1880 Sir John A. Macdonald, speaking as Minister of Indian Affairs, stated that government policy toward Indians was "to wean them by slow degrees, from their nomadic habits, which have become almost an instinct, and by slow degrees absorb them on the land. Meantime, they must be fairly protected."[13] In 1950 the minister, Walter E. Harris, announced a new Indian policy that echoed the words of Macdonald seventy years earlier: "The ultimate goal of our Indian policy is the integration of the Indians into the general life and economy of the country. It is recognized, however, that during a temporary transition period . . . special treatment and legislation are necessary."[14] In the intervening years interpretations of Indian policy followed the same theme. In 1920, for instance, the deputy superintendent-general of Indian Affairs spoke as follows to a special committee of the House of Commons on proposed changes in the enfranchisement provisions of the Indian Act: "our object is to continue until there is not a single Indian in Canada that has not been absorbed into the body politic and there is no question, and no Indian Department, that is the whole object of this Bill."[15]

After the end of the Second World War, when the period of settlement and treaty-making was long past and when the process of assimilation was well under way, the complete assimilation of Indians into the Canadian mainstream became a less pressing concern. In the post-war years there was an increased acceptance of cultural pluralism, and the positive aspects of Indian traditions began to be entertained. Nevertheless, the principle of assimilation that had guided Indian policy over the past hundred years was neither abandoned nor fundamentally modified.

The goal of assimilation raises the very sensitive issue of cultural genocide. The word "genocide," one of the most emotionally charged in the English language, must be used with caution. Nevertheless, the primacy of assimilation as a policy goal gives credence to Indian claims that cultural genocide has been at least an implicit goal in the administration of Indian affairs. When an outside observer concludes that "the extinction of the Indians as Indians" is the ultimate end of Canadian public policy,[16] the charge of genocide cannot be lightly brushed aside. In addition, Patterson notes that not only were bounties placed on the heads of the Beothuk Indians in Newfoundland, but the British General Jeffrey Amherst waged biological warfare against the Indians. He distributed to Indians blankets known to be infected with smallpox, when it was also known that the disease was often fatal to Indians due to their lack of natural immunity.[17]

Despite the zeal with which assimilation was pursued, the policy largely failed. Due to Indians' isolation on reserves, racial and linguistic distinctiveness, marginality to the labour force, and the gulf between native and European cultural patterns, Indians proved to be a difficult group to assimilate. A large part of the responsibility for the failure of assimilation must be laid at the feet of the broader Canadian society, for the obstacles posed by societal discrimination and prejudice were immense. Government policy tried to induce Indians into a mainstream that was unwilling to receive them.

Christianity

The policy of assimilation was buttressed by a number of supporting policies, one of which was the spread of Christianity to the Indian population. As Harper observed:

> In Canada the civilization of the Indian is made synonymous with his Christianization. Indian missions, in fact, enjoy government favour; the aboriginal religious and ceremonial practices are officially discouraged. Next to the attainment of the goal of self-support, the Indian's conversion from pagan belief to Christianity is the most important criterion for judging his fitness to assume an equal place in the white man's society.[18]

It must be remembered here that the entwinement of the Christian church with the administration of Indian affairs was virtually inevitable. In many cases missionaries spearheaded the first white contact with Indians in the interior of the continent and the missionaries were frequently the most successful in learning Indian languages and mores. Many missionaries worked vigorously to protect Indians and often found themselves serving as intermediaries between government officials and the Indians. It must also be borne in mind that the early church and missionary work in North America attracted some individuals of outstanding character and drive who were bound to leave their stamp on the policies of their times.

The church came to play a very important role in the education of Indians. In the early years, education was viewed, as it still is in many quarters, as an essential tool of assimilation. The responsibility for Indian education, however, was largely delegated by the government to the churches. In the long run this strategy was to prove unsatisfactory. Because the religious residential schools isolated Indians from other students, assimilation was impaired. Because their curricula

served as much as a vehicle for Christianization as for secular education, the secular education of Indians suffered in comparison to that
received by nonIndians. Finally, the residential schools were a source
of great disruption and antagonism within the native communities and
did little to enhance the value of education in the eyes of native
students. [19]

By the 1960s the traditional role of the church in Indian affairs was
drawing to a close. As a result of the increased secularization of the
Canadian society and of the almost total separation of church and
state, Christianization flagged as a policy goal. The education of
Indians passed into secular hands and by the mid-sixties the denomina-
tional residential school system was being abandoned. Although
education remained a vehicle for assimilation, it was no longer a vehicle driven by the churches.

Reserves and Self-Sufficiency
An important means of assimilation was the settlement of Indians into
agriculturally-based communities. Settlement allowed other instruments of assimilation, such as churches, schools, and limited local
government, to be brought into effect more readily. Moreover, to the
extent that settlement proceeded, large tracts of land formerly held by
Indians could be freed for nonIndians. [20] Indeed, the immigration boom
of the early twentieth century increased pressure even on the newly
founded Indian reserves and the government began actively to encourage Indian land surrenders and moved to make "excess" Indian
reserve land available for nonIndian settlement. In 1911 the Indian Act
was amended to allow for the expropriation of reserve lands for public
works. Speaking to the amendment, Minister of the Interior Oliver
"claimed that the whim of a band would no longer obstruct a
provincially-chartered railroad company from developing a certain part
of the country." [21] In the clash between nonIndian settlement and the
protection of Indian interests, public policy clearly came down on the
side of the former, although Indian interests were by no means totally
abandoned.

In the pursuit of assimilation the government tried to make Indians
as self-supporting as possible. This policy was not motivated solely by
the desire to limit public expenditures in support of Indians; the desire
to promote the integration of Indians into the Canadian economy was
also an important motivation. Yet here again the policy was frustrated
by the legislative restrictions of the Indian Act. The prohibition of
mortgages on Indian land and restrictions on the ability of outside
creditors to collect debts from reserve residents curtailed the infusion

of outside capital into the Indian economy. Self-support and fiscal self-management were also frustrated by the paternalism of Indian Affairs. Not only were band funds under the control of the department, but even the most straightforward financial and entrepreneurial enterprises by Indians required departmental approval if they involved contact with the nonIndian society.

An interesting step toward greater self-sufficiency was taken by the community development program launched by Indian Affairs in the early 1960s. This program sought to mobilize the Indian population, to create conditions of economic and social progress for the whole community by encouraging the maximum amount of community participation, initiative, and self-reliance. The program called for a change in emphasis from people administration to people development. To this end sixty-two community development officers were hired by Indian Affairs to work as resource persons and co-ordinators in the Indian communities. Despite or because of its early successes, however, the program quickly disintegrated in a welter of bureaucratic in-fighting and conflicts among the community development staff, Indian agents, senior bureaucrats, and factions in the Indian communities. The community development staff, torn between loyalty to their employer and to the Indian people, frequently found themselves as partisans on the side of the Indians against the government, and as such their support and effectiveness within the Indian Affairs bureaucracy rapidly dissipated. Concluding that the community development program threw sand in the gears of efficient administration, the Indian and Inuit Affairs Program moved to emasculate it.

Enfranchisement
The principal reward held out to Indians contemplating assimilation was enfranchisement. The equation of assimilation with enfranchisement and full citizenship was not an unexpected policy in a young country faced with the absorption of a large and polyglot immigrant population; in this sense Indian policy reflected a more general policy perspective within the society. However, the costs to be paid by an Indian seeking enfranchisement far surpassed those paid by immigrants to Canada.

The enfranchisement provisions of the Indian Act equated citizenship with cultural characteristics; only Indians who fit the dominant cultural mode could be full citizens. Indians who clung to native traditions or to reserve land clearly did not fall into this category. We can assume that in the eyes of policy-makers, ''rights'' as we know them today were associated with enfranchisement. Here we include such things as the right to vote, freedom of speech, the right to organize, and so forth. The ''rights'' embedded in the Indian Act and the treaties, on the other hand, were seen more as transitory means of protection rather than as inalienable rights as we would perceive such today. According to that line of thought, these lesser rights could be justifiably trimmed away when they were no longer needed as a means of protection. For example, reserve land that was not needed to support the Indian population could be made available to nonIndian settlement or farming; the Indian right to the land in this case was not equated with the more basic property rights associated with enfranchisement and citizenship. In effect, the types of Indian rights under debate today were probably not recognized as such in the nineteenth century.

As a lure for assimilation, enfranchisement clearly failed, for the rate of assimilation remained extremely low. Then, in 1960 all Indians were granted the vote in federal elections. It was recognized at last that full citizenship in Canada need not be conditional on complete assimilation into the Canadian society. The legitimacy of cultural pluralism and cultural distinctiveness for Canada's aboriginal inhabitants had been recognized, or so it seemed.

The Treaties
The first treaty between Indians and colonial officials in North America was signed in 1670 and the last Canadian treaty (by such name) was signed in 1923. During the intervening years numerous treaties of varying format and complexity were concluded. These generally included many or most of the following provisions: an agreement of peace and amity, the cession of land, initial payments to Indians, small annual payments in cash and/or goods, the designation of chiefs and councillors to negotiate and administer the treaty, guarantee of land reserved for Indians and/or right to use unoccupied territory in its natural state, and promises of government services such as education and health care.[22] Perhaps the major treaties in Canada have been the numbered treaties on the Prairies, starting with Treaty One in 1871 and ending with Treaty Ten in 1906, which opened the western territories for settlement and the construction of the Canadian Pacific Railway.

Reflected in the treaties are some policy perspectives that should be mentioned. For example, as the treaties were signed to extinguish Indian title to the land, they carried with them the explicit recognition of Indian ownership rights. Treaty Seven, to cite but one illustration, calls for Indians to ''cede, release, surrender, and yield up to the

30

Government of Canada" traditional lands in the then North-West Territories. Lands not so released remained as Indian reserves, the land being held in trust for Indian people by the Crown. It should be borne in mind that the various treaties are by no means identical in content and that no treaties were signed with Indians in Quebec, the Maritimes, and most of British Columbia. For registered Indians not under treaty – almost half of the registered Indian population – their only claim to their original lands is that based on aboriginal rights, that is, the rights of occupancy of the first settlers of the land where those rights have never been yielded to the Canadian government.

There is also room for confusion about the conception of "rights" that was brought to the treaty-making process by Indians and whites. As Smith points out, it can never be assumed that the treaties truly reflect the agreement and understanding of Indians.[23] The Indian perspective is set out by Cardinal. To Indians the treaties were "the beginning of a contractual relationship whereby the representatives of the Queen would have lasting responsibilities to the Indian people in return for valuable lands that were ceded to them."[24] In this respect Indian organizations argue that free Indian education in perpetuity has been paid for by the lands released by treaty. The government perspective at the time of the signings was quite different, although this conclusion is deduced from the Indian policies of the time rather than from the letter of the treaties themselves. To government officials, the critical feature of the treaties was that they ceded Indian ownership of the land; the treaties were more important for what Indians gave up than for the concessions given to Indians. Government officials also viewed the treaties as a means of providing transitional protection of an indigenous people who were faced with eventual assimilation or extinction. It is unlikely that officials at the time read into the treaties the scope and duration of responsibilities that Indians are claiming today.

It is also unlikely that the treaty-making process had the bilateral quality that is sometimes assumed or asserted today. Most of the treaties were approached by the government less as a matter of negotiation than as a "take-it-or-leave-it" proposition. Finally, it should also be noted that the conditions surrounding the signing of the treaties were often less than equitable and were not such as to ensure that Indian interests were fairly protected.[25]

The policy interpretations applied to the treaties have taken on a moral rather than a legal character. For example, the Indian chiefs of Alberta argued in *Citizens Plus* that treaty clauses promising machinery and livestock symbolized a lasting government commitment to economic development. Medicine chest clauses provide another example of legal interpretation. Treaty Six, signed in 1876, provides that ''a medicine chest shall be kept at the house of each Indian agent for the use and benefit of the Indians at the direction of such agent.'' The scope of this and similar clauses in other treaties has come under considerable debate. In 1935 the Treaty Six clause was interpreted by the Exchequer Court of Britain (Draver vs. the King) to mean that all drugs or medical supplies required by Indians should be supplied to them free of charge. However, in this decision testimony from Indians who were actually present at the signing of the treaty and at related discussions was critical; the letter of the treaty alone did not form the basis of the court decision. [26]

The evolution of Indian policy in Canada has been shaped by changes in the larger society, which have exerted significant pressure on Indians, on the administration of Indian affairs, and on the direction of this policy. A striking example of the impingement of external societal developments on the evolution of Indian policy is provided by the 1969 white paper, a document that renewed the assimilationist orientation of the earlier era. [27]

The 1969 White Paper
The 1960s witnessed the initial stirrings of Indian activism both in Canada and in the United States. The American civil rights movement indirectly called into question the legal segregation of Canadian Indians through the Indian Act, and civil rights advocates in Canada began to pay increased attention to the plight of Indians. Many Canadians felt that advances in civil rights, such as the provisions of the new Bill of Rights outlawing discrimination on the basis of race, colour, or creed, should apply equally to Indians as to other Canadians. Politically, a new Liberal government led by Pierre Trudeau, with his promise of a ''just society,'' was elected in 1968 and Canadians within and outside the government tried to reconcile the promise of the ''just society'' with the conditions faced by Canadian Indians. These various forces were not to leave Indian affairs untouched.

The new government was imbued with a strong liberal ideology that stressed individualism and the protection of individual rights. It adopted a new approach to Indian affairs that reflected a combination of North American ideological tenets that can be traced back to the American Revolution, Trudeau's personal ideological beliefs, and his deep antagonism to ethnic nationalism in Quebec. The new approach emphasized individual equality and de-emphasized collective ethnic survival. Indians as individuals were to be helped at the expense of Indians as a people. On June 25, 1969, Jean Chrétien, Minister of Indian Affairs and Northern Development, tabled "A Statement of the Government of Canada on Indian Policy" in the House of Commons.

That white paper proposed that the legislative and constitutional bases of discrimination be removed; the Indian Act was to be repealed. Rather than being legislatively set apart, Indians were to receive the same services as other Canadians and these were to be delivered to Indians through the same channels and from the same government agencies as serviced other Canadians. The unique federal government responsibility for Indians was to end. The Indian Affairs Program within DIAND was to be abolished and any residual responsibilities that were not transferred to provincial governments or to bands were to be transferred to other departments within the federal government. The white paper also recognized that any lawful obligations the government had incurred through the signing of the treaties must be recognized, although here the government expressed the very limited interpretation of treaty rights discussed above.

The white paper was also a response to values within the policy-making arena of the national government. It was designed more to protect the government from external criticism than to meet the aspirations of Canadian Indians as these were articulated by Indians themselves. In its emphasis on achieving contemporary equality for Indians, the white paper paid scant attention to the liabilities that had been accumulating for Indians from the inequalities of the past. Nor did the white paper acknowledge that discrimination "in fact" (*de facto*) may exist even when discrimination "in law" (*de jure*) has been abolished, and that as a consequence the special legal protection of minority rights may be necessary. As Weaver points out, the problem of reconciling demands for special status with the principle of equality is an old and enduring one for democratic societies; the white paper solution was to come down on the side of equality. The rights of the individual were placed above the collective survival of the group. [28]

Indian hostility to the white paper was crystallized in a number of documents, one of which was Cardinal's *The Unjust Society*. Cardinal charged that the new Indian policy was "a thinly disguised programme of extermination through assimilation," that the white paper postulated that "the only good Indian is a nonIndian." Cardinal was particularly opposed to the proposal to turn over the responsibility for Indians to the provincial governments. A second document, *Citizens*

Plus, was presented by the Indian chiefs of Alberta to Prime Minister Trudeau in June, 1970, and was introduced by the following excerpt from the Hawthorn Report:

> Indians should be regarded as "Citizens Plus"; in addition to the normal rights and duties of citizenship, Indians possess certain additional rights as charter members of the Canadian community.[29]

Through these and other similar documents, as well as through statements to the press, Indian organizations registered their unequivocal opposition to the white paper.

The 1969 white paper was the capstone of a policy of assimilation that can be traced back to the pre-Confederation years. Its rejection by Indians and its eventual retraction by the government in March of 1971 thus mark a watershed in the evolution of Indian affairs in Canada. Assimilation was at least officially placed aside as an explicit policy goal, although it may well continue as a socio-economic and cultural process and, Indians allege, as a hidden agenda behind federal government action. Formally, at least, the page was being turned on what had been the central theme of Indian policy over the past 130 years. The rejection of the white paper therefore opened up a new and confused policy era; the direction of Indian policy in the 1970s was suddenly "up for grabs." Yet, the development of alternative policies was to prove to be an incredibly complex process, in part due to a basic change in the composition of the policy-makers. Until the publication of the white paper, Indian policy had been formulated with very little Indian input and frequently in opposition to Indian goals and interests. In the 1970s and 1980s Indians were to be deeply involved.

An Indian Quiet Revolution

The years from the beginning of the 1970s to the present have seen Indians experience numerous social changes reminiscent of those of the so-called "Quiet Revolution" that transformed Quebec society in the 1960s. Although the Quebec changes were more profound and more rapid-paced and started from a very different base level of "development," the broad direction (decolonization), causes, and accompanying phenomena are quite similar. For instance, both populations have gone through a secularization of their educational system and in both populations the average level of educational attainment has increased significantly. In step with urbanization and educational change there has emerged a new Indian middle class, proportionately smaller than that in Quebec but in attitudes, skills, and aspirations not unlike the new Quebec middle class that was such a driving force for social and political change. Like the Québécois, Indians have been exposed to movements of national liberation throughout the world, and the examples have exerted an influence on Indian political thought, demands, and rhetoric. As Québécois nationalists stressed and defended the territorial sovereignty of Quebec, so too have Indians repeatedly emphasized the importance of Indian land, and of Indian control of Indian land. In addition, Indians, like Québécois, stress their unique cultural identity and at times have seemed to challenge the existence and value of a pan-Canadian nationality. Finally, demands for Indian government, or the transfer of the political authority of the federal government to Indian hands, parallel, in many respects, the Parti Québécois proposals for sovereignty-association.[30]

Although the term "quiet revolution" is a convenient label for summarizing the social transformation taking place among Indians, it glosses over important phases and variations that occurred during the period. The remainder of this section outlines the main developments of that era. Developments within the federal state and within the Indian population will be treated separately, because during that period the federal government and Indian organizations were often out of step, if not actually working at cross-purposes.

The federal state can be described as having experienced the Indian quiet revolution in three phases to date. The first phase might be called the *period of policy retreat*. This was the period from shortly after the release of the 1969 white paper until its withdrawal. Although the policy was eloquently defended by Prime Minister Pierre Trudeau using the language of the liberal ideology,[31] it came under vehement attack from Indian organizations and was officially abandoned. During the interim it overshadowed all other federal initiatives and made progress almost impossible on other issues such as Indian health and housing. The policy also stoked the glowing embers of Indian distrust of the federal government; the resultant fire consumed most of whatever goodwill had been created prior to the release of the white paper.

Clearly a new policy approach was needed. Yet the time from the withdrawal of the white paper until perhaps the late 1970s was a period of *turmoil and floundering* as the Department of Indian Affairs experienced a rapid succession of ministers and senior bureaucrats (deputy ministers and assistant deputy ministers), underwent significant organizational restructuring, offered a series of policy initiatives that were usually denounced by Indian organizations, and witnessed a variety of other federal government departments encroach on its domain (e.g., Secretary of State) or become more active in a "regulatory" manner (e.g., Treasury Board, Auditor General). This was also a period of considerable conflict within the department itself, as tensions between the "old guard" (veteran DIAND employees) and "new guard" (younger, innovative, more client-oriented employees) broke into open bureaucratic warfare. In addition, there was the bitter controversy surrounding Harold Cardinal's short tenure as senior departmental official in the Alberta region, and the highly strained relations between DIAND minister Warren Allmand and his deputy minister, Arthur Kroeger.

In the wake of the withdrawal of the 1969 white paper, DIAND groped for new policy thrusts. The first of these new policies involved the reversal, as a result of the 1973 Supreme Court of Canada ruling on the Nishga land claim, of the government's refusal to recognize aboriginal rights. Less popular with Indians was the policy contained in a 1976 cabinet-endorsed document entitled "The Nature of Government-Indian Relations." Since this document is critiqued elsewhere,[32] suffice it to say here that it not only fell short of Indian demands but actually ran counter to several of those demands. A second policy prepared for cabinet that same year encompassed all native people and was vehemently rejected by status Indians for a variety of reasons, among which one of the most important was the suggestion of curtailing funding for status Indians.[33] Another policy involved a process for the recognition and settlement of two distinct forms of Indian claims – namely, comprehensive claims (involving unextinguished aboriginal rights to large tracts of land) and specific claims (involving unfulfilled provisions in treaties; compensation for small parcels of land illegally expropriated from, or sold on behalf of, Indian bands; etc.). Although most Indian organizations to this day reject the policy's principle of extinguishing aboriginal title to land in exchange for compensation, some have submitted claims that have been processed under this policy. Finally, a fourth policy proposal (1978-79) was for a "charter system of Indian government" whereby Indian bands would negotiate a charter or band constitution with the federal government so as to remove certain aspects of local government from the jurisdiction of the Indian Act and from the arbitrary powers of the cabinet minister.[34] This, too, was rejected by the National Indian Brotherhood; NIB criticized it as mere "sandbox politics" in which Indians are expected to play at governing themselves while the minister retains the important powers.

The third phase experienced by the federal state during the period 1971-85 might be called the *quest for self-government and constitutional reform*. Modest steps in the direction of self-government were made in the late 1970s with the implementation of memoranda of agreement calling for individual bands to take over from DIAND the administration (and in some cases the designing) of various DIAND programs on their reserves. However, perhaps not until the recognition of aboriginal rights in the final constitutional package of 1981 or even until the creation of the Special Parliamentary Committee on Indian Self-Government (Keith Penner, MP, chairman) in 1982 did the federal government enter this phase in earnest. This phase witnessed yet another major change in the key policy actors, as DIAND lost its lead role to the newly created Office of Aboriginal Constitutional Affairs (OACA), to the Privy Council Office, and to the Department of Justice. In addition, the provincial premiers and their advisers and officials now became central participants, as did various native organizations representing the aboriginal interests of Inuit, Métis, and non-status Indians.

During this third phase the federal government and some status Indian organizations finally came to follow more or less the same trajectory, largely as a result of the main thrust of the recommendations of the Penner Committee. A fundamental act of convergence occurred when the Assembly of First Nations (AFN) dropped its demand for sovereign authority and indicated its conditional willingness to accept authority delegated from the federal government as the basis of Indian self-government.[35] However, not all provincial premiers were on this "track," as some of them (particularly in western Canada) were of the opinion that administrative, fiscal, or legislative reform, rather than the constitutional entrenchment of aboriginal rights to self-government, was the preferable course to follow. Added to the premiers' "go slowly" approach was an increased factionalism among aboriginal peoples (including between treaty and non-treaty sectors of the status Indian population). These factors and others combined to militate against a major constitutional breakthrough.

Apart from the recognition and partial protection of aboriginal rights, the main accomplishment of this third phase consisted of a constitutional amendment guaranteeing constitutional conferences on aboriginal rights until the year 1987. These conferences included delegations led by the Prime Minister, the provincial premiers, leaders of the main aboriginal organizations (excluding the Prairie Treaty Nations Alliance), and the government leaders of Yukon and the Northwest Territories. Although these proved to be valuable educational forums for the politicians and others, and although the very fact that they are held must be seen as a major symbolic gain for aboriginal peoples, at the time of writing deliberations had clearly reached an impasse with the failure to attain an agreement at the 1985 conference.

Although it is too early to be certain, it appears that the failure of the 1985 constitutional conference may mark the beginning of a fourth phase. The June, 1985, imposition of Bill C-31 (an Act amending the Indian Act) against the wishes of many status Indian leaders, the leaked April, 1985, report of Deputy Prime Minister Erik Nielsen's task force on native programs, and the introduction of the Sechelt Indian Band Act[36] suggest that the hallmarks of the last half of the 1980s may be fiscal restraint and a more piecemeal approach which is targeted at individual Indian communities and which therefore involves more modest challenges of consensus-building.

Indian organizations, communities, and individuals were going through a quite different transformation between 1970 and 1985. That development was galvanized by the release in 1969 of the federal government's white paper, which had the effect of uniting Indians and focusing their action to an unprecedented degree. In this regard it is important to realize that throughout most of the first half of the twentieth century, numerous factors militated against the establishment of Indian organizations at any level above that of the band.[37] Those factors included Indian poverty and adult illiteracy, interference by the Indian agent or the RCMP, a requirement of the Indian Affairs Branch that all grievances be routed through the local Indian agent, and a section in the Indian Act (1927) prohibiting political organizing. Other factors included the lack of the federal franchise; the geographic dispersal and, in many cases, isolation of the Indian communities; the linguistic diversity of Indians and lack of a shared second language; parochial identifications with a particular tribe or treaty; and the lack of explicitly articulated common objectives.[38]

Many of those obstacles no longer remained when the white paper was issued. In 1968 the National Indian Council (encompassing status and non-status Indians, as well as Métis) split into two organizations – the National Indian Brotherhood and the Canadian Métis Society. With that split status Indians, now represented by the National Indian Brotherhood (NIB), embarked on a period of *consolidation*. This involved securing resources (especially funding) and building a consensus among the provincial and territorial member organizations such as the Indian Association of Alberta and the Indians of Quebec Association. Consolidation was also pursued in Indian communities on reserves. Under the leadership of NIB president George Manuel bands were exhorted to tackle their social and economic problems by following the principles of collective endeavour (community development) as enunciated by Manuel's model, President Julius Nyerere of Tanzania.

Finally, the period of internal consolidation was characterized by a quest for legitimacy not only at the level of reserves and the level of the federal government, but also within the international community.

The mid-1970s was a period of contrasting behaviours. At the community level vigorous *protest and confrontation* with DIAND was rampant and a new generation of young and determined political leaders rose to prominence in band politics. Yet, while DIAND was virtually under siege in the regions, at Ottawa headquarters an era of *engagement* or co-operation, and some would say co-optation, was under way as NIB became heavily involved in federal government committees and task forces and in developing programs that could be implemented under the existing Indian Act. Two particularly noteworthy examples of such program development and engagement are to be found in NIB's policy and program of Indian control of Indian education and in the revival of the treaty-making phenomenon as manifested in the James Bay and Northern Quebec Agreement. In return for compensation and for the creation of various governing institutions on which the Cree Indians would have representation or control, the latter Agreement permitted construction of Quebec's massive James Bay hydroelectric power project, which flooded Indian land in the region. (Parts of the Agreement are discussed in Ponting's chapter on the economic development provisions of the new claims settlements.)

Another example of engagement was NIB's lobbying for, and participation in, a joint committee with the federal cabinet. This committee was born out of a September, 1974, physical clash between demonstrators and RCMP guards on Parliament Hill. Its three-and-a-half-year existence was marked by modest progress at best, infrequent meetings, and a high level of mutual frustration. It came to an abrupt end in April, 1978, when NIB announced its surprise withdrawal and denounced the government.[39]

More clearly than any other event, NIB's withdrawal from the joint committee signalled an end to the era of national-level co-operation and the beginning of a period of *disengagement and confrontation*, marked by increased distrust between NIB and DIAND and by each challenging the legitimacy of the other. DIAND's attempts to interest NIB in amending the Indian Act fell on deaf ears as NIB channelled most of its efforts into responding to the window of opportunity opened by Prime Minister Trudeau's constitutional initiative. Local protests and confrontations involving conservationists, sport fishing groups, and the federal Department of Fisheries and Oceans over Indian fishing rights in New Brunswick, British Columbia, and elsewhere, along with warnings and threats of racial violence, formed the backdrop to the early months of this stage. Such events could only have strengthened national Indian leaders' determination to entrench aboriginal rights in the new Canadian constitution.

Confrontation continued during the short-lived Clark government as Indians felt they were being shut out of the constitutional renewal process. For instance, a delegation of 300 Indian chiefs visited Britain to press their point but were denied an audience with the Queen as a result of instructions from the Clark government. With the re-election of a Liberal government determined to patriate and revise the constitution, Indians combined with other Natives (Métis, Inuit, and non-status Indians) to press on the federal and provincial governments their case for the recognition and elaboration of aboriginal rights. The strategy of engagement was revived and over the next four years Indians and other Natives bounced back and forth between strategies of engagement and confrontation as they were buffeted by stronger political winds emanating from other political storms. Since some of this is discussed later in this book, suffice it to say here that the first half of the 1980s saw aboriginal peoples (and their rights) excluded from the proposed constitution; then reincluded amidst literal tears of joy in parliamentary committee; excluded again in the November 5, 1981, constitutional "accord"; reincluded weeks later; fighting the new constitution in the British Parliament and courts; enmeshed in negotiations and discussions with the provinces and the federal government; and finally divided among themselves and locked in an impasse with the provincial and federal governments on the issue of Indian self-government.

Not surprisingly, such a roller-coaster ride took its toll not only on unity between status Indians and other Natives, but also on unity among status Indians themselves, where strains between those in western Canada who had signed treaties and those elsewhere who had not were never far below the surface. For instance, prairie treaty organizations balked at constitutional proposals that would give provincial governments (with whom they have no treaty or legal relationship) veto power over constitutional changes in Indians' relationship with the federal government. Indeed, treaty Indian organizations on the Prairies at one time balked at even proceeding down the path of constitutional reform, for they felt their professed status as sovereign nations to be irretrievably compromised by having Indians included in another nation's (Canada's) constitution. Consequently, in the 1980s the Assembly of First Nations (AFN), as the restructured[40] NIB is known, came to be essentially a shifting coalition into and out of which some western provincial Indian associations seemed to move on almost an issue-by-issue basis.

Such instability undermined the AFN's leadership, particularly in 1985 when prairie associations withdrew from AFN in response to George Erasmus's defeat of Saskatchewan politician David Ahenakew in the AFN presidential election. The instability of the national Indian organization, set in the context of a constitutional stalemate and explicit assertions from various other Indian organizations that "AFN does not represent us," reinforced the predisposition of new DIAND minister David Crombie (former mayor of Toronto) to work most closely with local rather than national political leaders.

The shift in emphasis to the reserve level may offer the greatest potential for concrete achievements over the short term to the end of the 1980s. At that level consensus is easier to build, objectives are usually more attainable, and a pool of leadership and expertise is building.

Attitudinal and Opinion Context of Indian Affairs

In the present Canadian political environment, where politicians are so heavily influenced by public opinion polls, it is important to know and understand the nature of public opinion toward Indians and Indian issues. Public opinion does serve as a very real constraint on policy-makers and thereby sets limits on social change. Rare is the issue, such as capital punishment, on which governments are willing to take a policy stand they know goes against the preferences of the majority of voters. In the face of an apparently (or potentially) hostile public, politicians will likely use public opinion as an excuse for inaction or as a rationale for the rejection of Indian demands. Interest groups that reject terrorism must either negotiate within the confines of prevailing public opinion or endure an especially arduous and costly journey en route to the even partial attainment of their goals. Accordingly, this section of the chapter has as its purpose the mapping of the attitudes and opinions of the Canadian mass public vis-à-vis Indians and Indian issues.

Prior to the mid-1970s, there was little social science research on Canadians' perceptions of Indians and views on Indian issues. The first study was Marlene Mackie's 1968-70 survey research in the Edmonton area on perceptions of Indians, Hutterites, and Ukrainians.[41] She found that the images of Indians were by far the least favourable of the three groups. Respondents' views of Indians emphasized poverty, lack of education, oppression by others, lack of ambition, lack of cleanliness, and excessive consumption of alcohol.

In the mid-1970s the federal government sponsored a national survey of the attitudes of majority-group members toward various ethnic groups. [42] Indians emerged at the bottom of an ethnic prestige hierarchy that ranked nine ethnic groups in Canada. Respondents on the Prairies were particularly negative in their assessment of Indians whereas French Canadians were more positive than the norm.

In 1976 Gibbins and Ponting launched the first in-depth national survey to focus almost exclusively on Indians and Indian issues. It dealt with respondents' knowledge about Indians, perceptions of Indians, general sympathy toward Indians, and opinions on various Indian issues (e.g., the Mackenzie Valley pipeline, Indian control of Indian education) of that period. Two less detailed studies were subsequently commissioned by the Department of Indian Affairs and Northern Development in 1979 and 1981. Other, more recent surveys have been conducted, although these contained just a few questions on Indians or Natives.

Several main findings emerged from the original Gibbins and Ponting study. [43] The first of these is that Indian issues are not a high priority with Canadians and that Canadians are not well informed about Indian affairs. We asked several questions pertaining to knowledge about Indian affairs in Canada. The most basic of these was a so-called "name recognition test" in which respondents were simply asked whether or not they were familiar with each respective name in a list of eighteen names. Many of the key individuals in Indian affairs were found to be virtually unknown. We also constructed a "knowledge index" using respondents' answers to questions such as: "What percentage of Canada's total population would you estimate is native Indian?" and "To the best of your knowledge, what level of government has the major responsibility for dealing with Canada's Indians?" Other questions asked respondents their understanding of the meaning of terms like "aboriginal rights" and the difference between "status" and "nonstatus" Indians. On only one of these dimensions (the level of government mainly responsible for dealing with Indians) is the Canadian public reasonably well informed. There is, however, a rough east-west gradient in levels of knowledge, with respondents living east of Ontario having particularly low levels of knowledge and those living to the west having somewhat higher levels.

A second principal discovery of the 1976 study is that, overall, the Canadian public is more sympathetic than hostile to Indians. We constructed a second index, which we called the "Indian sympathy index," to measure generalized sympathy, or lack of sympathy, toward Indians and Indian concerns. The index was based on ten statements (e.g., "Indians deserve to be a lot better off economically than they are now.") to which respondents were asked to indicate their degree of agreement or disagreement on a five-point scale ranging from strongly agree to strongly disagree. The distribution of scores approximated a normal or "bell" curve; the bulk of the respondents fell near the middle of the scale with very few respondents falling at either extreme. The distribution suggests a public disposition of neutrality or indifference toward Indian issues; there are very few extreme bigots just as there are very few extreme liberals. Although Francophones demonstrated a more positive outlook toward Indians and Indian issues than did Anglophones, Francophones were relatively less well informed about Indian issues than the Anglophone respondents. The greater degree of Francophone sympathy may therefore result from a form of minority-group identification with Indians rather than from a more acute grasp of the situation of Indians in Canada. In this light it should also be noted that, for the national sample, respondents who were relatively well informed about Indians were not, on the whole, any more sympathetic toward Indians and Indian issues than were respondents who were relatively uninformed. There was also no relationship between the degree of formal education and index scores.

Our third major finding was that the perceptions of native Canadians held by the Canadian public are complex and multifaceted. A small minority subscribes to views of Indians that are unquestionably pejorative: Indians are seen as lazy, lacking in motivation, factionalized, overly dependent on government handouts, and facing serious problems with the use of alcohol. On the other hand a much larger proportion of the Canadian public perceives Indians to be facing problems that are not of their own creation, such as a lack of economic opportunities, discrimination and prejudice, and an obstructionist government.

This leads directly to our fourth general conclusion, that is, there is considerable evidence that adult Canadians perceive the federal government to be an obstacle to the realization of Indian aims and aspirations. For instance, two-thirds of the respondents agreed (strongly or moderately) with the statement: "The federal Department of Indian Affairs tends to be more concerned with bureaucratic red tape than seeing to the needs of the Indian people." Only one in every nine respondents disagreed.

Our fifth general observation is that there was no evidence of a public opinion backlash against Indian protest. On the contrary, Canadians exhibited rather low levels of awareness of Indian protest; much of it went virtually unnoticed. However, the absence of a nationwide backlash does not preclude the possibility of one or more localized backlashes, particularly in areas of concentrated Indian population.

Our final general observation pertains to respondents' characteristics that tend to be associated with attitudes toward Indians and Indian issues. Two such characteristics stood out – namely the respondent's region of residence and language. Francophones displayed relatively low levels of knowledge about Indians, relatively low levels of awareness of Indian protest, and relatively higher levels of sympathy. In addition to language-related differences in knowledge about and sympathy for Indians, noteworthy regional variations emerged on a large number of questions. For instance, only 12 per cent of respondents from Atlantic Canada, but 32 per cent from the Prairies, perceived Indians to be characterized by what might be called "personality deficiencies" (e.g., lack of motivation). Similarly, on the aforementioned Indian sympathy index, respondents from Saskatchewan and Alberta scored very low on sympathy toward Indians, while British Columbia and especially Quebec scored quite high. Other social characteristics of respondents – age, gender, education, and federal political party identification – bore little relationship to attitudes toward Indians and issues.

On the basis of the federal government's partial replication of our study three years later, it can be said that in the adult Canadian population as a whole the average level of sympathy toward Indians was virtually identical in 1976 and 1979.[44] Gains in sympathy in some sectors of the population (e.g., Liberal Party supporters in the Atlantic provinces, British Columbia, and especially Ontario) were offset by corresponding declines in sympathy among Francophones. Quebecers nevertheless remained the most sympathetic sector of the population in their attitudes toward Indians.

Also, at the end of the decade there was still no evidence of polarization into supportive and hostile camps, and the Canadian public remained more sympathetic than resistant to Indian aspirations. This was particularly so with regard to Indians' claims for special cultural protections and for Indian control of Indian education. It also remained true that important differences exist in sympathy for Indians across the regions. However, some social characteristics which in the earlier study were unrelated to sympathy toward Indians had begun by 1979 to take on some differentiating ability. Perhaps most importantly in this respect, a significant gender gap emerged in attitudes toward

Indians, with women clearly exhibiting more sympathy than men. The gap between adherents of the three different mainstream political parties also widened, as did that between people in different income brackets.

The 1981 survey results[45] supported our 1976 generalization that Indian issues are not a high priority with Canadians. Furthermore, the clear impression left from inspection of those four questions asked in comparable form across the three surveys (see Table 1) is that levels of sympathy for Indians have undergone a significant decline, although on average they probably still have not declined to a point below the midpoint on the sympathy-hostility continuum. Similarly, a majority of the sample in 1981 agrees with the statement "the federal government has too much control over the lives of Indians," which reinforces our original observation that to a significant extent government is seen as an obstacle to the realization of Indian aims and aspirations. Various data not shown here support the earlier generalization that there is no polarization into two extreme camps. In addition, linguistic breakdowns (not shown) provided by the survey research firm for the fifteen questions asked in 1981 show that Francophones are still more sympathetic toward Indians than are Anglophones, although it appears that the gap continues to become narrower.

The pronounced regional variation in attitudes continued to exist into the 1980s. However, the respective ranks among the provinces changed. While Quebec remained most sympathetic and Saskatchewan very low in sympathy, Manitoba and Alberta exhibited increased levels of sympathy and British Columbia showed decreased levels of sympathy. However, systematic variations by sex and political party identification of the respondent, which were noted earlier, were not present in 1981. Religion, though, continued to play a differentiating role, as Catholics generally exhibited more favourable attitudes toward Indians than did Protestants. Finally, by way of reference to our earlier generalizations, the only indicator available in this survey suggests that Canadians remain poorly informed about Indian issues.

Thus, for the most part the several generalizations formulated on the basis of the 1976 study remain valid into the early 1980s, to the extent that we have been able to put them to the test in subsequent surveys. What, though, can be said about new dimensions of public opinion that have risen to prominence since the 1976 survey? To these we turn now.

Limitations of space do not permit us to discuss all of the questions and answers reported in Table 2, so we shall focus on a few highlights

Table 1

Attitudes toward Indians, 1976-81

Item	Per cent Supportive of Indians			Per cent Antagonistic toward Indians		
	1976	1979	1981	1976	1979	1981
Special cultural protection ('76, '79)/Special rights ('81)*	44	67	39	36	27	57
Indians deserve to be a lot better off economically than they are now.	72	64	60	12	28	34
At the present time, Indians receive enough financial support/backing from the federal government.	31	27	23	34	49	56
DIAND more concerned with red tape than with Indians ('76)/The federal government has too much control over the lives of Indians ('81).	65	–	51	12	–	32
Indians, not other governments, should decide what Indians are taught in school ('76, '79)/Indians should control their own government on Indian reserves ('81).	35	49	64	49	44	28
Indians should have political powers equivalent to provincial governments.**	–	–	39	–	–	47
Treaties should be renegotiated ('76)/Canada's responsibility to provide financial compensation for Indian land claims ('81).***	55	–	57	22	–	32

* 1981 phraseology was: Indians, as the first Canadians, should have special rights that other groups don't have.
** 1981 phraseology was: Any future claims settlement should include the establishment for the Indians of political powers equivalent to those held by provincial governments.
*** 1981 phraseology was: Canada has a responsibility to provide financial compensation for Indian land claims.

SOURCES: J. Rick Ponting, "Conflict and Change in Indian/non-Indian Relations in Canada," *Canadian Journal of Sociology*, IX, 2 (1984), p. 146; CROP Inc., "Attitudes Regarding Indians and Land Claims," CROP Omnibus 82-1, January, 1982.

contained in it and in other studies conducted in recent years. One of the most noteworthy findings in the table is the relatively large proportion (39 per cent) of the sample agreeing with the suggestion that Indian governments should have powers virtually equivalent to those of the provincial governments (question C). This question was posed just a few days or weeks after the provincial governments had been in the national limelight in developing the November 5, 1981, constitutional accord. It is probably safe to speculate that very few of the respondents would have much of an appreciation of the ramifications of province-like status for Indian governments. (See Chapter 16.) Also, the inclusion of the word ''political'' in the question might have led some respondents to differentiate in their own mind between political power and legislative power (jurisdiction); thus, some respondents might have been answering in terms of ''political power'' and others in terms of legislative power. Such a conservative interpretation of the results on this question is consistent with the low level of support expressed by respondents in this and other surveys when the suggestion is offered that Indians should have *special rights* that other groups do not have. For instance, we found in data not shown here that support for Indians plummeted and antagonism doubled when the phraseology of an item was changed from ''special cultural protection'' to ''special rights that other groups don't have.'' Similarly, in question H in Table 2 Canadians overwhelmingly agreed that Canada's native people should not be given special rights. Thus, even around the time when Indians' special rights were being enshrined in the very constitution of the country, the egalitarian norm in Canadian culture was so strong as to lead respondents to renounce the notion of special rights for Indians; hence, the conservative interpretation of responses to question C above.

Notwithstanding those findings, Canadians have come to hold the opinion that Indians can, and should be allowed to, govern themselves. This was found in a 1984 national survey commissioned by the Assembly of First Nations. Fifty-six per cent reported the opinion that Indians are capable of governing themselves (20 per cent described Indians as incapable of governing themselves) and a virtually identical number said that Indians should be allowed to govern themselves (31 per cent disagreed). However, a majority (52 per cent) were not even aware of the televised 1983 First Ministers and Aboriginal Leaders Conference at which constitutional aspects of this issue were the central agenda item. Yet, when the issue was presented to them, a plurality (47 per cent) agreed that the rights of Indians to self-government should be included in the constitution. One-quarter of the respondents disagreed and about an equal number expressed no opinion. Paradox-

Table 2

Attitudes toward Indians and Other Natives, Miscellaneous Survey Data, 1981-84

Question	Year	Sample	Strongly Supportive of Natives	Moderately Supportive of Natives	Neutral; Don't Know; No Answer	Moderately Antagonistic to Natives	Strongly Antagonistic to Natives	N
A. Indians should control their own government on Indian reserves.	Fall* 1981	National	33	31	7	16	12	1,994
B. On reserves, Indian governments should have powers similar to those held by other local government bodies.	Fall 1981	National	36	39	7	10	7	1,994
C. Any future claims settlement should include the establishment for the Indians of political powers equivalent to those held by provincial governments.	Fall 1981	National	13	26	13	24	23	1,994
D. Any future claims settlement should provide the Indians with a permanent share of the revenue gained from resource extraction.	Fall 1981	National	21	36	12	16	15	1,994
E. Any future claims settlement should provide for permanent Indian control over the land, its development, and exploitation.	Fall 1981	National	17	31	15	20	17	1,994

Per cent

F. After a claims settlement has been made, the federal government should continue to have obligations to Indians beyond what it provides to other Canadians.	Fall 1981	National	9	21	8	23	38	1,994
G. Various groups have proposed a number of additions to the protection of civil rights in Canada. Forgetting, for the moment, whether or not these items should be in a constitution, please tell me whether or not you support: granting native people limited rights to self-government.	1981	National	41	18	13	5	24	3,953
H. Canada's native people should not be given special status and rights – they should be treated just like the rest of us. **	1983	National	14	12	6	17	50	1,500
J. As you probably know, some of Canada's native people, that is, some Indian and Inuit groups, argue that their original rights to land have not been recognized and that they should now be compensated. Generally speaking, do you agree or disagree with this argument?	1983	National	–	52	3	46	–	1,500
K. Generally speaking, do you think Canada's native people should be given the power to control future development of certain areas of land?	1983	National	–	44	3	53	–	1,500

Per cent

Question	Year	Sample	Strongly Supportive of Natives	Moderately Supportive of Natives	Neutral; Don't Know; No Answer	Moderately Antagonistic to Natives	Strongly Antagonistic to Natives	N
L. Many different individuals and groups receive social services and benefits from government. Would you say native people should receive more or less social services and benefits from the government than they do now?	1981	National	*More* 54		*Same* 0	*Less* 29	*No Opin.* 17	1,500
	1983	National	45		9	31	15	1,500
	1984	National	46		7	28	19	1,500
M. Tell me whether the federal government has done an excellent, good, fair, or poor job at supporting Canada's native people.	Winter 1984	National	*Exc.* 6	*Good* 23	*No Opin.* 9	*Fair* 35	*Poor* 27	981
N. We would like to know how much effort you think government should put into . . . protecting the rights of native people. Remember that putting more effort into one of these areas would require a shift of money from other areas or an increase in taxes.	1981	National	*Much More* 12	*More* 37	*About Same* 41	*Less* 9	*Much Less* 2	3,753
O. . . . for each statement tell me how much it applies to your view of what it means to be a Canadian: recognizing the special place of native people in Canada.	Fall 1982	Six western Can. major cities	*Very Much* 41	*Some-what* 30	*Don't Know* 2	*Little Bit* 14	*Not At All* 13	2,408

ically, a large number (42 per cent) of those agreeing that the right to Indian self-government should be included in the constitution based their agreement on notions of *equality* (e.g., "deserve identical rights as other people"; "should have same/equal rights"). This suggests that the implications of the question escaped many of those who supported constitutional entrenchment.

The previously noted perception of the federal government as an obstacle to the attainment of Indian aims and aspirations is reinforced by a question on a 1984 survey in which a solid majority (62 per cent) characterized the federal government as doing a "poor" or "fair" job (versus 29 per cent saying "excellent" or "good") of supporting Canada's native people. Similar results were obtained in a 1981 survey conducted in the six major cities of western Canada and in the 1984 AFN survey. The AFN data show that that perception is rooted in an awareness of Indians' low standard of living, in a perception that Indians are unhappy, and in a belief that Indians should have more rights. Data from the aforementioned western Canada survey also show that the perception of the federal government as an obstacle to Indians is rooted in a belief that government does too much for Indians. For instance, 28 per cent of respondents in that survey said that government assistance to native people is "excessive" (versus 22 per cent saying "inadequate"), and when asked if any group receives too much government assistance, more respondents identified native people than any other group (i.e., 21 per cent for Natives and 7 per cent for the next most frequently cited group, the poor).

Another perception held by Canadians, which we noted in the 1976 survey results, is the victimization of Indians. More recent evidence suggests that these views have persisted into the 1980s in a sizable minority of the population. A 1983 "law and justice" national survey

---

Table 2
* The survey for questions A to F was conducted November 18-December 16, 1981, shortly after the nationwide controversy concerning the dropping of aboriginal rights from the November 5 constitutional accord.
** This question was originally asked on an eleven-point scale ranging from +5 (total agreement) to −5 (total disagreement). For our purposes these are recoded as follows: strongly supportive of Natives (−4, −5); moderately supportive of Natives (−1, −2, −3); neutral (0); moderately unsupportive of Natives (+1, +2, +3); strongly unsupportive of Natives (+4, +5).
SOURCES: CROP Inc., "Attitudes Regarding Indians and Land Claims," CROP Omnibus 82-1, January, 1982; Public Archives of Canada, Surveys G00012757, G0001264, G0001266, G0001267, G0001268; and miscellaneous data from the files of the Research Branch, DIAND.

probed various aspects of the victimization theme as it pertains to Natives' relations with legal institutions such as the police and the courts. Among the 40 per cent of respondents who felt that "the police in Canada are unfair to some individuals or groups in society," 29 per cent (or about 9 per cent of the entire sample) cited Natives when asked "Which particular groups of Canadians do you feel the police do not treat fairly?" Then, when given a list of eight particular groups, about another 10 per cent of the entire sample (or 30 per cent of those to whom this follow-up question was posed) identified Natives as one group treated unfairly by police.

In conclusion, to the limited extent that Canadians think about native people at all, they seem to be characterized by a certain degree of ambivalence. On the one hand, responses to a number of questions in Table 2 (questions D, E, G, J, L, N, O) garner majority or near majority support for Indians/Natives, even when explicit mention is made of increasing taxes or of shifting money from other areas and even when some special recognition for Indians is involved. There is, unquestionably, a reservoir of sympathy and support for Indians in the larger Canadian population. However, special *rights* or *powers* for Natives (questions C, H, and K) or continuing obligations after the settling of land claims (F) fall well short of being supported by even a plurality of Canadians. The contrasting answers to similar pairs of questions (E and K) capture this ambivalence well.

It seems that most Canadians recognize that injustices have been perpetrated against Indians and other native people and are prepared to acquiesce in the righting of those wrongs. Canadians are now prepared to have their government give special attention and symbolic importance to Indians/Natives, give special allocations of resources to address their problems, provide special protection to native culture (as part of the larger Canadian ideal of multiculturalism or cultural preservation), and devote special effort to the protection of the civil rights of Indians. Government can even "grant" limited special powers to the Indian collectivity to assist in Indian self-improvement, without running seriously afoul of nonIndian public opinion. However, despite a fairly widespread recognition of the gravity of the problems, in the minds of Canadians there is no sense of urgency[46] or priority in addressing them. Furthermore, the scope and extent of government action is circumscribed by Canadian norms of equality, such that Natives must not be seen to be receiving treatment that is too special.

Although levels of sympathy for Indians have apparently declined somewhat since the mid-1970s, there is no indication in the public opinion data that governments have gone anywhere near too far in dealing with Indians. The limits of public support are still to be tested, for the decline in sympathy has been neither a backlash nor a polarization, but rather an erosion. There exist ideological resources (e.g., the justification of policy changes in terms of Canadians' sense of justice and human rights or in terms of "getting the government off Indians' backs") that can be mobilized to halt or reverse that erosion, if Canadians can be convinced that the problems will be significantly diminished thereby.

Conclusion

In less than twenty years Indians have experienced changes of a magnitude that would have been utterly inconceivable in the late 1960s. The legitimacy of the paternalistic and ethnocentric policies and forms of administration that characterized the 200 years surrounding Confederation has been shattered. Once treated as second-class citizens by arrogant Indian agents and junior bureaucrats in government, Indian leaders at the local level now command audiences with cabinet ministers while their national leaders negotiate with prime ministers and premiers and meet with popes and monarchs. Once shunted to the political, economic, and geographic periphery of Canadian society, Indians now have aboriginal rights recognized in the constitution, undertake multimillion-dollar economic development projects on reserves, and lay claim to immensely valuable real estate scattered throughout the country.

Since the release of the 1969 white paper, Indian affairs have been in a constant state of flux or transition. Ironically, though, along some dimensions the wheel has come full circle. For instance, the national political organization in the mid-1980s, as in the late 1960s and early 1970s, finds itself in the midst of a crisis of legitimacy (and disunity) and of finances,[47] and the Department of Indian Affairs again finds itself in the midst of a major restructuring and a threatened dissolution. Reserve-level community development and devolution of authority from DIAND to bands once again appear to be of major importance. The leaked 1985 task force report of the deputy prime minister and the planned staff cuts at DIAND[48] raise the spectre of renewed federal government attempts to transfer federal responsibilities for Indians to the provinces.

The remainder of this book addresses some of the problems and concerns that have arisen in the transition toward decolonization, takes a measure of the change attained to date (e.g., social, demographic, economic), and examines new institutional arrangements that may come into play as Indians seek to regain some of the momentum for change – momentum which along some dimensions seemed to be dissipating by the mid-1980s.

Notes

1. The portion of this chapter dealing with events prior to 1970 is excerpted from Chapter One in J. Rick Ponting and Roger Gibbins, *Out Of Irrelevance: A Socio-political Introduction to Indian Affairs in Canada* (Scarborough, Ont.: Butterworths, 1980). Many of the citations in the original have been omitted here.

2. D. Bruce Sealey and Antoine S. Lussier, *The Métis: Canada's Forgotten People* (Winnipeg: Manitoba Métis Federation Press, 1975).

3. Quoted in A.D. Doerr, "Indian Policy," in G. Bruce Doern and V. Seymour Wilson (eds.), *Issues in Canadian Public Policy* (Toronto: Macmillan, 1974), p. 40.

4. Kahn-Tineta Miller *et al.*, *Historical Development of the Indian Act* (Ottawa: DIAND, 1978), p. 66.

5. Sally M. Weaver, "Segregation and The Indian Act: The Dialogue of Equality vs. Special Status," paper presented to the Canadian Ethnic Studies Association National Conference on Canadian Culture and Ethnic Groups, Toronto, 1973, p. 5.

6. Miller *et al.*, *Historical Development*, p. 66.

7. George Manuel and Michael Posluns, *The Fourth World: An Indian Reality* (Toronto: Collier Macmillan, 1974), p. 54.

8. Harold Cardinal, *The Unjust Society: The Tragedy of Canada's Indians* (Edmonton: Hurtig, 1969), pp. 43-44.

9. *Ibid.*, p. 45.

10. Harold Cardinal, *The Rebirth of Canada's Indians* (Edmonton: Hurtig, 1977), p. 97.

11. Allan G. Harper, "Canada's Administration," *American Indigena*, 5, 3 (1946), p. 297.

12. Allan G. Harper, "Canada's Indian Administration: Basic Concepts and Objectives," *American Indigena*, 4, 2 (1945), p. 132.

13. Miller *et al.*, *Historical Development*, p. 191.

14. *Ibid.*

15. *Ibid.*, p. 114.

16. Harper, "Basic Concepts and Objectives," p. 127.

17. See E. Palmer Patterson II, *The Canadian Indian: A History Since 1500* (Don Mills, Ont.: Collier Macmillan, 1972), pp. 63, 74.

18. Harper, "Basic Concepts and Objectives," p. 122.

19. Cardinal, *The Unjust Society*, pp. 87-95.

20. L.F.S. Upton, "The Origins of Canadian Indian Policy," *Journal of Canadian Studies*, 8, 4 (1973), pp. 51-61.

21. Miller *et al.*, *Historical Development*, p. 108.

22. Derek G. Smith (ed.), *Canadian Indians and the Law: Selected Documents, 1663-1971* (Toronto: McClelland and Stewart, 1975), p. xxvii.

23. *Ibid.*, p. xxviii.
24. Cardinal, *The Unjust Society*, p. 29.
25. *Ibid.*, p. 36.
26. R. St. J. Macdonald, *Native Rights in Canada* (Toronto: Indian Eskimo Association, 1970), p. 177.
27. For an excellent and detailed discussion of the formulation of the policy contained in the 1969 white paper, see Sally M. Weaver, *The Making of Indian Policy, 1968-70: The Hidden Agenda* (Toronto: University of Toronto Press, 1980).
28. Weaver, "Segregation and the Indian Act," p. 3.
29. The Hawthorn Report was a two-volume report of a study team commissioned by the federal government to survey Indian conditions in the mid-1960s. It was virtually a royal commission. See Harry B. Hawthorn (ed.), *A Survey of the Contemporary Indians of Canada: A Report on Economic, Political, Educational Needs and Policies* (Ottawa: DIAND, 1967, Part 1), p. 13.
30. For a more detailed discussion of similarities and differences in the situation of Indians and French Québécois, see Ponting and Gibbins, *Out Of Irrelevance*, pp. 321-23.
31. *Ibid.*, pp. 27-28, 327-31.
32. *Ibid.*, pp. 176-77.
33. See *ibid.*, pp. 177-78, for more detail.
34. *Ibid.*, pp. 189-90.
35. Personal conversation with an Indian leader who wishes to remain anonymous, February, 1985.
36. According to the draft of this statute given first reading in the House of Commons on February 5, 1986, it will remove the Sechelt Band in British Columbia from the jurisdiction of much of the Indian Act.
37. Hawthorn (ed.), *Survey*, pp. 364-65; James Frideres, *Canada's Indians: Contemporary Conflicts* (Scarborough, Ont.: Prentice-Hall, 1974), p. 112.
38. For a more detailed discussion of the founding of the National Indian Brotherhood and the history of its precursors, see Ponting and Gibbins, *Out Of Irrelevance*, Chapter 7.
39. See *ibid.*, pp. 257-69; Sally M. Weaver, "The Joint Cabinet/National Indian Brotherhood Committee: A Unique Experiment in Pressure Group Relations," *Canadian Public Administration*, 25, 2 (1982), pp. 211-39, for a discussion of the joint committee and its failure.
40. The NIB was restructured such that all of the country's chiefs became the voting members, in place of delegates from the various provincial/territorial member organizations.
41. Marlene M. Mackie, "Ethnic Stereotypes and Prejudice: Alberta Indians, Hutterites, and Ukrainians," *Canadian Ethnic Studies*, V1, 1-2 (1974), pp. 39-52.
42. John W. Berry, Rudolph Kalin, and Donald M. Taylor, *Multiculturalism and Ethnic Attitudes in Canada* (Ottawa: Minister of Supply and Services, 1977).
43. For a more thorough account of the findings of this study, see Ponting and Gibbins, *Out Of Irrelevance*, Chapter 3, and various articles by Gibbins and

Ponting or Ponting and Gibbins cited in the bibliography to that book. The sample consisted of 1,832 persons aged eighteen and over, randomly selected by professionally approved methods from among those persons living in the ten provinces. Indian reserves were excluded. Interviews were conducted in the respondent's home in the official language (English or French) of his/her choice.

44. See J. Rick Ponting, "Conflict and Change in Indian/nonIndian Relations in Canada: Comparison of 1976 and 1979 National Attitude Surveys," *Canadian Journal of Sociology*, IX, 2 (1984), pp. 137-58.

45. The authors wish to express special thanks to the following individuals for their cheerful and determined assistance in procuring the data reported in this section: Liz Fraikin and her staff at DIAND's Research Group, and Sue Gavrel, Pauline Charron, and Winston Gomes at the Public Archives of Canada.

46. On the aforementioned 1983 "law and justice survey," the opening question asked ". . . is there a particular law or area of law that you think should be changed in some way immediately?" Not quite half the sample replied in the affirmative. Only 0.4 per cent of them cited "Native or Minority Rights"; there was no list provided to respondents. "Capital punishment" and "drunk driving" were the two most frequently cited responses at 25 and 15 per cent of those citing any law, respectively.

47. The reference to financial crisis on the part of AFN alludes to the $2 million over-expenditure of budget that came to light in early 1985, to the deputy prime minister's April, 1985, task force recommendation to slash the funding of native political associations, and to serious allegations by AFN president George Erasmus that his predecessor engaged in highly corrupt spending practices while in office.

48. "Indian Affairs May Eliminate 1,500 Jobs," *Globe and Mail* (National Edition), October 3, 1985, pp. 1-2.

Chapter Two

The Socio-Demographic Conditions of Registered Indians

by Andrew J. Siggner

The Indian population in Canada is experiencing not only important political and legislative changes, but also noteworthy social, demographic, and economic changes.[1] In taking stock of these changes I shall at times draw from my earlier writing[2] for the historical context or longer-term trends, but the main emphasis will be on developments since the mid-1970s, including the extent to which opportunities have been opening for Indian people. Special attention will be devoted to one particular legislative change – the June, 1985, amendment to the Indian Act of Canada allowing for the reinstatement of a potential 76,000 persons as Indians.[3]

Size and Distribution of the Population

Historical records on the size of the Indian population are sketchy. Kroeber[4] estimates that prior to the arrival of Europeans, the total Indian population of North America was about 900,000 people, of whom about 220,000 were in what is now Canada. The introduction of firearms from Europe was one of several factors contributing to a subsequent decline in the Indian population. By the seventeenth century both intertribal warfare and English-French warfare, into which Indians were drawn as allies of the Europeans, were also taking their toll on the Indian population. Particularly devastating were the famines (e.g., that of 1879-80 on the Prairies) and epidemic diseases such as smallpox, scarlet fever, tuberculosis, and influenza, against which Indians had no natural immunity. Epidemics of these diseases were numerous and sometimes literally decimated the population they struck.

With the advent of Confederation in 1867, record-keeping improved somewhat. Shortly after Confederation the Indian population of what is now Canada was approximately 102,000. Over the next seventy years (to 1941), the Indian population apparently fluctuated between that level and about 122,000,[5] which represented from 2.5 to 1.1 per cent of the total Canadian population. Not until 1941 did the Indian population begin to show a pattern of sustained growth and not until 1966 did the Indian population of Canada again reach the size it had been just prior to European contact.

By 1981 the registered Indian population had reached an estimated 335,475, according to the count[6] from the Indian register maintained by DIAND. Indians' share of the total Canadian population amounted to 1.4 per cent. The most recent projections (assuming medium growth rates) envisage the registered Indian population reaching over 456,000 persons by 1996, or about 1.7 per cent of the total Canadian population.[7]

The distribution of the Indian population across Canada in 1984 is shown in Table 3. Here we observe that Indians are most numerous in Ontario and British Columbia, which between them account for four out of every ten Indians in Canada. The Prairie provinces account for another four out of ten and Quebec for one out of ten. However, as the table shows, when we rank the provinces and territories according to the proportion of the total provincial/territorial population composed of Indians, a quite different ordering from that just cited emerges. In the Northwest Territories and Yukon, registered Indians constitute a larger share (about 17 per cent in each) of the population than they do in any of the ten provinces. In fact, when all aboriginal peoples are combined together in the Northwest Territories, they make up the majority of the territorial population. In Manitoba and Saskatchewan registered Indians now constitute about 5 per cent of the provincial population, while in the separate provinces of central and eastern Canada, Indians account for 1 per cent or less of the provincial populations and are projected to remain at a similarly low level through 1996. The main gains in the Indian population as a proportion of the total regional population are expected to occur in the Northwest Territories and Yukon (combined) and in Saskatchewan and Manitoba. By 1996 registered Indians are expected to constitute 22, 7, and 6 per cent of the population in these three regions.[8]

Another important aspect of the geographical distribution of the Indian population is the proportion of Indian band members living on-reserve and the proportion living off-reserve.[9] The size and growth of the on- and off-reserve populations have policy and planning implications for several levels of governments (federal, provincial, Indian) that provide services to Indians in either type of location. The size, growth rate, and composition of the on-reserve population must also be a central concern to bands that aspire to self-government but whose pro-

Table 3

Regional Distribution of the Registered Indian Population and Indian Lands

	Atlantic*	Que.	Ont.	Man.	Sask.	Alta.	B.C.	N.W.T.	Yukon	Canada
Total Indian population, 1984**	13,590	34,335	77,313	52,049	54,188	43,436	61,730	8,530	3,638	348,809
% of total Indian population, 1984	3.9	9.8	22.2	14.9	15.5	12.5	17.7	2.5	1.0	100.0
% of total provincial/territorial population, 1984	0.6	0.5	0.9	4.9	5.4	1.9	2.2	17.2	16.5	1.4
% off-reserve, 1984***	28.2	14.4	31.9	26.7	34.0	24.7	35.9	7.2	24.5	28.7
No. of Indian bands, 1985	31	39	126	60	68	41	196	14	17	592
% of Indian bands, 1985	5.2	6.6	21.3	10.1	11.5	6.9	33.1	2.4	2.9	100.0
No. of reserves and settlements, 1985	67	33	185	103	142	90	1,610	29	25	2,284
% of reserves and settlements, 1985	2.9	1.4	8.1	4.5	6.2	3.9	70.5	1.3	1.1	99.9
Approx. total area of reserves, 1985 (× 1,000 hectares)****	30	75	699	218	615	657	338	14	3	2,649
Average area of reserve or settlement, 1985 (× 1,000 hectares)*****	0.4	2.3	3.8	2.1	4.3	7.3	0.2	0.5	0.1	1.1

* Includes a new Indian band established at Conne River, Newfoundland, in 1984.

** The official count from DIAND as of December 31, 1984, unadjusted for late-reported births and deaths (which would add about 2-3 per cent to the population). Such an adjustment would be unlikely to alter significantly the percentages shown in this table.

*** Off-reserve includes Indians living off reserves and off Crown land settlements.

**** 1 hectare = 2.5 acres; 1,000 hectares = 2,500 acres = 3.91 square miles. Therefore, the average size of an Indian reserve in Canada is 4.3 square miles. Many, however, are much larger.

SOURCES: DIAND, *Registered Indian Population by Sex & Residence, 1984* (Ottawa: Program Reference Centre, 1985); DIAND, *Schedule of Indian Bands, Reserves & Settlements, June 1, 1985* (Ottawa: Program Reference Centre, 1985); and Statistics Canada, unpublished post-censal estimates of Canada's population, August, 1985, forthcoming publication as Catalogue No. 91-210.

grams could be handicapped by the ineconomies of scale and the "shallowness" of the pool of local human resources, both of which are problems inherent in virtually all small populations. These two problems could be further exacerbated by a sizable or an extended migration out of reserve communities, all of which are already relatively small.

From the mid-1960s the proportion of the Indian population living off-reserve began to climb from its level of about 16 per cent, probably in response to employment opportunities, especially in the urban industrial areas of Ontario and British Columbia. Then, as urban economic growth slackened in the early 1970s, a movement back to the reserves occurred along with a diminution of the out-migration from reserves. Thus, as Figure 1 shows, the proportion living off-reserve ceased its rapid increase and levelled off in the mid-1970s at about 27 per cent before climbing to almost 30 per cent by 1981. In absolute numbers, the off-reserve population reached almost 100,000 persons in 1981.

What will happen to the size and growth rate of the off-reserve population in the last half of the 1980s will depend on demographic, social, housing, and economic conditions both on- and off-reserve. The on-reserve impact of the reinstatement to Indian status of perhaps 76,000 persons is potentially important but difficult to predict. Most of these are non-status Indian women (and their children) who have been living off-reserve. It is not clear how many of those eligible under the new Act will seek reinstatement, and of those, how many will seek residency on reserves or in Indian settlements. However, the amended Indian Act does allow Indian band councils to control band membership and therefore to control one aspect of on-reserve residence. From a policy perspective, it will be important to monitor the numbers and demographic characteristics of those reinstated, for they constitute a new component of growth to the Indian population and may affect planning and programs for both reserves and off-reserve jurisdictions.

Two (among many) important factors for the economic viability of Indian bands are their size and location. The number of bands with a population of 1,000 or more people has increased marginally from 13 per cent of all bands in 1977 to 16 per cent by 1981. However, as the recent projections contained in Table 4 show, the proportion of bands of this size is expected to increase to at least 25 per cent ((126 + 17)/ 578 bands) before the end of the century, assuming that no new bands are created. This table also shows that by 1996, 64 per cent (44.6 per cent + 19.2 per cent) of all Indians will be members of these larger

Figure 1
Registered Indian Population Living On and Off Reserve (and Crown Land), 1966-81

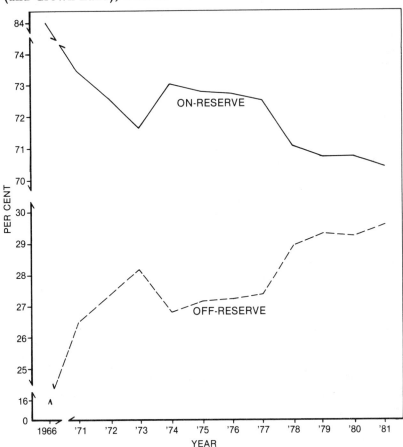

SOURCES: J. Perrault *et al.*, *Population Projections of Registered Indians, 1982 to 1996* (Ottawa: DIAND, 1985), Table 5.6; and A.J. Siggner, *An Overview of Demographic, Social, and Economic Conditions Among Canada's Registered Indians* (Ottawa: DIAND, 1979).

bands. This figure is up from 44 per cent in 1981. However, if the assumption that no new bands are created does not hold, for instance if small bands amalgamate with each other to form large bands, or if they amalgamate with existing large bands to form even larger bands (both of which may prove necessary for the success of self-government), the aforementioned 25 per cent could prove to be a conservative estimate. On the other hand, the number of small bands – those

61

Table 4

Distribution of Indian Bands by Membership Size and Region, 1981 and 1996

Region	No. of Bands and % of Population*	Band Membership Size and Year									
		1-499		500-999		1,000-2,999		3,000 +		Total	
		1981	1996	1981	1996	1981	1996	1981	1996	1981	1996
Atlantic	No.	23	15	3	9	3	5	–	–	29	29
	%	47.6	21.3	17.0	30.8	35.4	47.9	–	–	100.0	100.0
Quebec	No.	19	15	8	10	11	13	1	1	39	39
	%	15.8	10.2	16.8	16.9	52.0	57.0	15.4	15.9	100.0	100.0
Ontario	No.	75	65	23	23	14	22	3	5	115	115
	%	21.9	16.9	21.7	16.0	32.1	35.7	24.3	32.2	100.0	100.0
Manitoba	No.	26	12	16	23	18	21	–	4	60	60
	%	15.4	4.1	23.2	22.1	61.4	52.3	0	21.5	100.0	100.0
Saskatchewan	No.	22	13	28	23	17	30	1	2	68	68
	%	12.5	5.0	36.9	23.5	44.7	60.8	5.9	10.7	100.0	100.0
Alberta	No.	17	14	13	9	8	13	3	5	41	41
	%	9.7	6.7	24.4	13.0	34.3	36.2	31.6	44.1	100.0	100.0
British Columbia	No.	166	146	17	30	12	19	–	–	195	195
	%	54.0	39.2	21.1	25.4	24.9	35.4	–	–	100.0	100.0
Yukon and N.W.T.	No.	22	19	8	9	1	3	–	–	31	31
	%	43.8	33.6	41.1	39.3	15.1	27.1	–	–	100.0	100.0
Canada	No.	370	299	116	136	84	126	8	17	578	578
	%	21.6	15.3	34.4	20.9	33.8	44.6	10.2	19.2	100.0	100.0

SOURCE: J. Perreault, L. Paquette, and M.V. George, *Population Projections of Registered Indians, 1982 to 1996* (Ottawa: DIAND, 1985), Table 5.13.

with less than 500 persons – is projected to decline from 370, or 64 per cent of all bands, to 299, or 52 per cent of the total. The smaller bands will see their share of the total population of Indian individuals decline from about 22 per cent in 1981 to about 15 per cent by 1996 (again, assuming no change in the number of bands).

If economic opportunities do not materialize for this growing Indian population, particularly on reserves, the already serious unemployment problem and its related social problems will likely be exacerbated. Readers should also note that these national projections mask considerable regional variation. For instance, local economies of scale will be particularly difficult to realize in British Columbia and the Territories, where over one-third of the bands, compared to around 5 per cent of the bands in the Prairie provinces, are projected to still have fewer than 500 persons in 1996. Accordingly, for economic development, the demographic prognosis is not uniformly encouraging across the country.

The Demographic Transition

The demographic transition is a useful model to describe the historical trends in births and deaths for the Indian population. It has three stages. The first stage is characterized by high fertility and high mortality rates and, for the Indian population, this coincides with the first half of the 1900s. The second stage, which took place during the 1950s and 1960s, displayed a high fertility rate while mortality dropped off rapidly due to advances in sanitation and medicine. The third stage, which took place in the 1970s as urbanization and modernization (including contraception) had an impact, saw fertility rates declining and converging on the mortality rates.[10] In the latter half of the 1970s the birth rate for Indians, as measured by the total fertility rate,[11] began to decelerate despite the entry into child-bearing age of the Indian "baby boom" generation born in the early 1960s. The longer-term trend between 1968 and 1981 shows a convergence of the Indian total fertility rate with the Canadian rate (see Figure 2). Nevertheless, in 1981 the Indian birth rate, at 3.15 births per woman, re-

Table 4
* The ''% of Population'' data should be interpreted as in the following example of a cell from the table: in the Atlantic provinces in 1981, 47.6 per cent of the registered Indian population belonged to bands having 1-499 members; that is *not* to say that 47.6 per cent of the *bands* in the Atlantic provinces in 1981 fell in the 1-499 band size category.

Figure 2

Total Fertility Rate for Registered Indian and Total Canadian Populations, 1968-81

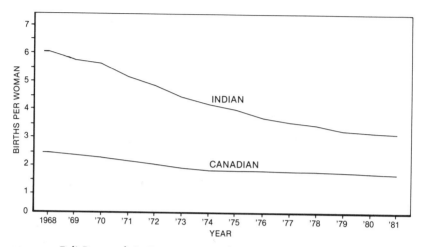

SOURCE: Bali Ram and A. Romaniuc, *Fertility Projections of Registered Indians, 1982 to 1996* (Ottawa: DIAND, 1985), Table 8.

mained almost twice as high as the Canadian rate (1.70 births per woman). [12]

One way to examine mortality of a population is to look at life expectancy at birth (not to be confused with average age at death). This indicator measures the probability of a male or female surviving to a certain age from birth, given the mortality experience of a population by age and sex. Indian male life expectancy at birth had reached 62 years by 1981, after hovering around 60 years for the previous two decades. This compared to a life expectancy of 72 years in the Canadian male population in 1981. Indian females, on the other hand, made greater gains as their life expectancy rose from 63.5 years in 1960 to nearly 69 years by 1981. [13] The life expectancy at birth for the Canadian female population in 1981 was 79 years.

Infant mortality refers to deaths of babies before reaching the age of one and is internationally used as an indicator of the overall standard of living of a population. Throughout the 1970s and into the 1980s, Indian infant mortality rates continued a decline that had begun by 1960. The number of Indian infant deaths per 1,000 live Indian births was 79.0 in 1960, 43.2 in 1970, and in the 1971-81 period continued the precipitous decline to 15.0 (see Figure 3). Mortality rates (not shown here) for most other age groups also maintained a trend of declining over the same period.

Figure 3
Infant Mortality Rates of Registered Indian and Total Canadian Populations, 1970-81

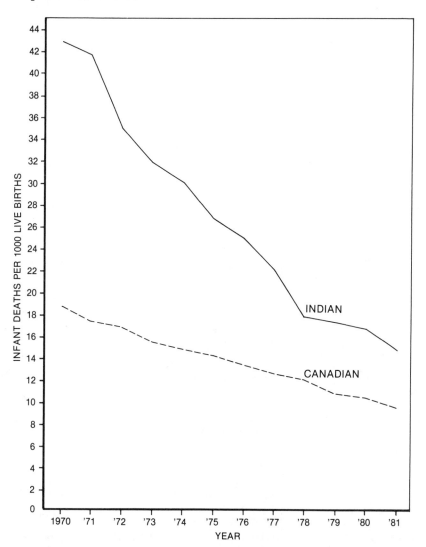

SOURCE: G. Rowe and M.J. Norris, *Mortality Projections of Registered Indians, 1982 to 1996* (Ottawa: DIAND, 1985), Table 4.

The Indian "standardized death rate" is a calculation of the death rate (per 1,000 population) the Indian population would have if it had the same age composition as the overall Canadian population. It is a good tool for making comparisons, because it lacks the biases of such other measures as the "crude death rate." The 1981 standardized death rate for registered Indians is 9.5 deaths per 1,000 population, or over half again as high as that of the overall Canadian population, whose rate was 6.1 per 1,000. [14]

The major causes of death for registered Indians are "accidents, poisoning and violence," often alcohol-related. Just over 174 Indian deaths per 100,000 population resulted from these causes in 1983, which was three times the rate for Canadians as a whole. However, seven years earlier, "accidents, poisoning and violence" were killing Indian people at a rate of 248 per 100,000, or four times the Canadian rate. Although many factors are likely associated with the decline in this so-called "cause-specific death rate" for Indians, it should not go unnoticed that significant alcohol and drug-abuse programs were implemented during this time period by various governments. All other major causes of death among Indians, except cancer, showed a decline in the 1976-83 period. The rates of death due to respiratory and digestive system diseases actually converged on the Canadian rates (see Table 5).

To summarize the mortality patterns among Indians, it can be said that Indian death rates have dropped significantly in recent years, but both general indicators and some "cause-specific" measures still compare unfavourably with those of the overall Canadian population. Indeed, in one of the most striking comparisons of opportunities in our data set, life expectancy tables show that as a consequence of health, social, and environmental conditions, life expectancy at birth for Indians is still nine or ten years less than for the nonIndian population.

Age Composition

With the decline in Indian fertility rates and the entry into the labour force age group of the Indian baby boomers of the 1960s, the share of the total Indian population under age 15 declined to 39 per cent in 1981 from 42 per cent just five years prior to that date and 48 per cent in 1966. If present trends continue, the share of children is expected to fall further to 34 per cent by 1996. [15] By contrast, the labour force aged 15-64 has been increasing its share of the total population from 46 per cent in 1966 to 57 per cent by 1981. On the basis of assumptions of

Table 5

Selected Causes of Death Among Registered Indians and the Canadian Population, 1976 and 1983
(deaths per 100,000 population)

Selected Causes of Death	Registered Indian		Canadian	
	1976	1983	1976	1982
Accidents, poisoning, and violence	247.7	174.3	66.8	57.5
Circulatory system diseases	153.3	141.5	355.2	326.4
Neoplasms (cancer)	54.0	56.0	151.5	172.0
Respiratory diseases	75.1	52.0	51.3	49.7
Digestive system diseases	34.5	28.1	27.2	28.2
Infections and parasitic diseases	18.2	6.9	4.4	3.8

SOURCE: J. Reed, *Indians and Inuit of Canada: Health Status Indicators* (Ottawa: Medical Services Branch, Health & Welfare Canada, 1985, draft), Tables B-85, B-86, B-98, B-110, B-122, B-134.

moderate growth, this group is expected to comprise 62 per cent by 1996. Numerically, the registered Indian labour force age group is projected to grow from 190,000 in 1981 to 284,000 by 1996. Throughout the 1980s, over half of this group will be in the young adult "family-forming" age group of 15 to 29, both on reserves and off.[16] The growth in the size of this group will exert important demographic pressures and will pose some significant planning issues in relation to job creation, housing, and social and welfare services.

The impact of adding a potential 76,000 people to the registered Indian population as a result of the amended Indian Act has not been considered in the projections described above. Their predisposition to reinstate and the pace at which they do so will have varying effects on the size, growth, age, sex, and geographic distribution of the registered Indian population, as well as its socio-economic composition. If all were to reinstate, and to do so before 1990 (two conditions unlikely to be met), the registered Indian population would increase by almost one-fifth.

The 1981 census data on the *non*-status Indian population indicate that this group had a smaller share of its population in the under-15 age category than the status Indians (35 and 39 per cent, respectively) and 63 per cent were in the labour force age group (compared to 59 per cent for status Indians). These 1981 shares for non-status Indians are about the same as those which the status Indian population is expected to have in 1996. However, it is important to sound a note of caution here because the characteristics of the non-status Indians as reported in the 1981 census may be different from those who actually decide to reinstate themselves as status Indians in years to come. [17]

Migration

Migration, as a phenomenon involving Indians, is influenced by many factors. Although Indians are widely believed to be highly mobile, both the 1971 and the 1981 censuses reveal that a slightly smaller portion of the Indian population than of the overall Canadian population had moved during the five years prior to the census. In the 1981 census these so-called "five-year migrants" constituted 19 per cent of Indians but 20 per cent of the total Canadian population. In absolute terms, though, the number of five-year migrants in the Indian population almost doubled (from 27,000 to 52,000) in the 1976-81 period compared to the 1966-71 period. [18]

Table 6 compares the origin and destination of Indians who had migrated in the five years preceding the 1971 and 1981 censuses, respectively. By way of illustration of how to read the table, from the top left corner of the table we note that 1 per cent of Indians who migrated from Indian reserves between 1966 and 1971 went to another Indian reserve, and 5 per cent who migrated from Indian reserves between 1976 and 1981 went to another Indian reserve. Also, among all Indian migrants interviewed for the 1981 census, 6 per cent of these were living in an urban metropolitan area at the time of the census and had migrated to there from an off-reserve rural area five years ago. Thus, the table enables us to see the relative sizes of these different migration "streams" for the five-year period prior to each of the two censuses and to discern the direction of the net flow.

The data shown in Table 6 indicate that in the five years leading up to the 1981 census, urban areas continued to be the preferred destination of Indian migrants (reading from the total of the "Urban Non-MA" and "Urban MA" columns: 26 per cent + 30 per cent = 56 per cent), just as had been the case in the five years leading up to the 1971 census (30 per cent + 25 per cent = 55 per cent). Importantly, though, Indian reserves also experienced an increase in their relative share of in-migrants (from 21 per cent in 1966-71 to 28 per cent in 1976-81). Overall, reserves contributed 17 per cent of those Indians who migrated in 1976-81 and acquired 28 per cent of all Indian migrants in that period, for a net gain of 11 per cent of all Indian migrants (compared to a net gain of only 21 per cent – 13 per cent = 8

Table 6

Percentage Distribution of Status Indian Migrants According to Their Places of Origin and Destination (1966-71 and 1976-81)*

Migrants' Origin		Migrants' Destination									
		Indian Reserve		Rural Non-Reserve		Urban Non-MA**		Urban MA**		Total	
		1971 %	1981 %	1971 %	1981 %	1971 %	1981 %	1971 %	1981 %	1971 %	1981 %
Indian Reserve	1966	1		4		4		4		13	
	1976	5		2		5		5			17
Rural Non-Reserve	1966	8		8		12		9		37	
	1976	5		4		6		6			21
Urban Non-MA**	1966	7		7		9		8		31	
	1976	8		6		8		8			30
Urban MA**	1966	5		4		5		4		18	
	1976	10		4		7		11			32
Total***	1966	21		23		30		25		99	
	1976		28		16		26		30		100

* The 1971 concept of migrants was adjusted to make it comparable to the 1981 concept, where the "quasi-return" migrants included in the 1971 census study (see sources below) were removed to construct the above table.
** "MA" refers to metropolitan areas with a population of 100,000 or more; "urban non-MA" refers to an urban area of less than 100,000 population.
*** Totals may not add to 100 per cent due to rounding.

SOURCES: Andrew J. Siggner, "Preliminary Results from a Study of 1966-71 Migration Patterns among Status Indians in Canada" (Ottawa: Department of Indian Affairs & Northern Development, 1978, mimeo), Table 17 and Chart 3.2.1; M.J. Norris, "Migration Patterns of Status Indians in Canada, 1976-81," paper presented at the Canadian Population Society annual meeting, Montreal, June, 1985, Table 4.

per cent during 1966-71). In other words, Indian reserves were net gainers of migrants, while all other areas were net losers over the 1976-81 period. Urban metropolitan areas had a net loss of 2 per cent of all Indian migrants in 1976-81, compared to a net gain of 6 per cent in the previous five-year period. Thus, while urban areas are the recipients of the greatest number of Indian in-migrants, they are also the contributors of an even larger number of Indian out-migrants.

Why has this important change in direction of Indian migration streams occurred? An individual's decision to migrate is usually a function of a variety of ''push and pull'' factors at the origin and intended destination of the migrant. These factors are often economic, demographic, and/or social in nature. For example, the downturn in the Canadian economy, and in particular in the urban economy, could be encouraging registered Indians to move back to reserves. However, another factor for potential migrants considering moving back to Indian reserves might be the amendment of the Indian Act. These legislative changes, which not only offer reinstatement of Indian status but also recognize Indian bands' right to control band membership and residency on reserve, have been under discussion for some years now. One might hypothesize that off-reserve persons affected by the Indian Act amendment may have decided to return to reserves in order to establish a period of residency prior to the change in the Act. Furthermore, in anticipation of increased competition for limited reserve housing and other amenities, status Indians living off-reserve might have been feeling some pressure to move back. Some support for this hypothesis comes from a DIAND study that found that a number of women and children were living on reserves who, under the old Indian Act, would not be considered as status Indians for various reasons. For example, there were 1,215 women (and their 1,250 children) who were legally married to non-registered males and living on reserves, and yet reporting themselves as status Indians.[19] In addition, in a recent study of status Indian migration, Norris found (in data not shown here) that the flow of female migrants from off-reserve to on-reserve locations in 1981 was twice as large as the female migration stream flowing in the opposite direction.[20]

Housing

Adequate housing is of pivotal importance in any person's life. Inadequate housing can subject the occupants to health risks from fire, poor sanitation, or exposure to dampness and chill. Overcrowded housing increases the risk of spread of communicable and other illness and is not conducive to the pursuit of home studies by students. Thus, an individual's housing situation has a major influence on his/her "life chances" such as the probability of completing high school, the probability of catching pneumonia, etc.

DIAND has recently completed an evaluation of on-reserve housing conditions and, while housing conditions in general still remain very poor (especially in rural and remote areas and in Manitoba, Ontario, and Saskatchewan), some improvements have taken place since the last major study in 1977. According to the 1985 study, almost half (47 per cent) of the housing fails to meet basic standards of physical condition; over one-third (36 per cent) is seriously overcrowded in terms of minimal standards; and 38 per cent of reserve housing lacks some or all of basic amenities (running water, indoor toilet, bath/shower).[21]

The improvements include a significant reduction in crowding problems since 1977, in that the average number of persons per house has dropped from six to five. (Nevertheless, the report still recognizes a growing demand for housing generated by the growth in the on-reserve population.) Between 1977 and 1984 there was also a substantial reduction (from 15 to 2 per cent) in the number of units considered unsalvageable. In addition, one-third more houses have basic amenities than in 1977 and there has been a significant increase in the supply of houses on reserves. Government housing programs clearly have had some impact.

Notwithstanding the above, the study concludes that an estimated $840 million is needed to correct the problems. The authors also note that current levels of funding are inadequate to resolve the housing problems within the decade and that diversion of resources to eliminate the existing backlog of need may hurt Indian bands which are about to enter a period of high population growth. Furthermore, the study did not appear to take into account systematically the changing age composition and net migration patterns on-reserve in order to assess future demand for housing; nor do the potential on-reserve impacts of the amendment to the Indian Act seem to be considered. Thus, although some important improvements in the housing situation of Indians have occurred since the late 1970s, housing still appears to present a significant hurdle to overcome in breaking the so-called "vicious cycle" of poverty.

Employment, Income, and Occupation Structure

When applied to the on-reserve Indian population, the concepts of "employment" and "unemployment" present thorny problems of measurement. For example, persons employed in seasonal occupations such as hunting and trapping often do not perceive these traditional activities as jobs, especially if they are carried out for subsistence. In addition, persons living on remote reserves do not often meet the government's definition of being unemployed (out of work, but seeking work in the week prior to the census or survey) when no work is available in their local area. With that proviso we turn now to the employment data from the 1981 census.

Census data indicate that among registered Indians aged 15 and over, only 38 per cent were employed in 1981 compared to 60 per cent in the general population. In fact, the majority (54 per cent) of the Indian population (compared to 35 per cent in the general population) in this age group is not in the labour force. The official unemployment rate is about two and a half times higher as well (17 versus 7 per cent). It is particularly high (24 per cent) among Indian youth aged 15-24.

The official unemployment rate in rural/reserve areas is slightly higher than in the urban non-reserve areas, at 18 and 16 per cent respectively. It is also interesting to note that the unemployment rate for females in urban non-reserve areas is about four percentage points higher than for the males, while the on-reserve rate for females is somewhat lower than that for females in urban areas. The reader will recall that more female migrants are moving to reserves than males and that most of these in-migrants are from the cities. The migration stream thus reflects the structure of economic opportunities at these women's present place of residence and at their considered destinations.

The occupational structure of the registered Indian population shows some important differences from the general population. Within the Indian experienced labour force, 52 per cent are engaged in so-called white-collar jobs, i.e., managerial/professional/technical, clerical, sales, and service occupations. The comparable figure in the general population is 64 per cent. Oddly, only 2 per cent of the Indian labour force is in such traditional activities as hunting, fishing, and trapping (although this low percentage may result from the reporting and conceptual problems mentioned earlier). The percentage of Indians engaged in occupations in the primary sector as a whole (including also agriculture and other forms of resource extraction) is 12 per cent, compared to 9 per cent in the general population (Table 7).

Some of the most interesting occupational data pertain to Indian females. For instance, Table 7 shows that Indian women share virtually the same percentage in the managerial/professional/technical category as women in the general population (26 and 25 per cent, respectively).[22] Proportionately and numerically, Indian women outnumber

72

Table 7

Distribution of Status Indians in the Experienced Labour Force* by Occupational Category, Sex, and Selected Types of Residence, 1981

Selected Types of Residence	Sex	Managerial, Professional, or Technical	Clerical	Sales	Service	Farming	Fishing, Hunting, Trapping	Forestry, Logging, Mining	Processing	Machine Production	Other
Total status Indians	T	19.2	12.4	4.1	16.1	3.8	2.1	5.8	5.3	7.7	23.5
	M	15.0	4.0	3.1	9.9	5.2	3.3	8.9	6.1	9.5	35.1
	F	26.0	25.6	5.6	25.9	1.6	0.3	0.9	4.0	5.0	5.2
Rural reserves	T	19.1	9.4	2.7	13.9	5.0	3.2	8.3	4.9	5.3	28.1
	M	13.7	2.8	1.9	8.8	6.7	4.6	11.6	5.6	6.0	38.6
	F	30.4	23.3	4.4	24.7	1.6	0.4	1.5	3.6	3.9	6.1
Urban non-reserve	T	20.2	16.4	5.3	18.8	1.6	0.9	2.8	5.5	10.4	18.1
	M	17.6	6.3	4.4	12.0	2.2	1.5	5.0	6.6	14.3	30.1
	F	23.2	27.8	6.2	26.4	1.0	0.3	0.4	4.2	5.9	4.6
Total Canadian population	T	24.4	18.9	9.0	12.0	4.1	3.5	1.4	4.1	10.7	15.2
	M	23.8	7.0	8.7	10.0	5.3	5.5	2.2	5.3	14.3	23.3
	F	25.3	36.3	9.4	15.7	2.2	0.0	0.1	2.3	5.3	3.3

* The experienced labour force is the total labour force minus unemployed persons who have never worked or who (in the case of this table) had worked only prior to January 1, 1980.

SOURCE: Census of Canada, 1981, special unpublished tabulations.

their male counterparts in this category as well. Again, perhaps related to the opportunity structure on reserves, the share of women in this category is twice as high as for men (30 versus 14 per cent). In fact, in all tertiary activities, Indian women outnumber men on reserves and in urban areas. It would appear that the majority of the experienced Indian labour force as of the 1980s is now engaged in tertiary occupations and that Indian women lead the way in terms of occupying the managerial/professional/technical category. This is, perhaps, one of the more encouraging findings in light of earlier studies on the socio-economic conditions of Indian women. [23]

The beginning of the 1980s witnessed some reduction in the disparity in the average annual income between status Indians and the general population. As Figure 4 shows, in 1980 the average annual income of the general population was one and two-thirds greater than that of the status Indian population; that was down from a threefold gap in 1971. For Indians residing on rural reserves or settlements in 1981, the income disparity with the general population was nearly one and three-quarters, while the comparable figure for the two populations living in urban areas was about one and a half. These differences in average annual income, while still significant, indicate an encouraging trend since the 1970s.

On a more discouraging note, the average annual income for Indian women was still well below that for Indian men in 1980. On reserves and settlements it was about $7,000 for males and only about $5,100 for females. In urban areas the disparity was even more pronounced with males receiving nearly twice the income of females ($12,300 and $6,400).

Significant differences exist between Indians and the overall Canadian population with regard to the source of income. In particular, government transfer payments supplied 35 per cent of status Indians (of labour force age) with a source of income in 1981 compared to only 16 per cent of the general population; also, 61 per cent of status Indians earned income through wages and salaries compared to 70 per cent of the general population. With respect to one form of transfer payment, social assistance, DIAND's own data indicate that the total social assistance payments (including administrative costs) increased from $34 million in 1970-71 to over $142 million by 1980-81, a growth of 315 per cent in ten years. [24] Most of these payments occurred on reserves and are attributed to increases in the number of family dependents and high utilization of social services as a result of unemployment. [25]

Figure 4
**Average Annual Income (all sources, 1980) for Status Indians and
All Canadians, by Sex and Selected Types of 1981 Residence**

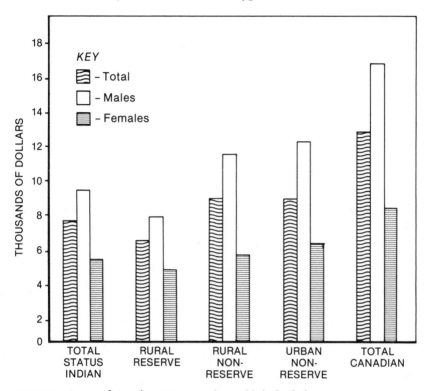

SOURCE: *Census of Canada*, 1981, special unpublished tabulations.

A small number of Indian bands have important sources of material wealth located on their reserves. Oil, gas, and mineral developments have resulted in a tenfold increase in the revenues to such Indian bands, but most of that wealth is located only in Alberta. Other mineral potential (e.g., gold, iron, copper, and asbestos) exists on 15-25 per cent of the reserves in the Atlantic, Quebec, Ontario, Manitoba, and Saskatchewan regions.[26]

Education

Indian education in Canada is in the midst of a radical change. Once in the hands of missionaries and other employees of the Christian churches, Indian education is now increasingly under the control of Indian com-

munities as a result of the gradual implementation of a policy originally formulated by the National Indian Brotherhood in the 1970s.[27] An
international perspective on this policy is provided in Jordan's article
in this volume. Suffice it to say here that under the policy of Indian
control of Indian education the classroom has become much more sensitive to the needs of Indian children. The curriculum is more relevant
to Indians' daily lives and culture; Indian teachers, Indian teachers'
aides, and Indian elders are now common in the classroom; and Indian
languages are being taught and in some cases used as the language of
instruction. It is not surprising, therefore, to observe that the drop-
out phenomenon has attenuated significantly; the retention rate for
Indian students from Grade 2 to graduation from Grade 12 as of
1984-85 was 31 per cent, up from 18 per cent in 1975-76.

It is, of course, important for Indian people to obtain post-secondary schooling in order to learn the many technical and managerial skills involved in directing and managing their own affairs.
Significant progress has been made in this regard. In 1971 barely 3 per
cent of the Indian out-of-school population had attained at least some
post-secondary education, but by 1981 the percentage had risen to
almost 19 per cent. There is still a twofold gap between the Canadian
population's attainment of post-secondary education at 36 per cent and
that of Indians, yet in 1971 the overall Canadian percentage was nine
times greater than the Indian figure.

There are dramatic differences in the educational attainment of
Indians living on rural reserves and Indians living in the urban areas of
Canada. Only about half as many (13 versus 20 per cent) of the out-of-
school Indian population on rural reserves had post-secondary education as compared to those in urban areas, although numerically they
were evenly split at about 11,000 each. Among those with this level of
school attainment, three out of four have their training from trades
and other non-university schools, while the remainder have at least
some university education or are university graduates. Census data also
show that as of 1981, 2,425 Indian women were enrolled in universities (including 1,005 part-time), compared to only 1,495 Indian men
(545 part-time), and a further 3,520 Indian women (compared to
2,315 Indian men) were enrolled full or part-time in non-university
post-secondary education institutions. In 1981, 1,435 Indian women
had one or more university degrees, as opposed to 1,170 men. Interestingly, among these graduates only 34 per cent of the women,
compared to 41 per cent of the men, were resident on reserve.[28]

In summary, major gains in educational attainment have been made
by the status Indian population since the 1970s.

Cultural Characteristics

The Indian population is a culturally diverse one. Given the historical interaction with the majority culture in Canada, the various Indian cultural groups inevitably underwent cultural change. Some would argue, and with reason, that such change was clearly involuntary. Today, maintaining cultural identity has become an important issue for Indian peoples across Canada. Therefore, measuring cultural retention and change becomes relevant to those who wish to develop programs and policy to ensure the continuance of cultural identity. One crude measure of such change is the ratio comparing the number of people using a given language at home with the number of people having that language as their mother tongue (the language first learned and still understood). If mother tongue were universally retained, then for every 100 persons who have Cree, for example, as a mother tongue, 100 should be using Cree as a home language (the language most often used in the home). Therefore, a ratio of less than 100 would tend to suggest that people have lessened the use of their mother tongue and use some other language in the home.

The 1981 census data in Table 8 show that the ratio of home language use to mother tongue for all aboriginal language groups is well below 100. For example, for every 100 status Indians with Ojibway as a mother tongue, only 71 were using it as a home language in 1981. On the other hand, and not surprisingly, for every 100 status Indians with English as their mother tongue, there were 119 using it as a home language. When the distribution of status Indians by home language is examined on its own, two out of three reported using English as their home language.

Data for some Indian languages suggest that they are in danger of extinction. For instance, in the 1981 census only eighty-five people claimed Kutenaian as their mother tongue, only 125 claimed Tlingit, and only 335 claimed Haida; only twenty-five people (average age 58) claimed Kutenaian as the language most often spoken at home.[29]

Despite the apparent increased use of English at the expense of other aboriginal languages among status Indians, in recent years there has been a resurgence of Indian interest in Indian culture. DIAND data, for example, indicate some significant changes at the primary and secondary school levels. Between 1979-80 and 1983-84, the number of students taking courses in which an aboriginal language is the medium of instruction over half of the time increased by 62 per cent. The data also show that the number of students taking an aboriginal language as

Table 8

Ratio of Home Language Use to Mother Tongue among Status Indians, 1981

Language	Ratio*	Language	Ratio*
English	118.9	Athapaskan	71.1
"Other Algonkian"**	94.6	Iroquoian	45.7
French	87.9	Salishan	43.3
Cree	82.1	All other languages	49.5
Ojibway	70.9		

* Ratio = (number of persons with that language as language most often spoken at home ÷ number of persons with that language as mother tongue) × 100.
** The Algonkian language group includes various dialects. The two most commonly spoken are Cree and Ojibway. Some others are Algonkin, Blackfoot, Malecite, Micmac, and Montagnais.
SOURCE: *Census of Canada*, 1981, unpublished special tabulations.

a subject or in a course using it as a part-time medium of instruction grew by over one and a half times in the same short period.[30] Such acquisition of an Indian language as a second language often shows up in neither the mother tongue nor the home language data.

Criminal Justice

In relation to their proportion of the Canadian population (about 2 to 4 per cent) native people – including status Indians, non-status Indians, Métis, and Inuit – are overrepresented in federal prisons, where they constitute 10 per cent of the inmate population.[31] This is up from 8.7 per cent in 1979.[32] In provincial and territorial prisons and jails, where inmates are serving sentences of less than two years, Natives are more heavily overrepresented, especially in the Prairie provinces and the North. For instance, 100 per cent of the female admissions to the Whitehorse Correctional Centre for Women and 20 per cent of all women incarcerated in British Columbia are Natives.[33]

With respect to type of offence, no change was observed between 1979 and 1983 in that approximately 48 per cent of native federal inmates were incarcerated for violent crimes (i.e., crimes against persons). Numerically, however, the number of Natives convicted of such crimes did increase from 385 to 508, a four-year increase of 32 per cent. It should be noted that despite the slight decline (from 76 to 74 per cent) in the proportion of the native inmate population in the 20-34 age group, this group's numerical increase accounted for two-thirds of the overall increase of native inmates between 1979 and 1981. This increase is not surprising in light of the rapid growth of the overall native population in this age group and the fact that this age group is also a "high-risk population" in terms of criminal offences (that is, it is disproportionately likely to commit criminal offences).

Most Indian crime is a direct result of alcohol abuse. Governments at various levels, including the Indian bands themselves, have been making major efforts to combat alcoholism and related abuses, in terms of both rehabilitation and prevention. However, Indian alcoholism, and therefore Indian crime, is inextricably related to the broader social, economic, educational, and cultural problems facing Indians. If and when substantial progress is made in combating the underlying causes of those problems, significant reductions can be expected in the incidence of Indian crime. In the meantime, various institutional innovations, such as recruitment of Indians to staff on-reserve police forces and the introduction of native court-worker programs, are continuing to be implemented.

In this era of government fiscal restraint, it is important that the effectiveness and efficiency of these various programs be assessed and that such assessments use appropriate statistical measures. Unfortunately, this is not always done. For instance, some measures might yield data suggesting that a program to combat crime has failed to have any impact in the desired direction (e.g., crime rates may have accelerated). However, the crime prevention program might actually be having positive results, but these may be masked by rapid growth in the size of the high-risk age group. Thus, age-specific indicators or standardization techniques (such as those described above in the section on mortality) are necessary. The same is true in the assessment of other programs, such as those designed to improve poor socio-economic conditions.

Conclusion

The period since the mid-1970s has actually witnessed several significant demographic changes in the Indian population, although Indians' 1.5 per cent share of the total Canadian population has remained almost unchanged. The overall birth rate has continued to decline, but its rate of decline has slowed in recent years, largely due to the entry of the 1960s Indian baby boom generation into the child-bearing age group. The Indian standardized death rate also continued to decline, although it was still 50 per cent higher than the Canadian death rate as of 1981. However, life expectancy did show signs of improvement for both Indian men and women, as it rose to 62 and 69 years, respectively.

One of the most intriguing demographic changes captured by the 1981 census was the small-scale de-urbanization phenomenon occurring, while Indian reserves and settlements are net gainers of migrants. This is a reversal of trends recorded in the 1971 census. Furthermore, 55 per cent of the migrants moving to Indian reserves were women. A number of factors were suggested to account for this pattern, although further research is required. For instance, with reference to one of many potential ramifications of the 1985 amendments to the Indian Act, speculation was offered that Indian women, fearing increased competition for limited resources on reserves as a result of the potential reinstatement of women who had lost their Indian status, might have decided to migrate back to reserves.

The Indian population aged 15-64 years has been growing rapidly. It is expected to increase throughout the remainder of the 1980s and the first half of the 1990s to reach 284,000 or more by 1996. With the expansion of this labour force sector of the population, pressure will build for a concomitant growth in employment opportunities. We did find some encouraging signals that the material well-being of Indians is improving. For example, the gap between their average annual income and that of the Canadian population closed over the 1971-81 period. Occupationally, Indians are now primarily employed in the tertiary (service) sector; only a small proportion are engaged in what might be termed "traditional" activities such as hunting and trapping. Indeed, the percentage of Indian women in professional/technical/managerial positions was on a par with that of Canadian women overall; numerically, Indian women actually outnumbered Indian men in this job category.

The findings on occupational distribution of Indian people correlate with the findings on educational attainment, where the percentage of out-of-school population with post-secondary training grew ninefold between 1971 and 1981. The policy of Indian control of Indian education should not be overlooked in explaining this improvement in the educational attainment of the population.

Even the criminal justice indicators give some grounds for optimism. One would have expected that as the Indian population aged 20-34 was increasing its share in the total Indian population, a similar increase would have been observed in the federal native inmate population, since this age group is at greatest risk. Yet, their share of the inmate population actually declined, on a proportionate basis, between 1979 and 1983.

In conclusion, it would appear that, indeed, some progress and improvement in Indian conditions have occurred in recent years, at least as measured by the various national demographic, social, and economic indicators used in this analysis. However, on many indicators of "well-being" Indians still lag significantly behind the norm for Canadians as a whole. Furthermore, important regional differences among Indians themselves also exist on some of these indicators.

Undoubtedly, as the young adult population enters the labour force age group and family formation stage throughout the 1980s and 1990s, issues such as on-reserve housing, employment, and economic development will continue to be major problems facing policy-makers and planners at all levels. The reinstatement of women and children and others who lost Indian status over the years will also have a variety of long-term effects on the socio-economic and demographic characteristics of the Indian population – effects to which program planning will have to adjust. From a statistical measurement perspective, however, it should be clear to planners that appropriate data-gathering systems should be put in place or existing ones enhanced if effective and efficient planning is to take place. The 1986 census, for example, coming as it does one year after the amendment to the Indian Act, should provide some important benchmark data to begin to assess the socio-economic and demographic impacts of this major legislative change.

Notes

1. The views, opinions, and interpretations expressed in this chapter are those of the author and do not represent those of Statistics Canada. The author wishes to express his appreciation to the staff of the Customer Services Section, Statistics Canada, for its assistance in obtaining several 1981 census special tabulations used in this analysis. These tabulations were specified by the author to exclude a small group of 1981 census respondents who, for the most part, were found to be of Indo-Pakistani background but who reported that they were "status Indians." It should also be noted that, for the most part, the 1981 census unpublished tabulations used here do not correspond exactly to the 1981 census customized data set on status Indians developed by the Department of Indian Affairs and Northern Development.

2. Andrew J. Siggner, "A Socio-Demographic Profile of Indians in Canada," in J. Rick Ponting and Roger Gibbins, Out Of Irrelevance (Scarborough, Ont.: Butterworths, 1980), pp. 31-65.

3. These persons are Indian women, and their children, who lost Indian status through marriage to non-registered males, as well as others who gave up their Indian status ("enfranchised") for a variety of reasons now deemed invalid. For a detailed discussion of this issue, see the chapter by Kathleen

Jamieson in this book. For a breakdown of the estimate of 76,000 persons eligible for reinstatement, see "Background Notes: Bill C-31, An Act to Amend The Indian Act" (Ottawa: DIAND, 1985), p. 3.

4. Alfred L. Kroeber, *Cultural and Natural Areas of Native North America* (Berkeley: University of California Publications in American Archaeology and Ethnology, #38, University of California Press, 1939).

5. It is not certain whether this apparent fluctuation was due to actual shifts in the size of the population as a result of epidemics, etc., or whether it was due to changes in the definition of an Indian, problems in reporting, or some combination of these.

6. This count is adjusted for late-reported events such as births and deaths.

7. J. Perreault *et al.*, *Population Projections of Registered Indians 1981 to 1996* (Ottawa: DIAND, 1985), p. 49.

8. *Ibid.*

9. Unless otherwise specified, the term "Indian reserve" is used to include both Indian reserves per se and Indian settlements on Crown land, which in most respects are treated as Indian reserves by the federal Department of Indian Affairs and Northern Development.

10. Siggner, "A Socio-Demographic Profile," p. 37.

11. The total fertility rate measures the average births per woman based on the age-specific fertility rates of a given population of women such as status Indian women.

12. Bali Ram and A. Romaniuc, *Fertility Projections of Registered Indians, 1981-1996* (Ottawa: DIAND, 1985), p. 19.

13. Perrault *et al.*, *Population Projections*, p. 25.

14. G. Rowe and M.J. Norris, *Mortality Projections of Registered Indians, 1982 to 1996* (Ottawa: DIAND, 1985), p. 14.

15. Perrault *et al.*, *Population Projections*, pp. 69, 82.

16. *Ibid.*

17. Statistics Canada, *Canada's Native People*, Cat. No. 99-937, Supply and Services Canada (Ottawa, 1984), Table 4.

18. M.J. Norris, "Migration Patterns of Status Indians in Canada, 1976-81," paper presented at the Canadian Population Society annual meeting, June, 1985, p. 8.

19. S. Klein and W. Wright, *The Development of Customized Status Indian Variables Using 1981 Census Data* (Ottawa: DIAND, 1985), pp. 31-38.

20. Norris, "Migration Patterns," p. 28.

21. EKOS Research Associates, *Summary Report: Evaluation of the On Reserve Housing Program* (Ottawa: DIAND, 1985), p. i.

22. General occupational categories, such as "managerial/professional/technical," may tend to hide real disparities in terms of job level and salary for a specific occupation contained in that general category.

23. Research Branch, *A Profile of Registered Indian Women in Canada* (Ottawa: DIAND, 1979).

24. Program Reference Centre, *Expenditures in the Social Services Program by Region and Category, 1970-71* (Ottawa: Indian and Inuit Affairs Program, DIAND, mimeo); Program Reference Centre, *Registered Indian Social*

Assistance Expenditures by Region, 1973-74 to 1980-81 (Ottawa: Indian and Inuit Affairs Program, DIAND, mimeo).

25. DIAND, *Indian Conditions: A Survey* (Ottawa, 1980), p. 28.

26. *Ibid.*, pp. 68, 69.

27. For a description of the policy of Indian control of Indian education and of the difficulties encountered in getting the federal government to implement it, see Harold Cardinal, *The Rebirth of Canada's Indians* (Edmonton: Hurtig, 1977), pp. 56ff.

28. All of the above education data in this paragraph were provided courtesy of Mr. Jeremy Hull, WMC Research Associates, Winnipeg. These data are preliminary tabulations prepared under contract to DIAND's Research Branch and are subject to verification prior to publication by DIAND.

29. Gordon E. Priest, ''Aboriginal Languages in Canada'' (Ottawa: Housing, Family, and Social Division, Statistics Canada, mimeo draft, 1983), Table 2 and Table 3.

30. Education Directorate, *Student Enrolment by Region Indicating Use of Native Language in School, 1979-80 and 1983-84* (Ottawa: DIAND, nominal roll, mimeo).

31. Policy, Planning and Systems Branch, ''Native Population Profile and Non-Native Population Profile Reports'' (Ottawa: Ministry of the Solicitor-General, 1984).

32. See Table 2.10 in Siggner, ''A Socio-Demographic Profile.''

33. Carol Pitcher LaPrairie, ''Selected Criminal Justice and Socio-Demographic Data on Native Women,'' *Canadian Journal of Criminology*, 26 (1984), pp. 161-69.

Chapter Three

Relations between Bands and the Department of Indian Affairs: A Case of Internal Colonialism?

by J. Rick Ponting

The Indian and Inuit Affairs Program (IIAP) of the Department of Indian Affairs and Northern Development (DIAND) is one of the most heavily criticized departments of the federal government.[1] Criticism has emanated from various official sources within the federal government and particularly from the department's clientele (Indians). The department has been criticized for a broad range of alleged and/or substantiated wrongdoings, including excessive spending and poor financial management and accounting practices, failure to live up to its trust responsibilities to Indians, excessive red tape, favouritism to some of its clients, paternalism in its relations with clients, interference in Indian politics, and other colonial behaviour and attitudes.

The central question that guided the research reported here was whether IIAP, in its relations with bands, has retained its colonial orientation and practices (perhaps manifested in different ways compared to a generation or more ago) or, conversely, whether the torrent of complaints from Indian band leaders can be explained by some other factor(s) such as excessive bureaucratization. The answer to this question is important over the short to intermediate term, for different answers have different implications for the future of the department, and particularly for the issue of whether IIAP should be abolished as per the recommendation of the Penner Committee.

The approach taken was to search the sociological literature for an inventory of behaviours that could be considered colonial in nature, and then to conduct in-depth interviews with Indian band chiefs and/or senior band administrators concerning their relations with IIAP/DIA.[2] Respondents were asked about: these behaviours, if present; other problems and frustrations in relating to DIA; and positive aspects of the behaviour and attitudes of DIA personnel. The senior DIA official in the region where most of the respondents were located was also interviewed at length and asked to respond to the criticisms and allegations. The researcher's own prior experience and the interview data were then searched for the best explanations of particular discrepancies between administrator's and clients' accounts of events, and indeed for the best general explanation of why discrepancies would occur at all. An explanatory model was formulated and found to fit rather well to a strikingly similar situation described in the sociological literature. As we shall see, the fact that the analogous situation did not involve Indians and did not have inter-ethnic or inter-racial contact as one of its salient dimensions calls into serious question the validity of explanations that stress colonialism or racism as the root of Indians' problems with DIA. Instead, bureaucratic factors and other factors such as social class loom large.

The research upon which this chapter draws was conducted primarily in a western province in the fall of 1984 and the spring of 1985. The modest research budget did not permit the kinds of checks on reliability and validity that are always desirable, especially in such a politically charged research setting. For that reason, and also because of the small size (eight bands) and regional concentration of the sample, no claim can be made that the conclusions are the authoritative explanation of DIA-band relations nationwide. Rather, their applicability to the rest of Canada must be viewed as tentative.

Indicators of Colonialism

In his seminal article "Internal Colonialism and Ghetto Revolt,"[3] Robert Blauner identified certain basic components of internal colonialism. He saw such colonialism as beginning with the forced integration of the indigenous people into the dominant society on terms controlled by the dominant society. Second, under his definition of colonialism the colonizing power carries out a policy that constrains, transforms, or destroys the culture (and, we might add, the economy) of the indigenous people. Third, racism as a system of domination (and a justifying ideology) is said to characterize the society. Fourth, the members of the colonized group are said by Blauner to be administered by members of the dominant power, especially in such a way as to be managed and manipulated in terms of their ethnic status.

James Frideres's treatment of the colonization of Indians in Canada compiles certain refinements to Blauner's model.[4] These include the notion of indirect rule (whereby nonIndians rule Indians through "puppet chiefs"), exploitation of Indians for their labour, and the establishment of a colour line (colour-based barriers to social mobility). Ponting and Gibbins[5] wrote not of colonialism per se but rather

Table 9

Empirical, Micro-level Indicators of Internal Colonialism

1. Inadequate preparation and/or resourcing for bands administering their own affairs
   e.g. – inadequate funds for training in modern skills of administration

2. Economic underdevelopment
   e.g. – inadequate resourcing of bands' economic development
   – refusal to relinquish control over economic development

3. Intemperate orientation toward risk
   e.g. – excessive risk aversion to the point of over-protectiveness
   – irresponsible exposure of bands to excessive risk

4. Flow of information
   e.g. – manipulation of information as a form of social control
   – excessive secrecy or over-burdening Indians with information
   – overly rigid (or frequent) accountability requirements
   – inadequate consultation with bands

5. Decision-making and control over allocation of scarce resources
   e.g. – excluding bands from decision-making
   – depriving bands of control over allocation of resources

6. Obstructionism
   – versus facilitation

7. Socio-fiscal control
   e.g. – manipulation of discretionary funds
   – withholding of funds

8. Divide-and-rule tactics
   – versus promotion of co-operation among bands

of forms of manipulation or social control exercised by the DIA bureaucracy over its Indian clientele. Particularly important were socio-fiscal control (based on control over the ''purse strings'') and technocratically based control, which might be called neo-paternalism.

Certain of the above dimensions either do not directly address the arena of interest here (the administration of Indian affairs) or are cast at a macroscopic level that takes us beyond the present concern with micro-level inter-organizational relations between bands and DIA. Thus, the questionnaire ignored those dimensions and focused instead mainly on the dimensions shown in Table 9. Space limitations will permit us to deal in depth with only a few of them.

One caveat should be mentioned before examining bands' experiences with DIA. Reference here is to the well-established fact that the very act of organizing creates power, that large, complex bureaucracies such as DIA create large amounts of power, and that in any bureaucracy there will always be some individuals who exploit opportunities to abuse the power for their own personal gain – sometimes at the expense of the clientele.[6] Such idiosyncratic deviant behaviour, while not condoned here, should be distinguished from policies, programs, and standard operating procedures that are positively sanctioned by the organization and/or virtually imposed by certain features of the organization's external environment. The former, individual deviance, does not constitute internal colonialism, but the latter two situations might.

Band Politicians' and Administrators' Perceptions of DIA

The eight bands selected for this study vary considerably along several important dimensions. They range in population size from slightly over 120 members to several thousand and in wealth from near poverty-stricken to fairly comfortable although not affluent. Geographically, they include rather remote (although not isolated), rural, semi-urban, and urban bands. Their chiefs range from having been relatively recently elected to having long-standing tenure in office, and from being politically "radical" to political "statesman" to virtually apolitical leaders or followers (at least in their relations with organizations external to the band). The bands also vary widely in their economic base, degree of program development, number of band employees, degree of financial autonomy from DIA, political "clout" with DIA and within Indian organizations, extent and severity of social problems on the reserve, and proportion of the band population living off-reserve. In addition, they are spread across two "regions" and five "districts" of DIA.[7]

We turn below to a consideration of selected dimensions listed in Table 9. In one sense it matters little how well founded an accusation or criticism is or how convincing a defence against an accusation is, for, in the well-known words of sociologist W.I. Thomas, situations are real if they have real consequences. Because Indian leaders take actions on the basis of such perceptions as were reported to this researcher, and because elected nonIndian politicians and DIA administrators take action in response to the actions of the Indian leaders, the latter's actions do indeed have very real consequences. Thus, new realities are created on the basis of the experiences, beliefs, and perceptions that emerge through the filters erected by those respective ideologies. Given the existence of these *different realities* it does not seem very productive to search for a single "true" account of a situation. Instead, this chapter tries to explain the divergent perceptions, without making judgements about their validity.

Preparation and Resourcing for Self-administration

Particular attention here was focused on administrative training and administrative resources. DIA does have a program specifically for band staff training and an occupational skills training program that can also be used for this purpose. Although some band offices display posters or notices of band management training programs offered through various organizations and institutions (Indian and nonIndian), bands vary considerably in the extent to which they have utilized the funds available from DIA. So, too, do bands differ widely in the administrative resources available to them at the band office. For instance, band administration offices vary from modern architectural showpieces to a corner of the living room in the chief's own house. Some bands have already computerized their administration to a significant extent using mini-computers and word-processors, while others are far from it or even antagonistic to the idea of computerization because of unhappy experiences they have had with DIA's use of computers. Significantly, library resources in support of administration proved to be practically non-existent in the band offices visited in this study, and budgets for hiring outside consultants were small to non-existent (in part because DIA views part of its role as providing advice).

A central feature of DIA is that it is a "money-moving department." That is, one of its main roles is to allocate and transfer money to recipient organizations. From this fact flow several important consequences. First, in an era of fiscal restraint, eligibility and accountability requirements may become prolific and rather rigid, which can give rise to complaints about a regulatory burden ("a sea of red tape") and to complaints about inadequacy of funds. Second, the degree of satisfaction experienced by a recipient organization such as a band will depend to a considerable degree on the political power and influence that band wields with the money-moving department and on the level of administrative-entrepreneurial and grantsmanship skills possessed by the band administrators. Variations across bands in these factors, and in such qualities as imagination, vigilance, and persistence, contribute to differing rates of success for different bands in their funding requests, and thus to Indians' perceptions that favouritism is shown by DIAND toward some bands.

Where the budget of a money-moving department is woefully inadequate to meet demonstrated needs of recipient organizations, the staff of the money-moving organization is placed in a very uncomfortable position. We should expect staff to develop coping strategies to deal with the strains involved. For instance, research on another social system, the criminal justice system, has found that service workers there try to bring some order to their work environment and cope with stress and uncertainty by "typing" (akin to stereotyping) their clients.[8] Such typing, which leaves the service worker in a better position to choose and deploy tactics to deal with clients, facilitates work by enabling the bureaucrat to process the client (in our case, the client band) as but one more instance of a broader category rather than as a unique case. Three different coping strategies suggest themselves. One involves the further elaboration of eligibility criteria so as to restrict client access to funds. Another involves attempts to limit the level of client demand by doing little to encourage or facilitate clients' acquisition of the grantsmanship and administrative-entrepreneurial skills that generate that demand. A third coping strategy involves an opposite approach that attempts to cultivate those skills but to direct them to other money-moving departments. When this researcher suggested that DIA was pursuing the second coping strategy, a senior DIA executive disagreed and responded by describing DIA's approach in terms that in essence describe the third strategy.[9]

Before leaving the question of preparation of bands for self-administration, an important allegation should be mentioned. This is the contention that in certain cases DIA has prematurely sloughed off its administrative responsibilities onto some bands before they are adequately prepared to assume those responsibilities; the alleged motivation for this is to make it likely that the bands will fail at self-administration so that (1) DIA will have to reassume responsibility; (2) other bands will be deterred from moving toward self-administration; and (3) the jobs of DIA staff members will be secured rather than phased out. Such a serious allegation is indicative of the intense distrust with which many chiefs view DIA. Not surprisingly, though, the perceptions of the DIA regional director-general (RDG) differed drastically from those of the persons who made the allegation. In the view of the RDG it was the bands' own outside consultants, not DIA staff, who were mainly responsible for propelling the bands toward greater autonomy. Interestingly, though, the chief who was most vociferous in his criticism of DIA on this case nevertheless blames DIA because, in his view, DIA is paying the consultants.

Economic Underdevelopment
One of the key factors enabling a colonized people to move out from under the control of the colonial administration is a degree of economic development, for economic dependency leaves a people subject to socio-fiscal control by outside administrators who control the

purse strings. Respondents were asked "How would you describe DIAND's economic development programs?" They were also asked to cite their main criticism of those programs and the main strong points of the programs. The question evoked a long litany of complaints and almost no specific positive responses (other than "They try" and "They are fiscally responsible").

The most widespread criticism is that DIA's economic development programs are grossly under-funded. For instance, for one large district containing a large number of bands, DIA's entire economic development budget for 1985-86 amounted to less than $10,000 per band. In the colourful words of one chief, DIA's economic development programs are "like the legendary Sasquatch – we hear about it but never see it." He added: "We've never had any results or co-operation from the Department."

The complaint of inadequate funds is often accompanied by one or more associated complaints: the inadequacy of funds to hire consultants to do adequate advance planning predisposes many economic development projects to failure; and the department's approach of merely providing "seed" (start-up) money is a "band-aid" approach that fails to come to grips with the enormity and gravity of the need. An example of the consequences of under-capitalization of start-up costs is provided by a band to which DIA granted sufficient money to plant a crop, but not to weed it; it consequently failed and left band leaders criticizing DIA for DIA's shortsightedness in funding and for creating unrealistic hopes among band members.

DIA strategies also came under attack from respondents. One criticism was that in its economic development strategy DIA vacillated between a preference for "megaprojects" and a preference for entrepreneurship. A related criticism was that DIA fails to provide sufficient funds for Indian entrepreneurs in comparison to band-owned enterprises. One strategy-related complaint, which illustrates the need for flexibility and the exercise of discretionary judgement by DIA bureaucrats, was that DIA policies are biased in favour of labour-intensive projects, whereas the band's competitors in the industry in question are mechanized and the band's project would be doomed to failure from the outset if it were to take a labour-intensive approach.

One can understand how DIA personnel might feel that they are in a "no-win" or "double-bind" situation when one hears complaints, as this researcher did, that DIA seems unable or unwilling to make long-range commitments to economic development, and then hears from a different chief that DIA's long-term economic development commitments to some bands preclude funding of his band's short-term needs (which arose later). DIA's hiring or staff development priorities also came under attack, such as in the criticism that DIA lacked staff expertise in the industry that dominated the region's economy and therefore was useless in assisting bands to move into that industry.

Criteria of eligibility also came under fire, as did various aspects of the DIA bureaucracy per se. Said one recently elected chief, who contended that his band had had various funding requests to DIA rejected "because we're an urban band":

> "Criteria." Now that's a fancy word. Two years ago if you had come in here and used words like that I probably couldn't even have comprehended your questions. Now I know that "criteria" are something that make money harder to get.

The DIA bureaucracy was criticized as well for inadequate consultation with bands, for being inefficient and top-heavy with administration (and thereby absorbing too much of the money that, in the view of respondents, should go to economic development), for "playing favourites" among bands, and for excessive red tape that deters entrepreneurs with low levels of formal education and excessively delays projects to the point where they are less viable when finally approved than they were when originally proposed.

The RDG's response to the criticism of inadequacy of funds is that federal economic development funds should be viewed as a *system*, of which DIA is only one component. He pointed out that he is attempting to enhance Indians' access to the other elements of the system – that is, to the funds available from other federal departments and agencies. He also stressed private-sector sources (e.g., chartered banks) of economic development funds.

The general tenor of his remarks suggested to this researcher that he had resigned himself to the unlikelihood of economic development becoming a significantly higher priority in DIA's budget. For instance, in response to the criticism that DIA lacked staff expertise in the dominant industry in the region, he pointed to his success (after encountering enormous difficulties) in getting the minister of the federal department responsible for that industry to include in his recent policy announcement an explicit reference to enhancing Indian participation in that industry as one of the goals of the policy. He also stated that in this field, and in another of the region's major industries in which he lacks funds for a sufficient number of professional staff, his objective is to get the bands to work with the appropriate other department of the federal government. Interestingly, the RDG stated his preference for his own economic development officers to be dealing mainly with questions pertaining to inventories of bands' human and other re-sources, rather than with questions of how much money is going to come from where.

In regard to allegations of DIA favouring one band over another, the RDG offered a different explanation. He argued that the vast differences in levels of grantsmanship and entrepreneurship from one band to another can result in even neighbouring bands achieving very different results with the same small amount of money, such that some bands view the more successful band as having benefited from DIA favouritism.

By way of final comment on the topic of economic development, it is worth mentioning the RDG's response to yet another criticism from a chief. The chief had reported to this researcher that DIA officials had discouraged his band from going ahead with a particular economic development project because, in the view of DIA, the project was not economically viable. The band nevertheless proceeded and, after much personal sacrifice by band employees of the enterprise, made it a profit-able venture. What the chief did not tell me, according to the RDG, was the constructive role played by DIA officials in other respects. The RDG contended that shortly after my interview with the chief, the chief told a meeting of Indian leaders that despite some bad advice from DIA, his band's enterprise would not exist today had the DIA bureaucrats not been there to help the band at a crucial moment.

Throughout the preceding pages various nuances of this "dialogue-at-distance" serve to remind us of the intensely political side to the relationship between DIA and its clients. On the Indian side, the rela-tionship is political in part because it has as its essence the distribution of what political scientists call "scarce values" – that is, valued goods (money and expertise) in scarce supply. The relationship is also political because the Indian chiefs are politicians seeking (re-)election to the band council or to leadership positions in other Indian political associations. On the departmental side, the relationship is political because DIA officials are striving to enhance, or avoid the erosion of, the department's credibility and prestige with superiors, with funding agencies, with legislators, and with other external critics. In a sense, the department is under siege, and that fact must influence its members' behaviour, just as the numerous pressing needs of the Indian constituency pressure the chiefs to state their case in the boldest of terms.

Flow of Information
Although the maxim "information is power" is somewhat over-stated, information is unquestionably an important resource contribut-

ing to one individual's or organization's power over another. Thus, the way in which information is disseminated and/or collected, particularly in a hierarchical relationship, can be symbolically important as a statement of the nature of power in that relationship. Below we shall consider communication, consultation, and information flows from bands' perspectives and from a DIA perspective.

Bands' complaints in this area are again legion. One complaint is that some bands get notice of a meeting only after the meeting has already been held, or get notice of the existence of newly available program funds only after the deadline for applying or after other bands have already been allocated all or most of the funds. DIA is also criticized for not giving bands enough lead time to be able to respond properly to some requests for information and for sometimes not giving enough advance notice to enable sound proposals to be formulated. Bands also complain that it is often well into the new fiscal year before a band will be notified whether its budget has been approved. Another finance-related complaint concerns the flow of information in the opposite direction; that is, bands are required to submit quarterly (rather than annual) financial statements to DIA on some programs. Furthermore, bands complain about the "legalese" and "bureaucratese" of the language, which make various policy circulars or memoranda of agreement very difficult for some band politicians and officials to understand. One final example pertains to DIA's alleged secrecy; that is, one chief complained that DIAND reserves the right to go through its files on a band to remove material before releasing the files to the band.

The complaint about different bands being notified at different times is particularly important because of its overtones of manipulation and favouritism. Interestingly, another chief pointed out that sometimes a band will learn about newly available funds before other bands simply because the first band may have had a representative in Ottawa on other business at the time that the coming availability of the new funds was first rumoured there. (Bands vary markedly in their ability to afford to send a representative to Ottawa.) The RDG also pointed out that he encourages his staff to communicate freely with clients and the general public, even to the point of accepting public-speaking engagements. In the context of such formal speaking engagements or the informal conversations immediately before and afterward, a band might receive information simply as a result of the DIA official attempting to do his job of facilitating bands' efforts and fostering good relations between DIA and the band, the RDG suggested.

The complaint about late notification of approval of bands' budgets is also worthy of special attention due to the difficulties that late notification poses for responsible financial management by bands. In response to this the RDG pointed to the complexity of the budgetary process, particularly insofar as it involves other levels of government and other federal departments. For instance, a band's budget may directly or indirectly involve funds from Canada Mortgage and Housing or from the Department of National Health and Welfare (DNHW). Those departments may have experienced cuts to their total budgets and at the beginning of the bands' fiscal year it may not yet have been decided by DNHW what proportion of those cuts will be allocated to DNHW's Indian health services branch. The DIA regional director-general also pointed out that procedural changes in bands' favour have been implemented in budgetary matters. For instance, to remove the necessity for a band to take out "overdraft protection" loans from its bank (sometimes at high rates of interest) while awaiting notification of whether the band budget has been approved by DIA, at the beginning of the fiscal year DIA now disburses to the band one-quarter of its previous year's budget. (However, bands anticipating budgetary cuts fear that under this arrangement they may be spending their way into a deficit position for the remaining quarters of the present fiscal year.)

Finally, let us address the question of DIA secrecy and manipulation of information by removing information from files made available to bands. Here the RDG pointed out that DIA files contain information involving private aspects of individual Indians' lives (e.g., information on illegitimate children or on the amount of an individual's loan). In addition to DIA's obligation to protect the rights of individual Indians, the RDG continues, DIA must protect community-level rights, such as a band's right to confidentiality concerning the size of its trust account. These factors, along with the fact that "we could and do get lawsuits from all sides and both sides," result in DIA reserving the right to limit access to DIA files and to remove material from band files before releasing the files to the band. Notwithstanding the above comment about lawsuits, the RDG contended that the removal of information from band files was unaffected by the possibility of further court cases being brought against DIA along the lines of the precedent set in the Musqueam case. In that case DIA was found negligent in the exercise of its trust responsibility to the Musqueam Band.

Other Dimensions of Internal Colonialism
To this point we have considered various allegations and complaints from bands along dimensions that can be considered indicative of the existence of internal colonialism. We have also considered departmen-

94

tal responses to some of the more serious of these complaints. Even though we cannot[10] carry that approach through for all of the remaining dimensions identified in Table 9, it is important to note the presence or absence and relative force of allegations and complaints pertaining to those other dimensions. Where they are present, chiefs communicate them to each other and those dissatisfactions thereby contribute to the formulation of a shared ideology that predisposes chiefs to perceive DIA's actions in a certain critical manner.

It is unlikely that a presentation of departmental responses[11] to particular allegations would alter those Indian judgements, for those judgements are formed on the basis of a whole constellation of experiences, observations, and stories extending back for generations. Furthermore, many of the DIA actions that give rise to Indian complaints of colonialism have their origin in structural features of the situation that are unlikely to change over the short term. Therefore, it is also unlikely that DIA behaviours will change drastically unless and until some major reforms are instituted in those structural features. This is the reality of the situation. Thus, the remainder of this section is mainly intended to demonstrate the multiplicity of pillars upon which Indians' critical conceptions of reality rest and to identify changes that have occurred in relations between bands and DIA over the last ten years.

An intemperate orientation toward risk was one of the dimensions identified in Table 9. This refers both to recklessness and to excessive caution that could unnecessarily slow the decolonization process. For the most part the former was not cited as a problem. One band administrator, though, contended that the history of the department has been to set bands up for failure, and cited a forestry program a few months prior to our interview as a specific recent example. Another cited DIA's transferral of programs to some bands without adequately preparing them. Excessive cautiousness on DIA's part appeared to be a more common occurrence, as some respondents identified projects where DIA's advice not to proceed was, in their view (albeit with "20-20 hindsight") or in their experience, faulty. Overall, though, risk-taking did not emerge as a major grievance, and some respondents cited instances where DIA's cautiousness proved to be better founded than the bands' enthusiasm.

Decision-making is a crucial dimension to consider, for one of the hallmarks of a colonial situation is that the colonial administrators occupy a disproportionately large amount of the decision-making "space," and thus leave the colonized people with little opportunity to make the decisions that will shape their own destiny. From the perspective of most respondents in this study, significant improvements have occurred on this decision-making dimension over the last decade, but much room for improvement remains, and this, of course, is one of the main *raisons d'être* of the Indian self-government movement. DIA's consultation procedures were perceived to have improved considerably, but consultation was not viewed as an acceptable substitute for the final authority to make a decision. Similarly, responsibility for administering DIA programs was seen by respondents as a poor substitute for having the responsibility and final decision-making authority on the *design* of programs. In many areas that authority continues to rest with DIA, although recent moves toward what is known as "block funding" will likely lead to bands taking on major responsibilities for program design decisions.

This account would be remiss if it did not make reference to the degree of change that has occurred over the last ten years in the realm of decision-making. For instance, one chief reported that ten years ago the band could not even have a meeting without a DIA representative being present. He also charged that in the mid-1970s a DIA staff member asked the band's signing authorities to sign a blank Band Council Resolution form, which is comparable to asking someone to sign a blank cheque. As political pressure on DIA has mounted, as Indians have acquired more education and training, as tribal councils have developed, and as modes of transportation and communication between bands and with DIA have improved, bands' decision-making responsibilities have grown, albeit within the limits to which the Indian Act can be stretched.[12] Numerous bands now design some of their programs (e.g., education, housing, river management, child welfare) and administer several others designed by DIA. However, even administering programs designed by DIA can mean that the bands' own officials or elected politicians now make the decisions on such important staffing matters as who will teach the band children in school and who will exercise the discretionary judgement as to whether or not a social assistance ("welfare") applicant meets provincial eligibility requirements.

Socio-fiscal control was another dimension of internal colonialism identified earlier. This refers to DIA granting, withholding, or otherwise manipulating funds – usually for political purposes – in an attempt to make the recipient or would-be recipient take a particular course of action or inaction that would otherwise not be taken. One indicator of this would be if DIA were initially to label certain funds as nondiscretionary but subsequently treat them as discretionary, or if DIA were to depart from established funding formulae. Although some respondents could cite examples of neither of these, some others reported the former to have happened, specifically with fire trucks, education, and/or housing. DIA departing from set funding formulae was not a common occurrence, judging by our respondents' observations. Nevertheless, one chief volunteered that his band had received funds that another band should have received, another complained about being the loser in such a transfer, and a third complained strongly that DIA frequently pulls money from an emergency contingency fund to appease a particular chief who has a reputation for taking his complaints to the mass media. One chief complained that if a band has capital (as opposed to operating) funds allocated to a construction project and has not started the project by November, DIA can reallocate that money to another band. (He did not mention that any such confiscation is supposed to be preceded by two warnings from DIA.) Overall, this researcher was left with the impression that socio-fiscal control is now viewed within DIA as being too blatant a tactic, so that it is less frequently used now than it was a decade ago.

Obstruction of initiatives issuing from the grassroots is another indicator of colonialism. Excessive "red tape," about which respondents frequently complained, can be one manifestation of obstructionism, as can the use of so-called "divide-and-conquer" tactics. The latter was a widespread complaint voiced by Indian leaders as recently as the mid-to-late 1970s, but it was not a common concern expressed in our interviews. Although it, too, thus seems to have waned considerably, the remarks of some respondents suggest that it is not entirely dead either as a behaviour of DIA or as an attribute of DIA in the perceptions of some chiefs. For instance, several chiefs alluded to what they viewed as DIA's favouritism toward large bands and pointed out how this has the effect of creating or exacerbating tensions in relations between large and small bands.[13] (It should be noted, though, that about half of the respondents replied in the affirmative when asked if DIA actually fosters co-operation among bands.) The allegation that DIA practises favouritism was one of the most frequently voiced grievances. Many of these complaints refer to incidents where other bands are adhering to the dictum: "the squeaky wheel gets the grease." One chief remarked, "Until two years ago DIA had barely heard of us, and so gave us the minimum." He contended that certain bands have favoured status with DIA, and that only they are told how to circumvent DIA's own rules.

In addition, various behaviours of DIA staff are perceived as patronizing by their Indian clients. For instance, one chief reported encountering such behaviour as recently as the week before our interview, when the band was "put down" by a DIA official over the band's choice of contractors on a particular project. On a different matter, a DIA official's question – "Are you sure that would be in the best interests of the band in the long run?" – was also perceived as patronizing by the band's chief. In general, though, from various comments, this researcher was left with the impression that band leaders and band administrators are treated much more respectfully by DIA officials than was the case a decade ago; band leaders, as elected politicians who have largely left behind the patron-client relationship their predecessors had with the Indian agent of an earlier era, are now in a position to demand or command respect from DIA officials whose careers they can now jeopardize or enhance.

This concludes our review of band grievances against DIA. We turn now to a brief consideration of a case study of relations between a government bureaucracy and its clients.

A Parallel Case Study of Government-Client Relations

Like DIA, the Newfoundland Workmen's Compensation Board (WCB) is a money-moving agency. It is responsible for certifying or rejecting workers' claims of having incurred illness or injury on the job, for judging the degree of the worker's functional impairment, and for granting the corresponding level of compensation payment or pension to those persons certified as having justifiable claims. In their book *Bureaucracy and World View*, Handelman and Leyton describe the enormous discrepancies that arise between the workers and the Board in their conceptions of "the reality" surrounding illnesses that miners believe to be caused by their work in the Newfoundland fluorspar mines. [14]

The background parallels between DIA and WCB begin with funding. Just as the Auditor-General's stinging criticisms and government budgetary restraint have led DIA to place much emphasis on fiscal responsibility and accountability, the WCB staff members are acutely aware that the indemnification payments they authorize come from a levy assessed on employers in the province; as one of the WCB officials remarked, "After all, it's industry we have to answer to." Moral considerations involving the value systems of the government officials also enter into both cases. WCB officials experience a dilemma in deciding where to draw the line between maximizing payments to injured workers, on the one hand, and "eliminating the work ethic entirely" or opening the way to "terrible abuse" on the other hand. In DIA the moral dilemma is sometimes expressed in terms of the dictum: "Problems aren't solved by throwing money at them." (This is also a convenient rationalization for underfunding programs or for making massive financial cuts to programs.) Both agencies, as money-movers, concern themselves with the potential for client abuse of their "largesse."

Both departments are besieged, and it is significant that this researcher and Handelman and Leyton independently struck upon this as an important factor explaining the tenor of government-client relations in these two different settings. Handelman and Leyton refer to "the intense and often contradictory pressures besieging the WCB from the public, media, unions, individual workers, government, industry, and industry's lobbyists such as the Canadian Manufacturers Association." A comparable list for DIA would read as follows: the public, media, band chiefs and councils, individual Indians, the Auditor-General, the Public Accounts Committee of Parliament, Treasury Board, the Penner Committee (on Indian self-government), the Deputy Prime Minister's 1985 Task Force on Government Spending, lobby organizations such as the Assembly of First Nations and the churches, various other Indian organizations (e.g., tribal councils), and to a lesser extent provincial governments and industry.

Another important factor independently identified by this researcher and by Handelman and Leyton was the structure of regulations in the situation. WCB officials are bound by the list of compensatable injuries cited by the Newfoundland legislature in the Workmen's Compensation Act and by the regulations promulgated under that Act. Likewise, DIA officials are bound by Treasury Board directives, by the archaic Indian Act, and by the provisions of the numerous other statutes and intergovernmental agreements that DIA administers.

The two client groups also share many similarities. Handelman and Leyton focus on two communities that were brought into an industrial mode of social organization (out of their feudal relations with the merchants) only relatively recently, which is to say, with the opening of the mines in 1933. Most Indian bands had their first ongoing exposure to the modern industrial welfare state even more recently. In both cases there arose what might be called de-collectivizing forces (e.g., competition for mining jobs or inter-band competition for DIA funds). Just as Indians were pushed to the sidelines of the modern industrial society (e.g., moved to reservations), miners stricken by one of the mining diseases (cancer, silicosis, and chronic obstructive pulmonary disease) find that they become unable to market their labour. Their sole marketable commodity is now their disease. It is only a slight exaggeration to say that for some of DIA's clients, their sole marketable commodity in their marginalized economic position is their ethnicity and their "affliction" (their poverty) itself. Both the afflicted Newfoundland mine workers and many DIA client bands find that their economic strategy must be to manipulate the benefits of the nation-state in order to gain an income. Their task is to seek out that to which they feel or know they are entitled, and to exploit the diverse social agencies or programs for whose benefits they are eligible. They regard public agencies as exploitable resources, like the rivers, the forest, or the farm. Grantsmanship, the ability to mount and document a convincing application for a government grant or pension, becomes an important skill in both situations because both bands and miners, as a basic survival strategy, have adapted to the system put in place by the dominant society.

However, to use the words of the Newfoundland researchers, many are "singularly ill-equipped for such a task" (that is, for the task of "working the system"). In both cases the social system is in transition from "traditionalism" to "modernism." The miners, frequently illiterate and uneducated, continue to perceive social relationships in personal terms and to interpret others' actions as a particularistic response to personal needs, rather than in terms of the implementation of formal regulations. For instance, workers often inaccurately perceive WCB's apparently arbitrary allowance of claims for a particular disease as the WCB relenting in their particular case because of their personal pressure on the Board, whereas the change has actually resulted from new legislation bringing a new category of disease under the Act. Their traditionalist world view renders imcomprehensible the impersonal, formal, and universalistic criteria of bureaucrats carrying out legislated mandates. The miner also continues to expect his patron – the priest, the politician, the doctor, and the lawyer – to negotiate with the outside world on his behalf.

Indian chiefs, also enmeshed in a social system in transition and well aware of the workings of the patronage system operated by Indian agents who were located on the reserves until the 1960s, often interpret the comparative good fortune of other bands in particularistic terms involving allegations of favouritism or patronage or malfeasance of DIA officials. While it would be naive to believe that these are totally absent in DIA (an organization also in transition), the behaviours in question are often merely instances of DIA officials following universalistic bureaucratic criteria or exercising the discretionary authority that to some degree must be vested in "street-level bureaucrats" in any large organization. However, an important difference between DIA and WCB, on the one hand, and other bureaucratic organizations, on the other hand, is that the DIA and WCB clients monitor their environment very closely and have ample opportunity to communicate to each other what they observe.

According to Handelman and Leyton, WCB staff members:

> must swim through an abrasive miasma of public and private pressures, knowing all the while that their actions will be consistently misunderstood, their motives continually questioned and their decisions almost universally reviled. [15]

The authors add:

> WCB officials are often astonished and hurt to learn of the reactions of the disabled workers and their families to Board decisions, for the officials do not see themselves as locked in battle with the people. To the contrary, they regard themselves as professionals and public servants. . . . [16]

In this researcher's experience both of these descriptions would have applied equally well to numerous DIA employees in the early 1970s. By the mid-1980s, relations had improved significantly, but Handelman and Leyton's descriptions nevertheless retain much of their validity for the DIA-Indians situation. In this regard we must not overlook the fact that various bands have called for the abolition of DIA and a parliamentary committee has endorsed their calls.

Distrust is a prominent feature in both situations. The Newfoundland researchers report that WCB officials are under "constant and unjustified critical pressure" and often react with bewilderment to the workers' distrust. Similarly, distrust has been a long-standing feature of Indians' orientations toward DIA. Recent events, such as the contradictory thrusts of the Prime Minister's remarks at the 1985 First Ministers Conference on Aboriginal Constitutional Matters and of the deputy prime minister's leaked task force report on government spending on native programs, fuel Indians' distrust and lead to its focusing on the government's agent, DIA.

Both the DIA bureaucrats and those at WCB sometimes slip into paternalistic modes of thinking. WCB officers' belief that WCB pensions and benefits should be restricted because they "may do more harm than good" is reminiscent of what was referred to earlier as DIA's neo-paternalism – that is, the belief of some DIA officials that because of their theoretical and technocratic "superiority" over Indians (based on their knowledge of the social and management sciences), they know what is best for Indians. This social scientism has its parallel in the place that medical science occupied in WCB officials' world view: they defend their assessments of workers' degrees of functional impairment as based on "precise and scientific calculations that are accepted internationally." In both situations the logic of science interferes with the officials' ability to recognize the logic of experience that their clients use. The divergent views of reality held by client and official are a product of the different systems of logic used in each group.

Not only the differences in logic of the clients and officials separate them, but also an incompatibility of languages. Reference was made earlier to Indian chiefs' complaints about "legalese" and "bureaucratese" rendering some DIA policy circulars incomprehensible to the bands. A comparable phenomenon was found in the Newfoundland case in written communications from the Board to the applicant. Whereas the miners argued their case in personalistic terms, [17] the WCB replies were written in a bureaucratically conditioned depersonalized style, using many words that most of the miners had never seen or heard before.

The final parallel to be discussed here is the experience of contradictions or inconsistencies and the importance attached to them by the clients. In the Indian situation the contradiction may be between the engineering and housing arms of DIA over the matter of lot specifications in a housing development; or it may be the inconsistency involved in one band having no band office or community hall, while another band of about the same size (therefore eligible for about the same amount in per-capita grants) has both. In the view of the first band chief, the situation is either inexplicable or else is a clearcut case of DIA favouritism. In the WCB situation, two miners with very similar symptoms will receive different judgements from WCB. This, too, will appear arbitrary and inexplicable to the miner who is unaware that two different diseases were involved in the two cases and only one is covered under the Act.

Conclusion

For this observer the parallels between the DIA-Indians relationship and the WCB-miners relationship are too numerous and striking to sustain the hypothesis that bands' perceptions of DIA behaviours result from the essentially colonial nature, per se, of those DIA behaviours. A highly similar situation to the DIA-Indian relationship exists in the WCB-miners case, and yet no racial or ethnic dimension is highlighted there and no allegations of internal colonialism are levelled there. Furthermore, in response to Indians' militancy, DIA is unquestionably changing for the better, as even our respondents acknowledged. In some respects those who continue to denounce DIA as a colonial apparatus are probably off-target in their criticism. That is not to say that reforms, indeed some sweeping reforms, are not warranted, for they surely are warranted and some (e.g., funding arrangements) are already being developed. Nor do I deny that abuse of power, malfeasance, and organizational politics occur in DIA just as they do in any large organization, and that clients sometimes suffer from these behaviours. Indeed, in any money-moving department the potential for abuse is great. What I am saying, though, is that more sophisticated explanatory models than the colonialism model need to be developed. Such models need to take into account social class considerations as well as bureaucratic, career, and organizational environment considerations. I am also suggesting that the Penner Committee's recommendation endorsing some Indian politicians' calls for the dissolution of DIA is too simplistic a solution for at least the short to intermediate term. Each of these points will be discussed in turn.

Explanations for the behaviours of DIA officials and for critics' perceptions of those behaviours as colonialism can be found at two levels. At the macro level we focus on two points: first, the fact that DIA is a part of, or an agent for, the larger Canadian state; and second, the maxim from the political economy school of thought that holds that the state, rather than being an impartial arbiter among competing interest groups, is actually biased in favour of the dominant classes in society. According to this perspective, the state performs three basic functions: (1) facilitating the accumulation of wealth; (2) legitimating (and therefore perpetuating) the distribution of wealth and power in society, especially to those social classes that are not the main beneficiaries in that distribution of wealth and power; and (3) preserving order through exercising the state's monopoly on the legitimate use of force.[18] Below we briefly consider the implications of these points in the context of Indian affairs in Canada.

Elsewhere I have argued that one of the unstated underlying purposes (latent functions) of DIA is *containment* or social control of Indians.[19] In particular, I argued that DIA seeks to channel Indian demands and aspirations for new political structures so as to keep them within the bounds of acceptability to cabinet, Parliament, and the Canadian electorate. This was illustrated by the comments of DIA's then-director of policy concerning DIA's 1978 proposals to revise the Indian Act. He said:

> I don't see that we can make much more extensive changes than what we are now proposing. We have to take the middle road approach between

what Indians want and what our masters – Parliament and the public – will accept.

In the view of many, the "need" for this containment function still exists, for Indians are in effect calling for new constitutional and legislative arrangements that were denied to Quebec in the Constitution Act of 1982 and that in some respects are tantamount to the sovereignty-association originally advocated by the Parti Québécois.

In the 1980s, the perceived need for containment of Indian demands and aspirations has been accentuated by the fiscal crisis of the Canadian federal state and of the larger capitalistic system in which it operates. At least over the short to intermediate term, Indian self-government may be considerably more costly (economically) than the status quo. Furthermore, the status quo itself has become extremely expensive, as the Indian and Inuit Affairs portion of the DIAND budget is projected to reach $3.6 billion in 1990-91 and all federal expenditures for all native peoples are projected to increase from the present $2.42 billion to $5.05 billion by 1990-91. To many members of the Conservative government's caucus, this is unacceptably high. They and most other major political and economic actors thus far seem to have failed to realize that most of the money funnelled into Indian self-governments would be recycled within Canada and probably in much more economically productive ways than is the case with the welfare payments that make up such a large proportion of DIA's annual budget (about one-fifth, as recently as the late 1970s). Finally, firms and corporations struggling in the midst and aftermath of the economic depression of the 1980s are sometimes wary of Indian self-government because of the competing firms and further regulatory encumbrances it will spawn. Thus, in the minds of many important actors in Canadian society, the need for containment of Indian demands and aspirations continues unabated.

This perceived need for containment is not lost on DIA officials at various levels of the bureaucracy. As the RDG reported, "We have been warned in fairly strong terms to back off from coming forward to Treasury Board for special [funding] submissions." This is the kind of constraint on daily work operations that gets conveyed, formally or informally, to those lower levels of the bureaucracy with which bands have most frequent contact.

From the perspective of political economy, Indians constitute a pool of surplus labour that occupies a very low class position in the system of stratification. Demands for Indian self-government challenge that distribution of power, prestige, and wealth and necessitate the redistribution of wealth from the more affluent sectors of the population to the fledgling Indian governments. DIA acts as a buffer between the government and the Indian people. In performing the second major function of the state, that of legitimating the existing system to those who are not its main beneficiaries, DIA can be expected to distribute government "largesse" to bands that are potentially the most vocal critics or challengers of the status quo, rather than allocating those resources evenly across all bands. However, since justice must appear to be done, funding formulae are devised and usually applied universalistically across all bands; it is in the distribution of discretionary funds (or in the reallocation of funds from the "non-discretionary" to the discretionary category) and in other instances of exercising that discretionary authority that must always be present in any system of formal rules and regulations, that DIA officials engage in behaviours that are perceived by bands to be favouritism. [20] Furthermore, because the state is at one and the same time attempting to fulfil two contradictory functions (facilitating the accumulation of wealth and legitimating the resultant inequalities in society), and because the demands placed on DIA from above ebb and flow over time, the probability of inconsistencies in the behaviours of DIA officials also increases.

According to this perspective, then, what is interpreted by some as a continuation or extension of racist colonial practice is actually attributable instead to class domination and to the state acting in the interests of itself and of certain social classes to the detriment of other social classes.

At the micro level of explanation we find a largely different constellation of factors that must be taken into account if we are to understand both the behaviours emitted by DIA and why they are perceived as colonialism by such critics as band chiefs. These factors are portrayed in diagramatic form in Figure 5. In this model the behaviours we are mainly interested in explaining are those located toward the right of the page – namely, paternalistic behaviours (real and/or perceived) and behavioural inconsistencies/favouritism. Three central factors in understanding those phenomena are: (1) the realization that, like many other government departments, DIA is in an intermediary position between its clientele and the larger government apparatus; (2) that DIA is under siege from both sides; and (3) that unlike many other government departments, DIA lacks both governmental support to "manage" its clientele and clientele support to

106

Figure 5
An Explanatory Model of DIA's Behaviour and Clients' Perceptions of Colonialism

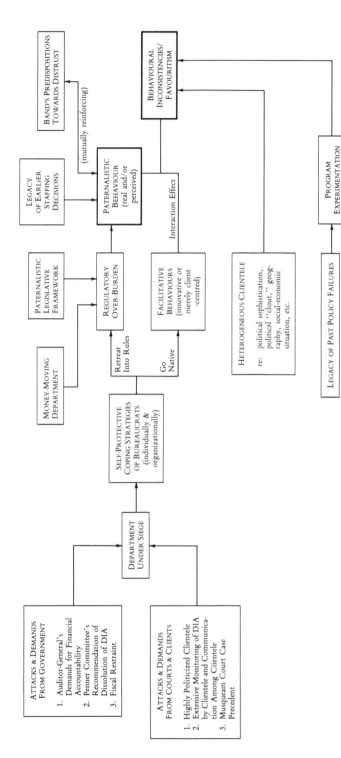

ward off government attacks. DIA's low prestige and poor reputation in government circles, and its reputation for having an "unruly" and non-prestigious clientele, handicap it in its attempts to muster allies within government in order to ward off both the strong criticism of its clientele and such hostile government recommendations as those of the Penner Committee and Nielsen task force. Despite having highly cordial relations with their RDG or with their district manager, band chiefs usually find it politically inastute to come to the aid of DIA when DIA is attacked by other chiefs, for some of the colonial stigma that DIA carries could rub off on them or political alliances with other chiefs could be jeopardized.

DIA officials cope with this state of siege by adopting one or more sets of strategies to protect themselves, their careers, and their minister. These strategies will likely be justified by what Kelly calls a "theory of the office," or a formally and informally transmitted ideology that provides a working typology of clients and becomes a basic ingredient of a department's official perspective.[21] Such an ideology not only helps the bureaucrat to make sense out of events, but also helps him/her to cope with stress and uncertainty by having readily available the criteria for initially classifying a client. Assigning a client band to one or another such category (e.g., "militant" or "troublemaker" versus "patsy") results in officials treating the client band in one or another different ways. This contributes to bands' perceptions of favouritism.

One coping response involves rigid and ritualistic adherence to the rules handed down from above. This rigid application of rules contributes to the excessive regulatory burden that already exists in the realm of Indian affairs by virtue of the paternalistic orientation of the Indian Act and by virtue of the fact that DIA is a so-called money-moving department. The second coping strategy, colloquially known as "going Native," involves facilitative behaviour calculated to win approval from clients rather than from superiors in the DIA hierarchy.

These two different types of coping behaviours (regulatory versus facilitative) can be understood as responses to the two different sources of stress faced by DIA staff; they are, therefore, contradictory or inconsistent. Furthermore, if a given individual vacillates between the two, the appearance of inconsistency will be exacerbated. Thus, the contradiction or tension in the work environment of the department sets up contradictory behaviours within the department – behaviours that clients perceive as favouritism or untrustworthiness.

The excessive regulatory burden that smothers Indian bands is prone to being interpreted as paternalistic by virtue of its very existence. The behaviours of bureaucrats who enforce those rules or regulations, or who refuse to bend them, are a second potential source of perceptions of paternalism. Indeed, the band leaders' distrust of DIA predisposes them to perceive overtones of paternalism in the behaviour of individual DIA staff members. Furthermore, the continued presence of an "old guard," the product of an earlier era of staffing decisions, in some cases provides ongoing substance to allegations of paternalism.

In addition, DIA has a legacy of policy failures that creates the need for further experimentation in the design and delivery of programs. Inasmuch as some bands are participating in these experiments and some are not, and because some bands may be taking on more responsibilities than others, there can also be inconsistencies in funding which are observed but not understood by other chiefs. For a department in transition in a field that is in even faster transition, experimentation will be widespread and inconsistencies will be numerous.

Finally, it should be noted that Indians in Canada constitute an enormously heterogeneous clientele compared to the clientele of most other government departments. Bands vary widely in terms of their political power and political sophistication, their geography, and the degree of need exhibited in their socio-economic circumstances. Such variety militates against consistency of treatment.

To the extent that this micro-level analysis is valid, it suggests that there are certain points in the model where reform could be introduced so as to reduce the incidence of real and perceived paternalistic behaviour and of inconsistent behaviour on the part of DIA officials. One such point of intervention is in staffing; early retirement or lateral transfers out of DIA could be offered to the older staff members who are most often criticized for alleged paternalism. More importantly, though, the excessive regulatory burden could be reduced, just as the federal government did with the Foreign Investment Review Agency and with the paper burden faced by small businesses. The most substantial steps in this direction would be to remove various powers the minister holds over a band and to institute a program of block funding or transfer payment where accountability is to the Indian community rather than to DIA. A more sustained effort to upgrade the grantsmanship skills of bands and to improve communications efficiency concerning newly available funds would also eliminate many complaints. Reforms suggested by the macro-level political-economy model, however, would so profoundly alter the existing distribution of power and wealth that they are unlikely to be seriously entertained by government until the political and economic costs of preserving the status quo become much greater than they are now.

In closing, I raise the question, "Would bands be better off without DIA than they are with DIA?" I am not yet convinced that this question can be answered in the affirmative. One concern must be that if DIA programs are reallocated to other departments, many of which will have no experience in dealing with Indians, major inefficiencies and even greater paternalism than under DIA might result as personnel in those departments make the long climb up a learning curve. Many mistakes of the past would likely be repeated. Another concern is that small bands might become even more disadvantaged (in comparison to large bands) than under the present regime. Indeed, the bureaucratic recrudescence or regrowth that would likely appear if DIA programs were to be administered by various other government departments could actually leave us with a larger, albeit decentralized, government bureaucracy for dealing with Indians. Furthermore, from a political-economy perspective, if, in the tug and pull of politics, DIA is dismantled but real Indian self-government is diluted or withheld as part of some larger political compromise within the government caucus, then nothing will have changed insofar as the fundamental character of class domination is concerned. Other departments of the state will simply take over the containment, social control, and legitimation functions that DIA has been performing.

Thus, in the view of this researcher, the dismantling of DIA would solve few of the problems involved in the daily lives of Indians and would likely exacerbate others. A more constructive first step would be the establishment of an "upgrading" program to address some of the class differences among Indian bands by bringing the most disadvantaged bands up to some minimum national standard of housing, infrastructure, and social services (including education and others) over, say, a five-year period. In such an endeavour there would still be a facilitating role that DIA could play, such as in helping bands acquire grantsmanship and negotiating skills. However, the keys to the success of such a venture would be that the decisions regarding specific uses of resources would have to be taken by local band members and their elected representative, the labour would have to come from local band members to the fullest extent possible, and the models would have to be provided by other Indian or aboriginal peoples. Such a community development approach would develop in band populations the experience and expertise that would increase the likelihood of successful self-government (if it ever comes) and of success in relations with state agencies and departments regardless of whether self-government comes or not. [22] It also offers the advantage of immediately addressing the pressing needs of the grassroots level Indian population.

Notes

1. The research reported in this chapter was made possible by grants from the Social Sciences and Humanities Research Council of Canada and from the Research Unit for Public Policy Studies in the Faculty of Social Sciences at the University of Calgary. The author also acknowledges the constructive suggestions offered by Drs. Roger Gibbins and Tullio Caputo.

2. The distinction between IIAP and the larger department (DIAND) recognizes that the interests of Indians and of IIAP administrators are not necessarily the same as the interests of department-wide administrators or of administrators in the Northern Development Program. However, the term "IIAP" has not caught on; thus, designations most commonly used by respondents – "DIA" or "DIAND" – to refer to IIAP will be used throughout this chapter.

3. Robert Blauner, "Internal Colonialism and Ghetto Revolt," *Social Problems*, XVI (1969).

4. James Frideres, *Native People in Canada* (Scarborough, Ont.: Prentice-Hall, 1983).

5. J. Rick Ponting and Roger Gibbins, *Out Of Irrelevance* (Scarborough, Ont.: Butterworths, 1980), pp. 144-47, 151-52.

6. See Charles Perrow, *Complex Organizations: A Critical Essay*, Second Edition (Glenview, Illinois: Scott, Foresman and Co., 1979), pp. 18-23.

7. Nationally, DIAND is divided into nine different administrative regions, most of which are coterminous with provincial boundaries. (The exceptions are the Atlantic, Yukon, and N.W.T. regions.) Regions are then subdivided into districts. The senior administrators of these are the regional director-general and the district manager, respectively.

8. See Lewis A. Mennerick, "Social Typing and the Criminal Justice System," in Delos H. Kelly (ed.), *Deviant Behavior*, Second Edition (New York: St. Martin's Press, 1984), pp. 339-56; Lewis A. Mennerick, "Client Typologies: A Method of Coping with Conflict in the Service Worker-Client Relationship," *Sociology of Work and Occupations*, 1 (1974), pp. 396-418.

9. As with many other aspects of this study, a conclusive assessment of which interpretation is more valid was not possible in a project intended to be merely exploratory in nature.

10. Not all of the allegations made by other respondents could be put to the RDG in the three and one-half hours this researcher spent with him. Indeed, our conversation was an interview, not a judicial cross-examination.

11. This observer personally found some of the earlier proffered explanations to be quite sufficient to "lay to rest" the allegation and other proffered explanations to be unconvincing.

12. From the perspective of the academic discipline of political economy, the Indian Act can never be stretched far enough; rather, as a control-oriented piece of legislation the Act needs to be discarded, not stretched. Political economists would submit the hypothesis that bands are allowed decision-making authority up to, but not including, the point where their decisions

would challenge the basic structure of power and privilege underlying their relationship with the larger Canadian society and its state.

13. One of the reforms instituted within DIA has been the widespread use of funding formulae intended to remove most or all of the discretionary allocation powers of DIA officials. However, funding formulae based on per-capita grants are, in a sense, inherently discriminatory against small bands, for small bands do not have the advantage of economies of scale.

14. This case study is taken from Don Handelman and Elliott Leyton, *Bureaucracy and World View* (St. John's: Institute of Social and Economic Research, 1978). Quotations cited in this chapter are from an excerpt printed as an article by the same title in Alexander Himmelfarb and James Richardson (eds.), *People, Power, and Process: A Reader* (Toronto: McGraw-Hill Ryerson, 1980), pp. 128-45.

15. *Ibid.*, p. 134.

16. *Ibid.*, p. 138.

17. The researchers quoted a 300-word letter in which the applicant made fifteen personalistic points such as "after working hard all my lifetime looking after my family. I don't think this is very considerate. I've been a Liberal all my life . . ."

18. See Leo Panitch, "The Role and Nature of the Canadian State," in Panitch (ed.), *The Canadian State: Political Economy and Political Power* (Toronto: University of Toronto Press, 1977), pp. 3-27.

19. Ponting and Gibbins, *Out Of Irrelevance*, p. 104.

20. Because it is relatively subtle, such use of discretionary authority replaces the much more blatant and/or coercive forms of intervention (e.g., use of divide-and-conquer tactics), which over the years came to be defined as illegitimate.

21. Kelly, *Deviant Behavior*, p. 3.

22. For a brief discussion of the potential adverse effect that such a massive assault on socio-economic and housing problems could have on self-government in some communities, see the concluding chapter of this book.

Chapter Four

Sex Discrimination and The Indian Act

by Kathleen Jamieson

Introduction

For more than a century Indian women in Canada have been the targets of legislation that has assigned them lesser fundamental legal rights than either Indian men or other Canadian women. This discrimination, long endured in silence, is now the focus of bitter debate – a debate that has overtones of sexism, ethnocentrism, paternalism, and racism. This chapter examines the development of the issue from an historical and sociological perspective, analyses the rationalizations offered for the discrimination, and describes some of its consequences for Indians in general and Indian women in particular.

Several sections of the Indian Act of Canada discriminate against Indian women, but the primary focus of recent debate has been on the membership sections of the Act, especially (the former) section 12.1.b. The membership sections define who is and who is not entitled to be registered as an Indian by the government of Canada, and thus who is entitled to whatever special rights accompany that status. Section 12.1.b stipulates[1] that an Indian woman who marries a nonIndian man loses her status as a registered Indian. In addition, according to another section of the Act, an Indian woman who marries a member of another band is transferred to the band of her husband regardless of her wishes. Conversely, an Indian man who marries a nonIndian woman does not lose his status as a registered Indian. Indeed, his wife acquires legal status as a registered Indian. These provisions of the Indian Act were upheld by the Supreme Court of Canada as recently as 1973.

Early legislation for Indians did not make such invidious distinctions

---

Excerpted from Kathleen Jamieson, *Indian Women and the Law in Canada: Citizens Minus* (Ottawa: Advisory Council on the Status of Women, 1978). Reproduced by permission of the Minister of Supply and Services Canada.

between male and female Indians. Not until after Confederation, in a statute of 1869, were the forerunners of section 12.1.b and other sex-discriminatory provisions incorporated into the legislation. Since then the provisions of the Indian Act that pertain to the Indian women have become increasingly restrictive in content and more punitive in tone.

The 1869 legislation was created primarily on the basis of the Dominion government's experience with the Iroquois and Algonquin groups of Ontario and Quebec. The great diversity of lifestyles and forms of social and political organization traditionally practised by the Indians west of Ontario, and even in Ontario and Quebec, were not taken into consideration by the lawmakers. For instance, whereas the Indian Act relegated Indian women to an inferior status, for many centuries before the nineteenth century (and possibly for part of that century as well) Iroquois society was matrifocal, matrilineal, and matrilocal. That is, descent was traced through women and after marriage the husband went to live with his wife's family. Each dwelling was owned by a senior woman. In the political sphere the senior matrons elected and deposed the elders of the highest ruling political body; hereditary eligibility to this council was through the female. The matrons are also said to have had veto powers in questions of war and peace. The men were absent for long periods on military or hunting expeditions.

Nineteenth-century Eurocanadian social organization and cultural values were clearly quite different from this in many fundamental respects. The "proper" role of women was highly circumscribed and in common law the wife was virtually the property of her husband. Not surprisingly, then, from this perspective the Indian married woman was seen as an appendage to her husband whether he be Indian or white. This situation persisted until the Indian Act revisions of 1951.

The legislation of 1869 clearly was not meant to reflect Indian customs. Indeed, Indians have never been a party to formulating any section of the Indian Act. Whatever objections Indians have made have been overruled or ignored. Significantly here, Indians in the East, and then in the West as the treaties were being made, were strongly opposed to legal discrimination against Indian women (and their children) who married nonIndians. However, the 1869 legislation that introduced this discrimination was intended to reduce the number of Indians and "half-breeds" living on reserves. This was part of the government's stated long-term policy of doing away with Indian reserves and of assimilating all native people into the Eurocanadian culture. Assimilation meant the phasing out of separate Indian status and the gradual absorption of all Indians into the Eurocanadian population. The culmination of this process was the act of enfranchise-ment, which signified that the enfranchised Indian was no longer an Indian in law, had become "civilized," and was entitled to all the rights and responsibilities of other Canadian citizens.[2] Thus, it is argued here, the 1869 discriminatory provisions did not arise out of some perceived need to protect reserve land, as some have contended, but rather as part of the government policy of assimilation. This policy is seen here as an integral part of a developing caste/class system in which Canadian society became more and more stratified and inequal-ity on the basis of race and social class became the organizing principle. The added dimension of institutionalized sexual inequality relegated Indian women to the bottom of this hierarchical structure.

Though Canadian legislation has provided sanctions only for the Indian woman in the event of interracial marriage, the expressed views of the majority of the Supreme Court justices in the 1973 Lavell case (described below) indicate both a continuing conservative approach to this whole question of race and sex and the deep prejudice these topics trigger in the Canadian public. The resultant inaction reflects these at-titudes and is reinforced both by the claims of some male-dominated Indian organizations that the Indian Act provisions reflected Indian custom and by the claims of others that Indians (not Parliament) should decide on the issue. Meanwhile, the victimization of Indian women continued.

According to St. Clair Drake,[3] the concept of victimization "im-plies that some people are used as a means to other people's ends – without their consent – and that the social system is so structured that it can be deliberately manipulated to the disadvantage of some. . . . The victims, their autonomy curtailed and their self-esteem weakened by the operation of the caste-class system, are confronted with identity problems; their social condition is essentially one of powerlessness." It is also typical that in such a system any attempt by the victim to alleviate oppression is seen as an attempt to subvert the system. An understanding of this provides the basis for unravelling and refuting the arguments for the continuing oppression of Indian women today.

We turn first to consideration of attitudes toward intermarriage in nineteenth-century Canada, after which we consider some of the highlights of the evolution of the Indian Act as it affects women.

Attitudes toward Intermarriage in Nineteenth-century Canada

Despite the fact that the Hudson's Bay Company explicitly prescribed strict racial segregation and eschewed the efforts at assimilation that characterized the earlier French regime, there developed during the eighteenth century a recognized form of marriage between Indian women and the white male fur traders employed by the Company. Indian women possessed a number of skills that made their economic contribution considerable and their presence indispensable both around the Company's fort and on journeys. Most important were the making of snowshoes and skin clothing, the cleaning and dressing of hides, and the preservation of meat – skills vital to survival in the Canadian winter and unlikely to be part of the repertoire of the average Hudson's Bay servant. Indian women also acted as interpreters, guides, and ambassadors to other Indian groups.

By the first quarter of the nineteenth century the Indian wives of "customary marriages" were being rejected by "men of station" (such as Governor Simpson and other senior managers of the Company). The influential writings of such men, and those of Simpson in particular, have contributed to the stereotype of the Indian woman as either the exploited concubine of the white man or a pawn that Indian men handed over to cement trading alliances with white men. Yet to characterize "customary marriages" as being primarily based on the sexual exploitation of Indian women does not accord with fact. Indeed, Simpson's own writings reveal him to have been "appalled" at the degree of control that the Indian and Métis women had over their white husbands.

The Evolution of Discriminatory Legislation

Pre-Confederation
The rejection of so-called "customary marriages" followed closely on the heels of the lessened military importance of Indians. For most of the eighteenth century Indians in general had been treated with the cautious respect accorded allies in war and partners in trade. After 1812, however, Indians ceased to be regarded as useful allies. In eastern Canada the fur trade was gradually being replaced by agriculture as the main base of the economy. With this change, increased importance was attached to European norms, including the British system of class and ethnic stratification. The ethnocentric ideology of "civilizing" the Indians came to displace military and economic motivations as the cornerstone of Eurocanadian relations with the Indians. From this evolved a fundamental shift in policy for Indians in Upper and Lower Canada after 1830. The main elements of the new policy were the inculcation of Christianity and the establishment of a sedentary way of life based on agriculture. A system of Indian settlements designating

special areas as reserved for Indians began to be regarded as the key to achieving these ends.

In 1841 a commission of inquiry was established to investigate the condition of Indians in Upper and Lower Canada. Its report offers valuable insights into the social system of the day, including the role of Indian women and attitudes toward Indian women. For instance, the commission reported in 1847 that Indian women were the main providers for their families. Notions of Indian inferiority were made explicit and the commissioners concluded that the Indians continued ''to require special protection and guidance of the Government.''

In 1850 legislation was set in place to determine who should have the right to live on Indian land in Lower Canada. This Act included the first statutory definition of who was an Indian. Significantly, all persons (male or female) intermarried with persons otherwise qualifying as Indian and living with Indians were entitled to Indian status, as were their descendants. The next year, however, this Act was amended to make the membership provisions slightly more restrictive. Under these amendments the provision granting Indian status to all persons intermarried with Indians was withdrawn and there was added a new section permitting only women (and their descendants but not the women's spouses) who married nonIndians to be considered Indian. A companion Act in Upper Canada applied ''to Indians and those who may be intermarried with Indians.'' A number of provisions of this Act, such as the inability to be bonded or held responsible for contracts, had the consequence of making an Indian a minor at law.

Attitudes in Canada were hardening in proportion to the increasing pressures of European settlement. The problems of the Indians were beginning to be viewed more and more as the result not of depredations on their land by Europeans but of Indian improvidence and lack of ''progress.''

In 1857, ''an Act to encourage the gradual Civilization of the Indian Tribes in the Province, and to amend the Laws respecting Indians'' was made applicable to both Canadas. The title clearly expresses its intent to expedite the process of ''civilizing'' the Indians through offering incentives to them to enfranchise. Enfranchisement was seen as a mechanism ''to facilitate the acquisition of property and of rights accompanying it.'' Ownership of property was the prerequisite for civil rights and responsibilities which were by definition indivisible from civilization. Thus enfranchisement, that ''quaint piece of legal Canadiana'' as one writer has called it, first appeared in legislation, offering as inducements land in fee simple and a lump-sum payment of a share of annuities and band funds. Only males could be enfranchised, and dependants were enfranchised with the male. The definition of Indian in this Act of 1857 for both Upper and Lower Canada was not that of the earlier Lower Canada Act but was the more inclusive designation of the Upper Canada Act: Indians or persons of "Indian blood or intermarried with Indians."

Virtually all subsequent legislation for Indians had three main functions: (1) "civilizing" the Indians – that is, assimilating them (and their lands) into the Eurocanadian citizenry; (2) while accomplishing this, the ever more efficient "better management" of Indians and their lands was always a goal to be pursued and, following on this, an important element in better management was controlling expenditure and resources; (3) to accomplish this efficiency it became important to define who was an Indian and who was not.

Post-Confederation

The British North America Act of 1867 contained only one mention of Indians – Section 91.24 gave to the federal government exclusive legislative authority for "Indians and lands reserved for the Indians." A statute in 1868 consolidated Upper and Lower Canada's legislation relating to Indians and in the process retained the more inclusive definition of Indian. Thereafter, there was a multiplicity of revisions to this Act. An Act of 1869 contained far-reaching changes, many of which involved the bestowal of extensive powers on the Superintendent-General of Indian Affairs (or his agent). In other provisions, on the death of an Indian his goods and land rights were to be passed to his children; the wife was excluded as her maintenance was seen as the responsibility of the children. A council was to be elected by adult males of each Indian settlement. If an Indian became enfranchised, his wife and minor children were automatically enfranchised. Most significant to our concerns here, though, was Section 6, which provided that "any Indian woman marrying any other than an Indian shall cease to be an Indian within the meaning of this Act. . . ." Her children in such a marriage also lost their status, and an Indian woman marrying an Indian from another band became (along with their children) members only of the husband's/father's band.

The Indian woman was here for the first time given fewer rights in law than an Indian man. Particularly punitive was the introduction of the proviso that she and her children would lose forever their Indian rights if she married a nonIndian, for she might then be obliged to leave the reserve since her husband could be "summarily ejected" at the order of the superintendent. Yet, despite such loss of status the

Indian woman who "married out" did not lose her right to annuities (such as they were).

The aforementioned Section 6 of this 1869 statute became the infamous Section 12.1.b of the 1951 Indian Act. It proved to be a source of great protest, bitterness, and divisiveness among Indians, and was extremely difficult to administer. With numerous refinements and embellishments it subsequently became far more restrictive than was ever envisaged even in its Victorian heyday. An examination of its underlying rationale is thus in order.

Previous legislation and the reports of special commissions of inquiry provide little evidence to suggest that protection of Indian lands from the encroachment of nonIndian males was ever more than a very limited and qualified intention of Section 6. Rather, statements in the House of Commons by the minister responsible for Indian affairs at that time suggest that Section 6 was primarily a muddled attempt to achieve the greater *administrative efficiency* and *easier management of budgets* that it was hoped would occur when the number of Indians to be administered didn't keep fluctuating. There appears to have been no "malice aforethought" – in fact, not much forethought at all about possible deleterious consequences for Indian women.

Administrative records of the period (and before) make it evident that a great deal of latitude was allowed for officials to implement their own moral convictions. For instance, commenting on the striking of members from a band membership list when those members have been absent without the consent or knowledge of the band, Superintendent David Thorburn wrote that such deletion is a definite rule of the department because such individuals, having not done their share of road labour, land clearance, and other work obligations, were not deemed to be entitled to the benefits to which resident band members are entitled. "Besides," he added, "we do not know what their behaviour may have been while absent." The Eurocanadian behavioural standards of the day were considerably more demanding for women than for men.

The statute of 1869, especially Section 6, plainly embodied the principle of assimilation. The number of Indians was to be gradually reduced. This was the "final solution" envisaged by everyone except the Indians. Furthermore, the Act embodied the principle that, like other women, Indian women should be subject to their husbands. In law their children were to be his alone.

Indian legislation after 1869 became increasingly restrictive. In the new province of Manitoba, land grants of 160 acres, or scrip valued at $160, were also offered to the Métis (half-breeds) in recognition and extinguishment of their aboriginal title. Those who accepted this land grant or scrip were considered by government to have made themselves ineligible to live on a reserve. Furthermore, in an example of internal colonialism and administrative racism, we have here the elaboration and imposition on native peoples of a set of categories and racial divisions that went against the expressed desire of the peoples. In some cases, it also went contrary to their perception of band affiliation, for the half-breeds were often (e.g., in negotiations for Treaty Four) viewed by the Indians as kinsmen.

The first Act to bear the title "Indian Act" was passed in 1876. It altered and elaborated on the definition of the term "Indian" by emphasizing legitimacy and descent through the male line. For instance, the previous definition of Indians in terms of "All persons of Indian blood" was changed to "Any male person of Indian blood" plus any child of such a person and any woman who is or was lawfully married to such a person. The Act goes on to restate that an Indian woman marrying a nonIndian "shall cease to be an Indian," but allows that she may retain her right to annuities. The definition of enfranchisement was made virtually synonymous with the ownership of private property (in contrast with the mere occupancy of reserve property, the title to which is held by the Crown). Enfranchisement and loss of status through marriage were seen as being different in that, unlike male Indians who enfranchised, the woman who married out did not have to be educated or civilized or prove she could survive in the white world. Responsibility for the Indian woman was merely transferred from the government to her husband. Section 72 of this Act also gave the Superintendent-General power "to stop the payment of the annuity and interest money of any woman having no children who deserts her husband and lives immorally with another man."

The Indian Act of 1876 was soon found to be inadequate. Indeed, the need to make almost annual amendments in the immediate post-Confederation period suggests that the fundamental premises on which the Act was based ensured that there would be enormous problems in administering it.

The Indian Advancement Act of 1884 and 1886 and the Franchise Act of 1885 endeavoured to accelerate the process of assimilation. The former gave some fiscal responsibility and other powers to band councils; the idea was that this would eventually lead to reserves becoming municipalities. However, the moral fitness of the Indians who served on the band council was to come under the scrutiny of the Superintendent, who could dismiss the chief and councillors if he so chose. The Federal Franchise Act of 1885 extended the right to vote in federal elections to all men, including Indian men. The extension of the franchise to Indians was withdrawn in 1896 after numerous protests that "wards," such as the Indians, were not legal persons (neither were women) and as such were not entitled to have such a responsibility. No representation without taxation was the crux of the argument.

In 1894 an amendment to the Act created an additional definition of an Indian for the purpose of the liquor control section of the Act. This new definition extended the term "Indian" to include cultural and behavioural dimensions when it included as Indian "any person, male or female . . . who follows the Indian mode of life, or any child of such person." Thus, when it suited the government a non-status woman and her children became Indians temporarily.

Early Twentieth Century
Controversial amendments in 1920 provided for compulsory enfranchisement of the more "advanced" Indians who were determined by boards of inquiry to be self-supporting. Testifying before a House of Commons committee, the Deputy Minister of Indian Affairs, scholar Duncan Campbell Scott, explained to Members of Parliament:

> Our object is to continue until there is not a single Indian in Canada that has not been absorbed into the body politic, and there is no Indian question and no Indian Department. That is the whole object of this Bill.

Of course, the woman who had lost her status through marriage was not affected by this part of the amendments since the procedure known as enfranchisement did not apply to her. However, she and her children continued to be subject to involuntary loss of status with the additions in the 1920 Act that the Superintendent could unilaterally, without her or the band's permission, commute her annuities, so cutting off entirely her last connection with her band.

It is interesting to note that an earlier provision of the Act required that an Indian widow had to be of good moral character in order to receive an inheritance. An amendment in 1927 stipulated that "the Superintendent-General shall be the sole and final judge as to the moral character of the widow of any intestate [lacking a will] Indian." In another section squatters on band land or other Indians not members of the band were to be evicted and jailed if they returned, even if only to fish. This had serious implications for Indian women who had lost their status as well as for other Indians.

The period between the Act of 1927 and the end of World War II saw no major changes in policy or legislation, although the compulsory enfranchisement clause of 1920, which had been dropped in

1922, was reinstated. In 1936, during the Great Depression, the Indian Affairs Department was absorbed by the Department of Mines and Resources; the focus was unequivocally on the development of mineral resources, not Indians. The "Indian problem" was pushed into almost complete obscurity.

The Post-war Period
In the wake of World War II and of the revelations of man's inhumanity to man, a wave of humanism washed briefly over North America. In Canada the condition of Indians was causing some concern and in 1946 a special Joint Committee of the Senate and the House of Commons, which sat until 1948, was established with broad terms of reference: to look at Indian Affairs and the Indian Act with a view to its amendment. Of the thirty-three MPs and senators on this committee, only one, Iva Fallis, was a woman. The chairman's first remark at the very beginning of the proceedings is rather interesting and was addressed to her: "I think we shall have it understood that whenever the masculine term is used it will indicate both masculine and feminine. I hope our lady member will agree to that." This decision, however, was not in the interests of clarity or precision, since a separate legal regime did exist for Indian women compared to Indian men – not only with respect to marriage and illegitimate children, but also, for example, with respect to exclusion from the right to vote in band elections and to partake in band business, the exclusion from rights to inherit, and a widow's exclusion from the right to administer her husband's estate.

Senator Fallis questioned the first witness to appear before the joint committee, the Director of Indian Affairs. His answer revealed the racist and ethnocentric views that persisted from the nineteenth century when he questioned "the moral authority of Parliament to deprive persons with 50 per cent or more white blood of the full rights of Canadian citizenship."

A number of representatives from Indian bands and associations (e.g., the North American Indian Brotherhood and Indian or native associations from the three most westerly provinces) submitted briefs and gave testimony to the joint committee. Some called for the abolition of the Act, while others, such as the Native Brotherhood of B.C., stated that women who had lost their status through marriage and who were deserted or widowed should be allowed to rejoin their band with their children. However, the Indian Affairs Branch expressed very different sentiments and, in a marked departure from the more enlightened nature of many of its other recommendations, the committee ignored Indians' representations on band membership.

In May of 1951, Parliament passed Bill C-79, which implemented some of the recommendations of the joint committee. In these amendments, the discretionary powers of the minister and governor-in-council were once more amplified. The nineteenth-century prohibition on Indian ceremonies and dances (the potlach and the sun dance) was removed, and the requirement of obtaining permission from the agent to travel or to sell produce was also omitted. Indian women were for the first time given the right to vote in band elections. The enfranchisement section and the membership section were greatly elaborated and altered. Both increased the disadvantages for Indian women who "married out." The sections dealing with estates and inheritance were also amended to affect the same women adversely. The consequences of these membership sections were to be profound for human relationships in Indian communities.

The membership section, in becoming vastly more elaborate, spelled out at length not only who was entitled to be registered as an Indian but also who was not. The mention of "Indian blood" was removed and the male line of descent was further emphasized as the major criterion for inclusion. In a similar vein are sections concerning descendants of those who had been allotted half-breed lands or scrip, who were not entitled to be registered. The result of this enactment was that attempts were made by the department to deprive whole groups of their Indian status on the basis that their forebears had taken half-breed scrip. This was so disastrous that public opinion forced it to a halt and this was amended in 1958 to allow those at that date registered as Indians to remain so.

The major change for an Indian woman who "married out" was that until this time she had to some extent had a dual status as an Indian and an ordinary Canadian citizen. Until 1951 she had usually retained the right to go on collecting annuities and band moneys if she did not choose to accept a lump-sum "commutation." Thus she would continue to be on the band list and to enjoy some band benefits as well as treaty rights (if her band had taken treaty), though she was no longer an "Indian Act" Indian. As of 1951, however, she was to be automatically deprived of both her Indian status and her band rights from the date of her marriage.

Involuntary enfranchisement for men was omitted from this Act of 1951, though voluntary enfranchisement for men and bands was retained. However, new clauses affecting Indian women who married nonIndians were inserted. Now, for the first time, on marrying a nonIndian they became subject involuntarily to the enfranchisement sections of the Act. In the woman's case the Act conveniently set aside provisions requiring that the Indian who chose to enfranchise obtain the consent of the band and be "capable of supporting himself and his dependents" and "capable of assuming the rights and responsibilities of citizenship."

An amendment in 1956 stated that the band membership (and hence the Indian status) of an illegitimate child of an Indian woman could be contested and that person be excluded from the band "if it is decided that the father of the child is not an Indian." The many anomalies and injustices thus visited on the children augmented the difficulties of women who married out.

The whole idea of enfranchisement was a patent anachronism by 1951, but the term has been perpetuated as a polite fiction that disguises the Act's blatant discrimination toward Indian women. For instance, on the issuing of the order of enfranchisement any property held on the reserve by the Indian woman marrying out must be sold or otherwise disposed of in thirty days. In exchange she is given twenty years of treaty money (if the band took treaty) plus "one per capita share of the capital and revenue moneys held by Her Majesty on behalf of the band." However, in the accounting procedures used, the base on which those entitlements are calculated is very narrowly defined, as we shall observe below.

Not surprisingly, voluntary enfranchisement has held little attraction for Indian women or Indian men. For instance, between 1965 and 1975 there were only 228 voluntary enfranchisements of Indian men and women, while during that same period 5,035 women and children experienced compulsory enfranchisement under Section 12.1.b of the Act. That is, only about 5 per cent of all enfranchisements were voluntary and 95 per cent involved women who had no choice. More recent data show voluntary enfranchisements to have virtually disappeared (e.g., there were only three in 1976) and involuntary enfranchisements under Section 12.1.b to account for over 99 per cent of all enfranchisements. That, in the past two years, only four Indians out of a population of some 280,000 have chosen voluntary enfranchisement is a telling commentary on the merits of enfranchisement in the view of Indians.

Consequences of Loss of Status

One of the arguments most frequently encountered by Indian women who have lost their status is that they have been financially recompensed for whatever they have lost. First and foremost, it should be stressed that no sum of money could ever compensate for their loss and that of their children. In addition, though, in all areas except the resource-rich parts of Alberta, the money received amounts to little or nothing. It consists of one per-capita share of band capital and revenue, plus, if she is a treaty Indian, a further twenty years' worth of treaty payments of $4 or $5 per year. Between 1966 and 1977 these payments averaged $261.80 per person enfranchised. The sums are very low in part because of the poverty of most bands and in part because of accounting procedures that do not include all band assets and investments (e.g., a hotel, a factory, farm machinery, and ranch animals are all excluded) when shares are being computed. These women are not permitted access to the band accounting books and also lack recourse through any appeals or investigative process. The consequence of this is that even a woman from a very rich band where oil "royalties" may average millions of dollars per year received a relatively small sum.

The amounts received under these provisions of the Indian Act vary enormously. At the low end of the range, the Attawapiskat Band in May, 1975, paid seven cents plus the eighty-dollar annuity, while some other bands paid nothing. At the other end of the range is Alberta, where the highest amount paid in 1976 was about $12,300. Interestingly, the Louis Bull Band on the wealthy Hobbema reserve paid about $9,200 per enfranchising person in 1975, but ten and twenty years earlier paid about $1,100 and $400 respectively. Clearly, the women and their children who were enfranchised from these bands ten or twenty years ago lost a great deal of potential income for which they have not been compensated. The same may be true of many of those who are being "paid off" today. In the jargon of economists, their "opportunity costs" (the benefits lost due to opportunities forgone) may be very high. A fair scheme of compensation would take into account all assets, including estimates of proven or potential unexploited natural resource wealth. The latter calculation is commonplace in resource-extraction industries such as the oil and gas industry.

Apart from financial losses, one of the more important benefits lost by these "non-status" enfranchised women and their children is in the field of education. Not only may the children be denied access to the cultural education programs offered in the reserve school, but they will also lose their entitlement to free tuition and supplies, a noon lunch supplement, sports equipment, and, at the post-secondary level, the educational allowance covering tuition, books, living expenses, travel, and clothing. Nor does the enfranchised former-Indian woman herself have the right to Department of Indian Affairs support in upgrading her own education.

Non-status women lose their eligibility for both off-reserve and on-reserve financial assistance for housing. More importantly, they lose their right to live on the reserve where they can be close to friends and family and the support they offer; the children and grandparents may also thereby be deprived of much of the contact that is often so vitally important to both generations.

Other benefits from which these women are excluded include: loans and grants from the Indian Economic Development Fund to start a business; exemption from taxation while living on the reserve; exemption from provincial sales tax on goods delivered to a reserve in certain provinces; free medicines to which the members of some bands are entitled; hunting, fishing, animal grazing, and trapping rights on (and under certain conditions, off) a reserve; and cash distributions derived from the sale of band assets or moneys surplus to band needs. Canadian Indians, but not non-status Indian women, may also be employed in the United States without a visa and have certain border crossing privileges under the U.S. Immigration and Naturalization Act.

The non-status Indian woman and her children often find themselves with identity problems that stem from their marginality; often they are socially rejected by white society and yet may not participate with family and friends in the life of their former community. Since by the late 1970s approximately one-half of all Indian marriages were to nonIndians (evenly split between Indian women and Indian men "marrying out"), Indian women who lost their rights and were forced to leave their communities found that nonIndian women were replacing them and conflict escalated between Indian men and Indian women.

The realm of inheritance of property and the right to live on the reserve has provided more opportunities than most for victimization of women (especially widowed or separated women). It has become a common practice on a few reserves to evict widowed or separated women who return to the reserve, often with several small children, to live in a family-held home. The acute shortage of adequate housing on most reserves and the intensity of inter-clan political rivalries on many of those same reserves combine to make the issue particularly volatile and the women particularly vulnerable to victimization.

Finally, the non-status woman may suffer the further indignity and deprivation of being refused burial with her forebears on reserve grounds that to her, too, are sacred. Thus, the deleterious consequences of this oppressive legislation extend from marriage (or earlier for her children) to the grave and beyond.

The Lavell-Bedard Case

Indian women became hopeful of change to the Act when in 1970 an Indian by the name of Drybones successfully appealed before the Supreme Court a conviction (under Section 94.b of the Act) for being found intoxicated off a reserve. His appeal was based on the contention that such a conviction was racially discriminatory and contrary to Section 1.b of the Canadian Bill of Rights, which guarantees equality before the law and equal protection of the law regardless of a person's race, colour, national origin, religion, or sex. The Canadian Bill of Rights seemed to overrule other Acts passed by Parliament.

In the case of Drybones it was clearly demonstrated that under the liquor provisions of the Indian Act an Indian was subject to harsher penalties for being found intoxicated in a public place than a nonIndian under the Liquor Ordinance of the Northwest Territories. The Supreme Court ruled that Section 94.b of the Indian Act was rendered inoperative because of the Canadian Bill of Rights.

Encouraged by the Drybones decision, Jeanette Lavell, an Ojibwa woman who had married a nonIndian, decided to contest the deletion of her name from the band list. She based her case on the grounds that such deletion constituted discrimination on the basis of race and sex; as such, it was contrary to the Canadian Bill of Rights and thus invalid in law. Lavell was joined in her case by Yvonne Bedard, an Indian woman who had lost her Indian status upon marrying out but who had subsequently separated from her husband. She was fighting the Six Nations band council's attempts to evict her from the reserve and from the house that had been willed to her by her mother.

The issue was taken up by various Indian and nonIndian politicians and became something of a political football. The Attorney-General of Canada intervened in court on behalf of the Indian organizations opposing Lavell and Bedard. By a controversial and puzzling five-to-four decision the Supreme Court of Canada judges ruled against Lavell and Bedard. Among the points contained in the majority decision were the following: (1) that equality before the law under the Bill of Rights means equality of treatment in the enforcement and application of the laws of Canada before the enforcement authorities and the ordinary courts of the land, and no such inequality is necessarily entailed in Section 12.1.b; and (2) Parliament has the right, under Section 91.24 of the BNA Act, to legislate as to how and by whom Crown lands reserved for Indians are to be used, and the Bill of Rights cannot take that right, as exercised in the passage of Section 12.1.b of the Indian Act, away from Parliament. That is, the Bill of Rights was deemed by the court not to take precedence over the Indian Act, and the Bill of Rights guarantee of "equality before the law" was construed very narrowly to mean equality in the administration or enforcement of the law, rather than to mean that all persons, no matter who they are, will be treated as having equal rights before the law. It is interesting to note also that Mr. Justice Ritchie, writing with the majority, could somehow contend that within the Indian sector of the population Indian women are not discriminated against before the courts or in the administration of the law.

The argument that Indian women face discrimination on the basis of race and sex was thus completely set aside in the majority verdict. Indian women faced with loss of status were left with no avenue of appeal except to Parliament, and alone they were politically powerless.

After the Supreme Court decision was announced the issue of sex discrimination in the Indian Act became even more highly politicized. The National Indian Brotherhood had taken a stance against Lavell and Bedard, and the federal Liberal government, anxious not to antagonize Indian organizations again so soon after the fiasco of its 1969 white paper, made little effort to remove the offensive provision from the Act. Indeed, the government gave an undertaking to the NIB that no part of the Indian Act would be changed until revision of the whole Act had been completed, after a full process of consultation. The result of this "gentlemen's agreement" was that a powerful blanket of silence was temporarily imposed on discussion of the status of Indian women. It became taboo and unwise in certain circles even to mention the topic.

After a few years, though, the unrelenting efforts of the national association of Indian Rights for Indian Women, and after 1978 the Native Women's Association of Canada, succeeded in forcing the issue back onto the government agenda. In this they were supported by such other women's groups as the federal Advisory Council on the Status of Women and the National Action Committee. The government's insistence that it would like to change the law but- to do ,so would be contrary to the wishes of the Indian people lost some of its force when, in 1977, NIB president Noel Starblanket went against the earlier NIB position by publicly declaring himself to be personally in favour of removing the discriminatory provisions of the Indian Act (Section 12.1.b). Nevertheless, the issue continued to divide the NIB internally and the NIB refused to allow any native women's organizations to be represented in the joint NIB-cabinet committee "negotiations." The government itself removed the Indian Act from the reach of the new Canadian Human Rights Act, which came into effect in 1978. Indian women were once again denied the basic human rights enjoyed by other Canadians.

One message emerges clearly from this – namely, that to be born poor and Indian and female is to be a member of the most disadvantaged minority in Canada today, a citizen minus. It is to be victimized and utterly powerless, and to be, by government decree, without legal recourse of any kind.

Postscript: Resistance and Change

The extent to which the Indian Act and the colonial system it enforces have warped family and social relations in Indian communities cannot be measured. Even if it seems that the Act has played an unintended role in preserving cultural enclaves that today provide a base for asserting aboriginal rights, there is abundant evidence that the social and psychological cost to all Indians, and Indian women especially, has been very high.

With the passage into law of Bill C-31 on June 28, 1985, the Indian Act was finally amended to eliminate sex discrimination. It also eliminates enfranchisement, provides for the reinstatement of those women who lost their status in the past, and gives the power to bands, for the first time since Confederation, to formulate and administer their own membership codes. This does not mean that the pervasive effects of the 117 years of legislative discrimination against Indian women will magically disappear. Indeed, it would seem that discrimination is deeply entrenched at the band level and is in many cases viewed as traditional, whatever was the case in the pre-European past. [4] However, there would also seem to be wide variations in the extent and practice of this discrimination – on the one hand, fairly egalitarian attitudes prevail in some British Columbia and northern groups; on the other, discrimination is very overt in some Alberta bands. In the 1980s as in the 1970s, these Alberta bands, with royalties from oil and gas, have continued to employ large numbers of lawyers to assist them in lobbying legislators and in preparing submissions to parliamentary committees in order to block any Indian Act amendments that would eliminate discrimination against women. Responses by bands and tribal groups to the amendments to the Act are therefore likely to vary considerably.

Between 1978, when the research for the book summarized above was completed, and 1985, when the Act was finally amended, there was a subtle change in the way that objections to change were expressed. The new form these objections took has some far-reaching implications. In a number of public forums the male-dominated organizations and their allies began to characterize the issue as one of individual rights versus collective rights. They argued that if the federal government took any action on membership it would violate the most fundamental premise of self-government, the right of the collectivity to decide on its own citizenship. Thus, although it became increasingly common for leaders of some of the male-dominated organizations to denounce Section 12.1.b in public forums, they were actually as adamantly opposed to the government taking action to eliminate it as they had ever been.

Indian women continued to protest strongly and lobby the government through one of two umbrella organizations, the Native Women's Association of Canada (NWAC) and Indian Rights for Indian Women (IRIW), or through provincial or local groups acting autonomously. With the aid of the feminist umbrella group, the National Action Committee on the Status of Women (NAC), with which IRIW is affiliated, and other allies, unremitting pressure was placed on government. However, although different Canadian governments promised from 1979 onward that the Act was about to be amended and although they chided Indian men for their sexism, Parliament itself continued to show extreme reluctance to take action to resolve the issue.

Important events between 1980 and 1985, which cumulatively contributed to the passage of Bill C-31, were:

- The finding by the United Nations Human Rights Committee, made public in September, 1981, that Canada had violated the human rights of Sandra Lovelace, a Maliseet woman from the Tobique Indian Reserve in New Brunswick. As a result of the operation of Section 12.1.b of the Indian Act she was denied the right to live on her natal reserve and enjoy her own culture – a right guaranteed to minorities under Article 27 of the International Covenant on Civil and Political Rights.[5] Canada made a commitment to the UN committee that it would introduce legislative changes before the House by mid-1981. Nothing changed.[6]
- The failure of the minister's 1980 "moratorium" allowing individual bands to apply for a ministerial dispensation in the suspension of the operation of Sections 12.1.b and 12.1.a.iv. Very few bands applied to have Section 12.1.b suspended.[7]
- The patriation of a new Canadian constitution with a Charter of Rights and Freedoms specifying sex as a prohibited ground for discrimination in two sections (15 and 28).[8]

- The 1982 recommendations of a special parliamentary committee on Indian women and the Indian Act. The committee recommended that several sections incorporating discrimination based on sex be eliminated from the Act. It further recommended that those women who had lost status, and their first-generation children, be reinstated to their bands.[9] On December 7, 1982, the Minister of Indian Affairs, John Munro, commenting on these recommendations, said in the House of Commons: "We intend to move with considerable haste on this question." They did not.
- The introduction of an amendment to the aboriginal rights section of the constitution guaranteeing equal aboriginal rights to male and female persons.[10] This section (Sec. 35.4), which could be as crucial as Section 15 in future court challenges, was promoted at the 1983 First Ministers Conference primarily by the Quebec Native Women's Association, which was given a front seat by the government of Quebec.
- In mid-1984, in the final days of the short-lived government of John Turner, a bill (C-47) to amend the Indian Act was finally brought forward. The bill passed quickly through the House but was defeated in the Senate. The bill was subsequently widely criticized as being very flawed, as a sop to feminists, and as having been pushed through without proper consultation with Indian groups.

When that bill, however flawed, was defeated, it seemed that the momentum that had been generated for change was completely lost. However, in the subsequent general election, the political power of women was strengthened by various factors, including the NAC-organized televised debates by the three party leaders on the topic of women's issues, the concurrent campaign of Geraldine Ferraro for U.S. vice-president, and speculation about "the gender gap" in voting patterns. Thus, the Indian women's case was strengthened, and in fact no momentum was lost. Women's groups continued their pressure. The Conservative government elected in the summer of 1984 did not have the same relationship with the male-dominated Indian groups that the Liberals had had. What finally triggered the changes, however, was the knowledge that on April 17, 1985, Section 15 of the Charter of Rights and Freedoms would be coming into effect.

Thus, on February 28, 1985, a second bill (Bill C-31, An Act to Amend the Indian Act) was introduced in the House of Commons by David Crombie, the Minister of Indian Affairs. After extended public hearings a substantially revised bill was finally passed four months later.

Given the history of the issue, Bill C-31 was probably as much as the women's groups could reasonably have hoped to achieve, although it presents most of the non-status women with a highly unsatisfactory "choice." Bill C-31 not only eliminated the sections that clearly offended against Section 15 of the Charter, but also abolished enfranchisement. This was a largely symbolic gesture since very few people have enfranchised in recent years. Under the amended Act, no one gains or loses status through marriage and those women who lost their Indian status because of sex discrimination in the previous Indian Acts are eligible upon application to the Department of Indian Affairs for reinstatement to band membership and for re-registration as Indians under the Act. The first-generation children and all those people who enfranchised for any reason, and their children, can also apply to be registered Indians but are not also entitled to band membership. Curiously and unfairly, all those who received a payment of over $1,000 from band moneys on enfranchisement must pay it back with interest before they receive any further disbursements from their band. [11]

Two broad categories of Indians who have different rights are thus created: (1) a charter group of those who had band membership on April 17, 1985, their children, and the reinstated women (minus their children); (2) a group who have registered Indian status but not band membership and thus, unlike those in the first category, do not have the right to live on an Indian reserve, share in resources, or take part in band politics.

The legislation provides that the under-age children of a reinstated woman may also reside with her on her reserve if she returns. No provision is made, however, for her husband or older children. Clearly, for many women this presents a painful dilemma if they do wish to return. Many others will not want to leave their home, friends, and employment. Another question is whether or not their bands will welcome them back. As far as many Indian women's groups are concerned, therefore, the revised Act does not go far enough.

Another key feature of the bill, intended, according to the Minister of Indian Affairs, as a step toward Indian self-government and an inducement to those who fought against government changes to the Indian Act, is that it provides that henceforth Indian bands will be able to decide who is eligible to be a member of the band. Bands may now formulate and apply their own membership rules with the approval of the majority of the members of the band. Thus, a third category of Indians may be created: those who have only band membership. To what benefits they may be entitled, especially if they reside off-reserve, is unclear. Bands have up to two years to formulate their own membership codes. If they have not done so during this period all those who regained status under the amended Act are eligible for band membership.

Those who do not have band membership have a limited ability to transmit status to their descendants; if they have one nonIndian parent and their children do not marry status Indians, their grandchildren will not have status. The discrimination is continued, therefore, between brothers' and sisters' descendants, in the sense that the grandchildren of Indian males who married out, but not of Indian females who married out, will have Indian status regardless of whether their parents marry an Indian or a nonIndian. It would seem that the result will be that over the long term this group will disappear and only those who have band membership will have status.

According to DIAND calculations, about 16,000 women and 2,000 other individuals are now entitled to have band membership in Canada's almost 600 bands.[12] The size of the bands varies but the average band size is now about 600 members. (The Department of Indian Affairs has calculated that the total number of those who are eligible to regain status, though not necessarily band membership, is about 76,000 to 86,000.)[13] With the uncertainty surrounding the numbers of people who may want to return and the concern that promised extra funds will not be forthcoming or will be insufficient, it seems likely that most bands will try to have membership codes in place in short order. It also seems likely that most of these codes will err on the side of exclusivity, given the scarce resources held by most bands, the extreme unwillingness to share extensive resources on the part of a very few other bands, and the recent history of discrimination against women. However, there also may be dramatic exceptions where the codes are quite inclusive, such as the code of the Nuu-Chaa-Nulth Tribal Council in British Columbia.

In addition to the feared adverse economic consequences to bands, it was argued in the various committee hearings that the implementation of the provisions in Bill C-31 allowing non-status women to return to their bands would have negative social and cultural consequences for bands. Yet, in recent years half of all Indian men have married non-Indians and these women have been integrated into the band, presumably without causing social and cultural disruption. (The bands and brotherhoods have not complained about this in their recent submission to government.) Thus, it is difficult to see why reinstated Indian women, who have family ties on the reserve and were brought up as Indians, could be more of a threat socially or culturally than nonIndians.

Some observers are now saying that the more articulate, politicized women who have obtained management and other job skills in urban areas might be a threat to male dominance and might disrupt established power structures on many reserves if they are permitted and wish to return. Thus, it does seem likely that there will be many legal challenges to this legislation both from those who believe that the Act did not go far enough in restoring rights and from those who claim that it went too far.

Through all the arguments and discussions in the special committee hearings and parliamentary debates there has run a common thread: the characterization of the issue as one of women's rights versus Indian rights in the 1970s and as individual rights versus collective rights in the 1980s. It seems not unlikely that some version of these arguments will surface in challenges to the Act or band codes through the courts. It is, therefore, worth considering them.

First, the argument that characterized the Indian women's struggle as demands for women's rights misses the point. Most Indian women were not feminists. What Indian women were primarily seeking was the retention or restoration of their special status, which they felt to be their inalienable right as indigenous persons. Yet, neither can "women's rights" be characterized as individual rights, even though the legal phraseology of human rights codes and the legal process involved represent them as such. If women are demographically half the collectivity and if in Indian communities all Indian women, as a group, stood to be affected by the various discriminatory provisions of the Indian Act, how can the rights of that half of the collectivity be construed as individual rights and the rights of the other (male) half as collective rights? The answer, I suggest, lies in inter-sex power relations and how they are expressed in our language and in our history, which still sees women as appendages to men.[14]

A second question is whether, in practice, the categories of individual rights and collective rights are indeed polar opposites as they tend to be portrayed in theory. Rather, just as the dichotomy between public and private spheres of life has now been shown to have limited analytic utility, I submit that the individual/collective dichotomy reflects Western philosophy's traditional preference for binary oppositions (opposing pairs). In practice what are presently understood to be collective rights and individual rights seem more often to be interdependent rather than contradictory. Trade unions provide one example of the complex ways in which individual and collective rights overlap or are interdependent. They function to protect those inside the unionized collectivity of workers from outside individuals or other collectivities, but through such mechanisms as seniority rules they might discriminate against women as a group and against minority groups. [15]

The concept of special status for Indians is slightly different, but along with Michael Asch I would argue that it is quite capable of being accommodated within present, evolving practices. [16] However, the development and analysis in Canada of concepts such as collective rights, special status, and affirmative action to correct structural inequality are relatively recent and not very advanced. Conversely, the concept of individual rights, though it often excluded women, is very old and well-developed in North America.

Finally, and more specifically here, the arguments have been made that the recognition of individual rights is not Indian custom and that equal rights for women with men is not Indian custom. Both these arguments assume homogeneity in Indian customs when all the evidence is that there was great variation. While it would be anachronistic to assert that Indian women had equal rights with men (or vice versa) prior to contact with Europeans, it can be said that in some Indian cultures there are indications of a high status for women.

Similarly, the question of whether individual rights are ''customary'' or not is also anachronistic, but evidence exists that in most West Coast societies, for example, all kinds of individual ''rights'' – implicit, symbolic, and material – existed and were recognized as such within the collectivity. [17] This does not mean that those things that we may believe to be individual rights today were recognized or that they were extended to all if they were. The point is that such comparisons with the past are very problematic.

Although there is a long way to go, in retrospect it is clear that there have been far-reaching improvements in the legal and social (though not economic) position of women in Canadian society over the past twenty years. However, Indian women seem to have benefited little from most of these improvements. Certainly infant and maternal mortality rates have decreased, but Indian women still live ten years less than other Canadian women; furthermore, a disproportionately large number of Indian women live on social assistance and with the constant and well-founded fear that their children will be apprehended by child-care authorities and put into permanent foster care. [18]

None of these circumstances is likely to be changed very much by the amendments to the Indian Act – although there undoubtedly are material benefits. Nevertheless, the healing process can now begin, as will the strengthening and affirmation of women's sense of identity and self-worth. These are necessary conditions for changing the situation of structural inequality, which virtually all native people now share.

Notes

1. Editor's note: The reader is reminded that the provisions of the Indian Act that discriminate against women were removed with the passage of Bill C-31 in 1985. The postscript to this chapter addresses these changes. The main body of this chapter will retain the verb tense originally used by Jamieson in her book. Even though the Act has been amended, the earlier discriminatory provisions have left scars on many individuals and on social and political relations in the Indian community. Furthermore, some Indian leaders remain adamantly opposed to the amendments enacted. Thus, Jamieson's piece remains valuable in helping us to understand consequences that will persist to the end of this century and beyond.
2. Until 1960 it was not possible to remain an Indian and simultaneously enjoy all the rights of a Canadian citizen.
3. St. Clair Drake, "The Social and Economic Status of the Negro in the United States," in A. Beteille (ed.), *Social Inequality* (Harmondsworth: Penguin, 1969), p. 299.
4. Kathleen Jamieson, "Plus ça change, plus c'est pareil? Les femmes autochtones et la question du gouvernement indien autonome et du droit contoumier," *Recherches Amerindiennes au Québec*, XIV, 3 (1984). (An analysis of testimony to the Sub-committee on Indian Women and the Indian Act.)
5. William Reeves's essay in this book deals with Article 27 in more detail.
6. Kathleen Jamieson, *Indian Women and Their Human Rights: A Guide to the Film Somewhere Between* (Vancouver: Legal Services Society of British Columbia, 1983), pp. 28-29.
7. *Ibid.*, pp. 24-25.
8. See Penny Kome, *The Taking of Twenty-Eight: Women Challenge the Constitution* (Toronto: Women's Press, 1983).
9. House of Commons Committee on Indian and Northern Affairs, Sub-Committee on Indian Women and the Indian Act, *First Report*, p. 40.
10. Sec *Canada Gazette*, Part II, Vol. 118, No. 14 (1984); or *Hansard*, June 29, 1983, pp. 26955-26956.
11. Loss of status through marriage and enfranchisement is recognized by this Act to have been unjust; the victims who have suffered social, psychological, and economic consequences should therefore be recompensed, not penalized. To pay back even a few hundred dollars may be impossible for many Indians.
12. *Background Notes: Bill C-31: An Act to Amend The Indian Act* (DIAND, 1985), p. 3. The 2,000 individuals include children deleted with mothers under Sections 109.2, 12.1.iv, and 12.2.
13. *Ibid.*

14. In *First Report* (p. 42), cited above, "collective right" and "individual right" are defined thus: "collective right: (1) right granted to an individual in a collective manner with the other individuals who are included in that group, and exercised jointly by the members of the group, and (2) rights of the collectivity as a whole, which cannot be claimed for the individual himself, but which can be claimed on behalf of the collectivity"; "individual right: rights belonging to all individuals in a state regardless of their membership in a group within the state." Rights and the history of the concept are discussed in Lawrence M. Friedman, "The Idea of Right as a Social and Legal Concept," *Journal of Social Issues*, 27, 2 (1971), pp. 189-98, and in Noel Kinsella, *Provincial Human Rights Legislation* (Ottawa: Employment and Immigration Canada, 1980).

15. See, for example, Harish C. Jain, *Race and Sex Discrimination in the Workplace: An Analysis of Theory, Research and Public Policy in Canada* (Ottawa: Employment and Immigration Canada, 1981), pp. 9-10, 39-52.

16. Michael Asch, *Home and Native Land: Aboriginal Rights and the Canadian Constitution* (Toronto: Methuen, 1984).

17. See, for example, the ethnographic work of Franz Boas on the Kwakiutl.

18. Patrick Johnston, *Native Children in the Child Welfare System* (Ottawa: Canadian Council on Social Development, 1983).

Part Two

Economic and Community Development

Editor's Introduction

When treaties were first signed with Indians in Canada the explicit rationale was one of moving Indians off of fertile land and other land of high economic value so that the land could be used for the economic benefit of the colonizers. Indians were deliberately relegated to the bottom rung of the ladder in a hierarchical system of economic exploitation that has been called a hinterland-metropolis system. Toronto and Montreal serve as hinterlands to foreign metropolitan centres like London and New York, while in turn the Prairie provinces are a hinterland to Toronto, and northern Alberta (and to a certain extent the Northwest Territories) is a hinterland to Edmonton and Calgary. Thus, like a child's playing blocks, these metropoli and hinterlands form a nested structure.

As occupants of the lowest position in this system of economic power relations, Indians have experienced major dislocations in the subsistence and trading economies they had prior to contact with Europeans. In most instances their technology was overwhelmed by European technology and when their labour as military allies, catchers of fur-bearing animals, guides, interpreters, intermediaries, etc. was no longer needed by the Europeans, they retreated or were pushed to the geographic margins of the respective regions. There, out of sight and out of mind of most Canadians, they lived in conditions that often parallelled those we associate with Third World countries today, especially insofar as their health was concerned. The capitalist economy no longer had a role for them as producers of needed goods, and their small numbers and low purchasing power rendered them unattractive as a market. In terms of the economy, they had become virtually irrelevant to Canadian society. For the most part lacking in industrial skills, and alienated from the capitalist economy by distance, ideology, culture, legal-bureaucratic barriers (the Indian Act and the Indian Affairs Branch of the federal government) and by the discriminatory behaviour of Eurocanadians, their income remained well below that of other Canadians and their local economies stagnated.

The penetration of the welfare state into their communities in the second half of the twentieth century brought mixed results, at best, as some improvements in health and living conditions were partially countered by the welfare dependency syndrome and its effects. Despite the fact that money coming into their communities from outside tended to exit the community again without being recycled and therefore without creating economic multiplier effects within those communities, Indian communities more often than not became a financial drain on Canadian taxpayers.[1] By the mid-1980s the budget of the Indian and Inuit Affairs Program of the federal government had exceeded $1.5 billion per year (of which only a tiny portion was devoted to Indian economic development per se).

During the twentieth century many of the potentially most economically productive lands on Indian reserves were leased to non-Indians. Sometimes, as testimony and documents before the courts have shown (e.g., in the 1985 Musqueam case in Vancouver), the staff of the Indian Affairs Branch either failed to exercise their trust responsibilities to get the best deal possible for the Indian band in question, or actually engaged in conflicts of interest or in criminal behaviour. In this way the economic development potential of those bands was further eroded and most of the economic surplus produced on those lands went to nonIndians. To this day, leasing revenues are still the main source of non-governmental revenues for some bands.

Economic development began to receive more attention from the Department of Indian Affairs and Northern Development (DIAND) around the mid-1960s as part of a larger program of community development. Many of these projects met with failure as they collided with vested economic and political interests within the band or between the band and DIAND. For instance, the Indian agent (or later officials in the district or regional office of DIAND) and the political elite or leading families on the reserve sometimes had reached a mutually beneficial accommodation that saw DIAND patronage funnelled to those leading families in exchange for their leadership in getting the community to co-operate with the department.[2] When community development projects challenged those accommodations or otherwise "rocked the boat" (threatened the stability of existing political-economic relationships), they usually met with strong protest from the local Indian elite and were accordingly snuffed out by DIAND.

Community Development

For various reasons community development is presently undergoing somewhat of a revival in the Indian realm. One reason for this revival is the pronounced difficulties that the federal government encounters in attempting to deal with the national Indian organization (the Assembly of First Nations) when the latter is unable to build and sustain a consensus among its members or, indeed, is unable even to keep its membership intact. Thus, the political incentive for the federal government, in its efforts to achieve visible accomplishments, shifts to the community level. Moreover, the present minister, David Crombie, as a former municipal politician who built a political reputation on his ability to work effectively with grassroots constituents, is probably favourably predisposed to a community-level orientation. The return to DIAND of Walter Rudnicki, one of the main architects of the department's 1960s community development thrust and now Director of Policy Development, reinforces the minister's proclivities. At the band level itself, various factors have combined to fuel the community development revival. Among these are: the political awakening and new assertiveness of numerous bands, the recognition and creation of opportunities, the positive examples (role models) provided by other bands, and the increasing depth and diversity of human skills in band populations.

Although in some respects community development might have been an "idea before its time" in the 1960s, the time now is ripe for it. In my opinion, it will be one of the main waves of the future, probably at least through the early to mid-1990s. In Chapter Eight Mackie expresses the same view and points out how it likely will be linked closely with economic development initiatives to produce what he calls "community-based economic development." This form of economic development contrasts markedly with that found by Driben and Trudeau in their study described below.

If community development is to be of major importance in the coming years, it is useful to have at least a rudimentary understanding of the concept and its evolution. Although throughout the first half of the twentieth century community development was occurring under other labels (e.g., "the co-operative movement," "the extension movement," "the self-help movement") in such places as the Canadian Prairies and in Moses Coady's Antigonish Movement[3] based at St. Francis Xavier University in Antigonish, Nova Scotia, the term "community development" did not come into widespread use until after World War II. Coined either at a Cambridge Colonial Conference in 1948 or in a dispatch that same year from the British Colonial Office to its Gold Coast (Ghana) office, the term was taken over by the United Nations in an influential 1955 publication[4] that defined community development as "a process designed to create conditions of economic and social progress for the whole community with its active participation and the fullest reliance upon the community's initiative." The UN publication, which followed on the heels of a large-scale program launched by the Nehru government in India in 1952, became the benchmark for subsequent development programs and policies and bestowed international respectability on community development.[5] Another major community development program was launched in the newly independent Philippines the next year. In 1959 a pioneering program among Canadian Indians was introduced by the government of Manitoba with the close involvement and strong support of Premier Duff Roblin.[6] From these experiences and others elsewhere in the Third World (e.g., Mexico in 1964), policy planners came to realize that the "model community" (that is, the developmental goal or condition "B" toward which a community now in condition "A" is trying to move) will differ from one country, or one part of a country, to another.[7]

Community development has evolved into many things: a process; a way of life in a community; a methodology or technology of problem solving, of working with people, and of delivering services; a social philosophy; a social movement; perhaps even an emerging profession. It means different things to different people. However, certain characteristics are common to most conceptions of the phenomenon. The most important of these are listed here. First, members of the community are expected to organize to help themselves and to participate actively in the organizations thus created. Second, community members are encouraged to develop a shared sense of responsibility for identifying their problems and for finding and implementing solutions to those problems; they are encouraged not to rely on outsiders to do this for them. Third, the proper role of outsiders is to provide materials and technical expertise; the community's development should be under its own control. Fourth, the norm of participation implies that discussion will be prolonged and that consensus will be sought to the fullest extent possible. Finally, community development as a philosophy has often tended to be based on a romantic, idealized notion of community that overestimates the potential for consensus in communities and underestimates the role of the state and of interest groups. However, these implicit assumptions began to change in the 1970s.

Community development, as an approach to problems, was widely acclaimed when it was introduced to Indian communities by the federal government in the mid-1960s. However, community development is no panacea for community problems[8] and it has a strong potential for engendering conflict and disruption in the communities where it is applied. Community development programs sometimes fail to solve problems and have sometimes created or compounded other problems (e.g., by introducing unrealistic expectations). Indeed, the animation phase – consciousness-raising, identification and articulation of the problem – is perhaps inevitably going to produce a disturbance in the community. This is especially so now that community development has evolved in the direction of identifying the *underlying causes* of community problems. Furthermore, community development is always political, in that it is guided by one or another ideology and usually creates some relatively autonomous centres of power. Thus, community development implies some degree of conflict over the distribution of money and power, sometimes within a community and usually between the community and external actors (including state actors) who hold economic or political power over the community. Community development is thus still an act of decolonization as it was in its early days under the United Nations.

The definition of community development cited earlier is one of over three hundred that can be found in the literature, and it does not capture the richness of the concept. More recently the Canadian Welfare Council has defined community development as:

> a process aimed at promoting citizen participation in social affairs, developing people's awareness of problems, enabling them to define their needs in relation to the total environment, making possible the enlightened choice among various options and channelling the results into effective action for social change.[9]

The Manitoba government has a more straightforward orientation that admits of economic activity and introduces, by implication, the notion of institution-building, which is an important concern of our next chapter. According to the Manitoba Department of Health and Social Development, the purpose of community development is: ''To assist people to develop economically and socially viable communities which can strengthen and support adequately individual and family growth and enhance the quality of life.''[10]

Around the world, communities or community development programs have followed various strategies or approaches to achieve these goals; among these have been the following approaches: confrontational, information-communication, adult education, skills training, economic development, and social animation. Different approaches are rooted, explicitly or implicitly, in different ideologies and in different types of social science. For readers who are practitioners in the field of Indian affairs, or who are studying to become so, this point is worth elaborating.[11]

The adult education approach to community development is rooted in the Western liberal ideology (with its emphasis on individualism) and in a social science that believes community development is best served by an (ostensibly) "dispassionate, objective, and systematic" quantitative assessment of social needs, which social scientists and community members then bring to the attention of those in power in the state structure. The social animation approach is based on a social science tradition (e.g., ethnography, symbolic interactionsim) that seeks to develop an understanding of society from "inside" the subject's world. This tradition, which is widely espoused by community development practitioners, argues that outsiders must take an empathetic approach to community problems and sees community development as occurring by organizing from within the group. German sociologist Jurgen Habermas views both of these approaches as inadequate and argues for a third scientific model, a critical science rooted in Marxist ideology, in which the goal is emancipation rather than quantification or "mere" understanding. Habermas argues that understanding and possession of facts are insufficient, for all the "objective" facts in the world will not change the world, and to understand suffering is merely the beginning of the amelioration of the conditions that cause it. To him, only a critical science that provides the correct analysis of possible alternatives (in addition to the pertinent facts and a sensitive understanding of conditions) offers the possibility of change. Thus, Habermas's critical social science adds a far-reaching political strategy to community development; it focuses on power and on the potential within communities for achieving power. From Habermas's perspective, this third type of social science and of approach to community development has the highest probability for achieving decolonization.

Contemporary community development in Canada, Britain,[12] New Zealand, and elsewhere is increasingly coming to be based on such a critical social scientific analysis of society. In Canada those Indians who are involved in community development, while seldom adopting the Marxist analysis holus bolus, do tend to adopt parts of it that are congruent with their experiences. Not surprisingly, they have often focused on the three-cornered relationship between the state, capitalism (especially big corporations, state corporations, and multinational corporations), and Indian communities as one of the areas in which critical social science has the most to contribute to their community development strategies. Community empowerment, local control, and the creation of viable alternatives (including employment alternatives) from among which Indian people can make choices are threads which we can expect to see woven through otherwise diverse community development projects in Indian communities across Canada in the 1980s and 1990s.

Those threads are much in evidence in the case study of community development presented as Chapter Five. That chapter deals with Kahnawake (formerly known as Caughnawaga), a Mohawk community that is one of the most institutionally developed Indian communities in Canada. There we observe not a government-sponsored community development program such as those of the 1960s, but rather a concerted, community-based institution-building effort that responds to locally defined needs, opportunities, and initiatives. External governments are at times used as sources of funding, at times supplanted, at times confronted, and at times treated as partners. (Such is likely to be the complexity of intergovernmental relations during and after the decolonizing period.) The discussion of the Kahnawake situation will deal in general terms with some of the aforementioned features of community development and then examine two realms of activity (justice and economic development) in more detail. The sociological concept of institutional completeness is also used to provide another perspective on community development there. The chapter ends by relating the Kahnawake situation to other trends and phenomena discussed elsewhere in the book.

Economic Development à la DIAND

DIAND's economic development efforts experienced an injection of funds after the 1969 white paper was released. As a proportion of the budget of the Indian and Inuit Affairs Program of DIAND, economic development funds increased from 4.4 per cent ($10 million) in the fiscal year 1970-71 to 8.5 per cent ($55 million) in 1977-78, only to drop back to 6.6 per cent ($45 million) the following year.[13]

These funds were usually channelled into small businesses such as sawmills, tourist camps, haulage firms, etc. The success rate of these ventures was poor. Driben and Trudeau[14] have done a case study of DIAND's attempts to revitalize the economy of a band in northwestern Ontario. Their findings are worthy of detailed mention because they stand in marked contrast to stereotypes some people hold about Indians.

DIAND spent over $1.5 million for economic development projects for that band, only to see all four projects fail. The researchers placed responsibility for these failures squarely on the shoulders of DIAND. They found that the department failed to set clear objectives for its programs, even to the extent of failing to have a clear definition of economic development itself. This led to a conflict between job-creation goals and goals of teaching Indians how to run a business. DIAND's approach was also marred by mismanagement, an improper use of incentives, and a failure either to monitor work in progress or to recognize the crucial role of individual initiative. Mismanagement took several forms, one of which involved bringing in outsiders (or worse yet, bringing in outsiders who lacked relevant job experience). Another form of mismanagement consisted of hiring too many employees, such that work became so diluted and depreciated that it was almost a meaningless chore.

The researchers also found a general paucity of consultation with, and accountability to, the people in the band, for DIAND rather than the band had control of the projects. As one respondent said of the DIAND economic development adviser, "he took away our pride. You see, it was always his ideas that were being developed and not ours." Furthermore, people came to see the businesses as "only a small step up from welfare" and concluded from DIAND's action in the community over the years that the government has lots of money to spend. As one report by DIAND itself concluded: "[V]arious individuals make use of the tourist camp equipment and abuse it, lose it, or steal it, knowing that it will be replaced [by government] and that no action will be taken against them." [15]

The Driben and Trudeau case study is just one example of many where DIAND's good intentions proved counter-productive and an economic development venture that was launched amidst widespread optimism turned out to be a failure. Complaints registered by Ponting's respondents in Chapter Three concerning the economic development efforts by a different administrative unit of DIAND lend support to the general thrust of Driben and Trudeau's findings. In short, in the minds of Indians DIAND's development efforts tend to be associated with red tape, inordinate delay, and, all too often, failure to live up to reasonable expectations.

Frontier Economic Development

In response to the "energy crisis" of the early 1970s, private-sector proposals were developed to build a pipeline through the Mackenzie River Valley of the Northwest Territories. Proponents contended that the pipeline would not only bring natural gas from Alaska and/or the Canadian North to markets in southern Canada and the United States but would also provide a major stimulus to the northern economy; northerners, Natives and whites alike, would reap the economic benefits through a bonanza of employment and entrepreneurial opportunities. In other quarters, though, considerable misgivings arose. Pushed

145

by the federal New Democratic Party, the minority Trudeau government in 1974 appointed Mr. Justice Thomas Berger of the British Columbia Supreme Court to conduct an inquiry into the probable social, economic, and environmental impacts of the competing proposals and to suggest terms and conditions that might be attached to any licence to build the pipeline so as to mitigate these impacts.

Berger was an astute choice for the task. A former leader of the B.C. provincial NDP, he could be assumed to be satisfactory to the federal NDP. As a key lawyer for the Nishga Indians in their famous aboriginal rights court case, he had won the respect of native people. As an esteemed member of the judiciary, he possessed an ability to be impartial that was calculated to forestall criticism from industry.

Berger conducted exhaustive and exhausting hearings throughout the North in every community likely to be directly affected by the pipeline and across southern Canada as well. His approach, listening to virtually anyone who wished to make a presentation, was heralded as a model of open government and participatory democracy. (Indeed, it drew on some elements of the community development philosophy.) In April, 1977, he submitted to the Minister of Indian Affairs and Northern Development the first volume of his report, *Northern Frontier, Northern Homeland.* In this controversial report Berger came down squarely on the side of the Natives in their conflict with the pipeline companies; he recommended that a ten-year moratorium be placed on the building of a pipeline in order to permit the native people of the region to strengthen their own indigenous economy and otherwise better prepare for the coming of the pipeline. (In a complex series of developments the pipeline as proposed was not built down the Mackenzie Valley. Instead, approval was eventually given for it to be built along the existing Alaska Highway, although the project became largely unnecessary with the subsequent discovery of vast amounts of natural gas in Alberta and B.C. In 1985 a pipeline running about half of the length of the Mackenzie Valley, from Norman Wells to northern Alberta, was completed.)

Although the main focus of this book is on southern Canada and on Indians rather than on all categories of native peoples, this section includes a précis of Berger's chapter on the economic impact of the proposed Mackenzie Valley Pipeline. Its inclusion here is warranted for various reasons, the most important of which is that Berger's message has much applicability to other economic development projects affecting Indians, including non-pipeline projects and megaprojects in the provinces, such as exploration and development affecting the Lubicon Lake Indians in Alberta. (With this in mind, the editor has changed many of Berger's references to "the North" to read instead "this region" and many of his references to "the pipeline" to read "the project" or "a megaproject.") The chapter on which this précis is based stands as a model of carefully considered economic development planning and is of historical value in and of itself.

In an epilogue written especially for this book, Berger outlines developments that have taken place in the North since the release of his report, such as the establishment of a wilderness park in northern Yukon and progress on native claims settlements. A leitmotif running through his epilogue, through the main body of his chapter, and through Ponting's subsequent chapter on economic development provisions of the new claims settlements (Yukon and James Bay) is that native hunting, fishing, and trapping ought to be preserved and fostered both as an important economic activity in the respective regions and as a source of protein for the human population.

Ponting's chapter in this section focuses mainly on the economic development provisions of the James Bay and Northern Quebec Agreement. More specifically, it focuses on the economic development aspects of the Agreement as those provisions pertain to the Crees rather than the Inuit. An interest in the extent to which the Agreement enhances the Crees' economic self-determination lies behind the selection of certain parts of the lengthy and complex Agreement for attention in that chapter. Thus, the power (advisory versus decision-making) of various boards or bodies created by the Agreement is a recurring concern, as is the membership of those organizations. Special rights and privileges of the Crees are noted throughout. The 1985 Yukon Agreement in Principle is approached from the same perspectives, but the absence of a final legal agreement necessitates that the discussion of the Yukon situation be conducted at the level of generalities. The chapter also includes a brief discussion of the problems and accomplishments associated with implementing the James Bay Agreement and concludes with an assessment of that Agreement. The assessment is neither enthusiastic nor wholly condemnatory. In the scholastic vernacular, the Agreement might be rated as a C + or B-. Notwithstanding its shortcomings, though, in its economic development provisions (at least) it remains a precedent for other contemporary claims settlements.

New Strategies, Old Constraints

This section concludes with a chapter by Cam Mackie, who, like Berger, brings a wealth of practical experience to his essay. As former assistant deputy minister (Development) for the Indian and Inuit Affairs Program of DIAND and as current director of the $345 million Native Economic Development Program of the federal government's Department of Regional Industrial Expansion, he knows whereof he speaks. He is, however, in a somewhat constrained position for the purposes of this volume in that his remarks must be couched at a level of generality that will neither compromise the confidential nature of his relations with his native clients nor provide information that might be of benefit to a competitor of any of his clients. Nor would it be realistic or fair to expect from a public servant a critical examination of his employer's record. Despite these caveats, Mackie's contribution is a useful one in several respects. First, it reflects some of the lessons learned from past successes and failures in the field. One specific example of such lessons is the realization of the importance of individual Indian *entrepreneurs* as prime movers of economic development projects, for in the past the usual operating philosophy had been that band-owned enterprises, rather than individual-owned enterprises, were likely to engender the most commitment from their employees and band customers. Another of Mackie's contributions is his sketching of some aspects of the history and quantitative dimensions of approaches to native economic development, including the strategy and intended role of the new organization he heads. A third contribution is his demonstration of the linkages between community development and economic development.

Finally, a few general points should be mentioned. First, it is important to realize that *the survival rate among most nonIndian small businesses is very low even in the best of economic times.* [16] Canada is not now in the best of economic times. In fact, the Canadian economy has only recently emerged from a recession so severe as to border on a depression. Not all sectors of the economy have fully recovered, and for some sectors (such as the oil industry of Alberta) conditions might get worse before they get better. Such conditions militate against the success of small businesses, Indian or nonIndian, especially where managerial skills and training are low. Furthermore, because many Indian reserves are situated in the midst of resource-extraction hinterlands, those reserves – as the bottom rung on the ladder of hinterland-metropolis relationships – will be among the first to be subjected to the adverse local effects of the inevitable bust in the boom-and-bust cycle that characterizes resource-extraction economies. With banks collapsing domestically, world oil prices falling, and protectionism running rampant in the main market for Canada's staples exports, Indian economic development projects may face a buffeting by a number of external economic forces over which Indians (and often Canada as a whole) have no control. When the internal particularisms (e.g., suspicion of those who try to "get ahead" economically, over-regulation by DIAND) of Indian economic development are considered as well, economic development for Indians throughout Canada should be expected to exhibit as high a failure rate as that exhibited by other newly established small businesses. In my opinion these factors do not justify the blind faith that the deputy prime minister's task force on government spending exhibited in Indian private enterprise as a major vehicle for pulling Indians out of poverty, especially given the severity of the spending cuts contemplated for Indian programs. Furthermore, governments should not lose sight of the fact that earlier in our history Indians were pushed to economically marginal lands; for many bands in contemporary times no amount of entrepreneurial drive, skills training, and injection of investment funds will permit the band to find an economic niche and prosper, because often there simply is no economic niche sufficiently beneficent to support more than a handful of people.

Notes

1. This perception of Indian communities as a financial drain on Canadian society is, of course, a short-term outlook that fails to take into account the ongoing value of the land which Indians ceded to Canadians.
2. Edgar Dosman, *Indians: The Urban Dilemma* (Toronto: McClelland and Stewart, 1972), p. 57.
3. See the National Film Board's film *Moses Coady* for an excellent portrayal of the Antigonish Movement.
4. Bureau of Social Affairs, *Social Progress through Community Development* (United Nations, 1955), cited in Jim Lotz, "Introduction: Is Community Development Necessary?" *Anthropologica*, IX, 2, Special issue on Community Development in Canada (1967), pp. 3-14. This issue was a helpful resource for my discussion of community development. From the same issue I have also drawn on Jean Legassé's "A Review of Community Development Experience in the World, 1945-67" (pp. 15-28). Other sources used were: Ian Shirley (ed.), *Development Tracks: The Theory and Practice of Community Development* (Palmerston North, New Zealand: Dunmore Press, 1982); James A. Draper (ed.), *Citizen Participation: Canada* (Toronto: New Press, 1971); T.R. Batten, *Communities and Their Development*, Sixth Edition (London: Oxford University Press, 1967).
5. John McCreary and Ian Shirley, "In the Rural Tradition: Anthropologists Come to Town," in Shirley (ed.), *Development Tracks*, pp. 28-49.
6. See Jean H. Lagassé, "The First Years of community development in Manitoba," in Draper (ed.), *Citizen Participation*, pp. 226-46.
7. Thus, the Kahnawake approach described in the next chapter is not necessarily well suited to all Indian communities in Canada.

8. For an incisive critique of community development, see Jim Lotz, "Does Community Development Exist?" in Draper (ed.), *Citizen Participation*, pp. 118-36.

9. Quoted in Freeman H. Compton, "Community Development Theory and Practice," *ibid.*, p. 383.

10. *Ibid.*

11. The discussion that follows is based on Chris Wilkes, "Development as Practice: The Instrument of Reason," in Shirley (ed.), *Development Tracks*, pp. 117-34.

12. See David Thorns, "In The Urban Tradition: Communion, Conflict, and Revolution," *ibid.*, pp. 50-68.

13. J. Rick Ponting and Roger Gibbins, *Out Of Irrelevance* (Scarborough, Ont.: Butterworths, 1980), p. 121. By the mid-1980s it had dropped further to a point where it once again accounted for only about 4 per cent of the budget of the Indian and Inuit Affairs Program. See Canada, *1986-87 Estimates – Indian and Northern Affairs Canada: Part III, Expenditure Plan* (Ottawa: Supply and Services Canada, 1986), pp. 2-10, 2-54.

14. Paul Driben and Robert S. Trudeau, *When Freedom Is Lost: The Dark Side of the Relationship between Government and the Fort Good Hope Band* (Toronto: University of Toronto Press, 1983), especially Chapter 5, "Why Band Businesses Failed." For some case studies of corporations' employment programs for urban native people, see Gail Grant, *The Concrete Reserve* (Montreal: Institute for Research on Public Policy, 1983).

15. Driben and Trudeau, *When Freedom Is Lost*, p. 70.

16. See Kenneth Barnes and Everett Banning, *Money Makers! The Secrets of Canada's Most Successful Entrepreneurs* (Toronto: McClelland and Stewart, 1985), p. 18.

Chapter Five

Institution-Building in an Indian Community: A Case Study of Kahnawake (Caughnawaga)

by J. Rick Ponting

The Mohawk Indian community of Kahnawake (pronounced Gon-uh-wog-uh and formerly written as Caughnawaga) is situated at the foot of the Mercier Bridge on the south shore of the St. Lawrence River, across from the suburbs at the west end of the Montreal metropolitan area.[1] The community includes about 5,400 Mohawks, about 90 per cent of whom at any given time reside on the reserve/territory[2] of 13,283 acres (5,900 hectares or about twenty-three square miles). It has by far the largest population of any Indian community in Quebec and is one of the largest in Canada. It also is reputed to possess one of the most developed or diverse institutional structures of any Indian community in Canada, which is the reason for its selection for the present study.

This chapter will explore the Kahnawake community as an example of a large-scale success story in community development. We shall examine how the building up of the institutions of Kahnawake relates to some of the central features of the community development phenomenon as described in the academic literature. In light of how far this institution-building has progressed at Kahnawake, it is appropriate that we consider also the extent and ramifications of what sociologists call "institutional completeness." This will involve providing an inventory and brief description of most of the institutions of the community. Two institutions – the economy and justice – will be selected for a more detailed examination. The chapter is presented with the intention of describing an Indian community,[3] dispelling certain stereotypes about Indians, and providing a glimpse of some possibilities for decolonization.

Methodology, History, and Social Setting

The present research has no pretensions to being the definitive anthropological account of Kahnawake; its purposes, as outlined above, are

151

much more limited. The description compiled here is based on eleven interviews involving thirteen persons from various sectors of the community. The interviews, held in November, 1985, ranged from forty minutes to three hours and twenty minutes and averaged over one and three-quarters hours. Interviewees were selected for the researcher by an elected chief (band councillor) in response to the researcher's requests to explore certain realms of activity. The elected council and community at large clearly had a vested interest in emphasizing certain aspects of the community and shielding me from other aspects. The researcher was "checked out" through informal Indian channels ("the moccasin telegraph") before his arrival and during the first day was accompanied in each interview by a liaison official, the aforementioned elected chief whose portfolio on Council is external affairs. After the first day, interviews were conducted with only the researcher and interviewee present. Documents were used to supplement interviews. The research was launched with an oral agreement that the first draft of this chapter would be submitted to the chief, who would be free to seek reactions from other members of the community. The agreement called for him to provide feedback (e.g., correct factual errors, suggest alternative interpretations where warranted) that the author could accept or not. However, for the protection of each party's interests, both the chief and the researcher held the right to veto the publication of the final draft.

Traditional Mohawk government at the community level is based on the matrilineal family unit and attends to the social, spiritual, and political needs of the community. There are three clans – Bear, Wolf, and Turtle – each of which is led by several clan mothers who have the responsibility of appointing a male to enact the directives and convey the needs of that family unit to the chiefs. Each clan has three chiefs and each chief is accountable to his clan mother who, in concert with the other clan mothers, can de-horn (impeach) an errant chief. This, however, is rare. Much emphasis is placed on reaching a consensus in debate and on collective consultation with the community members at public meetings, which are akin to a referendum. The community-level government is linked to a more encompassing level of government, that of the Mohawk Nation, which in turn is linked to the still more encompassing government of the Iroquois Six Nations Confederacy.[4] The Confederacy is governed according to the Great Law, which is a lengthy and sophisticated unwritten constitution recited every few years in a ceremony extending over a few days. The traditional ways are experiencing a revival at Kahnawake, but this revival is still in its early stages.

In 1716 the settlement of Kahnawake moved to the location it has now occupied for over 270 years. There the Kahnawakeronon (people of Kahnawake) were exposed to the missionary efforts of the Jesuits. This proselytization was to be of major and long-lasting importance. The Mohawks embraced the Jesuits' Roman Catholicism, which was first presented as merely a ceremony of songs (the Mohawk translation of "to go to church" literally means "to go and bring our song") and only later was embellished with rules, regulations, the introduction of the concept of sin, and schooling. The traditional government and traditional spiritualism were forced underground and their adherents were denigrated by the Catholic converts. In the community this profound cleavage, which has been accompanied by Catholic-Protestant divisions, has been partially bridged, but only partially and only since the mid-1970s. Although some bridging is occurring, there is also a cultural revival in the community, as some of the Christian and non-Indian ways of thinking and of doing things are being rolled back and the youth are being taught traditional Mohawk ways.

With the construction of the Victoria Bridge to Montreal in the mid-nineteenth century a pivotal event in the economic life of the community occurred. Men of the community were engaged in bringing sand through the rapids to the bridge site for the construction of the cement pillars. Their enthusiasm for going onto the steel girders to watch the workers, and their agility there, led to the hiring of some. This gave them an inroad in this demanding and well-paid occupation when the steel age and periodic construction booms occurred in North America. High steel work is to this day a common occupation in the community, and the men follow the jobs throughout North America.[5] The community thus has a brighter employment and income picture than most Indian communities in Canada, but it is also quite vulnerable to fluctuations in the larger world economic system.

Presently about 150 persons are employed full-time directly by the Council, another fifty by the hospital, over fifty in education, and twenty-five in social services. Council expenditures amount to approximately $10 million annually, with about 85 per cent of the revenue coming from DIAND. Over half of the men work in high steel, according to one estimate, and those women employed outside the home tend to work either in the community as teachers or nurses or in Montreal in clerical and stenographic jobs.

The main social problems appear to be a housing shortage and drug and alcohol abuse, all three of which are being combatted with locally devised programs. Child abuse and neglect are at low levels and only two or three children per year are taken into the protective custody of child welfare officials. Unemployment rates are much lower than on many reserves. As of November, 1985, ninety-eight families (involving 309 persons) and 266 individuals were "on welfare" (receiving Canada Assistance Plan payments) for economic reasons. The total number of families and individuals on welfare that month was 455, which encompassed 737 individuals (recipients plus their dependents) or less than 14 per cent of the Kahnawake Mohawk population.[6] The last two suicides were in 1982 and 1967; accidental deaths have been reduced to low levels; and no deaths by fire have been recorded since prior to 1970.

The community has a complex structure of locally staffed and locally controlled institutions, but these are heavily dependent on outside funding. There are several lines of cleavage in the community, although many individuals are able to relate well to people on the other side of a cleavage and the community is quite capable of taking concerted action. One important cleavage is between the Mohawks and the approximately 600 nonIndian leaseholders occupying much-needed housing on the reserve, particularly in a beach area on the riverfront. While race relations today are not fractious on the reserve, the nonIndians are clearly unwelcome and their tenure seems precarious. Another cleavage is between the Christian majority (especially the Catholics) and the perhaps 10 per cent of the residents who are strict traditionalists and follow the Longhouse ways. The harsh feelings that sometimes characterize this division are illustrated in the remarks of one of the traditionalists, who during the interview almost contemptuously referred to a former elected Grand Chief as "the mayor." Another interviewee offered the observation that there is barely a tolerance between the Longhouse people and the council elected under the provisions of the Indian Act. However, he also pointed out both that this situation has improved in the 1980s and that on major decisions the elected council now consults with the traditionalist leaders and seeks ratification from a community meeting. The band manager and several of the elected chiefs (councillors) are now sensitized to the traditional values. However, among the traditionalists there are two "groups," one much larger than the other.[7] This cleavage seems to be based more on personalities and politics than on religious ideology. Despite the cleavages, the community is replete with voluntary organizations and volunteered labour, both of which attest to a considerable degree of social cohesion. Tragedies and external threats, such as those represented by Quebec's language legislation (Bill 101), by the killing of a young reserve man by Quebec provincial police, and by the collapse of a bridge that killed thirty-one of the community's high steel workers, bring the community together and evoke a response of collective solidarity.

Aspects of Community Development

In describing community development at Kahnawake, we must address the question of whether Kahnawake is in fact a community or is merely an aggregate of individuals and families. A community may be defined as a network of reciprocal interpersonal and inter-organizational relations, wherein the actors are individuals, families, and their organizations, and wherein there exists a shared sense of belonging to the group. Kahnawake is clearly a community. Its kinship, service, cultural, economic, and mutual aid networks are extensive and overlapping. Organizations created by the Kahnawakeronon are abundant and persisting, and the shared Kahnawake identity is conspicuous, commonly displayed, and instilled in the children in the schools. The defining features of community are variables that can wax and wane in intensity with changing social, economic, and political circumstances, but in the mid-1980s they are present to a high degree in Kahnawake.

Creation of a Collective Sense of Responsibility
In community development theory, community development can only succeed if the community members take on a shared sense of responsibility for identifying their problems and for finding and implementing the solutions to those problems. The dependency engendered in the people during the earlier colonial regime under the Department of Indian Affairs and its predecessors is an insidious social force that militates against community members taking on responsibilities themselves; under DIAND Indians very often come to expect others to do things for them rather than doing those things for themselves. For instance, the chief of a western Canadian band (who was interviewed in the course of research for Chapter Three) recounted how band members used to come to the band administration office expecting the administration to do minor household maintenance chores for them. Similarly, at the 1985 Canadian Indian/Native Studies Association Conference one Indian panelist contended that most of the people of his reserve do not want the challenges and responsibilities entailed in self-government, for they have reached an accommodation with the status quo and do not want to be bothered or to have that accom-

modation upset. In a later conversation with the author he suggested that the band council was not doing enough to delegate responsibilities (decentralize power) so that band members would acquire experience with discharging responsibilities and making the attendant decisions.

Vestiges of this problem of getting community members to take on responsibilities can be found at Kahnawake, according to an interviewee who is well placed to know. However, Kahnawake has already gone a considerable distance in overcoming this problem, for most institutions in the community have been formed at local initiative and are staffed by local residents. Often, volunteers play a prominent and demanding role (e.g., the Combined Schools Committee, which functions essentially like a school board, and the volunteer fire brigade), especially in the infancy of a project, such as the Survival School, the radio station, the project to convert the school curriculum into Mohawk, and even the peacekeeping force. Another example of taking on responsibilities involves extended families taking child-rearing responsibility for children removed from their parental home by child welfare authorities. Finally, community members have accepted financial responsibilities for various projects by purchasing raffle tickets ("At any given time we have raffles going on for various activities," said one band official.) and by authorizing a withdrawal from the band's trust account (e.g., the $250,000 withdrawal for the $1.5-million arena project now under construction). Thus, Kahnawake is characterized by a rather well-developed collective sense of responsibility, although that sense does not extend in the direction of establishing a business tax or an income tax for revenues earned on reserve; in the words of one politician, "Taxation of our people is a 'no-no.'"

Self-help and Active Participation of the Community
The foregoing discussion of the assumption of responsibilities attests to the community members' commitment to principles of self-help and to the active participation of the members of the community. Further evidence of the participatory orientation is to be found in the Council's practice of holding community meetings to discuss major issues. Community meetings have been used as a crucial feature of the decision-making process on such important issues as the membership code (which determines who has the right to vote in elections), the firing of the police force when they refuse to enforce a Council order to shut down the local quarries, the establishment of a Kahnawake high school, and others. Participation occurs as well on an informal level in

the monitoring of the behaviour of officials, such as the behaviour of the radically new peacekeeping organization.

Self-help, with accompanying local control, is a highly valued principle among the Kahnawake leadership. This can be seen in the fact that the community has taken over responsibility for various programs formerly controlled externally. Perhaps the best examples of this are the hospital and the peacekeeping program. The latter was formed after Kahnawake successively withdrew from programs controlled externally by RCMP, the Quebec provincial police, and the Amerindian Policing Services. Now, provincial police do not come on the Kahnawake territory without being requested or asking permission. Another example is to be found in the child welfare field. Although the Council does not exercise control in this realm, it has signed an agreement with the regional social services centre to deliver all the services the latter would normally deliver. This arrangement of delegated power "does not sit well politically" with the Council but does circumvent a provincial law that authorizes the provision of social services only by regional social services centres. Such an arrangement also permits the Kahnawake social services program to operate under its philosophy of borrowing some methods from nonIndian models while developing other methods to better suit local Mohawk needs. For instance, the director of social services reported that when encountering a traditionalist client it is standard procedure for social services staff to consult with elders and to ask them to intervene first and to provide ongoing support to the social services team thereafter.

The Mohawk heritage of mutual aid involves an extension of self-help outward from the community. Many manifestations of this can be found at Kahnawake, such as in the assistance rendered by the radio station to other Indian radio stations attempting to get established and in the Kahnawake station's "radio-thon," which raised over $6,000 in cash and a large volume of new and used clothes for needy Indians in South Dakota. [8]

Thus, the principles of self-help and community participation are well established at Kahnawake. When implemented in institutions that are also under the control of the Kahnawakeronon, the result is that the symbols produced by those institutions reflect the community back to the community in a meaningful way. For instance, the radio station includes a local history program and an open-line show on which much reminiscing occurs, and the reception area of the Survival School administration building is adorned with pictures of the sacred eagle rather than with the pictures of the Queen and Prince Philip often found in nonIndian public schools.

Locally Formulated Programs and Objectives

For community development activities to be sustained it is important that the objectives and programs be formulated locally rather than imposed from the outside. This means that the programs will be tailored to local conditions, personnel, and resources and also that the local residents will develop a sense of ownership of, and pride in, their projects. At Kahnawake this aspect of community development is much in evidence, although there are exceptions. Among these exceptions are some of the social services programs still operated under a DIAND policy manual, and two federally funded and controlled elementary schools. Yet, even within those two schools there are programs formulated by Kahnawakeronon. Particularly noteworthy here is the curriculum development project, in which a team of six persons is involved in developing curriculum materials for instruction of various courses in Mohawk.

The community-controlled Survival School (grades seven through eleven) is another outstanding example of local initiative in education. When it became apparent in September, 1978, that Quebec's Bill 101 would require that the Kahnawakeronon obtain special ministerial permission to continue to send their students to an English-language high school in a neighbouring community, the Kahnawakeronon balked and accelerated by five years their plans to build their own high school. The Kahnawake students were pulled from the off-reserve school, and with almost no funding a makeshift school was created using temporary facilities and accredited teachers who volunteered their time. Today the Mohawk-controlled Kahnawake Survival School is an impressive institution whose forty-member staff (including twenty-five Mohawk teachers) offers a full Mohawk-oriented program to approximately 200 students.

Finally, with regard to locally formulated programs and objectives, it is significant that one of the eleven elected chiefs was at pains to point out to this researcher that even though some of the programs in the community appear to be products of the Council and administration, often it has been the grassroots members of the community who have taken the initiative.

Focus on Underlying Power Relations

As noted in the introduction to this section, the practice of community development has evolved to the extent that it now tends to include an analysis of the underlying causes of social problems, including the distribution of power in a community or society. At Kahnawake this is present, although not in the form of a radical political move-

158

ment (like the former Company of Young Canadians) engaged in confrontational tactics for the sake of political consciousness-raising. Rather, the critique of the present power structure takes the form of the anti-colonial ideology prevalent among the Indian leadership here and throughout much of Canada since at least the early 1970s. It seems also to be tinged with a mild populist critique of capitalism.[9] The anti-colonial political ideology appears to be a widely shared understanding that forms the basis of the daily work of many people in the community; Kahnawakeronon are beyond the stage of needing to verbalize this ideology repeatedly, except when legitimating proposals for new programs, and instead are quietly involved in their daily work in trying to change those power relations or to make successful the community empowerment that has already occurred. This work and the ability to present *choices* to the Kahnawakeronon are a large part of what self-determination is all about at Kahnawake.

Under a federally funded program the Kahnawake social services department employs two community health representatives (CHRs) trained in community development, proposal writing, and other more explicitly health-related areas such as suicide prevention and first aid. In a departure from the role played by CHRs in most Indian communities, the CHRs at Kahnawake have been involved in such community development areas as improving sanitary conditions and combatting other environmental threats (e.g., toxic chemicals dumpsites) to community health. However, community development efforts launched by the social services department generally do not take a confrontational approach. As one interviewee expressed it, in its community development efforts the social services department:

> has not taken the textbook approach of motivating the people to rise up. Rather, the approach has been to sensitize as much of the community as possible and to influence community leaders without them knowing it. The community would not accept a high profile "fire and brimstone" confrontational approach. Rather, the social services people get elected leaders to adopt social services' priorities as their own.

Institutional Completeness

"Institutional completeness" is a sociological concept referring to the extent to which a racial or ethnic or national group has created the organizations and other institutions that enable members of that group to meet their daily needs without having to turn to others outside the group.[10] Among the institutions involved are religion, the polity, mass media, recreation, commerce and services, health, welfare, education, and others.[11] A high degree of institutional completeness both increases the social cohesion of a group and serves what social scientists would call "boundary-maintenance" functions. That is, it serves to set the group and its members apart from the larger society; it reinforces the group's own culture and the members of the group become less reliant or dependent on the larger society and therefore less integrated into it. The degree of institutional completeness of Indian communities is thus an extremely important feature of those communities.

A high degree of institutional completeness requires a sufficiently large population base not only to sustain the institutions once created, but also to yield the "social entrepreneurs" (and commercial entrepreneurs) who have the aptitudes and inclination to build those institutions in the first instance. Although many Indian communities lack that so-called "critical mass" of population, the same cannot be said of Kahnawake. Kahnawake has developed a large number of community-based institutions to serve the Kahnawakeronon. In Table 10 they are listed and briefly described.

From the table it can be seen that Kahnawake is by no means characterized by the state of social disorganization that, in the stereotyped views of some nonIndians, is believed to prevail on Indian reserves. Instead, a dense network of interdependent organizations meets a large proportion of the daily needs of the Kahnawakeronon and contributes a sociological vitality to the community. These institutions reinforce community members' identity as Mohawks and as Kahnawakeronon and also serve other purposes. For instance, they offer convenience, employment, a source of pride and challenge, service attuned to the special needs of Indians, and a channel for the recirculation of money within the community. Furthermore, many of them provide experience at self-government, proof of Indians' ability to manage their own affairs, and/or a launching pad for mounting challenges to the legal status quo through unilaterally exercising sovereignty in fields where it has not been "granted" or delegated by nonIndian governments.

Description of Selected Institutions: Justice and the Economy

Numerous cases of institution-building command the respect of an outside observer and as such call for attention in a forum such as this. The enthusiasm of the young staff of the radio station, the determined dedication of the curriculum development team, the vision of the plan-

Table 10

Community-based Institutions of Kahnawake

Karonhianonha School
nursery to Grade 3; half-time immersion at lower levels; Mohawk language and culture offered as subjects studied; federally controlled

Kateri Tekakwitha School
multi-denominational; grades 3-6; English as language of instruction, but Mohawk and French are offered as courses; federally controlled

Early Childhood Learning Centre
a social services program in special education for handicapped and learning-disabled children

Kahnawake Survival School
nineteen buildings spread over 174 acres; grades 7-11; community controlled, full academic program, but emphasis on Mohawk culture in curriculum and elders are used as resource persons

Indian Way School
offers instruction in academic subjects and in the traditional ways of the Longhouse people and is entirely under their control

Combined Schools Committee
the elected educational authority exercising responsibilities of a school board

Curriculum Development Project
translates and otherwise converts school curriculum into Mohawk

Housing
council has responded to severe housing shortage by constructing an eighteen-unit multi-family housing project (expandable to forty families)

Alcohol and Drug Abuse Program
newsletter; regional film library and resource centre; produced two videotapes (on the topics of fetal alcohol syndrome and family violence); sponsoring of dry social events; presently developing a new treatment centre; created role-models program for Indian youths

Child Welfare
Kahnawake social services department provides foster care, home care, institutional care, and counselling and family therapy; staff of social workers is almost entirely from Kahnawake

Awards
Alwyn Morris (1984 Olympic gold and bronze medalist from Kahnawake) Award of Achievement in sports or the arts, community involvement, and education

Volunteer Fire Brigade
forty volunteer firefighters with vehicles and equipment

Conservation Officers
eighteen volunteers who patrol the territory enforcing Kahnawake's laws concerning fishing without a licence, small game poaching, woodcutting, and polluting

Community-based Institutions of Kahnawake

Cultural Centre
intended to facilitate awareness of Kahnawake's history and culture within and outside the community

Kahnawake Historical Society
a group of individuals committed to preserving the history and culture of Kahnawake

Public Library
contains over 1,000 books, including a comprehensive collection on North American Indians

Radio Station CKRK-FM
about 30 per cent of broadcast time is in the Mohawk language

Recreation Program
facilities include youth centre, teen drop-in centre, and various sports venues; programs include clubs and leagues in various sports

Religious Organizations
Roman Catholic, United, Pentecostal, Jehovah's Witness, Bahai, and Longhouse

Social Clubs/Service Organizations
Knights of Columbus, Moose Lodge, Royal Canadian Legion, Golden Agers' Club, Marina, Handicapped Self-Help Club

Kateri Memorial Hospital and Out-Patient Clinic
accredited hospital under Mohawk direction; most employees are Mohawks

Court
jurisdiction has so far been limited to minor offences

Peacekeeping
nineteen paid members of peacekeeping force; community-controlled; enforce Criminal Code of Canada and Kahnawake laws on Indians and nonIndians in/on the territory

Local Government
twelve-member Mohawk Council elected under the Indian Act is the legislative arm of local government; heavy use of community meetings for ratification

Mohawk Self Insurance
a form of workers' compensation scheme in which persons employed on the territory participate in lieu of the provincial scheme

Commercial Enterprises
numerous small businesses such as barbershop, building contractors, funeral parlors, gas stations, taxi firms, restaurants, laundromats; also, three companies working off-reserve, two steel-fabricating companies, four golf courses, warehouse shelving manufacturing plant, and others

Chamber of Commerce
a recently formed organization of local businesses

ners of the Survival School, the originality of the social services staff – these and other examples of the social lifeblood of the community lie at the root of institutional success stories that merit a book of their own. However, the social scientist should not (or not primarily) choose his/her examples for their public relations value but for their pedagogical value or their value in stimulating research. Accordingly, the present account will focus on two other institutions: one has repeatedly failed to live up to hopes and expectations; the other is presently enjoying success (although of a somewhat precarious nature). We turn first to the economy.

Economic Development
According to a Council document, [12] over 90 per cent of the estimated $25-30 million in personal income that flows through Kahnawake immediately leaves the community in the form of goods and services purchased. This occurs despite the fact that, as of December, 1984, there were reportedly 109 businesses in the community. The Council has pursued various economic development opportunities, but the record is at best a checkered one. It ranges from the abject failures of a trap factory and a $75,000 "Celebration Centre" (a tourism development also known as "Fort Courage") in the 1960s to an ambitious joint-venture golf and country club that by the mid-1980s was showing signs of flourishing.

Recent economic development efforts include the tourism project (1967), a 1979 housing construction firm owned by the Council under the name Kahnawake Building Systems, a 1981 proposed dairy farm and milk processing plant, the aforementioned golf and country club, and a 1984 enterprise to build foundations for houses. A brief description of some of these follows.

Kahnawake Building Systems (KBS) was launched under an $85,000 federal Local Employment Activity Project (LEAP) grant that enabled the band to hire three band members to do an extensive market study. Unfortunately, the persons employed lacked the requisite skills to conduct a definitive market analysis. The study concluded that a market, mainly other Indian reserves in Quebec, did exist (at least at that time) for the homes KBS would manufacture, and a further $250,000 was obtained from LEAP for operational costs over the next three years. A $70,000 grant from DIAND was negotiated to erect two prototype homes, for at that point the band still did not have a product to market. The prototypes, said to be of high quality, were completed in April, 1982, but not until August, 1983, was the first contract signed with an outside buyer. The firm possessed proven expertise in construction but was weak in sales and management skills. Consequently, the firm was largely unsuccessful in penetrating the market on other reserves. Other reasons for the failure of the firm can also be identified. Specifically, the fact that the firm was not incorporated created potential legal problems (e.g., if a house were faulty, whom could the buyer sue?) that undermined sales efforts. Second, the firm's factory was located on land leased from the band and the Council charged an extremely high rent in order to recover the money on the project "up front." Adherents to the belief in the importance of incentives have also contended that the lack of incentives generated a lackadaisical attitude that pervaded the whole project. Said one interviewee: "It was a government program with guaranteed funding and the employees felt, 'Hey, we don't have to work too hard.' " The bottom line was that houses that should have cost perhaps $40,000 were costing closer to $60,000, and the project was folded at a loss of $164,000 to the Mohawks.

The dairy farm and milk processing plant of the early 1980s was never implemented due to the inability to procure adequate financing. Much preparatory work on the $1.5-million project was done with the assistance of the director of economic development, who himself holds a Master of Business Administration degree. Land sites were procured both for the farm and for the growing of forage crops for the dairy herd. Commitments for financing totalling $300,000 were procured from the Council and from outside sources. Commitments from retailers were also obtained to look after the distribution of the products. Extensive work was done in keeping the Kahnawakeronon informed as the project evolved, for this was to be a band enterprise with important social benefits. The political lobbying so essential for such an ambitious project was done successfully to the point where there was strong and extensive support for the project both on Council and at the community level. However, the project was never implemented; it simply required too much start-up capital.

The new Mohawk Hills Golf and Country Club was also endorsed by the community and the Council contributed $53,000 in a joint venture on this project with a Mohawk entrepreneur. DIAND also contributed funds (approximately $125,000) in the form of a fifteen-year loan from the Economic Development Loan Fund. Unlike most of the aforementioned projects, marketing is not a problem because public relations and marketing skills are the forte of the particular Mohawk entrepreneur involved. The project, though, has had to navigate through other troubled waters. For instance, the Council found that in practice it had far less control than it had on paper; the entrepreneur, who lacked stong management skills, made most decisions on his own and failed to make payments during the first few years. DIAND at one time wanted to foreclose on its loan, although now that the project is experiencing some financial success DIAND seems content to keep the project alive in the hope of being able to retrieve at least the principal on its loan. At the time of writing the Council had not decided whether to take the risk of exercising its option to convert its loan to the entrepreneur into shares that would give the Council almost one-third ownership of the project.

The Kahnawake radio station provides a good example of the marriage of community development and employment creation. Although making a profit is not part of the station's mandate, it does generate a substantial cash flow (about $200,000 annually) through its advertising revenues. This enables it to employ seven full-time staff members and fifteen part-time staff. The station's country-and-western programming in the evenings generates the revenue to sustain Mohawk-oriented programming in the daytime hours. [13] That daytime programming fosters a Mohawk identity and helps to preserve the Mohawk heritage. The numerous Kahnawake community service announcements the station broadcasts also help to sustain various institutions in the community.

The community's less than enviable overall record of economic development has led to some re-examination of the fundamental parameters of economic development and to a taking stock of lessons that can be learned from these experiences. One, among several, of the lessons learned is the need to exert very close control over any external consultants who might be used. This is consistent with the fundamental principles espoused in the academic literature on community development. Related to this is an acute sense of caution vis-à-vis DIAND and other governmental advisers, for they are accountable to their minister rather than to the Kahnawakeronon. In the (paraphrased) words of the Kahnawake economic development director, when asked to comment on the role of DIAND in Kahnawake's economic development:

> They've been more concerned with their loan/loss ratio than with economic development on reserves. DIAND's Indian Economic Development Loan Fund disbursed a lot of money in the early 1970s, with many losses, because the DIAND staff was not professionally qualified and know little about reserve life. They encouraged Indian projects to take more money than they should; for instance, they'd take a $15,000 project and make it into a $100,000 project. Now, in response to all the losses they've

suffered from those bad loans, they're being too selective and a lot of projects that are above average are being refused. In each era they're responding to the political pressures and priorities of the time, not to Indians' needs. Nevertheless, I'm working very closely with DIAND now; they're our major recourse for money, since Indian land cannot be used as collateral. I've taken over the role of the DIAND district business officer (for instance, formulating business plans), although at first they said "You can't do that." . . .

We have to write almost a thesis to secure funding. Also, I sometimes have to deal with DIAND people who don't know what an industry is all about – they're just not competent. In negotiations last month on a particular project, *forty-five* minutes into the conversation the DIAND person said "What type of an enterprise are we talking about here?"

Changes in strategy are another product of the re-examination of economic development at Kahnawake. The Council's concern about businessmen obtaining too much control or power appears to be fading. For instance, after a year of discussion, meetings, and resistance, Council eventually acceded to the request of the newly formed Chamber of Commerce and passed a Band Council Resolution supporting the principle of individual enterprise. Council is now more favourably disposed to arguments that entrepreneurship, with its incentive element, offers advantages that collective enterprise (band-owned) does not. For instance, when KBS failed, Council decided to leave house-building to individual contractors. Similarly, one interviewee predicted that the coming years will see some privatization of some of the tasks now performed by the Kahnawake Public Works Department.

In the community there is an emerging conviction of the need to gain greater economic self-determination before undertaking any ambitious new economic development projects. There is also an increasing realization that economic development and self-government are, to a degree, interdependent. The approach favoured in an analysis done by the Council's economic development program staff is the creation of a "people's bank," which would be essentially a *caisse populaire*. The need for such a banking institution is reflected in the fact that in 1984 $7 million in cheques were cashed on the territory. Now that the Catholic Church has stopped cashing cheques, people go outside the community to cash their cheques. It is felt that a *caisse populaire* in Kahnawake itself would make people more likely to bank their money and less likely to spend it. The *caisse populaire*, which has been approved by the Council, would be affiliated with the *Caisse Populaires*

Desjardins but under the immediate direction of a board of directors from Kahnawake. Current thinking also calls for including in its structure a position to be called the Indian Trustee. The Indian Trustee would be an Indian who would hold in trust collateral seized from the borrowers who fail to make payments on their loans. This is an attempt to address the problem of banks being reluctant or unwilling to loan to Indian individuals, firms, and bands due to provisions of the Indian Act (Section 89.1) that prohibit the seizure of Indian land and buildings. Overall, apart from its retail service function, the *caisse populaire* should make an important contribution to the community by making more money available for commercial loans and by shortening considerably the time required for getting approval of loan applications.

Formal legal incorporation of a firm is another tool of economic development offering certain advantages (e.g., limited liability, easier access to bank loans through eliminating the need for the Minister of Indian Affairs to co-sign loans), but incorporation is a highly controversial issue among the Kahnawakeronon, in part because corporations are subject to taxation of their corporate income. More importantly, though, a corporation could fall outside the control of Council. Furthermore, to opt for incorporation is to make a symbolically significant concession for it negates the special status to which Indians have a moral and constitutional right[14] and it can be seen as a step toward assimilation.[15] Yet a belief in the need to be adaptable (while maintaining a Mohawk identity) appears to be a widely shared feature of the Kahnawakeronon world view and an argument in favour of incorporation can be made in terms of adaptability. Thus, the issue will not be an easy one to resolve. It has the potential to leave a residue of ill will.

Kahnawake is situated on land of prime industrial and commercial value. It stands in the middle of a large concentration of population and in close proximity to the busy Dorval airport, which in turn has excellent connections throughout North America. The community has the St. Lawrence Seaway literally on its doorstep and excellent rail and highway connections. It is also within a thirty-minute drive of the heart of Montreal. In light of these features it has one of the most outstanding potentials for economic development of any Indian community in Canada. Yet, something has held it back, has kept it from realizing that potential. That ''something'' is a complex constellation of personnel, social structural, legal, political, bureaucratic, and sociocultural factors.

According to the director of economic development at Kahnawake, one of the most important factors pertains to personnel. The scarcity of indigenous professional expertise in such areas as marketing, accounting, and management has not only been a major problem in the various economic development ventures at Kahnawake, as described earlier, but has also been a major problem in most Indian communities across Canada. Joint ventures with outsiders would provide one way of dealing with this problem, but the Council and the community are very wary (a socio-cultural factor) of joint ventures with outsiders because of past unpleasant experiences.

An important social structural constraint is the fact that only about 15 per cent of the territory (reserve) is collectively owned, while the remaining 85 per cent is held in private hands by individuals (mainly Mohawks) under certificates of possession. Thus, a particular ideal site for a business may not be available because it is in private hands. This takes us into the legal realm, where a more important obstacle to economic development has been the inability to use land and buildings as collateral due to the aforementioned Section 89.1 of the Indian Act. Whereas off-reserve firms usually need only place 20 per cent down as their own equity in a firm (they may borrow the remaining 80 per cent), on-reserve ventures often would need to have much more than 20 per cent equity to pay for expensive buildings because their buildings cannot be used as collateral for a loan. This leaves less money for equipment and working capital and thereby changes the priorities of the firm from what they would otherwise be.

Political and bureaucratic factors are enormously important in economic development. Reference has already been made to the shifting priorities of DIAND,[16] and to that we can add the fact that in dealing with governments the Kahnawakeronon have had to deal with a multitude of programs, each with its own priorities. These programs and departments have exhibited little, if any, co-ordination and sometimes are in direct competition with each other. At the community level, where elections are held every two years, the turnover in the membership of the Council and the reluctance of the Council to make decisions immediately prior to an election and in the three or four months after an election militate against the establishment of a local economic climate conducive to economic development.[17] Furthermore, the priorities of the Council and its constituents have been more social than economic; faced with a shortage of funds, the Council has been more inclined to give housing loans than business loans, because the development of that community infrastructure is seen as more important (and perhaps less risky) than economic development.

Finally, socio-cultural obstacles must be overcome for economic development ventures to succeed. Reference was made earlier in the chapter to the DIAND-induced dependency mentality that makes some Indians shy away from taking on responsibilities in the hope that others will do the work for them. This same orientation is sometimes brought to economic development by would-be entrepreneurs who expect the economic development staff to do the research and project design work for them; the staff decline to do so and the project sometimes proceeds no further because of these incompatible expectations. Another socio-cultural obstacle is the community's egalitarian ideology, which leads to the censure of those who, it is perceived, seek to stand ''above'' the others in the community. Said one interviewee about the resentment and hostility sometimes directed at the entrepreneur or the manager of a successful Indian firm:

> It's improving now, but even today some people will say ''I'm not going to support him. I'm going outside.'' . . . People tolerate local business more now, but the resentment is still there. In the past we were a communal people, living in communal homes, farming communally. . . . For some reason, people think that getting into this [economic development] is not conducive to our culture, that it's the white man's ways. . . . [Others] don't feel secure at first in procuring a service from our own people. They don't trust our own people to be good enough or professional enough, although after a while they feel more comfortable in going to them.

Like the dependency mentioned above, this denigration of the in-group is an indication of a colonial mentality. The same orientation leads Canadians to spurn Canadian artistic performances until they are acclaimed in New York or Los Angeles. It does not die easily, for it is ingrained in the value system of a culture. Thus, indigenous economic development at Kahnawake is vulnerable to attack from both the traditionalists and the assimilated.

Notwithstanding these obstacles, the prospects for the future economic development of Kahnawake are actually fairly bright. Barring a return to economic recession by the larger Canadian economy, and looking ahead to the mid-1990s, it is reasonable to project that the *caisse populaire* will be firmly established and actively involved in making business loans to entrepreneurs seeking to fill the present void in service organizations in Kahnawake. Joint ventures with Kahnawakeronon and/or with outsiders will probably be more common, especially in manufacturing and tourism, and a small industrial park could be established. By these measures the Kahnawakeronon will probably have made some significant strides toward their economic development goal of having control and effective management of the local factors of economic production so as to increase the economic self-sufficiency of the community. That in turn will provide the revenue base to permit the creation or reinvigoration of various other non-economic institutions within the community.

Justice
Economic development proceeds with caution and lags behind many other fields of development at Kahnawake, but in the area of justice the community has taken some bold (although not uncontested) initiatives that place justice at or near the vanguard of Kahnawake's developmental drive. The community's justice program is breaking new ground that de facto is extending the scope of Indian sovereignty in Canada.

The justice program has undergone massive changes since the RCMP was asked by the Council in 1969 to provide policing on the reserve. When the RCMP began its gradual withdrawal from Quebec in the mid-1970s, the provincial government provided much the same services through its Special Constables Program. However, these native Indian constables laboured under a 60-40 per cent federal-provincial cost-sharing regime that left the Mohawk Council with little control. Even its successor program, the province-wide Amerindian Policing Services (APS), provided little local control,[18] and by the end of the 1970s the Kahnawakeronon had decided to break away from APS and go their own way. This generated an extremely adverse reaction on the part of DIAND executives who, in a classic case of socio-fiscal control, cut off funding. Similarly, the provincial government accused the Kahnawakeronon of operating illegally as a militant, radical group. All of the local police staff from APS were fired by Council and replaced by forty self-selected volunteers who, in the words of one interviewee, "played at being police." This person went on to describe the situation as "complete chaos," a view that some other interviewees did not share.

In 1981 the composition of the twelve-person Council changed significantly with the election of five new members who, in the opinion of some, were less reluctant than their predecessors to make decisions that might "ruffle feathers." A major restructuring of the justice field was undertaken to deal with problems of poor management, lack of training, and lack of guiding philosophy. The demotion and dismissal of various officers engendered much community dissension, including an unsuccessful move to impeach three of the five new Council members. The community's fear of quick changes dictated that thereafter even minor changes would have to be made slowly. In 1985, however, the Justice Committee of five elected chiefs (band councillors), whose mandate is to co-ordinate and oversee the entire justice system at Kahnawake, was restructured in a way that reduced the representation of the elected politicians to a minority and even brought onto the committee a representative from the Kahnawake social services department.

The system is funded by a $400,000 grant from the federal government and by revenues from fines levied by the local court. The system includes nineteen paid members of the peacekeeping force, eighteen volunteer conservation officers, a forty-man volunteer fire and ambulance brigade, three justices of the peace, and a prosecuting attorney. All except the latter are Natives.

Working relationships with other police departments are described as excellent at the lower levels but strained at the political level. To paraphrase one interviewee:

> By making other Indian bands aware of our approach we have become a thorn in the side of governments. I have various legal opinions from the province saying our peacekeepers are illegal and cannot carry their firearms. But these are only opinions. I can get other opinions saying the opposite and I tell the province not to bother me with opinions, that if they don't like what we're doing they should have appealed the Fortier decision. That was a 1982 test case involving two young fellows drinking and driving and Justice Guy Fortier ruled that our peacekeepers are peace officers under the Criminal Code and have the authority to do what they're doing.

On a day-to-day operational basis relations with other police departments range from the formal (e.g., setting up a road block at the request of another police department) to the informal ("Sometimes external police forces will call us and say 'Come and get this guy off our backs before we charge him.' "). The Kahnawake peacekeepers do not enforce provincial laws, except the provincial highway code, which has been adopted as a band by-law. They patrol the provincial highways passing through the territory.

The peacekeeping force and conservation officers bring into bold relief the issue of Indian sovereignty and jurisdiction. Presently a major limitation to the Kahnawake justice system is that its courts hear only cases involving minor offences such as offences under the Indian Act, common assault, vagrancy, breaking and entering, cruelty to animals, and infractions of Kahnawake by-laws (including the provincial traffic act). Lobby efforts to get the federal government to increase the

171

Kahnawake court's jurisdiction have been unsuccessful, in part because such a change would necessitate that the government pass a separate statute. Having exhausted the conventional avenues in seeking to extend the Kahnawake court's jurisdiction, the Kahnawakeronon will make incremental changes to extend that jurisdiction unilaterally. These are, in effect, legal challenges to external governments. Through cumulative case-law precedents they could bring a redefinition of this important dimension of Indian sovereignty, especially if the provincial government continues not to take up the challenge through appeals to higher courts.

The Kahnawake peacekeeping system as it currently stands already raises important issues of sovereignty and constitutional rights. For instance, if a nonIndian living outside the territory refuses to appear for a court date at Kahnawake, the Kahnawake peacekeepers will go out and make an arrest outside the territory. Sometimes the accused will offer resistance to arrest, but according to the director of justice at Kahnawake, there has never been an instance of a nonIndian police force not backing the Kahnawake peacekeepers in such a situation. Furthermore, because of the fact that there is no jail at Kahnawake, accused persons who are convicted and sentenced to jail terms are handed over to authorities at provincial jails in Montreal. Those provincial authorities accept the transferees and incarcerate them. Thus, by their co-operation with the Kahnawake peacekeepers in depriving persons of their liberty, provincial authorities give their tacit approval to the Kahnawakeronon extending their sovereignty in these forms. [19]

In 1986 we can expect to see unilateral action by the Kahnawakeronon to extend their jurisdiction into the realm of impaired driving, seizure of vehicles, breach of payment, and other civil (noncriminal) matters, as part of a larger design of moving toward complete self-sufficiency in justice matters. If they are challenged in the courts and lose, they will still have recourse to negotiations. In any such negotiations the Kahnawakeronon ultimately would hold an important bargaining chip – namely, the ability to block nonIndian commuters' access to the Mercier Bridge. In the words of the Kahnawake director of justice: "If nonIndians don't like what we're doing, they can cease using the Mercier Bridge to get into Montreal and can drive twenty miles farther to take the Cartier Bridge." However, the situation would have to have deteriorated quite drastically before such a move would get majority approval on Council.

It is useful to note both the advantages that the present system offers in comparison with the earlier arrangements and the directions in which it is likely to evolve in the future. One of the main advantages is that the community can formulate policing policies that are independent of the provincial attorney-general and in so doing can ignore various aspects of provincial policy (such as filing formal reports on minor accidents or filing statistical reports with Statistics Canada). The Kahnawake authorities can also hire, fire, promote, and demote all personnel (including justices of the peace). There are also economic advantages to the present arrangements, such as the ability to patronize Kahnawake businesspersons when filling the gas tanks of the peacekeeping vehicles and the ability to retain in the community the revenues from court fines. Most importantly, though, the present system has the potential ability to serve justice better because of its sensitivities to local personalities, problems, traditions, and opportunities (e.g., the knowledge that the best way to deal with a particular offender is to remand him in the custody of his uncle rather than to incarcerate him). While some of these advantages have accompanying drawbacks, such as the system's vulnerability to political interference and to broad-based community pressures, it does enjoy majority support in the community, at least for the time being.

The future of the justice system at Kahnawake is unclear. On the one hand there likely will be a push for extending the frontiers of local sovereignty. In addition, in the words of the justice director:

> We're headed in the direction of our dreams, and if the community allows us to continue in five or ten years we'll achieve those dreams. . . . Specifically, we'll have native legal counsel for both defence and prosecution, we'll have total jurisdiction from dog bites to murder, we'll have a local jail, an expanded [numerically] and better paid peacekeeping force, better equipment, and the recognition and support of our concept by outside governments.

However, the present system is very controversial within the community. It is not above the feelings of jealousy, resentment, and envy that are so pronounced in small communities characterized by a high degree of institutional completeness and dense networks of interpersonal interaction. Accordingly, it is very fragile, and for its continuity and development it is heavily dependent on a small number of elected chiefs, especially its main advocate, the justice director. If he and his supporters on Council suffer electoral defeat, as he almost did in the 1984 election, the system could be totally revised.

Conclusion

A single chapter cannot fully convey the vibrancy and complexity of a community of over 5,000 persons. Nevertheless, the portrait of Kahnawake sketched here demonstrates the potential of some Indian communities and the constructive uses to which that potential can be put. The portrait also reveals some of the dynamics of contemporary community development. This chapter concludes with some reflections on community development as prompted by a consideration of the Kahnawake case.

The Kahnawake situation illustrates the importance of consciousness-raising events and of a capable Indian political leadership if community development is to proceed. Not only here, but also in some bands studied in Chapter Three, this researcher encountered situations where a change in the elected leadership of a band resulted in a major turnaround in the band's orientation and fortunes, at least in certain realms of activity. It would be grossly misleading and insensitive to argue that Indians have been primarily responsible for their own misfortune; however, it would also be misleading and naive to deny that in some cases the local Indian leaders have pursued their own interests ahead of the collective interest of their constituents. Some Indian bands are highly complacent and support chiefs and councillors who preserve the status quo and do not demand that band members take on more responsibilities. Such bands often benefit considerably from a jolt that shatters that complacency. In Kahnawake a combination of Quebec's Bill 101, the killing of a local Mohawk by the Quebec provincial police, and the election of five new chiefs (councillors) provided the jolts that shook the community to its foundations. The resultant stimulus to development was powerful and enduring. The fact that development did not always proceed smoothly (e.g., the controversy in Kahnawake over the justice reforms and over legal incorporation) is a rebuke to those who would idealize and romanticize the notion of ''community'' by making unwarranted assumptions about the ease of consensus-building or about the extent to which consensus prevails in a community.

Although from an outsider's viewpoint many Indian communities would be said to need the change that community development entails, a fear of change is often widespread in those communities. As Mackie implies in Chapter Eight below, and as has already been noted in the present chapter, this conservatism is often reinforced by petty jealousies, rivalries, and resentment. These are sometimes passed down across generations. Regardless of their origins, these sentiments often contribute to the pace of community development being painfully slow.

At various points in this book the topic of community size arises, often in conjunction with the ineconomies of scale inherent in serving a small population. In Chapters Sixteen and Eighteen it is argued that the consolidation of population (e.g., through political-administrative amalgamation) should be seriously considered by numerous Indian bands. The Kahnawake case study demonstrates the substantial collective achievements of which Indians are capable when the demographic base is sufficiently large. However, the Kahnawake case also illustrates the formidable obstacles standing in the way of the consolidation of some Indian populations. For instance, on various issues the Kahnawakeronon seek to develop a common Mohawk position with two other Mohawk bands (Kanestake and Akwasasne) of which the brothers, sisters, cousins, aunts, and uncles of Kahnawakeronon are members. However, the cleavages and jurisdictional barriers to be overcome are numerous. The location of the Akwasasne or St. Regis reserve (straddling the international border and the provincial border) would invoke the involvement of the governments of Canada, the United States, New York State, Quebec, and Ontario in certain undertakings that might be contemplated between the three Mohawk councils. Second, there are the divisions at Kahnawake between the two traditionalist groups, and between those Longhouse people and the mainly Roman Catholic non-traditionalists. Kanestake is predominantly Protestant (Anglican and Pentecostal). While the traditional ways and values are making a comeback at Kahnawake, at Kanestake the Longhouse followers are a tiny minority who are very much in disfavour. Under these circumstances it is remarkable that the three communities have had any success at all in presenting a united front on various issues.

Our examination of the Kahnawake experience reveals that economic development on-reserve is not a prerequisite to community development. At Kahnawake the expansion in the organizational density or institutional completeness of the community has occurred in the absence of major economic development successes. The entrepreneurial skills of community members have surfaced not so much in the collective commercial ventures of the band as in very small businesses and in grantsmanship, political lobbying, and construction of viable community organizations of a non-commercial nature. Added to these has been a pool of skills (of the high steel workers) that has provided well-paid off-reserve employment. Some of the income from that employment has been recycled within Kahnawake and some has been redistributed as, in essence, a voluntary tax (in raffles and radio-thons) in support of various community organizations and their projects. Thus, one difference between Kahnawake and many other Indian communities is that Kahnawake now has in place a (growing) cluster of Indian-controlled commercial and non-commercial organizations that can capture some of the income (wages, salaries, and transfer payments) of the community members, rather than having that income spent externally in ways that have no economic or social-multiplier effect within the Indian community.

The processual aspects of community development at Kahnawake are also noteworthy. Although leadership is a vital necessity for Indian development to occur at any level, it is risky for the Indian leadership to get too far ahead of its grassroots constituents. There comes a point where "far ahead" becomes "out of touch." For the most part, the Kahnawake leadership seems to have avoided this pitfall by various means. These include taking principled stands, exerting leadership by example, drawing on volunteer labour, and especially submitting major issues to decision or ratification of the community at community meetings. Furthermore, the delegation of responsibility (e.g., to the Justice Committee, the Combined Schools Committee, etc.) has broadened the leadership base and thus blurred somewhat the distinction between leaders and the rank and file. In these respects the Kahnawake experience exemplifies some of the main tenets of community development, such as the principle of active participation of the community and the creation of a collective sense of responsibility. This experience can be instructive to other bands.

Finally, the Kahnawakeronon have demonstrated to other bands that greater self-determination can be attained within the existing legal and constitutional order if a band is able to develop the institutional completeness of its community and then is prepared to pursue both aggressively and doggedly the expansion of the jurisdictional domain of those institutions. In the Kahnawake case that expansion has sometimes occurred through intergovernmental negotiation and agreement and sometimes through the unilateral assertion of sovereignty. In either case the developmental efforts have acquired a momentum based on an earned self-confidence and on the credibility that comes from demonstrated competence. For some bands afflicted with alienation, a few successes of this nature could be a powerful tonic. Such successes also provide a source of hope to those discouraged by the constitutional impasse of the mid-1980s. In addition, a high degree of institutional completeness, such as that enjoyed at Kahnawake, can both enhance social solidarity within a community and also serve to set boundaries on the interaction patterns of community members. (For instance, a high school student attending the Kahnawake Survival School is more likely to marry another Mohawk than is a Kahnawake resident attending a predominantly nonIndian school off the territory.) Those boundaries, and the institutions within them, help preserve the ethnic group as a sociologically and culturally distinct entity.

Kahnawake is not a typical Indian community, if indeed such an entity exists at all. Kahnawake is unusually large, unusually well located, has a large proportion of its labour force employed in a highly skilled occupation, and its leaders to a substantial and increasing degree are in touch with their Indian heritage. Although its successes at community development are relatively recent and have not been uniform, they have not been entirely dependent on the unusual resources just listed. Thus, although I am not suggesting that other bands should blindly adopt Kahnawake's pattern for development, the Kahnawake experience does offer development lessons and models for the consideration of other bands.

Notes

1. I wish to express my sincere appreciation to the people of Kahnawake for their time and kind co-operation, without which this chapter would not have been possible. I especially wish to thank Chief Billy Two Rivers for his generous assistance and gracious hospitality. Outside of Kahnawake, the contributions of Marjory Ponting, Michael Harrison, and colleague Dr. G.L. Symons were instrumental in bringing this research to fruition.

2. Officially, the Kahnawake ideology rejects the Indian Act vocabulary of "reserve" and "band." What the Indian Act calls a "reserve" the elected Mohawk leadership of Kahnawake calls a "territory." Instead of referring to their people as a "band," these leaders use the term "the Mohawk Nation of Kahnawake." The band council elected under the Indian Act is called "the Mohawk Council," and the word "Council" will be used in this chapter to refer to it. The chief councillor elected under the Indian Act will be termed "the Grand Chief," while the elected councillors are called "chiefs," in accordance with local practice at Kahnawake.

3. For an insider's description of life in Kahnawake, as viewed from the perspective of one family, see Johnny Beauvais, *Kahnawake: A Mohawk Look at Canada and Adventures of Big John Canadian, 1840-1919* (Kahnawake, Quebec, 1985). This book also contains numerous interesting photographs.

4. The other five nations are the Oneida, Onondaga, Cayuga, Seneca, and Tuscarora.

5. This pattern of migratory labour has been a contributing factor in the spread of the English language in the community.

6. Forty-three individuals and a further nine families involving twenty-one individuals received social assistance for health reasons in November, 1985, while thirty-nine unwed mothers and their forty-nine children also received social assistance (shown in official records as "social reasons").

7. The elected political leaders reject the term "factions" to describe these two "groups" of traditionalists. They point out that the smaller of the two traditionalist groups is not recognized by the traditional council of the larger Mohawk Nation and therefore dismiss it as a mere "splinter group."

8. Another radio-thon reportedly raised $35,000 in community donations for a new ambulance for Kahnawake.

9. A hint of the anti-capitalist strain is to be found in the remarks of one of the elected chiefs. In contrasting accountability in the traditional Mohawk political system with accountability in the larger Canadian political system, he commented on the influence the banks, multinational corporations, and holding companies have on nonIndian governments in Canada.

10. See Raymond Breton, "Institutional Completeness of Ethnic Communities and the Personal Relations of Immigrants," *American Journal of Sociology*, LXX, 2 (September, 1964), pp. 193-205.

11. The concept of "institutional completeness" differs from the concept of "total institution" (mentioned in Chapter One) in that a total institution is characterized by coercion, whereas in a situation of institutional completeness the community members have the option of using or not using the array of institutional services available to them. Also, the two situations normally differ in the locus of control over the institutions – that is, in whether control rests individually or collectively with members of the community served, or conversely, with some external authority.

12. Kahnawake Arena Committee, *Proposal: Kahnawake Arena* (Kahnawake, Quebec: Mohawk Council, January, 1984).

13. In the evenings the station has a substantial audience in the west-end suburbs of Montreal.

14. As one interviewee remarked, "Incorporation is a cause for great concern because corporations are governed by federal and provincial legislation and the basic philosophy of a corporation is an alien and foreign body governed by rules established outside, not by our people."

15. The unhappy experience of Alaskan Natives who took the corporate approach to a land claims settlement helps substantiate that view. See Thomas R. Berger, *Village Journey: The Report of the Alaska Native Review Commission* (Toronto: Collins, 1985).

16. Not until 1985 was economic development accorded a sufficiently high priority at DIAND to have its own assistant deputy minister.

17. This phenomenon is by no means restricted to Kahnawake.

18. The director was non-native and disputes arose over representation and allocation of funds among the Crees, Montagnais, and Mohawks.

19. Turning to the case of Indians taken into custody by the Kahnawake peacekeepers, one interviewee asserted that the Kahnawakeronon will not permit the Charter of Rights and Freedoms to be imposed on them in the sense of protecting Mohawks from Mohawk law.

Chapter Six

The Probable Economic Impact of a Mackenzie Valley Pipeline

by Thomas R. Berger

In practice it is not possible to separate rigidly the narrowly economic from the more broadly social sphere, for the development of the non-renewable resources of any region can bring serious pressures to bear on the population there. Gradually more and more people give up one kind of work, and relinquish the way of life associated with it, in favour of another kind of work and life. They often feel that they have had very little choice in the matter. Where that relinquished way of life – such as hunting, fishing, and trapping – is a preferred or culturally important lifestyle that offers a means of self-identification and a source of self-respect, the devaluation of that way of life can have widespread and dismaying consequences. These adverse consequences are exacerbated if the industrialized economy offers rewards that are only short-term.

Although many southern Canadians do not realize it, an economy based on the seasonal harvesting of renewable resources is still a vital part of the native society in the North. Although many native people have taken advantage of opportunities for wage employment in the non-renewable resources sector, often in order to obtain the cash they need to equip themselves for traditional pursuits, we must not lose sight of the fact that large-scale projects based on non-renewable resources have rarely provided permanent employment for any significant number of native people. However, the real danger of such projects lies not so much in their continued failure to provide ongoing jobs for native people, but rather in the highly intrusive effect such projects may have on native society and the native economy, including among

Abridged from Thomas R. Berger, *Northern Frontier, Northern Homeland: Report of the Mackenzie Valley Pipeline Inquiry*, Vol. 1 (Ottawa, 1977), Chapter 9.
Reproduced by permission of the Minister of Supply and Services Canada.

other things the failure to recognize and to strengthen the native economy and native skills.

The fact must be faced that in the short term the interests of northern native people are in conflict with the interests of governments and industry, which view technologically sophisticated "megaprojects," such as a Mackenzie Valley Pipeline, as a panacea for the economic ills of the region. In the short run, highest priority should in fact be given to strengthening the native economy and its associated values and preferences so that its very foundations are not undermined by the intrusive effects of pipeline construction. Only by this means can we ensure that native and non-native interest will not be in conflict in the long run.

Much of Canada's history is related to the export of "staples" – such as fish, fur, lumber, pulp and paper, wheat, minerals, oil and gas – from successive geographic frontiers or hinterlands to the advanced industrial metropolises of France, Britain, the U.S.A., or Canada itself. As Harold Innis[1] has written: "Each staple in its turn left its stamp [on the economic, political, and social structure], and the shift to new staples invariably produced periods of crises in which adjustments in the old structure were painfully made. . . ."

The impact of exploration for oil and gas (the new export staple) is quite different from the impact of the fur-trade economy of an earlier era. For instance, unlike the oil and gas economy, the fur-trade economy did not require that the native participants yield up their land; nor did it require that they become wage-earners. The fur trade did, though, bring the native peoples within the purview of the larger world economic system and into the metropolitan sphere of influence. The influences of that larger world economic system were also felt with the subsequent construction of DEW (Distant Early Warning) line stations after World War II, with the development of base metal mining in the 1960s, and with the construction of highways and railways. Whenever an area or community became involved in these activities whose origins were in the external metropolitan cities, the staple left its mark on the economic and social lives of the native people.

Now the era of oil and gas exploration has arrived. Such exploration does not need local labour; as with mining it is the land and adjacent waters, not the people who live on it and use it, which have become important. Thus, because the oil and gas industry does not depend on the native people, they cannot depend on it. And if they can no longer rely on the land for their living, they will cease to have any essential relation to any form of economic activity.

The history of metropolis-hinterland relations in Canada is one of frontier projects being developed to enrich the metropolis rather than the communities on the frontier. The same pattern is the likely prospect that a Mackenzie Valley pipeline offers, for the conditions for secondary economic growth in the North in terms of "ripple effects," "spin-offs," or "multipliers" are largely absent. The necessary condition for such secondary growth is the retention, within the frontier region, of earnings and of returns on capital. The fur trade and the mining industry took their profits out of the region and the oil and gas industry, as the new staple industry, will do the same.

Objectives of Economic Development

One of the federal government's own criteria for northern development is "that native northerners should derive early, visible and lasting benefits from economic development."[2] Although I can recommend some terms and conditions that would cause a Mackenzie Valley pipeline to meet the first two of these criteria, no terms and conditions can guarantee the third criterion. Indeed, it is my judgement that the social costs of the project would outweigh any economic benefits which northern Natives may derive from it, especially since there are very few who possess the capital, the knowledge, and the inclination to take advantage of the business opportunities that would arise.

We must ask some fundamental questions. What is the purpose of the project? In whose interests is it being undertaken? How should the economic gains be shared? Can the negative impacts be ameliorated or mitigated? We must even ask, if one of our objectives is to provide gainful employment for Natives, is the project the best way to do it?

We must also disabuse ourselves of the notion that the regional economy could become self-sufficient if this megaproject were built. The present economy of the region is scarcely conducive to such self-sufficiency in that it is not structured to capture and contain a significant proportion of the income that is generated by major investment there. Most goods and industrial labour are still imported into the region from the south. By and large these individuals and firms from outside exhibit little or no commitment to the region. They do not, generally, bank their money there or invest surplus earnings in any way that would expand employment within the region; nor do royalties, profits, or taxes stay in the North. Thus, the region's economy will not become self-sufficient, regardless of what support systems are devised for it. Indeed, regional interdependence is part and parcel of Canadian economic life.

The goal of providing real and lasting benefits to the native people of the region can thus be reached not through trying to make the regional economy self-sufficient, but rather only if we are prepared both to postpone construction of this project and to diversify the regional economy by strengthening the renewable resource sector. From a native point of view, it is dubious whether development that is conceived as transformation of the region's economy from a traditional base to an industrial base can be said to be real development at all. It is my judgement that the interests of the native people, as they themselves perceive them, should take priority now.

The Mixed Economy

Although the economy of the region is often considered to be a dual economy consisting of a native sector and a white sector, there are in reality four sectors: subsistence, trading of renewable resource produce, local wage employment, and industrial wage employment. As part of their accommodation to change, native people have absorbed, and are now even dependent upon, some elements of the economy of the newcomers. Overlapping or mixed economic forms are now integral to the native economy. The question we face, though, is how will the mix look as a result of the pipeline?

Many native families still derive a living – or the greatest part of a living – from the land. Said one native woman in her testimony to the Inquiry:

> I still go out in the bush every year. Sometimes its hard for me and yet I still do it because I just love being out in the bush and making our living, because that is the way that I was brought up.

In some ways wage employment has been useful to the native economy and compatible with the attainment of many native aspirations. In other ways, though, wage labour has had adverse effects on the traditional life. For instance, employment in a settlement may put a family at a great distance from its hunting and trapping areas. Another way in which the two are disparate is that in the native economy the individual or family combines production, exchange, and consumption activities, at least during certain parts of the year, whereas in the cash economy based on specialization and production for the market, the three activities tend to be divided.

In the region today the lives of many native families are based on an intricate economic mix whereby they hunt and fish at certain times of the year, and at other times of the year they work for wages for government, on highway construction, or for the oil and gas industry.

However, if opportunities and pressures to take industrial wage employment expand, the native economy may be completely transformed and perhaps debased and overwhelmed. Migrant native industrial workers, following the industry where its opportunities take them, cannot also be hunters and trappers. Yet the native economy should be preserved – and not merely as a curiosity, but rather because the native peoples have demonstrated that their economy is not only a link with their past, but also the basis of their plans for the future. The continued viability of the native economy should be an objective of economic development in the region, not its price.

Impact and Returns

Natives' experience to date with large-scale industrial development in the region has not been a happy one. Various development projects, of which the Pine Point lead-zinc mine and the Pointed Mountain pipeline near Fort Liard are but two relatively typical examples,[3] illustrate this point poignantly. Clearly, the principal beneficiaries of the presently proposed project will be southerners, not the people who live in the North. This section undertakes an examination of claims to the contrary – claims that native people will find jobs in the project, that local businesses will get contracts, and that the territorial governments will receive tax revenues from the project and its associated economic developments.

Two notes of warning should be issued from the outset of the analysis. First, experience in Alaska, on the James Bay project, and already on this project demonstrates that large-scale frontier projects usually cost very much more than was initially estimated. Furthermore, the influx of workers is sometimes much larger than estimated (e.g., 24,000 workers during the 1975 and 1976 construction seasons on the trans-Alaska pipeline, as opposed to the estimated 6-8,000). Thus, our predictions below will probably understate the costs, changes, and impact of the pipeline. Second, we must not forget that long-run impacts cannot usually be reversed: if we opt now for a regional economy that is dominated by the oil and gas industry, that is the economy we shall have for many years to come.

We turn first to short-run economic problems. The influx of workers, and of those seeking work, from southern Canada will have an adverse impact upon the supply-demand ratio and that in turn will drive prices up. Existing supply lines (e.g., river barges unable to travel in winter) do not permit northern merchants to replace depleted stocks easily or cheaply. Capacity in housing, retailing, community services, and local public works cannot be expanded quickly. Although proponents of the project have claimed that the movements of the workers and supplies they will need are controllable and will, in fact, be controlled, the Alyeska pipeline experience in Alaska suggests differently. There, attempts to dissuade workers from flocking to the area were not effective; they came anyway in search of high-paying jobs. The high pay on the project also attracted qualified workers away from lower-paying jobs in both the public and private sectors of the Alaskan economy and swelled the budgets of the state and local governments.

We can obtain some idea of what would happen to a town such as Hay River, Fort Simpson, or Inuvik by examining the experience of Valdez, Alaska. In three years its population roughly trebled, the structure of its labour market changed drastically, and salaries had to be raised to meet local inflation and prevent loss of personnel. Although the state provided some funds to help communities deal with the impact of the project, the funds were insufficient and too late, and worse yet, many of the problems they were intended to alleviate could not be solved merely by the injection of cash (e.g., because materials and skilled personnel were not available). Prices, especially rents, rose greatly and persons who had formerly not been part of the paid labour force – such as married women, Natives, and high school students – entered it. Job turnover was high as workers tried to make more money to meet the rising cost of living. Persons with relatively fixed incomes sustained losses, sometimes severe, in real income.

We should not overlook the fact that the Alyeska project, although it was very large, is smaller in relation to the Alaskan economy than the presently proposed project would be in relation to the economy of the Northwest Territories. The N.W.T. economy is much less able to absorb the kinds of impacts that such large projects inevitably generate. Although the pipeline company would exercise a measure of control over the movement of its own personnel, materials, and equipment in an attempt to minimize the impact, the activities of the company and its contractors would give rise to a great number of secondary and tertiary activities over which those companies would have little control. I do not see any way that these effects could be prevented.

In considering the long-term impact of the project, we must remember that once an energy corridor is established other pipelines would be built along it, too. So the pipeline must be regarded as a threshold: once crossed, there is no turning back.

The Alaskan experience is also instructive with respect to long-term impacts. There, government services proliferated and the greatly expanded population created a demand for more and more such services and at an improved level of quality. Oil was expected to flow at what proved to be an unrealistically early date; thus government access to royalties and tax revenues was delayed. The state government is now on a treadmill. It has created services and a bureaucracy that require very large sums of money to maintain them. There is only one source from which enough money can be obtained and that is the oil and gas industry. The government must, therefore, support further oil and gas exploration and development, and pipeline construction, even though it may have misgivings about them.

Alaska's native people have been drawn into the Alaskan economy, although by peculiarly American features of their land claims settlement. The native family that wants to continue a life of hunting, trapping, and fishing is not encouraged. The land that they use for these purposes is sought by developers, including native developers, as almost all of the Alaskan economy now focuses on a single activity: the continued search for, and development of, oil and natural gas.

Yet, staples like oil and gas are notoriously susceptible to cycles of boom and bust, and non-renewable resources must eventually run out. In either case – declining prices on world markets or depletion of the resource – or even after the completion of the construction phase of a megaproject, painful and disruptive problems may arise both in sloughing off expanded capacity and in adjusting to lower levels of income. These, too, must be considered part of the long-term impact of the project.

We must also bear in mind that control over the region lies outside the region. Within the N.W.T. there will be little control over the rate or direction of developments, and in the minds of some the low level of economic diversification of the region does not afford the luxury of putting the brakes on oil and gas development once it has begun.

For its budget the government of the N.W.T. is presently heavily dependent on subsidies from the government of Canada; such loans, grants, and transfer payments constitute more than 87 per cent of its budget. The costs of providing increased health and social services necessitated by the project will be high and normal programs in the fields of health, education, welfare, recreation, game management, and justice will have to be expanded and diversified. These costs come first and the benefits, in the form of government revenues, come much later. Yet even the revenues might be far less than many people realize.

That is to say, if the existing taxation mill rate per foot of pipeline is applied to the new pipeline it would yield only about $984,000 per annum in tax revenue, although taxes on ancillary facilities such as compressor stations would increase the total tax revenue. Nevertheless, these revenues to the territorial government are so low as to be insignificant. They would come nowhere near meeting the aforementioned social costs of the project.

Proposals to increase tax revenue through levying a throughput tax on natural gas travelling through the pipeline are unrealistic insofar as American gas travelling through the pipeline is concerned, for such a tax is precluded by treaty between Canada and the United States. Furthermore, the power to tax personal and corporate income in the N.W.T. is also unavailable, for it is held exclusively by the federal government. Thus, it is clear that unless there is a fundamental redistribution of taxation powers between the federal and N.W.T. governments, the territorial government will be even more dependent on the federal government than it is now.

A somewhat closer examination of the impact of the project on the native economy is also warranted here.[4] One important consideration is the project's impact on income distribution within small native communities, where local custom calls for food obtained from the land to be shared with others in the community. Because such produce is shared more readily than is money, the shift toward a money economy has created new possibilities for poverty. Those in want are more likely to stay in want and inequalities within native communities may become more pronounced, even while average per-capita income in the community rises. Economic "development" and concomitant decline in the native economy will make native communities poorer in some ways as they become richer in others.

Furthermore, the intrusion of large-scale labour recruitment into the social life of small native villages will be total rather than selective. Indeed, because the men whose lives are most firmly committed to the harvesting of renewable resources also suffer from recurrent cash problems, these men – and even whole communities – who have the strongest cultural and personal links with the land will be the ones who are most firmly pushed toward participation in industrial activity. The loss of those links with the land will only exacerbate the various costly problems a megaproject inflicts on the communities directly associated with it. The problems to which I refer here include congestion, shortage of housing, separation of families, alcoholism, familial and other violence and crime, and problems of mental health; their costs are economic, social, psychological, and spiritual.

You may question my pessimism and suggest that if native people cannot be painlessly transformed into industrial workers on the project, they will nevertheless inevitably become involved as industrial workers, albeit painfully. The fact of the matter, though, is that if the North continues to be regarded solely as a frontier for industrial development, there will *not* be an assimilation that is either more or less painful. On the contrary, the North will be not only an industrial frontier, but also the home of a demoralized, confused, and increasingly angry people who believe that they have been oppressed and weakened ever since white men came to their homeland. The impact of pipeline construction in the near future on the native economy would be serious and perhaps irreparable. All northerners seek a diversified economy, but the possibility of diversification, which depends on strengthening the renewable resources sector, will be lost if we build the pipeline now.

Employment and the Pipeline

Government's tendency to ignore the existence of the native hunting, fishing, and trapping economy leads to an inflated estimate of the number of unemployed Natives in the region. That goes hand in hand with a willingness to justify construction of the project on the basis of the jobs it will provide to Natives. While there are unquestionably Natives in the region who are properly viewed as unemployed or underemployed, I venture to say that no one knows for sure how large their numbers are.

I think we can assume that, through a scheme of preferential hiring, native people who want to work on the pipeline will be given the opportunity to do so; but let there be no doubt that the work offered to them will not solve the long-term problem of native employment as it is understood by government officials. There are only 200-250 permanent jobs in the operation and maintenance of the pipeline once construction is completed. As for the pipeline construction jobs themselves, it took a generation for Canadians to replace Americans in the highly specialized, highly skilled jobs that comprise the Canadian pipeline construction industry. Skilled jobs in pipeline construction will not be available to Natives because they do not have the requisite training for those jobs. Even if some of them were to qualify for these jobs, once the project is completed they would have to travel to other parts of the world to pursue their specialized trades. There will thus be severe restrictions on the type of work native northerners can do on the project. Most would be employed in various unskilled capacities, such as cutting brush.

It is all very well for the proponents to say that there will be employment for everyone, but the pipeline contractors and the unions – not the proponents – will be controlling the hiring. In a letter to this Inquiry the unions made their views plain: they stated their unwillingness to make any commitments with respect to northerners' participation, and recommended that instead of northerners being trained in pipeline construction they be trained in the other building and construction trades (e.g., for the building of compressor stations). This position is entirely at variance with the position taken by one of the proponents, Arctic Gas. Not only is Arctic Gas's position not tenable, in my view, but the alternative advanced by the union is also doubtful, for no evidence has been advanced to show that there will be a significant number of opportunities for native people to acquire long-term skills on gas plant or compressor station construction.

Even to the extent that semi-skilled jobs – mainly as operators of trucks and heavy equipment – are available to Natives, there will be no long-term need for any considerable number of these operators once the project is built. In fact, there is already a surplus of native heavy equipment operators.

We can learn from the Alaska experience and overcome some of the problems (e.g., unions requiring Natives to register at hiring halls far from the home community and to be at the hiring hall when the call for employment is made) that the native people in Alaska had in finding employment on that project. However, I do not pretend that any scheme for native preference in hiring would necessarily be wholly effective in placing native people on the job. Once construction is under way, the unions will have a degree of control over hiring that will make it likely that their own hiring rules will be enforced, rather than any procedure recommended by this Inquiry, even if the latter has the force of law through the sanction of Parliament.

To reiterate an earlier point, after the project ends those Natives who do acquire jobs and the skills that go with them will return to their home communities where they might never again have occasion to use those skills. How many heavy equipment operators are needed in a small, remote native community that may have only one piece of heavy equipment? Because past megaprojects (e.g., DEW line construction) intruded into the local native economy and inhibited its normal functioning, the native people who had worked on those projects often found themselves left with reduced, rather than expanded, opportunities when they returned home. There is danger of the same outcome with the presently proposed project. The result will be that many of the self-employed native hunters, fishermen, and trappers will become unemployed. That is to say, the extension of the industrial system creates not only employment but also unemployment and subsequent resort to welfare.

Experience in the Mackenzie Delta shows that although seasonal industrial employment there has provided an extremely useful opportunity for native people to acquire cash to supplement their income from hunting, fishing, and trapping, it has nevertheless led to the undermining and to some extent the abandoning of the native renewable resources economy. The presently proposed project would offer seasonal employment for only two or three years, but it would intrude throughout the region in a way that would threaten the native economy to a much greater extent than has occurred in the Delta – indeed, to an unprecedented extent. Seasonal employment will then be of little use to those who wish to maintain their traditional native economic life, for the very possibility of that economic life will have been removed.

An understanding of the economic costs outlined in this chapter and of the considerable associated social costs, which have thus far been only cursorily discussed, compels the conclusion that construction of the pipeline now would irremediably compromise the goals embodied in native claims in the region. Clearly, the pipeline should not be built now. However, I speak of the postponement of the project, not its cancellation.

There are those who contend that without this project there will be no economic development in the N.W.T. I find that point of view to be an oversimplification; it reflects a decade of insistence by politicians and the oil and gas industry that there can be no form of northern development except in a pipeline and that, ergo, without a pipeline there will be no development in the North. Yet, if the pipeline is not built the northern economy will not come to a sudden halt. Indeed, the program of modernizing and expanding the native economy, for which the native people have called, could be undertaken. Other industries, including the large government bureaucracy, will carry on largely as before. Furthermore, a decision to postpone this project would not mean that oil and gas exploration in the region would end. Inuvik and perhaps other Delta communities would suffer a serious setback, admittedly, but the losses experienced by businesses that have geared up under the assumption that permission to build the project would be granted would be as attributable to the raising of those expectations as to the postponement itself. Assuming, as I do, that a pipeline will eventually be built, the setback might not be as severe as many northern businesspersons have predicted. In the interim, the postponement will afford the native communities and economy the opportunity to adjust so as to mitigate the impacts that even a slower-paced industrial development will create.

Epilogue

The Mackenzie Valley Pipeline Inquiry provided a focus for consideration of the consequences of the advance of the industrial system to Canada's last frontier and beyond, a focus for consideration of the necessity for the preservation of the northern environment and, above all, a focus for consideration of the rights of the native peoples living on the frontier. The Inquiry had to weigh the value of establishing large-scale extractive industry in the midst of native communities trying to preserve traditional values and to re-establish local self-sufficiency.

We had been committed to the view that the economic future of the North lay in large-scale industrial development. There had been generated, especially among northern business, an atmosphere of expectancy about industrial development. There had always been a traditional renewable resource sector in the North, but instead of trying to strengthen it, we had, for a decade or more, followed policies by which it would only be weakened or even destroyed. We believed in large-scale industrial development and depreciated the existing economic base. Indeed, people who tried to earn a living by hunting, trapping, and fishing had often been regarded as unemployed.

I recommended that we should postpone the construction of such a pipeline for ten years, in order to strengthen native society, the native economy – indeed, the whole renewable resource sector – and to enable native claims to be settled.

This recommendation was based on the evidence of the native people. Virtually all of the native people who spoke to the Inquiry said that their claims had to be settled before any pipeline could be built. It should not be thought that the native people had an irrational fear of pipelines. They realized, however, that construction of the pipeline and establishment of the energy corridor would mean an influx of tens of thousands of white people from all over Canada seeking jobs and opportunities. They believed that they would be overwhelmed, that their native villages would become white towns, and that they would be relegated to the fringes of northern life. The government of Canada rejected the Arctic Gas pipeline proposal and decided that, if a pipeline were to be built, it should be along the Alaska Highway route, that is, along the alternate route that I urged.

Almost a decade has passed since I wrote *Northern Frontier, Northern Homeland*. Even though my recommendation that no pipeline be built was followed, progress has not abandoned the North. There has been a good deal of progress, though not in terms of large-scale projects.

As a result of the decision to postpone the construction of the pipeline for ten years, a number of developments have taken place in the Northwest Territories. I urged that an international wilderness area should be established comprising, on the Canadian side, nine million acres in the northern Yukon and, on the American side, what was then the nine-million-acre Arctic National Wildlife Range. Together these two areas would provide for the long-term well-being of the Porcupine caribou herd and other wildlife. I urged that, in northern Yukon, preservation of the wilderness and of the caribou herd would plainly be in keeping with the interests of the native people on both sides of the border. However, certain essential conditions had to be observed: native people would have to be guaranteed the right to live, hunt, trap, and fish within the park. I also suggested that they should play an important part in the management of the park and, in particular, of the Porcupine caribou herd. The government of Canada concurred and in 1978 Hugh Faulkner, the Minister of Indian and Northern Affairs, withdrew 9.8 million acres of northern Yukon, saying: "I have concluded that the conservation values of the region exceed the development potential and we must reserve all land north of the Porcupine and Bell Rivers." This withdrawal was facilitated because the environmental interest was united with the native interest. The Inuvialuit – the Inuit of the western Canadian Arctic – urged a withdrawal prior to the final resolution of their claim. And on July 25, 1984, as part of the Inuvialuit Claims Settlement Act, a national wilderness park was established with special management and hunting, fishing, and trapping provisions for the native peoples. In 1980, much of the nine million acres on the Alaska side of the boundary was designated wilderness.

The native people had testified overwhelmingly that they wanted their land claims settled before the pipeline was built. Although I said that, with appropriate environmental safeguards, a pipeline could be built from Canada's Mackenzie Delta up the valley, I said this should not be done for ten years, to provide an opportunity for land claims to be settled.

In 1979, the native majority on the Legislative Council for the Northwest Territories took over the council. Since 1983, the leader of the government is a native person, the only Native who leads a government in any province or territory in the country. Measures have now been taken to strengthen the renewable resource economy in the N.W.T.

Then, of course, there has been the COPE (Committee for Original Peoples Entitlement) settlement of 1984. This settlement is the best land claims settlement that any native organization has achieved anywhere in North America.

Negotiations are taking place between the Dene Nation and the Métis and the government of Canada to settle their land claims in the Northwest Territories. These negotiations have not yet resulted in final agreement, but it should be remembered that many sub-agreements relating to fish and wildlife have already been reached. I said that settling land claims would take time – ten years – and that is exactly what has happened.

In the early 1980s, when Esso Resources put forward its proposal for an oil pipeline from Norman Wells to the Alberta border, the Dene Nation was consulted; indeed, the federal government consulted the government of the N.W.T. and the Dene Nation, and all sat down with the industry and worked out an agreement. The Dene are not happy with the way the agreement has turned out, but the important thing is that they were treated as important players in decision-making regarding resource development.

There has been a renewed emphasis on the possibilities of the development of renewable resources. The report "Fish, Fur and Game in the Northwest Territories," issued in September, 1980, by the Science Advisory Board of the Northwest Territories, discussed the importance of wildlife as a source of income and food. In its report, the board said that "intensive management can increase substantially the fish and wildlife that can be harvested" and that "the economic importance of fish, game and furs can be greatly expanded." The report concludes that the fish and mammal resources of the Northwest Territories could provide sufficient protein for a human population in the Northwest Territories two to four times as large as the present one. Of course, there must be a greatly expanded program of wildlife management and a carefully regulated harvest, and native people in the North must become actively involved in resource management. To achieve these objectives, a school of renewable resource management technology has been established at Fort Smith, N.W.T.

The Dene, the Métis, and the Inuit are advancing proposals for two new political units in the Northwest Territories. Their proposals are far-reaching, including entrenched guarantees for aboriginal representation in whatever new political institutions emerge and entrenched

192

guarantees for aboriginal rights. Whatever their outcome, they are evidence of a renewed determination and a new capacity on the part of native peoples in the North to establish a distinct and contemporary place for themselves in Canadian life. The native people are now a political force to be reckoned with in the North and in the country.

Notes

1. Harold Innis, *Empire and Communications* (Toronto: University of Toronto Press, 1950).
2. Hon. Jean Chrétien, remarks introducing the *Statement of the Government of Canada on Northern Development in the 70s*, Minutes of the Proceedings of the House of Commons Standing Committee on Indian Affairs and Northern Development, March, 1972.
3. Editor's note: For an elaboration of these two case studies, see pages 123-25 in vol. 1 of Berger's report and Paul Deprez, *The Pine Point Mine and the Development of the Area South of Great Slave Lake* (Winnipeg: University of Manitoba Centre for Settlement Studies, Series 2, Research Report No. 16, 1973).
4. Editor's note: Berger's report also considered the probable impact of the pipeline on non-native businesses in the North. The aforementioned "treadmill" effect was one of the consequences Berger predicted for the non-native business sector.

Chapter Seven

Economic Development Provisions of the New Claims Settlements

by J. Rick Ponting

As noted in Chapter One, a major objective of the federal government's policy toward Indians for most of the last century was the assimilation of Indians into the larger, nonIndian society. This included their economic assimilation, and because Canada was primarily an agricultural society in the nineteenth century, a major thrust of those assimilative efforts was to make farmers out of Indians. This was reflected in various treaties, where provisions were made for a rudimentary form of agricultural economic development on Indian reserves. However, the different treaties were by no means identical in their provisions; some of the later treaties were slightly more attractive to the Indians, including in their economic development provisions, than were the earlier ones. Most treaties did provide for Indians to retain hunting, fishing, and trapping rights and provided some supplementary benefits (e.g., twine for nets, ammunition, some implements) to assist, if not sustain, Indians in these activities.[1] Although such modest support did contribute to the subsistence level of living for some, it could hardly be considered economic "development" if the latter is taken to mean expansion with accumulation of surplus and growth of opportunities. For others the treaties proved woefully inadequate to carry the Indians through periods of economic depression and recession.

The new land claims settlements of the 1970s and 1980s were designed to provide more than token economic support to Indians. They were framed to do so in a manner that would carry Indians forward with both a viable traditional sector for those who chose that way of life, and an adequate share of political-economic power or local influence to be used to protect Indian interests and to create enduring economic opportunity of a non-traditional type. The purpose of this chapter is to describe the main economic development features of the James Bay and Northern Quebec Agreement of 1975, which in impor-

194

tant respects serves as a prototype for modern claims settlements. Brief attention will also be given to the 1985 Agreement in Principle for Yukon. Throughout the discussion of the James Bay Agreement the remarks refer to the Cree Indians rather than to the Inuit, who are also part of the Agreement.

To summarize the economic development provisions of this 454-page document[2] is a difficult task, for the ten pages explicitly devoted to the economic and social development of the Crees are by no means the only sections having major ramifications for economic development.[3] Since land is a crucial resource in much economic development, let us turn first to those provisions of the Agreement pertaining to land allotments and land-use rights.

Land Allotments and Land-use Rights

The agreement creates three categories of land. Category I lands for the approximately 6,000 Crees at time of signing[4] amount to about 2,140 square miles (about 547,315 hectares, or the equivalent of a block of land approximately 35 kilometres wide by 160 kilometres long). These are lands in and around existing settlements. The important issue of mineral and other sub-surface rights was resolved by having the rights remain with the Quebec government but also by giving the native people the right to veto the Quebec government's exercise of those rights. By implication, this enables the Crees to negotiate certain development terms (e.g., to mitigate any adverse impact of such development on the local community, to extract employment concessions from a mining company) in exchange for suspending their veto. The Agreement (Sec. 5.1.10.a) explicitly states that compensation must also be paid for the use of such mineral or sub-surface rights, in effect a royalty. Subject to some constraints,[5] the Crees also have the right to use and commercially exploit the forests on Category I lands without having to pay stumpage fees to Quebec.

Category II lands for the Crees amount to almost exactly 25,000 square miles (6.39 million hectares). These are lands where the Crees have the exclusive right to hunt, fish, and trap. These lands are administered jointly by the Crees and the non-native Municipality of James Bay for purposes of policing, fire protection, zoning, etc., although the municipality will have no voice in matters concerning hunting, fishing, and trapping. Mining and industrial developments are permitted on these lands and the lands may otherwise be appropriated by Quebec for development purposes, although in the latter case the Crees are entitled to replacement lands or, if they prefer, to monetary compensation. On both Category II and Category III lands the Crees must pay stumpage fees for commercial cutting of forests. The Crees' hunting, fishing, and trapping rights on Category II and III lands are subordinated to the right of the Quebec government and its agencies, such as Hydro-Québec, to develop the land.

Category III lands constitute the vast bulk of the territory. All people have access to these lands under ordinary provincial laws and regulations, although the Crees do receive some special consideration by being entitled to hunt, fish, and trap year-round and by having certain species reserved for their use.

Financial Compensation

The financial compensation provisions of the Agreement are complex and are presented here as the total compensation for *both* Crees and Inuit. The reader should bear in mind that the financial benefits are divided proportionately between Crees and Inuit on the basis of population (approximately 6,000 Crees and 4,000 Inuit at time of signing).

At the time the Agreement was made public, much media attention was given to the amount of financial compensation involved – about $250 million. However, readers should bear in mind several important points. First, the payments in question are for the *extinguishment* of all aboriginal rights and claims, for the renouncing of the right to collect royalties or mining duties (past, present, or future), and for the forfeiture of the right to try to block the James Bay hydro development project in the courts. Second, the payments are spread over a twenty-year period. Third, the value of the settlement was eroded considerably by inflation, especially in the first five years after signing. Finally, by standard accounting procedures money received at some time in the future is considered to be of less value (even if there is no inflation) than the same amount of money received in the present; thus, to take this factor into account, a discount rate of approximately 5 per cent per annum should be applied to moneys received in the future.

Payments are made in the form of grants from the governments of Canada (43.67 per cent) and Quebec (56.33 per cent) and royalty payments on power generated by the James Bay Energy Corporation. The first $75 million has been paid over the ten-year period since the implementation of the Agreement. The second $75 million is payable as royalties on power generated, but even if those royalties do not amount to that sum (e.g., due to turbine generators not being brought into operation), the Quebec government is obliged to pay this second $75 million in instalments by December 31, 1996. The third $75 million is in Quebec government debentures issued between 1975 and 1979, which mature twenty years later. The compensation payments themselves are non-taxable and are paid to a Cree- or Inuit-controlled legal entity rather than to individuals. The federal and Quebec governments are represented on the boards of directors of these entities.

Harvesting Provisions

One of the primary objectives of the harvesting provisions of the Agreement is to guarantee the continuation of the traditional economy based on hunting, fishing, and trapping on as large a scale as in the past.[6] One mechanism designed to help achieve this is the newly created Hunting, Fishing, and Trapping Co-ordinating Committee (HFTCC), an expert body of twelve members charged with the responsibility of reviewing, managing, and in certain cases supervising and regulating the hunting, fishing, and trapping regime set in place by the Agreement. The committee is in part a consultative body to the federal and provincial governments, yet with respect to certain large mammal species (moose, caribou, and black bears) it is empowered to make decisions that are binding on federal, provincial, and local governments. On most species HFTCC does not have such power, yet the Agreement is extraordinary in that it requires the responsible federal or provincial minister to consult with the committee and "to respect the views and positions of the Co-ordinating Committee" (Section 24.4.36, p. 373). Similarly, in another section (24.8.8.c, p. 383) pertaining to outfitters the Agreement states: "Save for reasons of conservation, the responsible Provincial Minister shall not unreasonably refuse the recommendation of the Co-ordinating Committee when approved by the Cree local government concerned. . . ."

In light of the influence and power of the HFTCC, it is worth noting its composition. The Crees, Inuit, Quebec, and Canada each appoint three members, while the James Bay Development Corporation (a subsidiary of the provincial Crown corporation Hydro-Québec) appoints one non-voting member. An illustration of the level of detail at which the negotiating teams operated in formulating the Agreement is to be found in Section 24.4.4 (p. 367) where the voting procedures are established for HFTCC. For instance:

a) When matters of exclusive provincial jurisdiction are being dealt with by the Co-ordinating Committee, the members appointed by the Provincial Government shall each have two (2) votes, and the members appointed by the Federal Government shall not vote. . . .

d) When matters relating to the area of primary interest of the Crees [defined in Sec. 24.13.2] are being dealt with by the Co-ordinating Committee, the members appointed by the Crees . . . shall each have two (2) votes and the members appointed by the Inuit . . . shall each have one (1) vote.

On tie votes the chairman gets a tie-breaking second vote; the chairmanship and vice-chairmanship rotate among all four "parties" on a four-year cycle. This entire section of the Agreement also demonstrates that highly particularistic, mutually satisfactory accommodations can be reached to meet the needs of governments and specific Indian communities, albeit at an enormous cost in terms of legal fees and precious time and energy of the Indian leaders involved.

All regulations pertaining to the hunting, fishing, and trapping regime established by the Agreement must be submitted to HFTCC before enactment by the government concerned. Among other responsibilities, HFTCC also supervises the outfitting industry for non-native hunters, acts as a clearinghouse for information (e.g., game inventories) on hunting, fishing, and trapping, recommends conservation measures to governments, and has the right to participate in environmental impact assessment hearings. In addition, each individual member of HFTCC has a veto over any provincial or federal government changes to the list of species reserved exclusively for the Crees and Inuit.

The Agreement contains numerous other provisions pertaining to the hunting, fishing, and trapping economy. For instance, it guarantees the "principle of priority of Native harvesting"; gives the Crees and Inuit the exclusive right to operate outfitting facilities on certain lands and (for thirty years) the right of first refusal to operate as outfitters on certain other lands; gives the Crees and Inuit the exclusive right to operate commercial fisheries in certain areas or for certain species of fish; requires that a minimum of control or regulations be applied to the Cree and Inuit people and that the control applied to the Crees and Inuit be less restrictive for them than for non-Natives.[7] Also, the Agreement (Sec. 24.3.24) requires the governments of Canada and Quebec to assist the Crees and Inuit "in establishing trappers' associations, as well as a Native-controlled and run trapping industry, including . . . such [functions] as marketing, promotion, registration, collection, transportation, grading, dressing, dyeing, manufacturing, etc." Quebec and Canada are also obliged to "provide for the training of a sufficient number of Native people as conservation officers" and to "modify, when necessary, the criteria required for acceptance as a trainee and [to] establish and fund special facilities, courses and training programs" (Sec. 24.10.2). Such Cree and Inuit conservation officers would then be given enforcement powers as game officers, fisheries officers, and the like under the relevant federal and provincial statutes.

Section 30 creates an income security program (guaranteed annual income) funded by Quebec for Cree hunters and trappers. The purpose of the program is to ensure that hunting, fishing, and trapping will constitute a viable way of life for the Crees, at the same time ensuring that the program offers effective incentive to pursue harvesting (rather than transfer payments) as a way of life. The program is subject to various eligibility requirements (Sec. 30.2) and to a somewhat complex formula (Sec. 30.3) for the calculation of benefits.

Other Economic Development Provisions

Under the Agreement, numerous other organizations were created to advance or facilitate the economic development of the Crees. One of these is the James Bay Native Development Corporation (JBNDC), a subsidiary of the Quebec government's James Bay Development Corporation. Among the objectives, the JBNDC lists such items as investing in various projects for Cree economic development and assisting, promoting, and encouraging "the creation, diversification, or development of business, resources, properties, and industries within the territory with a view to stimulating maximum economic opportunities for Cree people and contributing to their general economic well-being" (Sec. 28.3.1.a). Particular types of business envisaged include outfitting, tourism, native arts and crafts, road maintenance, fuel distribution, forestry, mining, and others.

The Agreement also committed the governments of Canada and Quebec to assisting the Crees (with funding and technical advice) in establishing a Cree Trappers' Association, a Cree Outfitting and Tourism Association, and a Cree Native Arts and Crafts Association, if feasible. To take but one of these as an example, the Agreement calls for feasibility studies to be undertaken in respect to the Cree Trappers' Association. The feasibility studies are mandated to make recommendations in ten different areas, of which two are "improved trapper capability including measures to increase availability of and sources of funds for equipment, supplies, and transportation" and "fur marketing and promotion to increase the trappers' returns including fur collection services."

A Joint Economic and Community Development Committee, involving two members appointed by each of Quebec and Canada and five members appointed by the Cree Regional Authority,[8] is established under Section 28.8. Its purpose is to review and make recommendations concerning the various programs for the promotion of the social and economic development of the Crees (e.g., training programs, job placement and recruitment services, awarding of contracts, programs to assist Cree entrepreneurs in obtaining funding or capital or technical expertise).

In addition, both Quebec and Canada pledged themselves to take measures to enable Crees to qualify for jobs created by existing or planned developments in the territory and for jobs in government services.

Other Related Features of the Agreement

Although various other features of the Agreement would be important to an understanding of the broader nation-building effort under way in the James Bay area,[9] our present more limited focus on economic development makes the provisions dealing with the environment particularly important. Indeed, it was the prospect of massive environmental degradation from the James Bay hydro project that led to negotiations on an Agreement in the first instance, and it would make little sense to have developed such an elaborate hunting, fishing, and trapping regime if the ecosystem were to be left vulnerable to massive disruption that would further undermine the Cree economy. Thus, the Agreement creates two environmental bodies, the Environmental and Social Impact Review Committee and the James Bay Advisory Committee on the Environment. The latter is a thirteen-member body of four members appointed by each of Canada, Quebec, and the Cree Regional Authority, plus the chairman of HFTCC. Its voting procedures and rotating chairmanship and vice-chairmanship are similar to those of HFTCC. The committee has the right to be consulted and to make recommendations before any environmental or social protection regulations are made for the territory. As well, it is mandated to examine and make recommendations concerning the environmental and social impact assessment and review mechanisms and procedures. However, the committee does not have the authority to veto regulations, to impose its own regulations, or to enforce any regulations.

Most types of development in the area are subject to automatic prior study and then ongoing monitoring by the Environmental and Social

Impact Review Committee (ESIRC). [10] This committee, which serves in place of the similar body required elsewhere in Quebec or Canada by provincial or federal legislation, respectively, assesses the statement of environmental and social impact that a proponent of certain types of development is required to submit. The interested Cree communities or their governments may then make oral or written representations to the committee. [11] The committee makes recommendations to the administrator [12] on whether or not the proposed development should be allowed to proceed and, if so, under what terms and conditions (including, if appropriate, preventive or remedial measures). It is the administrator who has the power to make the actual decision, although if she or he is willing to accept any recommendation from ESIRC or wishes to modify an ESIRC recommendation, she or he must consult with ESIRC to explain and discuss the reasons for such a course of action. Significantly, the provincial cabinet has the authority (Sec. 22.7.2) to overrule the administrator's decision by authorizing a development that she or he turned down or by altering the terms and conditions established by the administrator.

General Comments on the James Bay Agreement

The negotiators went to considerable lengths in attempting not just to facilitate but also to promote the economic development of the James Bay Crees. These elaborate provisions contrast markedly with the almost fleeting attention that economic development received in the treaties of an earlier era. The 1975 Agreement's efforts to protect the traditional Indian harvesting economy also contrast with either the efforts at economic assimilation or the rudimentary provisions in support of the traditional harvesting economy found in some of the treaties of an earlier era. However, we must not lose sight of the caveats mentioned at the outset of this discussion. Nor should we allow the complexity of the provisions to blind us to the ultimate fact that most of the provisions of the Agreement give the Crees the power to advise, recommend, or be consulted, rather than the power to make final decisions. Perhaps that is all the Crees could expect to achieve under the circumstances, but the Agreement was nevertheless repudiated by other Indian leaders when its terms were made public.

In the view of the then-president of the National Indian Brotherhood, George Manuel, a serious flaw in the Agreement is the fact that it extinguishes the Crees' aboriginal rights. He was particularly concerned that this and other features would be used as precedents for negotiations on the comprehensive claims of Indians elsewhere in Canada. His concern proved justified, as there are many parallels, including the extinguishment of aboriginal rights, in the 1985 Yukon Agreement in Principle. Manuel also criticized the Agreement on the grounds that it was a significant step toward the implementation of the infamous, and ostensibly retracted, 1969 white paper, in that it transferred to Quebec responsibilities that formerly rested with the federal government.[13]

Andrew Delisle, president of the Indians of Quebec Association, offered similar criticism and went on to charge that the Agreement is a violation of the federal government's responsibilities for the protection of Indian rights, especially those of "other Indian peoples not a party to the final agreement but directly affected." Conversely, Billy Diamond, Grand Chief of the Crees of Quebec and one of the prime movers throughout the negotiations and since, defended the Agreement as one that "will protect our way of life and give our children a choice between the traditional way of life and the non-native way of life."

This is not the place for an evaluation of the overall Agreement, but it can be said that the Agreement has stimulated intensive efforts at constructing what in many respects is virtually a new society. The Cree Regional Authority has taken a very active role in this institution-building and has established numerous commercial and non-profit entities, including a commercial airline, Air Creebec Inc., and a construction firm, Cree Construction Company (Quebec) Ltd. Despite the facts that some serious problems of implementing the provisions of the Agreement have occurred, particularly with respect to health and sanitation provisions not discussed in this chapter, and that the flooding for the James Bay hydro project caused serious disruption and dislocation, and despite the extinguishment of prior aboriginal rights, the Agreement has served to provide some degree of self-determination and choice of economic lifestyle in the face of what would have been an unmitigated social and economic disaster for the Crees if the hydro development (and other developments) had gone ahead without the Agreement.

The 1985 Yukon Agreement in Principle

James Frideres's chapter in this book describes the key features of the 1985 Yukon Agreement in Principle. At time of writing only a thirty-four-page summary of the Agreement in Principle (AIP) was publicly available, due in part to concerns that premature release of the document might close some options presently open to the "beneficiaries" (Yukon status and non-status Indians) in their selection of lands. In addition, the AIP is presently being renegotiated. Thus, it is neither possible nor appropriate to analyse the 1985 AIP in the same amount of detail as the James Bay Agreement. Instead, at a general level some broad features of the 1985 Yukon AIP are identified here and compared to the James Bay Agreement (JBA).

One of the potentially most important economic development issues is that of sub-surface mineral rights. This was handled in JBA by leaving ownership with Quebec and by giving the Crees a veto over the exercise of that ownership. In Yukon no agreement was reached on this issue.

Almost as important is the level of compensation. The 10,000 Crees and Inuit of James Bay will get $250 million over twenty years; if the AIP provision on this item is not changed, the approximately 5,500 Yukon beneficiaries are to receive $380 million ($130 million in 1982 present value), also over twenty years, for surrender of their aboriginal claims and interests, plus $160 million ($54 million in 1982 present value) over twenty years as compensation for the cessation of programs of the federal Department of Indian Affairs and Northern Development. Yukon Indians will also get an unspecified amount of money in support of the operation of Indian band administration.

Thus, some important similarities and differences exist vis-à-vis JBA. The most important similarity is the absolutely crucial feature whereby undefined aboriginal rights are extinguished in exchange for financial compensation and circumscribed, legally defined rights regarding hunting, fishing, trapping, and land use. An important difference is that Yukon beneficiaries, but not the James Bay Crees, have given up the right to receive programs and services from DIAND.

Both agreements also provide for the establishment of beneficiary corporations, under the control of the beneficiaries, to be responsible for the management of the financial compensation funds. Various other structures are also established in both agreements for land use planning and environmental impact assessment; preliminary indications suggest that the Crees may have slightly more power on these bodies than the Yukon beneficiaries will have on the comparable organizations in Yukon. As Frideres notes, though, during the present negotiations this may change in the direction of more power for the Yukon beneficiaries than they had in the 1985 AIP. In both agreements, most of the powers of the boards and organizations on which beneficiaries sit are advisory or consultative, rather than involving decision-making, standard-setting, or enforcement. For instance, in both cases final responsibility for wildlife management rests with the "external" government (Quebec or Yukon).

In both agreements the beneficiaries are given exclusive rights to harvest game on their lands, are given favoured (but non-exclusive) treatment concerning fish and wildlife quotas, have their rights take precedence over sport fishing, and are given rights of first refusal to some other economic opportunities (e.g., outfitting licences in the James Bay territory, trap-line licences in Yukon).

In the published summary of the Yukon AIP, no mention was made of certain other features found in JBA, such as those listed earlier in this chapter under the heading "Other Economic Development Provisions."

This is a very cursory treatment of the economic development aspects of the two agreements. More detailed analysis awaits the public release of a full-fledged legal document for Yukon. From the present vantage point, though, it seems safe to conclude that the basic approach to economic development is quite similar in the two cases.[14] The James Bay Crees were in a slightly stronger bargaining position, because their suit attempting to challenge the massive James Bay hydro project was already before the Supreme Court of Canada at the time the final negotiations were in progress. Whether that makes a substantial difference in the deal they were able to strike remains to be seen.

Concluding Comments

A general assessment of the economic development provisions of the James Bay Agreement is now in order. To make that assessment more meaningful, a few observations are offered on the implementation of those provisions. Those observations are mainly from the perspective of the president of CREECO (Cree Regional Economic Enterprises Inc.), the holding company established as a profit-oriented firm to oversee the operation of the collectively owned commercial enterprises of the Crees.[15]

The economic development provisions of the Agreement have not escaped the serious problems of implementation that have plagued other sections of the Agreement, although certain economic development provisions have proceeded reasonably well. Compensation payments, for instance, have been paid on schedule by the provincial and federal governments, and the principle of native priority vis-à-vis harvesting of wildlife has generally been respected.[16] Similarly, the environmental protection provisions, which have important economic ramifications, are reported to have worked to the general satisfaction of the Crees although with some noteworthy exceptions. Furthermore, numerous small businesses (mainly local service-oriented firms such as gas stations, restaurants, and laundromats) have been established as all but one of the communities have adopted the private enterprise orientation. By way of final example, both collective commercial entities (CREECO and Air Creebec Inc.) established by the Cree Regional Authority are operating at a profit.

On the negative side, implementation has been impeded by various factors, perhaps the most important of which is the transfer of funds. For instance, the James Bay Native Development Corporation was established in 1978 but has not performed as expected by the Crees because, according to the president of CREECO, the government of Quebec has made available only about $4 million of the $50 million it committed.[17] Under other sections of the Agreement the Crees have encountered roadblocks rooted in a difficulty in getting the federal and provincial governments to come to agreement on budgetary allocations. Furthermore, in such a complex agreement there are bound to be conflicting interpretations of some important provisions. This has happened with the JBA, for the government of Quebec has reportedly balked at providing funds, envisaged in the Agreement, in those instances where no pre-existing program is in place to address a particular need, and has sometimes refused to launch a new program in response to those needs. These kinds of financial problems, exacerbated by government delays of six to eight months in some cases, have led to the belief among some of the Cree leaders that such agreements should contain provisions establishing various section-specific pools of implementation funds.

Problems of finances and of federal-provincial co-ordination have not been the only ones to encumber the implementation phase. Other problems stemmed from Quebec civil servants' unfamiliarity with Cree society and culture, in that they had had little or no occasion to work with the Crees prior to the signing of the Agreement.[18] Consequently, they have been inclined to try to slot the Crees into existing programs and existing service-delivery mechanisms used for the non-Indian population in Quebec. This has been resisted by the Crees where such an approach fails to take into account their special needs, circumstances, and traditions. Similarly, a degree of paternalism has sometimes characterized the Quebec (and federal) government's orientation to planning, in that government attempted to play a much larger role in planning than Cree leaders felt was appropriate. This violation of one of the basic tenets of community development theory led the Cree leaders to view some of the provincial planners as more of an obstacle than a resource. In addition, implementation has been impeded as relations between Cree authorities and provincial bureaucrats became strained. The perception exists among the Crees that provincial bureaucrats are resisting implementation because they feel that the Crees are "getting too much for free." [19] Finally, implementation has been marred also by a conflict of values surrounding the trappers. While the Crees are of the opinion that some of the most important needs of the trappers are social rather than economic, the federal and provincial governments have placed priority on the trappers' economic needs under the Agreement.

This sketch of problems in implementing the economic development provisions of the Agreement is admittedly general and one-sided. Nevertheless, it does illustrate the point that, despite the considerable intelligence, legal expertise, and forethought that go into negotiating such agreements or treaties, implementation problems will always arise. In practice, those problems take the agreement in directions different from those anticipated by the signatories. This is anticipated in public policy literature, where the implementation phase of the policy cycle is often viewed as merely a continuation of the politics and power struggles that constituted the policy-formulation (or in this case, agreement-negotiating) phase. [20] From that literature and from the James Bay case there are lessons to be learned for future negotiations, such as in Yukon. In particular, if there is to be a reasonably close fit between the policy/agreement as designed and the policy/agreement as implemented, the interests of the bureaucrats who will implement policy must be taken into consideration at the bargaining table, however distasteful that might be. Also, one of the features built into the implementation regime should be the role of a "fixer," a person strategically situated (e.g., at a senior level of one of the important organizations) to learn about implementation problems and endowed with sufficient power, authority, legitimacy, and discretionary funds to be effective at resolving disputes and lubricating resistance. [21] Such a person is not a magician who can turn every bad or lopsided provision of an agreement into a workable and fair one, but across a large number of problem areas this person can have a net salutary effect that can make the agreement much more effective at the grassroots level and much more palatable to the bureaucrats who implement it.

We turn now to the task of assessing the economic development provisions of the JBA on other grounds. For a non-economist, non-Native who was not a party to the negotiations to make such an assessment is rather presumptuous, and I do so at my peril. However, some criteria can be formulated and applied, and there is some utility to making such criteria explicit for use by the reader in assessing future claims settlements.

A fundamental criterion for assessing any comprehensive claims settlement must be the adequacy and security of the resource base, where resource base includes the land, non-renewable resources under it, renewable resources such as fish and wildlife, and fiscal compensation and transfer payments. Here the JBA gets a mediocre rating. Category I lands are of very modest amounts and their renewable and non-renewable resource potential remains to be proven. However, sufficient security for renewable resources probably exists, not only in the preferential harvesting rights for the Crees, but also because HFTCC has the regulatory power to establish the native and non-native kill limit for large mammals and because individual HFTCC members have a veto over changes to the list of fish species reserved exclusively to native people. The Agreement also guarantees native people levels of harvesting equal to levels for all species at the time the Agreement was signed. Security of the resource base is also enhanced by the Cree veto over Quebec exercising its sub-surface rights to Category I lands and by other provisions not discussed above that pertain to man-made changes in the water levels in the river systems. [22] When the modest guaranteed annual income provisions are considered as well, the security of the resource base is further enhanced. Overall, then, the Agreement receives a high score on security of resources. The compensation payment, however, merits a much less favourable rating: its value has been severely eroded by inflation and by discounting over twenty years. It is, in my opinion, not a lot of money to receive for the extinguishment of rights held since time immemorial.

A second major criterion for assessing a comprehensive claims settlement is whether it permits individuals a viable choice of pursuing traditional or contemporary occupations. The James Bay Agreement scores well on this criterion, particularly insofar as the perpetuation of the traditional economy is concerned. This takes us to a third criterion, the existence of adequate provisions for representation before and participation in decision-making bodies having jurisdiction over economic development matters (broadly defined). Here the Agreement rates well on representation, but rather poorly on decision-making participation. The Crees will have ample opportunity to make their collective will known before numerous bodies, but most of those bodies are merely advisory or consultative in nature. With few exceptions, the actual decision-making authority rests elsewhere, although the propensity of such decision-makers to rule against the advice of their advisory and consultative bodies is an empirical matter.

Finally, the ability to raise capital has been a hurdle over which various Indian economic development projects have tripped in the past. Bankers are reluctant to loan money where, in the event of default on the loan, they cannot seize collateral due to restrictions in the Indian Act pertaining to the seizure of Indian lands. Although JBA stipulates that some of the Category I lands of the Crees are taken out from under the jurisdiction of the Indian Act, this is largely irrelevant. Few banks would be interested in seizing a building and the land on which it rests because of the remoteness and/or small size of most of the Cree settlements. At least as importantly, though, the lump-sum compensation payments provided under the JBA should produce sufficient capital (especially if invested prudently) to meet most of the small and intermediate capital needs the Crees have through to the end of this century. Beyond that, though, needs may outstrip the supply of capital, especially if there is a large population increase.

These are not the only criteria that can be brought to bear. Other persons might attach more importance to such factors as skills training for the labour force, taxation powers for local governments, or non-obstruction of entrepreneurs. However, in the opinion of this author the four criteria discussed here are more important, and on them the economic development provisions of this prototype claims settlement agreement rate a mediocre score at best.

Notes

1. Derek G. Smith (ed.), *Canadian Indians and the Law: Selected Documents, 1663-1972* (Toronto: McClelland and Stewart, 1975).
2. The treaties of the nineteenth century were usually only three to five pages in length.
3. For one summary of the entire Agreement, see *Indian News*, 17, 7 (special issue devoted entirely to the Agreement).
4. As of 1985 the Cree population of the communities involved ranged from 339 in Chibougamau to 2,095 in Chisasibi (formerly Fort George). The total population was 9,342 persons in nine communities, for an average of 1,038 persons per community.
5. For instance, commercial cutting by the Crees must be in keeping with the development and marketing plan accepted by the Quebec Department of Lands and Forests.
6. For a graphic portrayal of this traditional lifestyle, see the National Film Board film *The Cree Hunters of Mistassini*. Mistassini is one of the Cree communities covered by the Agreement.
7. In light of such explicit racial discrimination (affirmative action) the reader can appreciate the importance of Section 25 of the Charter of Rights and Freedoms, which protects existing aboriginal rights including those contained in treaties or land claims agreements such as the James Bay and Northern Quebec Agreement.
8. The Cree Regional Authority comprises the chief of each of the Cree

communities, plus one other member of each of those communities. It is an example of what could be called a "supra-level" Indian government. Among other responsibilities it appoints Cree representatives to all of the bodies established by the Agreement, gives consent (where required) on behalf of the Crees, and co-ordinates and administers programs on Category I lands.

9. Reference here to "nation-building" is to such features as the creation of the Cree Regional Authority as a form of limited self-government; the establishment of a Cree Regional Board of Health and Social Services and of a Cree Regional School Board; the designation of the native tongue, French, and English as official languages of local administration; and the provision of education in the students' mother tongue.

10. The Agreement includes a list (Section 22, Schedule 1) of all developments that are automatically subject to the requirements of having an impact assessment done, and a second list (Section 22, Schedule 2) of developments automatically exempt from that requirement. Any other proposed development not contemplated in either of these two lists is considered by a six-member Evaluating Committee that advises the administrator (see note 12, below) on his/her decision as to whether that development shall be subject to assessment and review by the Environmental and Social Impact Review Committee.

11. An interesting potential case of conflict between individual rights and the collective rights of a Cree community is resolved (Sec. 22.6.12) in favour of the collective rights of the community. That is, the local government is given veto power over interested individuals who wish to make a presentation to the committee. The freedom of speech of those individuals is curtailed by the rights of the community. Although it should be noted that various regulatory bodies (e.g., the National Energy Board) are empowered to decide who shall have leave to intervene (e.g., to question witnesses) they may be required to accept written submissions from any interested party. Thus, the provision in question appears to be a significant departure from practice elsewhere in Canada, and is clearly a departure from the widely acclaimed procedure used by Mr. Justice Berger in the hearings that preceded the issuing of the report discussed in the previous chapter. Whether Section 25 of the Charter of Rights and Freedoms can be used by a Cree government to protect its veto power, if challenged by an individual wishing to make a submission that the Cree government is blocking, is a matter yet to be tested in the courts.

12. The administrator is usually not a Cree. In the case of matters respecting provincial jurisdiction, the administrator is the Director of the Environmental Protection Service of the provincial government (or anyone authorized by the provincial cabinet). In the case of matters involving federal jurisdiction, the administrator is anyone authorized by the federal cabinet to exercise the functions of the administrator in the Agreement. Only in the case of the proposed developments on Category I lands is the administrator likely to be a Cree, for in such cases the administrator is the Cree local government administrator responsible for the protection of the environment.

13. The reactions of Manuel and others cited here are taken from *Indian News*, 17, 7, p. 6.
14. Although important differences do emerge in areas other than economic development, they are not our concern here.
15. Interview with the author, December 16, 1985.
16. However, as the Cree population expands and more Crees seek to enter the wildlife harvesting economy, it has been necessary to employ conservation measures such as reducing one's total harvest or sharing one's trap line with another family.
17. The James Bay Native Development Corporation, known as La Société de développement d'autochtones de la Baie James, has functioned mainly as a source of funds for entrepreneurs starting local small businesses.
18. This is precisely the same kind of problem envisaged in the concluding part of Chapter Three in the discussion of abolishing DIAND and transferring responsibility for providing services to Indians to other departments.
19. To the extent that this orientation is held by the Quebec public servants, it bespeaks a fundamental value conflict directly parallel to that discussed in Chapter Three. That is, similar orientations to that ascribed here to the Quebec public servants were found on the part of the staff of the Newfoundland Workmen's Compensation Board and the staff at DIAND, vis-à-vis their respective client groups.
20. Eugene Bardach, *The Implementation Game* (Cambridge, Mass.: M.I.T. Press, 1977), p. 38.
21. *Ibid.*, pp. 273-78. For further discussion of the implementation of public policy, see Jeffrey Pressman and Aaron Wildavsky, *Implementation*, Second Edition (Berkeley: University of California Press, 1979); Walter Williams, *The Implementation Perspective: A Guide for Managing Social Service Delivery Programs* (Berkeley: University of California Press, 1980).
22. The drowning of thousands of migrating caribou in 1984 due to a sudden change in the level of a river they had to cross was blamed by some on an upstream hydro dam, while others claimed that the dam prevented a worse disaster. If the former were to be proven true, it would provide yet another example of problems of implementing legal agreements that look good on paper.

Chapter Eight

Some Reflections on Indian Economic Development

by Cam Mackie

A recent conference on native women and economic development was the first conference for almost half the women there. Most of them were successful businesswomen whose companies included construction, restaurants, fine art stores, clothing manufacturing, consulting services, fishing lodge operations, and so on. The majority of the successful businesses had never received any financial support from government. They had done it the hard way, on their own initiative.

Like these successful women, many other Indian business leaders have contributed to their own economy and, indeed, to the economy of a whole country. Four B Manufacturing, owned by two brothers of Tyendinaga Reserve, sews shoe uppers for Bata and other shoe companies. The Sawridge Motor Hotel in Jasper, Alberta, owned by Sawridge Holdings of the Sawridge Band, creates jobs and income for both Natives and non-Natives. Tanizul Timber Ltd., owned by the Stewart Trembleur Band of B.C., has the largest tree-farm licence ever issued by the provincial government and is the source of timber and jobs for many people in the surrounding communities. These and many more companies and businesses are strong models for success. This chapter identifies the main ingredients for Indian business success and briefly describes some examples, but it is not a "how-to-do-it" manual.

Economic development occurs when a unique set of circumstances comes together. Briefly, the conditions are these:

1. There exists a *vision* or goal of individual and/or group economic self-reliance.
2. Individual *leadership* is exercised to achieve financial self-sufficiency, accumulate wealth, or build a powerful organization.
3. A conscious or unconscious *need* exists for a product or service among a sufficiently large group of potential buyers.
4. Sufficient *equity, capital, technology, raw materials,* and/or *human skills* can be brought together.

211

5. There is an acceptance of the idea that *profits* are required to create wealth for reinvestment so that *growth* in quantity and/or quality continues to occur.

If those are the general characteristics, what has the experience of the last twenty-five years taught us about specific situations? First, economic development on an individual, band, or regional level does not occur in a vacuum. The most successful business development experience has occurred in connection with other large-scale investments by outside organizations on reserves close to regions where economic growth is occurring at a reasonably steady pace. Major northern investments in resource exploitation have provided the engine that has driven much small, medium, and large-sized aboriginal business development. Where revenue from gas and oil discovery has been used wisely, long-term economic growth has occurred. Trucking and other transportation services have grown because of mines or hydroelectric development. Shopping centres have been successful where there is a large population of Indians and nonIndians. In larger urban areas that are expanding steadily, aboriginal economic development through small business creation and through individual enterprise has also taken place.

With the exception of a small number of service or retail businesses (e.g., hairdressing, small grocery or general stores, arcades, etc.) and building trades businesses related to construction, some aboriginal communities are too small to support many businesses by themselves. On the other hand, resource exploitation, where there is a strong outside market for the product, can be successful. Fishing and lumbering, while they have their ups and downs based on fluctuations of supply and demand in markets, and agriculture, particularly in the Prairie provinces, illustrate this point.

Second, the characteristics of business leaders, no matter what the social or cultural background, are different from those of political, religious, or educational leaders. Few people move comfortably in more than one field, and those who do find that to be successful in each they must act differently. Entrepreneurs are psychologically able to take risks, to see opportunities, to be decisive, and to create conditions within which other people do the things necessary to contribute to the success of the enterprise. Consensus may be useful to achieve a common perception of the vision, but it is no substitute for knowledge, skill, and decisive leadership.

Successful entrepreneurs in aboriginal communities often must assemble support from many people and organizations in order to proceed. This can involve much red tape, delay, Catch-22 situations, and other frustrations that often lead to a dissipation of energy and prevent the entrepreneur from concentrating his/her time and efforts on the primary objective of economic viability and profit-seeking.

Knowledge of good business practices is a must for any entrepreneur or economic development leader, as the Kahnawake economic development case studies illustrated. The simple maxim, ''If you haven't got it, buy it,'' applies in almost every field. Accounting and financial practice, marketing, legal requirements, techniques of purchasing, and the like all can be enhanced by having access to expertise. This may be available through government programs, hired consultants, or CESO (Canadian Executive Services Overseas – an organization of retired businesspersons who usually lend their expertise gratis to indigenous peoples' development efforts). Driben and Trudeau's research, cited in the introduction to this section, highlights the desirability of aboriginal control over such expertise.

While such expertise may be available inside or outside the local Indian community, perhaps the most important ingredient for future aboriginal economic success is the development of skilled, trained, and experienced aboriginal entrepreneurs. Access to every sort of training, from the two-week basic management programs offered by many community colleges and universities to MBA degrees from the top universities, will be required in the future if aboriginal economic self-sufficiency is to be achieved. Two encouraging developments in this regard are the Donner Canadian Foundation's funding of a university-level native management program and the emergence of native consulting firms that offer courses on the fundamentals of band management and business practice.

Third, economic development involves the exchange of goods or services for money. This, of course, means that someone must have something to sell (labour, knowledge, raw materials, finished goods) and someone must want to or be persuaded to buy. Every community has something to market, including the skill, knowledge, and ability of its human resources. The first steps are to take stock of what is available and to consider how resources can be exploited for the best long-term benefit. This can occur in many ways, including making a five-year plan, doing an opportunity analysis, and looking at what has been successful in the past or in similar communities elsewhere.

Past Experience

In a sense, economic development on Indian reserves both ended and began with the establishment of reserves. The economic process of barter, of sharing the products of the kill, of exchange of meats for fruits and vegetables, of the manufacture of implements and their use in trade to a large extent all ended with the establishment of the reserves. For approximately seventy-five years the economic development strategy of the federal government was to provide Indian people with a minimum of individual and personal support and through education in residential schools to achieve a level of integration with the larger society. Some attempts were made to establish an agricultural base, but for the most part up until the early 1960s little of substance occurred that would lead to any form of economic self-sufficiency.

During the mid-1960s, there emerged a program of community development that essentially became the vehicle for a wide-scale political awakening among aboriginal leaders. It taught organizing skills that reinforced a confrontation mentality. The Department of Indian Affairs and Northern Development itself seemed well organized to continue a confrontational mode.

During the early 1970s, DIAND established a loan fund (the Indian Economic Development Fund, or IEDF) and implemented a strategy of creating large-scale growth centres, motels, shopping centres, and major investments in forestry. This was consistent with regional economic development strategies being employed for non-aboriginal economic development in Canada at the same time. These were expected to promote growth in many communities. By 1976, 80 per cent of all DIAND's economic development funds, whether in loans or grants and contributions, was going to support fifty-five major projects, of which only five were assessed to be viable economic units in their own right.

While it is difficult to capture all of the data that would demonstrate the level of total investments made in Indian businesses over the years, Tables 11, 12, and 13 do provide some measures for recent years. Table 11 shows the number and dollar value of economic development applications approved in the form of direct loans from IEDF during the period 1978 to 1985. (For various reasons, an applicant whose application has been approved might not proceed; thus, some of the offers shown in the table were not accepted.) The number of approval offers issued fluctuates wildly from year to year, with no clear trend emerging. The same can be said about the dollar value of those

214

Table 11

IEDF Approval Offers, by Fiscal Year and Region, 1978-79 to 1984-85: Direct Loans Only

	Atlantic	Que.	Ont.	Man.	Sask.	Alta.	B.C.	Yukon	N.W.T.	Total
Direct Loans: Number										
1978-79	16	18	35	138	36	31	32	5	2	313
1979-80	10	22	39	94	56	17	14	6	0	258
1980-81	23	28	52	138	42	18	27	4	0	332
1981-82	30	34	59	38	48	25	41	3	0	281
1982-83	8	16	31	21	29	53	14	3	0	175
1983-84	18	20	8	118	47	65	37	2	0	315
1984-85	15	13	6	72	38	24	13	3	0	184
Total	120	151	230	619	296	233	178	29	2	1,858
Per cent	6.5	8.1	12.4	33.3	15.9	12.5	9.6	1.6	0.1	100.0
Direct Loans: Value ($'000s)										
1978-79	179	187	609	1,307	370	473	621	53	33	3,833
1979-80	129	426	379	1,202	605	284	291	93	0	3,410
1980-81	288	404	1,380	2,175	637	347	656	89	0	5,975
1981-82	490	595	1,246	615	794	343	1,036	71	0	5,189
1982-83	222	295	406	351	435	566	453	69	0	2,889
1983-84	460	290	117	1,651	921	961	1,089	42	0	5,331
1984-85	249	197	116	1,108	999	928	630	62	0	4,289
Total	2,017	2,394	4,253	8,409	4,761	3,902	4,776	479	33	31,116
Per cent	6.5	7.7	13.7	27.1	15.4	12.6	15.4	1.5	0.1	100.0

SOURCE: Program evaluation of Indian Economic Development Fund, DPA Group, June, 1985.

loans. In addition, there is considerable variation across regions in both the number and dollar value of approval offers for these IEDF loans. For instance, Manitoba is heavily over-represented: although it has about 15 per cent of the total Indian population in Canada and about 10 per cent of all Indian bands in Canada, it received fully one-third of the loan approval offers and over one-quarter of the amount of money in these offers. Conversely, British Columbia and Ontario are significantly under-represented.

Table 12 includes the direct loan data plus investments in the form of contributions and loan guarantees. These aggregate figures are slightly more stable than those in Table 11, although a dramatic decline did occur in 1984-85 as the effects of an earlier change in DIAND's strategy (see below) began to filter through the system. It should also be noted that the inter-regional distribution of IEDF financial support takes on a slightly different character in these aggregate figures compared to its character in the figures for direct loans alone. In the aggregate figures Quebec and, to a lesser extent, Alberta join Manitoba in being significantly over-represented (compared to both their proportion of the total Canadian Indian population and their proportion of the total number of bands in Canada) in the dollar value of approved offers. British Columbia and Ontario are still under-represented. The reasons for these inter-regional discrepancies are probably numerous and could include regional differences in culture, opportunities, awareness, entrepreneurial skills, grantsmanship experience and skills, DIAND staff orientations, and political factors, to name just a few. One final observation to be made here is that prior to the 1984-85 fiscal year the IEDF was committing about $23 million per year to Indian economic development, which if spread evenly across the 578 bands in Canada would be able to help one project in each band to the extent of about $39,000.

Table 13 reminds us that IEDF is not the only source of funding assistance for Indian economic development. Indeed, during the first half of the 1980s IEDF provided only about one-half of the funds on the projects it assisted. This table also gives us some insight into the human side of this funding program. That is, during the first half of this decade the projects in which IEDF participated had the potential of creating about 4,600 full-time or part-time jobs, or about two and one-half full- or part-time jobs per project (excluding ripple effects outside the project), although projects in B.C. and the North, for example, tended to be somewhat more labour-intensive than in Saskatchewan, Alberta, and the Atlantic provinces. For the country as a whole, each of the full- or part-time jobs thus created involved an investment of over $19,000, of which almost $10,000 came from IEDF.

216

Table 12

IEDF Approval Offers, by Fiscal Year and Region, 1978-79 to 1984-85: Direct Loans, Loan Guarantees, and Contributions

	Atlantic	Que.	Ont.	Man.	Sask.	Alta.	B.C.	Yukon	N.W.T.	Total
*All Offers: Number**										
1978-79	124	100	102	200	125	147	88	21	5	912
1979-80	69	75	141	182	180	218	56	17	19	957
1980-81	136	101	233	235	198	102	23	19	31	1,068
1981-82	132	163	205	158	182	103	255	20	8	1,230
1982-83	35	106	117	198	257	154	33	16	17	1,030
1983-84	33	119	66	356	216	151	66	7	17	1,033
1984-85	n.a	116	76	223	102	43	25	5	0	687
Total	≈600	780	940	1,552	1,260	918	546	105	97	≈6,910
Per cent	8.9	11.5	13.8	22.8	18.5	13.5	8.0	1.5	1.4	100.0
All Offers: Value ($'000s)										
1978-79	790	9,738	1,455	2,243	1,264	2,870	1,651	216	109	20,337
1979-80	436	11,340	1,901	2,870	2,010	4,446	1,032	243	372	24,650
1980-81	934	2,583	3,814	6,727	1,981	4,925	1,880	359	314	23,517
1981-82	885	2,950	3,334	5,186	3,255	3,820	3,408	212	142	23,152
1982-83	826	2,010	1,682	4,983	5,081	3,980	2,334	214	195	21,306
1983-84	619	2,646	813	6,711	3,761	4,992	3,287	143	203	23,175
1984-85	345	1,335	1,203	5,838	2,157	2,199	879	80	0	14,036
Total	4,835	32,602	14,202	34,558	19,509	27,232	14,471	1,467	1,335	150,173
Per cent	3.2	21.7	9.5	23.0	13.0	18.1	9.8	0.9	0.9	100.0

* Not all offers are accepted. Loans, etc. to Indian institutions are included in relevant provinces.

SOURCE: Program evaluation of Indian Economic Development Fund, DPA Group, June, 1985.

Table 13

Profile of Economic Development Projects in which IEDF Participated, 1980-81 to 1984-85, by Region

	Total Country	Atlantic	Que.	Ont.	Man.	Sask.	Alta.	B.C.	Yukon	N.W.T.
Projects assisted (No.)	1,880*	104	138	329	401	190	382	250	42	44
Total investment** ($ million)	88.3	2.2	8.1	11.8	20.2	7.3	9.9	19.4	3.4	6.1
Total IEDF funding*** ($ million)	45.2	1.7	4.5	7.8	12.5	3.7	7.5	4.9	1.6	1.0
IEDF as % of total	51	77	56	67	62	50	76	25	47	17
Potential jobs**** (No.)	4,610	196	360	901	950	298	726	834	127	218
Potential jobs/project	2.5	1.9	2.6	2.7	2.4	1.6	1.9	3.3	3.0	5.0
Investment/job ($)	19,160	11,070	22,380	13,050	5,081	24,590	13,600	23,230	27,090	28,070
IEDF funding/job ($)	9,800	8,520	12,430	8,010	3,150	12,250	10,390	5,840	12,810	4,680

* 1,490 projects were in operation as of June, 1985.

** From all sources.

*** Including direct loans, loan guarantees, and contributions.

**** Includes both part- and full-time jobs.

SOURCE: IEDF special tabulation.

However, even in southern Canada these figures on total investment per job varied enormously across the country, from a high of around $25,000 in Saskatchewan to a low of about $5,000 in neighbouring Manitoba.

Throughout the 1970s and 1980s successful individual entrepreneurs have emerged. Max Gros-Louis in Quebec, working from his reserve close to Quebec City with his own arts and crafts sales and distribution operation, is one good illustration. Others are the Derrickson family in British Columbia and Fred Gladstone and his cattle business in Alberta. Willie Wilson in Ontario took advantage of many government programs, hired expertise, and set up a number of successful businesses, including a sawmill, general store, and laundromat.

The notion of participation and the need for fairly equitable distribution of resources emerged from the community economic development experience and from the concentration of efforts on major projects. In the early 1980s the Indian Affairs strategy shifted to distribution of economic development funds on a regional, tribal, or band basis for use largely by local economic development officers for salaries and expenses. The amount of money available for investment directly into specific enterprises was further reduced by the need to build and develop infrastructure in primary resource industries, most notably agriculture.

In October, 1983, the Native Economic Development Program (NEDP) came to fruition with the appointment of an advisory board of aboriginal people from all parts of the country. After considerable deliberation, the board gave its advice to the government; this resulted in the current NEDP. As recommended, the NEDP followed a strategy of attempting to create a pool of capital under the ownership, control, and management of aboriginal people through a series of financial and economic development institutions, including trust companies, loan companies, development corporations, and venture capital operations. All of these institutions were to have the shared characteristics of being in a position to invest or lend money to Indian businesses, from which they would receive a return. In this way, they would continue to accumulate a capital base from which economic development could occur long after NEDP itself was finished. The same initial investment would be multiplied in value over a number of years. As loans are paid off or interest is paid on investments, this money would be used for new loans and investments. If managed well, these loans or investments would lever funds from other individual and commercial sources.

The second element of the program focuses on those communities in which little or no economic activity is now occurring. This community economic development element is intended to bring together the knowledge of the last twenty-five years in a concentrated approach to twenty-five to thirty-five communities, determine the most successful approaches required, and be the basis for further policy recommendations to the federal government. Essentially, this process should provide an opportunity to concentrate efforts on identifying specific business opportunities, ensuring that human and other resources are available, and putting in place appropriate financial support.

The third element of NEDP is designed to support the first two. Its primary functions are to fund marketing analysis, to fund research into new products, and to fund the education of highly skilled aboriginal people to take on major and senior management roles. In addition, it has a minor capacity to support specific business proposals, which ultimately the major financial institutions would be in a position to support.

Finally, NEDP seeks to bring together all of the available resources of the various federal government departments and programs to focus their efforts in support of aboriginal economic development.

Table 14 shows the number and dollar value of funding requests to NEDP from its inception to October, 1985. These figures are broken down by province and by the three elements of the program described above. Readers are reminded that about one-fifth of the proposals received by NEDP have the potential for being supported in whole or in part, and that the data presented in the table are for all aboriginal peoples, not just for status Indians. The table demonstrates that the second element, "community-based economic development initiatives," is dwarfed by the other two elements, insofar as both applications received and dollar value of those applications are concerned. Those other two elements are approximately equal in terms of funds requested, but the vast majority (79 per cent) of all proposals received are for the "special projects" (e.g., market analysis research, product development research) element of the program. Two other highlights of the table should also be mentioned. One is the extremely heavy recourse to the program that Albertans hope to have; applications from Alberta alone amount to 38 per cent of the funds requested. This large figure comes not because Albertans have submitted a large number of applications but because the dollar value of a small number of applications is very large. Discounting the dollar value of these few unrealistic applications would place the average value of applications from Alberta on a par with the other Prairie provinces. However, the total amounts requested go considerably beyond the total funds available in the program. Nevertheless, the number of proposals arriving monthly has not diminished. Instead, the competition for NEDP

Table 14

Projects Accepted for Consideration of Funding by NEDP, by Program Element and Province, to October, 1985 ($000s)

Province	Element I: Financial/Economic Institutions		Element II: Community-based Economic Development Initiatives		Element III: Special Projects		Total	
	No.	NEDP Funding Requested	No.	NEDP Funding Requested	No.	NEDP Funding Requested	No.	NEDP Funding Requested
British Columbia	15	63,300	16	700	133	77,400	164	141,400
Alberta	10	93,000	3	–	53	193,800	66	286,800
Saskatchewan	17	53,400	5	–	72	23,600	94	77,000
Manitoba	15	5,800	8	1,500	80	30,300	103	37,600
Ontario	15	42,600	11	800	103	26,100	129	69,500
Quebec	12	79,300	3	200	48	13,000	63	92,500
Newfoundland	1	100	1	300	11	2,200	13	2,600
New Brunswick	2	400	1	200	12	1,800	15	2,400
Nova Scotia	3	300	1	–	21	2,300	25	2,600
Prince Edward Island	1	–	1	–	2	200	4	200
Yukon	1	7,200	3	300	7	3,100	11	10,600
Northwest Territories	4	19,000	2	300	16	8,700	22	28,000
Total	96	364,400	55	4,300	558	382,400	709	751,200

funds has grown, for the quality of the proposals received has begun to improve significantly as applicants become aware that the program seeks to fund only strong business proposals.

Major gaps exist in government support for economic development. Most important is the still limited investment in primary resource exploitation, particularly in the renewable resources of forestry, fishing, agriculture, and trapping. While the acceleration of business development and business opportunity will provide many new jobs and create wealth for future investment purposes, much needs to be done to fulfil the highest potential of aboriginal communities in the midst of and surrounded by rich natural resources. The situation with regard to agriculture on reserves illustrates this point. A recent NEDP study of Indian agriculture in Ontario and the four western provinces found that there are approximately 1,650 Indian-operated farms on reserves in these five provinces. Table 15 shows the location of these farms by province and their estimated annual sales, the latter of which amounts to approximately $35 million per year. The land involved is widely distributed in each province and appears, on average, to be of approximately the same quality as other farmlands in those five provinces. Although its potential productivity is influenced by such factors as climate and access to markets, it has been concluded that the potential production (valued at current prices) could be increased from current levels to approximately $200 million.

The large difference between actual and potential production is attributable to a number of factors. For instance, much of the land is undeveloped or underdeveloped and typically requires clearing, breaking, draining, fencing, or other improvements before any output or full potential output can be achieved. Second, investment in buildings, machinery, livestock, and other factors of production is generally low

Table 15

Farms on Indian Reserves in Ontario and the West

Province	Number of Farms	Estimated Sales ($ million)	Acres	Hectares
Ontario	137	1.0	153,000	61,200
Manitoba	225	4.0	170,000	68,000
Saskatchewan	640	15.7	1,000,000	400,000
Alberta	450	8.3	919,400	367,800
British Columbia	200	6.3	130,000	52,000
Total	1,652	35.0	2,372,400	949,000

and must be increased before full output can be reached. Third, access to technical information is limited and a shortage of developed farm management skills exists. Fourth, farmers' limited access to short-, medium-, and long-term credit adversely affects the ability of farmers to apply appropriate levels of capital investment to the land. Furthermore, the land-tenure agreements in some cases on some reserves discourage or prevent the development of viable farms. Finally, some of the land is presently rented to nonIndian farmers. If the full potential of farms on Indian reserves were to be realized, it would provide the equivalent of almost 6,000 full person years of employment on an ongoing basis.

Illustrations of Success

At present, there are well over 750 successful Indian businesses in Canada with new ones forming rapidly. The following cases illustrate successes in a number of fields but they should not necessarily be considered the most successful. At best they illustrate what clear vision, persistence, and individual leadership have achieved.

Recalma Enterprises Ltd.
Recalma Enterprises Ltd. was registered as a business in British Columbia in 1978. Its purpose is to own net gear and general equipment for two vessels, the *Sea Lock* and the *Quilicum Producer*. In addition, in 1979, the *Gulf Grenadier*, an ocean-going groundfish trawler, was added to the firm's fleet.

The firm is operated by a father and son who are members of the Quilicum Indian Band and hold elected offices in the band. Over the years the father and his wife have operated a number of businesses where they have acquired experience with a wide variety of labour relations, union, and other business issues.

The crews on the seiners *Sea Lock* and *Quilicum Producer* are Natives. The *Gulf Grenadier* is required by law to have on board a ticketed master, mate, and engineer. The standards of the industry establish that a skipper has the right to hire all crew members except the engineer. The current skipper is from Newfoundland and has hired six non-Natives as crew. Another member of the owner's family works on the *Gulf Grenadier* and expects to have his ticket soon. This will result in more Natives having an opportunity to work on the boat.

The *Gulf Grenadier* is used for formal training in conjunction with Malaspina College in Nanaimo, B.C. Upon completion, successful trainees can be offered full-time positions on the *Gulf Grenadier* and share fully in the profits of the venture. Eventually, two full native crews are expected to work the *Gulf Grenadier*. Associated businesses include the Quilicum Indian Band Processing Plant, which will be supplied by the *Gulf Grenadier* and other ships of Recalma Enterprises.

This privately owned business has taken advantage of opportunities to expand and develop. It now provides income for its owners and jobs for people of its community. It is an Indian example of the old adage: "If you give a man a fish, he will eat today. If you teach a man to fish, he will eat forever. If he can catch enough fish and sell, he can feed the rest of us too!"

Pimee Well Servicing Ltd.
Pimee Well Servicing Ltd. is a company owned by the Tribal Chiefs Association of Northeastern Alberta. All of the issued shares are held in trust for each band by the chief of the band. For a number of years, the Tribal Council and various bands have sought opportunities to develop businesses associated with the oil industry. Following much discussion, an agreement was reached between Pimee Well Servicing Ltd. and Esso Resources. Funding was received from a number of sources, including a large equity investment by the bands themselves. In brief, the agreement with Esso guarantees a market for Pimee services for three years at going market rates. Esso further guaranteed to buy back the service rig and associated equipment at fair market value at the end of the three-year period if Pimee so requested. In addition, Esso agreed to provide an experienced tool-push (a rig worker) and an experienced manager during the training period for each of the four skilled positions on the rig.

At the end of the three-year agreement, Pimee will have fulfilled its contractual obligations to Esso Resources, will have a crew trained in the operation and management of a well-servicing rig, and will have the opportunity of bidding on ongoing contracts. In addition, the Tribal Chiefs Association of Northeastern Alberta will have gained a presence in the oil industry.

This project illustrates both the persistence required and opportunities that exist for the development of joint ventures with existing major non-native corporations. The jobs created are well paid and provide access to other positions in the oil industry. The potential for growth of the business in the area is high and the level of equity invested in the project by the Tribal Chiefs Association and individual bands assures a commitment to its success. Many examples of similar Indian-owned companies related to resource extraction exist. Sinco Trucking Ltd. in Saskatchewan and Neegan Construction Ltd. in northern Alberta have followed similar patterns.

Chippewas of Rama Ltd. (455457 Ontario Inc.)
The Chippewas of Rama is a share capital company wholly owned by the Rama Band in Ontario. The corporation was established in 1979 to own and operate the Rama industrial mall. The mall contains 40,000 square feet of space and the land tenure is by virtue of a land surrender and lease that has another forty years to run. The mall has been fully leased since it was opened.

The Rama Band has an on-reserve population of approximately 350 and is located near Orillia, Ontario. By using a portion of its land to provide space for industrial development as well as for other uses, the Chippewas of Rama have ensured that employment for band members will continue to be available. Over 100 jobs, of which approximately 60 per cent are filled by men and women of the Rama Band, have been created as a result of the band's initiative.

There are various other examples of Indian economic development ventures that could be cited, such as the use of clay deposits for the manufacture of bricks, the sale of sand and gravel deposits, the use of reserve lands for recreational purposes, and the use of land adjacent to major urban areas for golf course development (a tough business, as many can attest). In some situations, business and political leaders must look at the major resources available to them, as the Chippewas of Rama have done. A willing work force and land used to create an opportunity for small or medium-sized industry can be brought together for wider benefit. In some cases this can be done using the principles of community development.

Community Economic Development

The concept of community development places much emphasis on the participation and involvement of community members in identifying and resolving community problems. The concept of economic development emphasizes entrepreneurship, return on investment, and financially self-supporting activity. Combining the two makes a very powerful tool for community change. From a business point of view, the participation element usually takes the form of shared ownership, partnerships, or employer-employee joint ventures. Leadership lies with a board of directors whose members hire officers to manage within the bounds of good management practice. Freedom to respond to opportunities and to make decisions that will not be routinely called into question characterize the day-to-day action of business.

The community development process has often achieved a high degree of consensus among community members in identifying commonly held concerns and in resolving them over time through a process of gathering information, sharing analysis, testing options, taking action, and reassessing the effects of that action on the perceived problem. This process is characterized by open communications and by a leadership that varies depending on the membership of the community and the issue to be resolved.

Economic development in many Indian communities needs to draw on the aforementioned community development processes. Without a process of preparation, participation, identification of economic options, and the commitment of substantial numbers of people in the community, many Indian economic development activities will not succeed. Often, economic development will necessitate major changes in the way in which people participate in the economy or in the traditional use of physical resources. For instance, some people will have to change from a reliance on seasonal hunting and trapping to a primary reliance on steady wage or salaried work, and some reserve lands will come to be used for purposes of nonIndians' recreation rather than for traditional purposes. Such major changes will be successful only if widely accepted and if there is a commitment on the part of many members of the band or community to participate in, and work on, the new activities.

If any level of economic self-sufficiency is to be reached by many aboriginal communities, the skills and knowledge gained through twenty years of community development practice in Canada must now be applied in concert with the application of business skills and the attempt to create economic opportunities. Freeman Compton, long a contributor to the community development process and practice, has written: "I am just like any man; I do best those things I plan." Community-based economic development is one of the waves of the future for Indians in Canada, and it will require thoughtful planning on the part of those involved.

Part Three

Aboriginal Rights and Claims

Editor's Introduction

The concept of aboriginal rights is a shifting one that is subject to different interpretations across different aboriginal groups in Canada, across different nonIndian governments, and across time. Indeed, the concept has become politicized and is still evolving in the minds of aboriginal political leaders and strategists. With new political, legal, constitutional, and judicial developments, nonIndian governments also change their conception of aboriginal rights, sometimes quite drastically over a short period of time.

The Meaning of Aboriginal Rights

There is no concrete entity to which we can point and say "This is aboriginal rights." Instead, rights are socio-political-legal constructions with a foundation in the moral order of a society. Furthermore, societal conceptions of morality change over time. To take an example from outside the realm of Indian affairs, only in the 1980s has there emerged the notion that adopted children have the *right* to know something about their "natural" parents. In fact, this is still contentious in some quarters, as are some much longer-established civil rights. Given that state of flux and contention, any definition or description presented here must be recognized as merely one interpretation.

Aboriginal rights are the rights held by the descendants of the original peoples of Canada by virtue of their ancestors' occupancy of the land since time immemorial.[1] In the broadest contemporary usage of the term, those rights are multi-faceted. A crucial component of aboriginal rights is the right to retain one's aboriginal identity and culture rather than being subjected to forced assimilation. (Jordan's chapter addresses this dimension.) This implies not only certain educational rights, but also the right of a child to be raised in his/her aboriginal culture if placed in an adoptive or foster home. Included among aboriginal rights is the right to be free to choose between a non-aboriginal way of life and an aboriginal way of life. Such a right is violated if economic or other societal developments (e.g., clear-cut logging, strip-mining, flooding from hydroelectric dams) ruin the natural environment and ecosystem on which the aboriginal economy depends.

Another aspect of aboriginal rights is the right to have self-governing aboriginal institutions that provide at least as much self-determination for aboriginal peoples as is enjoyed by other Canadians. The National Indian Brotherhood (forerunner to the Assembly of First Nations) has listed twenty-four jurisdictional areas that would fall under the domain of Indian governments: (1) band constitutions; (2) citizenship; (3) land; (4) water; (5) air; (6) forestry; (7) minerals; (8) oil and gas; (9) migratory birds; (10) wildlife; (11) fisheries; (12) conservation; (13) environment; (14) economic development; (15) education; (16) social development; (17) health and welfare; (18) marriage; (19) cultural development; (20) communications; (21) revenues; (22) justice; (23) Indian law enforcement; and (24) local and private matters. In these areas – the list is virtually exhaustive – Indian law would prevail on Indian territory, and that law might differ significantly from nonIndian law.

As is implied in the foregoing, aboriginal rights involve the right to an adequate land base so that the other aspects of aboriginal rights are not nullified in practice once they have been recognized in law. That land base takes on not just political and economic significance, but also spiritual significance, as Little Bear's chapter below attests.

Finally, since most of these aspects of aboriginal rights have been violated down through Canada's history, aboriginal rights include the right to compensation for past infringements on these rights. The creation of new opportunities to overcome existing disadvantages of aboriginal peoples and to provide attractive alternative paths of development for the future is an approach to compensation that is widely regarded by Aboriginals and non-Aboriginals alike as appropriate.

Legal Aspects of Aboriginal Rights

From the above we can see that aboriginal rights involve far more than just the land claims that so often attract media attention. Land, however, is a crucial component and accordingly is the main focus of attention in the Little Bear chapter. In that chapter the author examines legal aspects of aboriginal land rights in a broad context and from an Indian point of view. Even the reader who has little interest in law may find Little Bear's eloquent description of aboriginal philosophy to be enlightening. Furthermore, his discussion of the standards of international law, of British law, and of Canadian disregard for those well-established standards also conveys important insights that can help us understand the sense of grievance that fuels the determination brought to the constitutional bargaining table by aboriginal leaders.

By way of background to Little Bear's chapter, it is useful to bear in mind the ethnocentrism that has characterized the Canadian courts' approach to aboriginal rights and the approach of Britain before that. As Michael Asch has observed,[2] ethnocentrism has been at the heart of the British orientation to aboriginal rights, has carried through in Canadian court rulings to the present, and will die a slow death. Asch points out that it was easier for the British to recognize ongoing legal rights in newly acquired territories if the local inhabitants had traditions and values similar to those of the British. To get their rights legally recognized in court, aboriginal peoples have had to demonstrate that their law at the time of first contact with the Europeans was recognizable in British eyes (because of its similarity to British law). Asch notes, though, that Canadian legal traditions have developed primarily around the proposition that the aboriginal peoples of Canada were too primitive to have such a legal system. He goes on to say that the decision of the Supreme Court of Canada in the 1973 Calder case (discussed in Little Bear's chapter) represented a major breakthrough in ruling that some Indians (in this case the Nishgas) did have such "advanced" legal systems; however, it was also a continuation of ethnocentrism in that it remains necessary for aboriginal rights claimants to prove to the courts that they were "civilized" at the time of first contact with the Europeans. Asch finds this same ethnocentric strain appearing in the judgement issued by the Supreme Court of Canada in the 1980 Baker Lake case dealing with the aboriginal rights of the Inuit.

Another important point of context for Little Bear's chapter is the Royal Proclamation of 1763, for many Indian peoples in Canada trace their aboriginal rights to this document. As Gibbins notes in his chapter below, this Proclamation has been deemed sufficiently important to have been incorporated into the new Canadian constitution. Indeed, it has been called the Magna Carta of Canadian Indians. The Proclamation, issued by the King of England, reads in part:

> [W]hereas it is just and reasonable, and essential to our interest and the security of our colonies, that the several nations or tribes of Indians with whom We are connected and who live under our protection should not be molested or disturbed in the possession of such parts of our dominions and territories as, not having been ceded to or purchased by us, are reserved for them . . . as their hunting grounds. We do therefore . . . declare it to be our royal will and pleasure that no governor or commander-in-chief in any of our colonies of Quebec, East Florida or

West Florida do presume, upon any pretense whatever, to grant [permission to survey and settle upon] lands beyond the bounds of their respective governments. . . .

And We do further declare it to be our royal will and pleasure for the present as aforesaid, to reserve under our sovereignty, protection, and dominion, for the use of said Indians, all the lands and territories not included within the limits of our said three new governments or within the limits of the territory granted to the Hudson's Bay Company. . . .

And We do hereby strictly forbid, on pain of our displeasure, all our loving subjects from making any purchases or settlements whatever, or taking possession of any of the lands above reserved, without our special leave and licence for that purpose first obtained.

And we do further strictly enjoin and require all persons who have either wilfully or inadvertently seated themselves upon any lands within the countries above described, or upon any other lands which, not having been ceded to or purchased by Us, are still reserved to the said Indians . . . to forthwith remove themselves from such settlements.

And whereas great frauds and abuses have been committed in purchasing lands of the Indians . . . [We do] strictly enjoin and require that no private person do presume to make any purchase from the said Indians of any lands reserved to the said Indians . . . ; but that, if at any time any of the said Indians should be inclined to dispose of the said lands, the same shall be purchased only for Us, in our name, at some public meeting or assembly of the said Indians to be held for that purpose. . . .

Little Bear's chapter discusses two landmark Canadian court cases in which this Proclamation became a central issue. In the first of those cases certain phrases quoted above come to life to take on pivotal significance in the resolution of the case.

Aboriginal rights are not just a concoction of ambitious Indian lawyers and politicians. As Little Bear notes, they are now recognized by the highest court in our land, as well as internationally. They have also been formally recognized in such land claims agreements as the James Bay and Northern Quebec Agreement (1975), where nonIndian governments have paid sums of money to extinguish those rights. Similarly, the negotiating stance of the federal government in other land claims negotiations (e.g., Yukon) has explicitly recognized the existence of aboriginal rights and sought to "buy them out." More importantly, Section 35.1 of the Constitution Act, 1982, states that "The existing aboriginal and treaty rights of the aboriginal peoples of Canada are hereby recognized and affirmed" and the constitutional amendment proclamation (1983) enshrined in the constitution a series of conferences, involving the Prime Minister, the provincial premiers, and aboriginal leaders, whose purpose was to deal with the definition and identification of those "existing aboriginal rights."[3] This is far removed from the position taken by the federal government in its 1969 white paper on Indian affairs, where aboriginal rights were dismissed almost casually. It is also far removed from the Constitution Act (British North America Act) of 1867, in which no mention was made of aboriginal rights and the only mention of aboriginal peoples was in Section 91.24, where "Indians and the lands reserved for the Indians" were listed among the responsibilities falling under the federal government's jurisdiction.

Sovereignty

One of the issues that has arisen in conjunction with the legal aspects of aboriginal rights is that of sovereignty. Like the term "aboriginal rights," the term "sovereignty" or "sovereign authority" has different meanings for different users and at different times. "Sovereignty," however, evokes emotional responses that "aboriginal rights" does not, for in the minds of nonIndian politicians the term sovereignty is associated with the threat posed to Canada by the sovereignty-association platform of the Parti Québécois in Quebec. The term is also of major significance to those Indian leaders who believe that because Indians never surrendered their right to self-government, Indian governments today retain sovereign authority. To them some implications of this are, first, that as sovereign nations they should not have their rights cited in the constitution of another country (Canada), and second, that it is inappropriate for the federal or provincial government to delegate powers to Indian governments as if Indian governments are of a subordinate nature. Thus, adherents to this position do not seek to have powers granted or delegated to them by other governments in Canada, but rather to have Canadian governments pass "confirmatory legislation" that recognizes Indian governments and enables Canadian governments to engage in relations with them.

Although some proponents of this position, such as the Assembly of First Nations, have recently softened their stand, other organizations, including the Prairie Treaty Nations Alliance, have not. The rhetoric adopted by some of the latter is forceful and articulate and appears to be designed as much to instil or reinforce a sense of pride among Indian constituents as to stake out a position in negotiations with non-Indian politicians. One example is to be found at the 1984 First Ministers Conference on Aboriginal Constitutional Matters, when Chief Billy Two Rivers of the Kahnawake Mohawk Council said:

The Haudenosaunee Six Nations Confederacy have no desire to separate from Canada, since the Confederacy have never been part of Canada. . . . [T]he new constitution that has been granted to the Parliament of Canada by Great Britain will have no jurisdictional authority within our territories or over our people. Our people are citizens of our nation and do not seek citizenship within the nation of Canada.[4]

Another example is to be found in the earlier thought of the Assembly of First Nations. The following passage, from the Declaration of the First Nations, adopted by the AFN in 1980, touches on the spiritual dimension of Indian demands for the recognition of Indian sovereignty:

We the original people of the Land know the Creator put us here. We have maintained our freedom, our languages, and our traditions from time immemorial. We continue to exercise the rights and fulfill the responsibilities and obligations given to us by the Creator for the Land upon which we were placed. The Creator has given us the right to govern ourselves and the right to self-determination. The rights and responsibilities given to us by the Creator cannot be altered or taken away by any other nation.[5]

A final example is the Dene Declaration issued by the Dene of the Northwest Territories (1975). It is explicitly cast in a decolonization framework:

We the Dene of the Northwest Territories insist on the right to be regarded by ourselves and the world as a nation. . . .

As once Europe was the exclusive homeland of the European peoples, Africa the exclusive homeland of the African peoples, the New World, North and South America, was the exclusive homeland of Aboriginal peoples of the New World, the Amerindian and the Inuit.

The New World, like other parts of the world, has suffered the experience of colonialism and imperialism. Other peoples have occupied the land – often with force – and foreign governments have imposed themselves on our people. . . .

Colonialism and imperialism are now dead or dying. Recent years have witnessed the birth of new nations or rebirth of old nations out of the ashes of colonialism. . . .

The African and Asian peoples – the peoples of the Third World – have fought for and won the right to self-determination, the right to recognition as distinct peoples and the recognition of themselves as nations.

But in the New World the Native peoples have not faired so well. . . .

The Dene find themselves as part of a country. That country is Canada. But the Government of Canada is not the government of the Dene. The

Government of the Northwest Territories is not the government of the Dene. These governments were not the choice of the Dene, they were imposed upon the Dene. . . .

And while there are realities we are forced to submit to, such as the existence of a country called Canada, we insist on the right to self-determination as a distinct people and the recognition of the Dene Nation. . . .

We the Dene are part of the Fourth World. . . . What we seek, then, is independence and self-determination within the country of Canada. This is what we mean when we call for a just land settlement for the Dene Nation.

Although the topic of sovereignty could sustain a separate book of its own, I shall close this discussion of the term with just a few additional comments. First, we should bear in mind that sovereignty is a malleable concept. As Boldt and Long have written,

> The history of the doctrine of sovereignty is the history of competing and often conflicting claims to the legitimate exercise of authority. The various doctrines of sovereignty represent ethical-philosophical rationalizations of particular power arrangements – rationalizations that were developed by or on behalf of those in power or those seeking power. Each state developed its own theories of sovereignty to justify particular internal social arrangements, whether religious or secular, absolutist or relative, political or legal, coercive or popular, hierarchical or egalitarian. Thus, theories were framed to legitimate the Crown or eliminate the Crown, to justify the power of the state or proclaim the power of the people. . . .[6]

It is important, as well, to realize that the element of hierarchical authority implicit in European concepts of sovereignty is missing in the original Indian world views. As Boldt and Long point out,[7] Indians invested their customs and traditions – not their chiefs or elders – with the authority to guide their behaviour. For Indians to adopt European, "democratic," hierarchical forms of government in order to claim sovereignty and in turn counter the destructive effects of Eurocanadian society is to violate some fundamental Indian values. In some Indian communities it might also relegate members of the community to the periphery of decision-making and create an Indian political-administrative elite with a vested interest in maintaining the externally imposed authority structure. Other models, based on the community rather than on the state, may be needed.[8]

The Aboriginal Right to an Aboriginal Identity

Equally as fundamental as the legal and sovereignty aspects of aboriginal rights is the aboriginal right to an aboriginal identity. This is addressed in Jordan's chapter, where she examines, in an international context, education as it relates to aboriginal identity.

Education is one of the most influential societal institutions for instilling an identity in children. In contemporary society it is also a virtual prerequisite for those who seek to enjoy a freedom to choose an occupation that maximizes stimulation, challenge, and fulfilment and minimizes monotony. Increasingly, advanced education is becoming necessary for the acquisition of those research, legal, and administrative and other skills needed by aboriginal communities to increase their level of self-determination and to fulfil the potential offered by the legal recognition of aboriginal rights.

Until the mid-1970s, and to a certain extent even today, education functioned more to undermine aboriginal rights than to bring them to fruition. The content, staffing, mode of delivery, and atmosphere of Indian education were the antithesis of learning as it occurred in Indian society. Education was explicitly designated as a vehicle for the ethnocentric colonial policy of assimilation. As such, it succeeded in alienating many Indians from their formerly positive self-concept, thereby introducing a certain bifurcation of identity. For many Indians that split identity (Indian and nonIndian) created confusion or guilt or lack of self-confidence, alienated them from their culture and their parents, and caused them to leave school early, ill-equipped to function well in either society. Some are still struggling with the effects of this whole phenomenon today. Thus, while some Indians seek to reclaim Indian lands or sovereignty or legal rights, others are involved in an individual or community struggle to reclaim their Indian identity. Jordan recounts how this pattern has occurred among various indigenous peoples abroad and discusses their efforts to take control over the education of their children as a first step toward making that education work for them rather than against them.

She frequently refers to "theory" and "theorizing." In so doing, she is not speaking of grandiose intellectual endeavours by genius philosophers or aboriginal Albert Einsteins. Instead, she is referring to a much more common phenomenon, that of seeking to develop an understanding of "what's going on" in a situation (an understanding of how that situation "works") and then developing a plan of action to change, cope with, or otherwise respond to that situation. In that sense, all public policy and programs of reform, including educational policy and reform formulated by aboriginal peoples, is theorizing or hypothesis testing. That is, policy formulation and implementation is based on a causal model that hypothesizes that factor "A" causes or influences factor "B," and therefore that an increase in the amount of factor "A" present will produce some degree of change in the desired direction in factor "B."

Jordan's survey of the decolonization of education in three countries also offers some lessons for those pursuing decolonization in other institutional spheres. One of these involves the pace of change. She points out that in some communities the need for reform was so great and so urgent that it caused people to move forward with reforms at a pace too rapid for those reforms to be absorbed and consolidated by the communities. Thus, the reforms were jeopardized and, in some communities, presumably overturned. The optimum pace at which reform should be implemented is a matter of judgement, and one of the contributions of Jordan's chapter lies in that reminder to practitioners.

Other comments made by Jordan are also equally applicable to the broader phenomenon of Indian government. For instance, she points to the importance of community size, not only in regard to the shortage of highly skilled persons in small communities and in regard to the fact that some of the most creative teachers may be drawn away from teaching to fill other developmental roles inside or outside their local community, but also in relation to the curtailed opportunity structures that highly educated people encounter in small communities. She points, as well, to a danger implied in the above remarks on sovereignty. That is, rather than offering self-determination through the creation of distinctively aboriginal structures, local control can (under some circumstances) be reduced to the mere management of a white program, a white organization, and white methodologies. The fact that her observations are based on more than one country makes them all the more worthy of close consideration.

Aboriginal "Claims": Terminology, Ideology, and Action

James Frideres's chapter below is entitled "Native Claims and Settlement in Yukon." As innocuous as that title or the phrase "aboriginal claims" may seem, the very term "claim" and the present "claims settlement" process can prompt impassioned debates in Indian political circles. Past governmental behaviours have both produced the need for a claims settlement process and generated the distrust that lies behind the rejection of the current claims settlement regime. It is useful to be aware of some of the detail of the ideology of distrust that forms the backdrop against which the Yukon Agreement in Principle is being received in some parts of Canada, including some Yukon communities. That distrust is a pervasive feature of the government-Indian relationship and affects people's perceptions of unfolding events in that relationship. It has also become mobilized as a political resource in the presidential politics of the Assembly of First Nations.

The main proponents of the ideology of distrust are those Indians whose suspicion of nonIndian governments has led them to be very wary of most nonIndian proposals. These Indian leaders reject the term "claim" as a code word or shorthand designation for a much broader governmental orientation that their rhetoric labels "genocidal." Other vocabulary used in conveying this world view includes such words as "assimilation," "extinguishment," and "municipalization." Adherents to this ideology diagnose the main threat to Indians as being the government's alleged attempts to implement the assimilationist 1969 white paper. The Office of Native Claims, a branch of the Department of Indian Affairs and Northern Development, is viewed as one of the main vehicles for this policy.[9] Evidence for this belief is found in its basic policy of negotiating the *extinguishment* of aboriginal rights in land claims settlements. Furthermore, because the Office of Native Claims does not concern itself exclusively with the grievances of status Indians and instead deals with the claims of other native peoples as well, this is taken as proof of its alleged mandate to dilute the special rights and legal status of registered Indians (especially treaty Indians), preparatory to responsibility for Indians being transferred to the provinces. Indians, however, have no special legal arrangements with the provinces. For instance, unlike the federal government, the provinces have no legal trust obligations to Indians. Thus, Indians believe that they would quickly come to be treated like any other citizens if jurisdictional responsibility were transferred from the federal government to the provinces. That equal status, as opposed to special status and the implementation of aboriginal rights, is viewed as inherently assimilative.

The "municipalization" component of this ideology is also traceable, in part, to the Office of Native Claims. In the view of adherents to this ideology, settlements negotiated by the Office of Native Claims have tended not only to extinguish aboriginal rights but also to reduce

Indian nations to the status of mere municipalities, or less, in the eyes of the law. This is also the likely outcome of participation in constitutional negotiations, according to this belief system, for such negotiations are not likely to recognize contemporary Indian sovereignty; instead, they are likely to lead to the delegation of powers from federal or provincial governments to Indian governments in the same manner that municipalities, as mere creations of provincial governments (under such legislation as the Municipalities Act of Alberta), have powers delegated to them by the province. That the present Minister of Indian Affairs and Northern Development is a former municipal mayor who has emphasized local Indian community development rather than promoted the recognition of sovereign Indian governments is taken as further confirmation of the validity of this view. Specific developments in the field, such as the proposed creation of near-municipality status for the Sechelt Band of British Columbia under the terms of federal Bill C-93, or the contents of the leaked report of the deputy prime minister's task force on native programs are also selected to buttress the conspiracy theory. Finally, in this world view pragmatic Indian politicians who are prepared to reach accommodations with nonIndian politicians, in order to extract the best deal possible at the present time to meet the pressing needs of their Indian constituents, are dismissed as "sell-outs" who are merely paying rhetorical lip service to the idea of opposing the government's scheme while actually collaborating with it.

Hence, quite apart from the term "claim" being perceived to be weaker than the term "aboriginal rights,"[10] it is often shunned by Indians because it evokes a set of concerns, observations, allegations, and interpretations that are highly charged both emotionally and politically, in part because they strike at the very integrity of some Indian and nonIndian leaders.

The sources of the grievances registered by Indians in the "claims" process are varied. Neither those sources nor the restitution sought is restricted to matters of land. Some grievances, for instance, pertain to treaty obligations the government has never fulfilled. Under the federal government's claims policy, first enunciated in 1973, these are now labelled "specific claims."[11] Included under this rubric are such matters as monetary compensation (with interest) for cattle or ammunition or twine explicitly mentioned in a treaty but which was never provided by the federal government. These settlements vary in size from tens of thousands of dollars per band to several million dollars. Some land matters also fall in the "specific claims" category, such as those cases where reserves were never created despite provisions in the treaty calling for them or cases where the boundaries of a reserve have been reduced without the consent of the band. Compensation in these cases usually takes the form of land.

A final example of the variety of localized grievances held by Indians is provided by the federal government's violation of its trust responsibilities. Legally, when the federal government acts on behalf of Indians in transactions with third parties it is obliged to seek the best possible deal for the Indians. However, in various instances government employees ostensibly acting on behalf of Indians actually deceived the Indians, were careless in exercising their responsibilities, had a personal conflict of interest in the transaction, or otherwise failed to demand fair market value for the goods or property rights being exchanged. These instances, such as the government's leasing of Musqueam Band prime land to the Shaugnessy Golf Club in Vancouver at prices below market value, provide the basis of other legal claims against the government.

The federal government's 1973 land claims policy established a second category of claim, in which, in the government's opinion, the following criteria are met: treaties were never signed, aboriginal rights were never extinguished, and the territory in question was traditionally used and occupied by the native people involved. Several such cases have been or presently are being negotiated, including: the Naskapi-Montagnais-Innu Association in Labrador; the Labrador Inuit Association; the Naskapi Indians in Schefferville, Quebec; the James Bay and northern Quebec Crees and Inuit; the Dene and Métis of the Northwest Territories; the Committee for Original Peoples' Entitlement (COPE) representing the Inuvialuit of the western Arctic; the Inuit Tapirisat of the eastern Arctic; the Nishga Tribal Council in British Columbia; and the Council of Yukon Indians about which Frideres writes. The thrust of the comprehensive claims policy is "to exchange [read extinguish] undefined aboriginal land rights for concrete rights and benefits" such as are described in the chapters on Yukon and James Bay. To redress at least partially the imbalance of power in these negotiations, the federal government advances moneys from the anticipated compensation payments, thereby enabling the claimant organizations to hire the requisite legal expertise and conduct the historical and anthropological research to buttress their claim. To date, both sides have usually preferred to negotiate a settlement rather than submit to the more risky (albeit potentially more beneficial) process of a court case. The Nishga claim cited by Little Bear is one of the exceptions to this trend.

In Frideres's chapter we see how the peculiar system of land tenure in Yukon and the aspirations of the Yukon government to cast off its colonial status have led to unique features in the Agreement in Principle that has thus far been negotiated. Of particular importance is the so-called "one-government" approach, under which no reserves, per se, are established and Natives will actively participate in the Yukon government. In most respects, however, the Yukon Agreement in Principle is patterned after the James Bay Agreement, as has been discussed in Chapter Seven. Frideres here takes us through the parameters and processes that have shaped the initial Agreement in Principle in Yukon and that will likely shape its renegotiation.

The Constitutional Situation

As noted earlier, aboriginal rights are now recognized in the Canadian constitution. Gibbins's discussion of Canadian Indians and the constitution examines the process by which that constitutional recognition came about. In large measure he attributes constitutional entrenchment to larger political forces external to Indians. Significantly, he notes that those external forces have virtually dissipated, and along with them has gone the momentum for further constitutional change that would identify and define the content of the rights recognized, and more specifically, might recognize a right to self-government.

Gibbins identifies a central issue relating to the constitution, how the courts would interpret the word "existing" in Section 35.1. Some observers anticipate a highly restrictive interpretation that would almost neutralize the term "aboriginal rights" in the present and future. Others argue for a permissive interpretation that would recognize the right to self-government as an existing aboriginal right that has never been surrendered by most Indian tribes or nations. The metaphorical term used to describe this issue is the "empty-box-versus-full-box interpretation."

A second crucial issue is the role of the provinces in aboriginal rights. Bringing aboriginal rights into the constitution has perhaps altered the bilateral legal relationship (e.g., through treaties and through the trust relationship) between status Indians and the federal government. That is, amendments to the aboriginal rights provisions of the constitution are subject to the same approval formula as any other amendments. The provinces have thus acquired a voice, a vote, and in the case of Ontario and Quebec, almost a veto, over future constitutional change involving aboriginal peoples. This was recognized in advance by Assembly of First Nations strategists and deemed by them to involve lesser costs than being left out of the constitution altogether. Some others disagreed.

Although Gibbins places considerable emphasis on the "full box" interpretation of Section 35.1, in other respects his chapter is somewhat pessimistic in tone. For instance, he downplays the political gains that native politicians have made with their constituents and the gains Natives have made in educating the provincial premiers and bureaucrats as to the needs, history, and capabilities of Indian peoples. Over the long term these inroads with the political elite of the country are potentially one of the more significant gains to have come from the constitutional process for Indians. Admittedly, though, the lasting significance of these educational gains is tied to the effects of turnover in the ranks of the provincial premiers. In 1985 we witnessed the arrival of new premiers in the three most powerful provinces (Ontario, Quebec, and Alberta), and forthcoming elections in British Columbia, Saskatchewan, and New Brunswick all offer the prospect of installing new governments. It remains to be seen whether these political changes will nullify those advances made with the earlier premiers, or conversely, will remove political obstacles. [12]

One further point made by Gibbins should be stressed; that is, constitutional change is not a panacea to Indians' problems, and much progress across a wide front can occur without constitutional change. Various aspects of local community developments at Kahnawake and elsewhere demonstrate this fact. The time has now come, I believe, for Indian organizations at least to consider a change in strategy from one of maximizing constitutional gains to one of constitutional "damage control" while simultaneously building the institutions of local communities that can test the constitutional limits of Indian governments through the unilateral assertion of sovereignty on a daily basis. Such an incrementalist strategy recognizes that some of the most important changes in Indian affairs in the past have come when Indians have been caught up in stronger political currents or have been able to ride the coattails of other, more powerful political actors. [13] Such a strategy permits the time to mend political fences, cultivate new allies (such as the Haida nation in British Columbia did with environmentalists in 1985), and seek together to generate a new wave whose crest Indians can ride.

Notes

1. Some Indian peoples associate their aboriginal rights with a particular territory they and their ancestors occupied not since time immemorial, but since contact with nonIndians (or with other Indians who were displaced by nonIndians) impelled them to migrate there.
2. Michael Asch, *Home and Native Land: Aboriginal Rights and the Canadian Constitution* (Toronto: Methuen, 1984), pp. 42-54.

3. Some Indian organizations oppose these conferences on the grounds that the "definition and identification" exercise will lead to aboriginal rights being limited.

4. First Ministers' Conference on Aboriginal Constitutional Matters, Ottawa, March 8-9, 1984, unverified and unofficial verbatim transcript, pp. 256-57.

5. As if to attest to the aboriginal view of the world as being cyclic in nature, the wheel has come full circle on religion and aboriginal rights. That is, the British in the era of early contact justified the violation of aboriginal rights with a religious ideology, and the aboriginal peoples now use a religious ideology to justify their attempts to reinstate their aboriginal rights.

6. The quotation is from a pre-publication draft of the authors' stimulating article "Tribal Traditions and European-Western Political Ideologies: The Dilemma of Canada's Native Indians," *Canadian Journal of Political Science*, XVII, 3 (1984), pp. 537-53. The quotation does not appear in the published version.

7. *Ibid.*, pp. 548-50.

8. *Ibid.*

9. The Office of Native Claims is also reviled because it both sets the rules of the claims settlement process, including even which claims will be accepted as valid, and is one of the parties to the settlement negotiations. This is seen by Indian organizations as inherently unjust, especially given the arbitrary manner in which the Office of Native Claims is perceived to exercise its authority to deny the validity of a claim.

10. In this ideology the term "claim" connotes that the grievances are merely a contention rather than a valid fact. Furthermore, in aboriginal affairs the term "claim" has been promoted by the federal government's Office of Native Claims. To accept that term is to accept implicitly not only the legitimacy of the present claims settlement regime in general but also the legitimacy of the federal government, the defendant in most of the claims, arrogantly appropriating unto itself the right to establish the rules of the game and the eligibility of "claims" for compensation.

11. For a discussion of federal land claims policy, see Asch, *Home and Native Land*, p. 65. The original policy documents issued by DIAND are: "Statement on Claims of Indian and Inuit People," DIAND press release, August 8, 1973; *Native Claims: Policy, Processes, Perspectives* (Ottawa: Queen's Printer, 1978); and *In All Fairness: A Native Claims Policy* (Ottawa: Queen's Printer, 1978). For one history of the "claims" process, see Research Branch, *A History of Native Claims Processes in Canada, 1867-1979* (Ottawa: DIAND, 1980).

12. One could argue against the removal-of-obstacles hypothesis on the grounds that the political incentives for the new premiers may be little different from those faced by their immediate predecessors.

13. Examples of this phenomenon have been changes to the sex discrimination provisions of the Indian Act (in part in response to pressure from the United Nations) and the constitutional entrenchment of aboriginal rights (in response to momentum generated in large part by Pierre Trudeau, the NDP, and the women's lobby). Even the hated white paper of 1969 was largely a response to events external to the realm of Indian affairs.

Chapter Nine

Aboriginal Rights and the Canadian "Grundnorm"

by Leroy Little Bear

Although persons unfamiliar with law often think of the law in "black and white" terms – something is either against the law or it is not – there is, in fact, an enormous area of grey in any set of laws. Law and rights are often matters of opinion and interpretation. The courts, especially the Supreme Court of the land, in rendering their judgements often provide reasons for their decisions. Included in those reasons are norms, or standards, or criteria, or decision rules by which future cases are to be judged. These norms are not necessarily "cast in stone," for they may be modified or superseded by competing norms that emerge as circumstances, paradigms, and moral standards change. (A paradigm is a way of conceptualizing and thinking about a phenomenon. It determines the way in which people even approach that phenomenon.) The purpose of this chapter is to present an exposé of the norms (that is, the standards or decision criteria) and paradigms in the political and legal philosophy of aboriginal people, in British common law, and in international law. These will be compared with the standards and paradigms used by Canada to deal with the issue of aboriginal title to land. We shall find that what prevails in Canada is what might be called the "Grundnorm approach," which, in the writing of constitutional theorist Hans Kelsen,[1] refers to the fact that whatever a government can "get away with" (in terms of changing the constitutional law of the land merely through its administrative and legislative actions) might well be held by the courts to be legal, even though it might not conform to the written constitution or to international legal norms.[2]

In his writings on property rights, the famous British legal expert Lord Blackstone once observed that we rarely take the trouble to consider the origin or foundation of what we take to be our rights to own property. He writes:

We think it enough that our title is derived by the grant of the former proprietor, by descent from our ancestor, or by the last will and testament of the dying owner, not caring to reflect that (accurately and strictly speaking) there is no foundation in nature, or in natural law, why a set of words on parchment should convey the dominion of land. . . . These inquiries would be useless and even troublesome. . . .[3]

It would be difficult to find a more appropriate comment to describe Canada's title to lands in North America, for Canada has for the longest time attempted to avoid the issue of how it gained title from the Indian nations who were the original occupants. Instead, Canada has acted as though it legitimately purchased the lands from the Indians.

The question of tribal title is an issue of political and legal theory. It is possible to describe the debate as a conflict between two world views, but it is more appropriate to discuss it in terms of western European legal philosophy and paradigms. The pivotal issue in this controversy and this chapter is: how could nonIndian nations acquire title to land in North America without actual military conquest or outright purchase of the lands from the Indian nations? We begin by describing the standards of property rights in aboriginal law, but to understand the property concepts of any society one must have some appreciation of the overall philosophical premises that are basic to its culture – the premises that the society uses to relate to the world. Accordingly, we shall examine these premises in aboriginal cultures.

The Aboriginal Peoples' Standard

In contrast to the Western (occidental) way of relating to the world – namely, a linear and singular conception – the aboriginal philosophy views the world in cyclical terms. A good example of linear thinking is the occidental conception of time. Time is conceptualized as a straight line. If we attempt to picture "time" in our mind, we would see something like a river flowing toward and past us. What is behind is the past. What is immediately around us is the present. The future is upstream, but we cannot see very far upstream because of a waterfall, a barrier to knowing the future. This line of time is conceptualized as quantity, especially as lengths made of units. A length of time is envisaged as a row of similar units. A logical and inherent characteristic of this concept of time is that once a unit of the river of time flows past, that particular unit never returns – it is gone forever. This characteristic lends itself to other concepts such as "wasting time," "making up time," "buying time," and "being on time," which are unique to occidental society.

Another characteristic of this linear concept of time is that each unit of time is totally different and independent of similar units. Consequently, each day is considered a different unit, and thus a different day. Every day is a new day, every year is a new year. From this we can readily understand why there is a felt need in Western culture to have names for days and months, and numbers for years. In general, Western philosophy is a straight line. One goes from A to B to C to D to E, where B is the foundation for C, and C is the foundation for D, and on down the line.

Native people think in terms of cyclicity. Time is not a straight line. It is a circle. Every day is not a new day, but the same day repeating itself. There is no need to give each day a different name. Only one name is needed: "day." This philosophy is a result of a direct relationship to the macrocosm. The sun is round; the moon is round; a day is a cycle (daylight followed by night); the seasons follow the same cycle year after year. A characteristic of cyclic thinking is that it is holistic, in the same way that a circle is whole. A cyclical philosophy does not lend itself readily to dichotomies or categorization, nor to fragmentation or polarizations; conversely, linear thinking lends itself to all of these, and to singularity. For example, in linear thinking there is only one "great spirit," only one "true rule," only one "true answer." These philosophical ramifications of Western habitual thought result in misunderstanding holistic concepts, as Westerners relate themselves to only one aspect of the whole at a time.

The linear and singular philosophy of Western cultures and the cyclical and holistic philosophy of most native peoples can be seen readily in the property concepts in each society. Indian ownership of property, like Indians' way of relating to the world, is holistic. Land is communally owned; ownership rests not in any one individual, but rather belongs to the tribe as a whole, as an entity. The members of a tribe have an undivided interest in the land; everybody, as a whole, owns the whole. Furthermore, the land belongs not only to people presently living, but also to past generations and future generations, who are considered to be as much a part of the tribal entity as the present generation. In addition, the land belongs not only to human beings, but also to other living things (the plants and animals and sometimes even the rocks); they, too, have an interest.

Although the native conception of title to land is distinct from the

British concept in important ways, the two do have some points of overlap. The native concept of title is somewhat like a combination of different British concepts (the FSD, FSSCS, and FT concepts discussed later in this chapter). To Natives it is as though the Creator, the original one to grant the land to the Indians, put a condition on it whereby the land remains Indian land "so long as there are Indians," "so long as it is not alienated," "on the condition that it is used only by Indians," etc. In other words, the Indians' concept of title is not equivalent to what today is called "fee simple title" (see below); it is actually somewhat less than unencumbered ownership because of the various parties (plants, animals, and members of the tribe) that have an interest in it and because of the above-noted conditions attached to the ownership.[4] Finally, a point raised above must be emphasized: that is, the source of Indians' title to their land can be traced back to the Creator, who gave it not only to human beings, but to all living creatures. In other words, deer have the same type of interest in the land as does any human being.

This concept of sharing with fellow animals and plants is one that is quite alien to Western society's conception of land. To Western society, only human beings have a right to land, and everything else is for the convenience of humans. Yet, the concept of Indians sharing the land ownership with fellow living things is not entirely unrelated to the concept of social contract that has been put forward by such occidental philosophers as Rousseau and Locke. However, whereas Rousseau's and Locke's social contract encompasses human beings only, the Indian social contract embraces all other living things.

The question inevitably arises as to just what the Indians surrendered when they signed treaties with European nations. First, the Indian concept of land ownership is certainly not inconsistent with the idea of sharing with an alien people. Once the Indians recognized them as human beings, they gladly shared with them. They shared with Europeans in the same way they shared with the animals and other people. However, sharing here cannot be interpreted as meaning that Europeans got the same rights as any other native person, because the Europeans were not descendants of the original grantees, or they were not parties to the original social contract. Also, sharing certainly cannot be interpreted as meaning that one is giving up his rights for all eternity.

Second, the Indians could not have given unconditional ("fee simple") ownership to Europeans in any land transactions in which they may have engaged because they did not themselves have fee simple ownership. They were never given such unconditional ownership by their grantor (the Creator), and it is well known in British property law that one cannot give an interest greater than he or she has.

Third, Indians could not have given an interest even equal to what they were originally granted, because to do so would be to break the condition under which the land was granted by the Creator. Furthermore, they are not the sole owners under the original grant from the Creator; the land belongs to past generations, to the yet-to-be-born, and to the plants and animals. Has the Crown ever received a surrender of title from these others?

Fourth, the only kind of interest the native people have given or transferred must be an interest lesser than they had, for one can always give an interest smaller than one has. [5] Thus, from all of the above we can readily conclude that, from their perspective, the Indians did not surrender very much, if they surrendered anything at all.

Thomas Berger, in a recent study of the Alaska Native Land Claim Settlement Act, summarizes the viewpoint of the native people of Alaska. His remarks can be applied readily to other native people. Writes Berger:

> The European discoverers, their descendants, and the nations they founded, including the United States, imposed their overlordship on the peoples of the New World. The Europeans came, and they claimed the land. No one has ever advanced a sound legal theory to justify the taking of native land from the Natives of the New World, whether by the Spanish, the Portuguese, the French, the Dutch, the Americans, or – in Alaska – by the Russians.
>
> Certain European powers claimed, by virtue of discovery, the exclusive right to purchase land from its original inhabitants. [However,] the rule of discovery depends upon the concept of native sovereignty: only if the original inhabitants had the right to sell their land could the discoverer exercise his right to purchase it. . . .
>
> Before and after contact native peoples of the New World governed themselves according to a variety of political institutions; they were acknowledged to be sovereign as distinct peoples. [6]

In summary, the standard or norm of the aboriginal peoples' law is that land is not transferable and therefore is inalienable. Land and benefits therefrom may be shared with others, and when Indian nations entered into treaties with European nations, the subject of the treaty, from the Indians' viewpoint, was not the alienation of the land but the sharing of the land.

The British Common Law Standard

An underlying premise of the British property system is that no one can own land in the same way that one can own a book. Also, possession forms a large part of ownership. Since one cannot own land in the same way that one can own a book, a system has been devised by the British to give symbolic ownership. This system is known as the estate system. Under this system, one can only have an interest in the land, and that interest is called an estate. The British common law developed a hierarchy of interests or estates. At the very top is "a fee simple absolute," the largest estate in British law. This possession is said to be of infinite duration, freely alienable, and without any other outside interests impinging upon it. A "fee simple absolute" transfer can be symbolized as "A" (grantor) to "B" (grantee) and his heirs.

Lower in the hierarchy come the so-called "defeasible estates." The first defeasible estate is technically known as "fee simple determinable (with a possiblity of a reverter)" or FSD for short. This legal jargon simply refers to the type of ownership obtained when "A" (a landowner in fee simple absolute) grants to "B" with a condition or limitation attached which will cause the ownership rights of "B" to come to an end if a certain event happens (or, otherwise stated, the ownership rights of "B" remain so long as that certain event does not happen). An example of a condition that might be attached is that liquor not be sold on the premises. The interest retained by the grantor is known as "a possibility of a reverter." The grantee has all the same rights in regards to the land as if she held a fee simple absolute title, except for the one condition; hence, she is said to have a lesser interest than one having a fee simple absolute title.

Although there are various other types of estates in British law,[7] only one more will be described here. It is another type of defeasible ownership and is called "fee simple subject to a condition subsequent" (FSSCS). The main difference between this and the FSD is that under FSD the grantee's interest automatically terminates on the happening of an event (as soon as the condition is broken, the title reverts back to the grantor), whereas under FSSCS the fee does not automatically revert back to the grantor on the happening of an event or when the condition is broken (the grantor or his heirs must exercise the right to re-enter the premises before the title reverts back; if the right of re-entry is not exercised, ownership remains with the grantee despite the condition being broken).

Some observations can be made about the British system of property ownership as discussed to this point. First, the system is linear vertically (hierarchically linear). It is also very singular, in that it is geared to individuals' ownership of land. Second, an underlying goal of the system is to facilitate transferability of the different interests. Third, the system necessitates an extensive and complicated registry and that makes it possible to trace previous owners chronologically. If one went back far enough to the original source or original owner one would discover that it is the Crown or the Monarch. In other words, the source of the title to the land is the Crown, whereas for Indians it is the Creator.

Although the above types of ownership existed in British law, the British usually took quite a different and highly ethnocentric orientation to the inhabitants of a territory conquered or purchased by England. If the people in the territory were "civilized," their existing laws were viewed by the British as remaining in effect until altered by the British monarch (or, after the Restoration, by Parliament). If the inhabitants of the territory were "savages" or "pagans," it was presumed by the British that they had no law, and English law filled the vacuum at once. If the territory was uninhabited "desert," the Englishmen going abroad to occupy it were deemed to have taken their law with them "as their birthright."[8]

Under the British law of nations there existed a legal norm known as the *principle of discovery*. In describing this principle, Henderson argues that the rights gained by a country that "discovered" a part of the New World were actually rather limited. The right of discovery merely gave the discovering country the right to trade with the aboriginal inhabitants and to seek their voluntary relinquishing of their existing rights. Only by such a voluntary disposition (relinquishing) from the North American Indian nations could nonIndians claim property rights in the New World. Indeed, British colonial governors in the New World had clear instructions to respect native land rights and to acquire territory only by purchase or by treaty of purchase. Military conquest was never asserted as the legal justification for acquiring tenure from the Natives, although such conquest (e.g., over the French) was used to take over from other European nations the rights (discovery rights) that they had acquired by virtue of their earlier discovery of the territory.

Henderson quotes a revealing remark made by Mr. Justice Chapmen in stating the legal position of the British Crown in the case of The Queen vs. Symonds (1847) in New Zealand:

> Whatever may be the opinion of jurists as to the strength or weakness of native title . . . it cannot be too solemnly asserted that it is to be

respected, and that it cannot be extinguished (at least in times of peace) otherwise than by the free consent of the native occupiers.[9]

Henderson points out also that British philosopher John Locke provided a further basis for the recognition of aboriginal rights under the British legal philosophy. Locke postulated that in the original condition of humankind, the original state of nature, human beings lived without political superiors and the relation of states to each other was one of independence. These independent states were equal in the sense that none had dominion or jurisdiction over any other. Native governments of the New World were characterized by Locke as independent states under (aboriginal) "kings" or "rulers," and those who have the supreme power of making laws in European countries are to the Indians simply "men without authority."

Locke argued that when Indian nations entered into treaties (what he called "treaty federalism" or "treaty commonwealth") with the American nations, those treaties and the bonds they established were limited to specific purposes rather than being a comprehensive subordination of Indians' will to the will of the nonIndians. This is his so-called *principle of contractual treaty of commonwealth*.

These principles, the contractual principle of treaty commonwealth and the principle of discovery, vested existing rights of native governments in the British law of nations.[10] The British standard recognizes the norm of international law, which is to say it recognizes the ownership of the land to be with the Indian nations. In recognition of this ownership of land by the Indian nations, Britain's way of protecting its discovery rights was to enter into "treaty commonwealth" with the Indian nations and, more specifically, treaty commonwealth by treaties of protection. In the law of nations the status of such protected states was well defined. As early as 1760 it was established (e.g., in the writings of Swiss legal theorist Emerich Vattel) as a general principle that protected states remain sovereign, and until/unless annexation occurs, the international sovereignty of the native governments of the New World continues intact under those treaties of protection with the Crown. It is within this whole context that Indian treaties and other documents such as the Royal Proclamation of 1763 should be read.

The International Law Standard

International law pertaining to aboriginal peoples was much influenced by the famous Spanish jurist Vitoria, who believed in the fundamental equality of the rights of all human beings.[11] Pope Alexander V had given Spain the discovery rights to huge expanses of North America, on the basis of the early landings of the Spanish explorers. When other countries wanting to trade with the Natives contested the geographical scope of the discovery rights granted by the pope, the pope asked Vitoria to decide the case. Vitoria ruled against the pope; he severely curtailed the geographical extent of Spain's discovery rights by making those rights localized to the vicinity actually explored by the Spaniards. He based his decision on his conviction that Indians are human beings who have their own laws and government; hence, the pope has no authority over them. He ruled also that the "aborigines" were the true owners of the land before the Spaniards' arrival, and that neither "discovery" nor the actions of the pope could give the Spaniards rights over the "aborigines." This doctrine of aboriginal rights was quickly affirmed by the Roman Catholic Church and later by the Spanish Crown. The vitality of this doctrine, and its legitimacy in the law of nations, was confirmed by its adoption by other prominent European jurists such as Gentillis, Grotius, and Pufendorf (who wrote from the late sixteenth century to the eighteenth century, respectively), and it is now universally entrenched in the international covenants on human rights. However, this doctrine of aboriginal rights did allow for the indigenous nations to voluntarily give up their protected rights in agreements with the European nations.

Another of the foremost jurists in the early "post-discovery" era, J.L. de Palacious Rubios, enunciated a doctrine that came to be widely accepted among nations and held that those who used Indians as slaves or conquered people or otherwise mistreated them must make due restitution to them. The sole right of the Crown, he held, was to bring the Christian faith to the Indians, not to exploit them.

Thus, the international law standard basically states that Indian nations were the true owners of the land, and that discovery, the rights of the pope, or the fact that Indians were not Christians was not sufficient basis for Europeans to claim outright ownership of Indian lands. The only legitimate means by which European nations could get title from the Indian nations were through purchase and the voluntary transfer of title from one party to another.

The Canadian Standard on Aboriginal Rights

One case has singularly set the standard for Canada on how it is to treat the issue of aboriginal title. This is the so-called St. Catharine's case, the case of the St. Catharine's Milling and Lumber Company vs. The Queen.[12] The case was actually a boundary dispute that came to revolve around the issue of the kinds of rights Indians had in the lands in dispute. It was by no means a case launched by Indians in an attempt to clarify their rights. Rather, it was a dispute about where the proper western boundary of Ontario is located.[13]

In 1870 the province of Manitoba was created out of the Northwest Territories, and the next year Ontario and the federal government entered into discussions about the boundary. The federal government argued that it was further east, while the Ontario government argued that it was further west. Two years later Treaty Three, which covered the area in dispute, was signed. The dispute was referred to arbitration and it was subsequently held that the area covered by the treaty was in Ontario. The federal government did not accept the decision and went ahead to enlarge the boundaries of Manitoba to cover the area in dispute. In 1883 the federal government issued a licence to the St. Catharine's Milling and Lumber Company to cut timber. Now, when the province of Manitoba was carved out of the Northwest Territories the federal government decided to retain the natural resources; thus, it believed that it owned the natural resources within the Treaty Three area. Ontario sued the company and asked the court to order the company to cease its logging operations and to pay Ontario for the value of the timber already taken.

The pivotal issue became one of the nature of Indian land rights and the effect of the treaty. The federal government argued that the Indians had had a complete proprietary interest in the land surrendered by the treaty, that they had transferred their interest in the land to the federal government in the treaty, and therefore that the federal government could issue a licence. The highest court of appeal, the Judicial Committee of the Privy Council (in Britain), ruled against the federal government. The ruling traced Indian title to the land back to the Royal Proclamation of 1763, but characterized the Indian interest in the land as merely "a personal and usufructuary right, dependent on the good will of the sovereign." That is, Indians could use the land, but did not have absolute ownership rights in fee simple. The Indian title was held to be subject to the ultimate ownership of the (federal) Crown, and as such was subject to the provisions of Section 109 of the British North America Act of 1867, which required that Crown land of the Province of Canada be distributed to, and brought under the ownership of, the Canadian provinces (in this case, Ontario) created at the time of confederation in 1867. The title was held to be less than a full fee simple interest because it contained restrictions not found in full fee simple ownership rights. (For example, while the fee simple interest is fully alienable, the Indian title could be alienated only to the Crown, and whereas a fee simple interest cannot be unilaterally revoked by the Crown, the Indian title could.) With regard to the effect of the treaty, the ruling held that the Crown had underlying ownership rights over the land and had acquired full title (no restrictions). That is, once the Indians surrender their title to the land (or otherwise have it extinguished), all encumbrances are removed and the federal Crown's interest becomes complete (unrestricted). The decision also characterized the Indian interest as a "mere burden" upon the Crown's present proprietary ownership rights. Thus, according to the standard set for the future by this decision, Indian nations in Canada could not claim "allodium rights" (that is, absolute ownership without being subjected to any superior rights of others) to land. As Elliott points out, one significant feature of the St. Catharine's decision was that the rights of the (federal) Crown under the Royal Proclamation of 1763 extended as far as the right to terminate the Indian ownership rights at will, for the tenure of the Indians was declared in the Proclamation to be at the "will and pleasure of the sovereign" and to be "for the present."

The next most important case regarding aboriginal title is the so-called Nishga case, Calder vs. the Attorney General of British Columbia.[14] The Nishga Indians occupy a territory in and around the Nass Valley of northwestern British Columbia. They have occupied the area since time immemorial and have hunted, fished, and otherwise used the area pursuant to their traditional lifestyle. They never agreed to the assertion of ownership over the territory by the province of British Columbia. In 1888 a spokesman for the Nishga nation told a royal commission visiting the Nass Valley:

> What we don't like about the government is their saying this: "We will give you this much land." How can they give it when it is our own? We cannot understand it. They have never bought it from us or our forefathers. They have never fought or conquered our people and taken the land in that way, and yet they say now that they will give us so much land – our own land. . . . It has been ours for thousands of years. . . . We have always got our living from the land. . . . we have always depended on the land for our food and clothes.[15]

Thus, the Nishgas based their claim to the Nass Valley on occupancy since time immemorial and on the fact that they have never engaged in any activity, such as signing a treaty, to extinguish their aboriginal title. However, the B.C. government refused to recognize occupancy from time immemorial as a legal basis for title. In 1973, the Supreme Court of Canada decided the case, with seven judges present. Of the seven, three ruled that whatever title the Nishgas may have had had been extinguished by "adverse acts"[16] on the part of the Crown.

However, three judges agreed with the Nishgas that their aboriginal title had never been extinguished. The seventh and deciding judge ruled against the Nishgas on a technicality: the Nishgas had not obtained the permission of the Crown to bring suit against the Crown.

Justice Judson, speaking for the three judges against the Nishgas, stated emphatically that the Royal Proclamation of 1763, upon which the Nishgas' case was in part based, did not apply to the Nishgas, for the Nass Valley and the whole of B.C. were outside the geographical scope of the Proclamation. He also reiterated the interpretation that the Judicial Committee of the Privy Council had made (in the St. Catharine's case), namely, that the Indian title rested on the goodwill of the sovereign and hence could be extinguished by the Crown. Justice Judson concluded:

> This is not a property right, but amounts to a right of occupancy which the Sovereign grants and protects against intrusion by third parties, but which right of occupancy may be terminated and such lands fully disposed of by the Sovereign itself without any legally enforceable obligation to compensate the Indians.

Mr. Justice Hall, speaking for the judges who agreed with the Nishgas, did not disagree with Mr. Justice Judson that Indian title can be extinguished by treaty or by competent legislation.[17] However, he argued that extinguishment cannot be implied but must be explicit. He said:

> Prima facia . . . the Nishgas are the owners of the lands that have been in their possession from time immemorial and, therefore, the burden of establishing that their right has been extinguished rests squarely on the respondent (i.e., B.C.).
>
> Once the aboriginal title is established, it is presumed to continue until the contrary is proven.
>
> It would . . . appear to be beyond question that the onus of proving that the Sovereign intended to extinguish the Indian title lies on the respondent (i.e., B.C.) and that the intention must be clear and plain. There is no such proof in the [present case]. . . .

In Justice Hall's opinion, the British Columbia government was not competent to extinguish the Indian title, as this can be done only by the federal government.

The significance of the Calder case lies in the fact that it recognizes prior occupancy as a basis for aboriginal title and in the fact that it recognizes that aboriginal title can exist without the Royal Proclamation of 1763. When the St. Catharine's and Calder cases are taken together, the scope and extent of aboriginal title can be summarized thusly:

1. Aboriginal title is a personal and usufructuary interest, recognizable in Canadian law.
2. Its existence can be traced either to the Royal Proclamation of 1763 or it can be based on possession from time immemorial.
3. Its continuing existence is at the goodwill of the Sovereign, and aboriginal title can be extinguished at the whim of the Sovereign.
4. The Sovereign is not necessarily obligated to pay compensation for the extinguishment of aboriginal title.

In point number three above we find an answer to the central question of this chapter. How could nonIndian nations acquire title to land in North America without actual military conquest or outright purchase of the lands from the Indian nations? The answer, in Canadian jurisprudence, is that the Indians' title was extinguished at the whim of the Sovereign and that it can be extinguished when the Sovereign demonstrates a clear and plain intention to do so. The problem with this answer, though, is that it begs the question – it still does not tell us how the Sovereign acquired title from the Indians, in light of what we know about British law and norms of international law that run contrary to the Canadian practice.

Since Calder, there have been other cases dealing with aboriginal title, but these add little to the Calder decision and do little to change the effect of the St. Catharine's case.[18] Canada, to a large extent, has attempted to deal with aboriginal title outside of the court system, which explains the lack of clear precedents other than the two cases discussed above. One can say that Canada has always had a claims policy in the form of the Royal Proclamation of 1763, which stipulated that purchases of Indian lands should be carried out at public meetings of the Indians and that only the Crown can purchase from Indians. In accordance with this broad general policy, Canada has utilized the treaty process as a means of extinguishing Indian title to large areas of Canada. However, regardless of the manner in which Indian title has been extinguished or has been claimed to have been extinguished, the Canadian standard or norm has remained as established in the St. Catharine's and Calder cases.

Conclusion

One can readily see from the aboriginal rights standard that the assumption made in the St. Catharine's case that the Crown has always had underlying title does not make sense, for philosophically and legally one cannot own an interest in something that one does not know exists. Also, when was the starting point to the Crown's underlying interest? The Crown's interest could not have originated prior to the discovery of the Americas. An interest in the lands of the Indian nations could have come about only via treaty or purchase, but for the Indians the treaty relationship revolved around the notion of the "sharing," not the alienation, of the land.

Under the international law standard the Indian nations were recognized owners of the land. The discovery rights of the European nations were merely rights against other *European* nations and did not divest the Indians of any interest. The St. Catharine's case would have been consistent with the development of international law on aboriginal rights if the decision had limited the Crown's underlying title to such discovery rights, but it did not do so. Instead, the decision accorded to the Crown a title that was superior in law to the Indian title; the Indian was a "mere burden" on the Crown's interest. When the burden is removed or otherwise extinguished, the Crown's interest becomes complete.

The St. Catharine's decision, even within the context of British common law, is out of line. The British common-law approach to aboriginal title was one of acceptance of the international law standard. In recognition of this standard the British entered into treaties with the Indian nations.[19] It is within this context that the "protectionist" phrases of the Royal Proclamation of 1763 should be understood. That phraseology is as follows:

> And whereas it is just and reasonable, and essential to our interest and [to] the security of our Colonies, that the several Nations or Tribes of Indians with whom we are connected, and who live under our protection . . . .

However, it seems that the outcome of this protectionist language instead has been the guardian/ward type of trust relationship. An implication of the guardian/ward relationship is that the Indians are under the extraordinary authority and control of the federal government, yet this is totally inconsistent with the concept of "treaty commonwealth by treaties of protection." The latter concept refers to the protection of a weaker nation by a stronger nation; this protection does not imply surrender of the sovereignty of the weaker nation.

Indian treaties and their legal status within Canadian law are another example of Canada's deviation from the British, aboriginal, and international norms. Canadian law does not recognize Indian treaties as agreements between two sovereign parties, but even if they were they would not be legally binding because there is no implementing legislation for them.[20] Indian treaties are not recognized as contracts. Indians cannot sue the government for non-performance of its treaty obligations because a treaty has been held to constitute only a "personal obligation" on the part of the Crown's representative.[21] The most that can be said of Indian treaties is that they are "mere promises and agreements."[22] To the framers and judicial interpreters of Canadian law, the existence of an Indian treaty does not make much difference in the relationship between an Indian nation and Canada with regard to land title.

In 1982, when Canada patriated the constitution and included in it Section 35 – "The existing aboriginal and treaty rights of the aboriginal peoples are hereby recognized and affirmed." – there were glimmers of hope that Canada will now adhere to the norms and standards of international law and British common law. Section 35 presents an excellent opportunity for Canada to correct prior Canadian judicial precedents and to construe aboriginal and treaty rights on concepts of law rather than on perspectives of race, politics, and social class. It remains to be seen, however, whether the present government or future governments have the determination to overcome judicial and administrative constructions of aboriginal rights and treaties. Henderson observes:

> The federal government's willingness to equalize the involuntary losses of the aboriginal peoples and to attempt to make restitution will be the litmus test of the recognition of aboriginal and treaty rights in the Canadian constitution.[23]

However, because of the controversy revolving around the word "existing" in Section 35, Indian nations are more and more convinced that Canada will continue to follow its own norms and standards. The government's interpretation is that Section 35 recognizes only those rights that have been legally recognized but does not apply to rights that, according to Canada, have ceased because of the fact that they have been extinguished or superseded by law.

Thus, the Canadian approach seems to be aptly characterized as a "Grundnorm approach" – that is, whatever the government can get away with may in the future come to be held to be legal, just as it has in the past, regardless of the fact that it is inconsistent with standards in aboriginal, British, and international law.

Notes

1. Cited in Michael Valpy, "Zimbabwe Constitution Undercut by Precedent," *Globe and Mail*, date unknown.

2. Readers not familiar with law should note that I am distinguishing here between formal constitutional reform, which requires the participation of the provinces and adherence to the amending formula set out in the constitution, and mere legislative change that the federal (or provincial) government can implement on its own without the participation of the provinces. Thus, the sentence in the text implies a hierarchy with the constitution at the top, other legislation in the middle, and administrative behaviour at the bottom.

3. Lord Blackstone, *Commentaries on the Law of England*, 2d, book 2, 1765.

4. To say that Indians' view of land ownership was not equivalent to fee simple title is *not* to say that Indians were incapable of conceiving of a fee simple ownership of land.

5. We shall see below that in British law the types of ownership are arranged hierarchically. Thus, the reference in the text here is to the fact that if one holds the type of ownership found at, say, the second-from-top level of the hierarchy, one can give up those lesser ownership rights found at the lower levels of the hierarchy.

6. Thomas R. Berger, *Village Journey: The Report of the Alaska Native Review Commission* (Toronto: Collins, 1985), pp. 138-39.

7. For instance, there is the Fee Tail (FT) estate, which has now been phased out of British common law. Under fee tail ownership, the class of heirs capable of inheriting the property was limited to those who are lineal descendants. If and when the line of lineal descendants ran out, the ownership rights came to an end.

8. James Youngblood Henderson, "Canadian Legal and Judicial Philosophies on the Doctrine of Aboriginal Rights," in Menno Boldt and J. Anthony Long (eds.), *Quest for Justice: Aboriginal Peoples and Aboriginal Rights* (Toronto: University of Toronto Press, 1985), pp. 191ff. Henderson is a legal strategist for the Grand Council of the Mic Mac Nations in Cape Breton. He holds a B.A. degree from California State University at Fullerton and a J.D. degree from Harvard University. He is of Chickasaw and Cheyenne tribal background and has written widely on aboriginal rights.

9. N.Z.P.C.C. 387, p. 390.

10. There was a third principle, the *proprietary principle of purchase*, which Henderson discusses but which has been omitted here as it is of lesser importance. The discussion above on British common law and British law of nations is distilled from Henderson, "Canadian Legal and Judicial Philosophies," pp. 191-203.

11. This section is distilled from *ibid.*, pp. 187-89.

12. (1888) 14 Appellate Cases 46 (Judicial Committee of the Privy Council).

13. The account below is distilled from W. David Elliott, "Aboriginal Title," in Bradford Morse (ed.), *Aboriginal Peoples and the Law: Indian, Métis, and Inuit Rights in Canada* (Ottawa: Carleton University Press, 1985).

14. (1973) Supreme Court Reporter, 313, 4 Western Weekly Reporter, 1.

15. *Ibid.*

16. The phrase "adverse acts" has a specific meaning here. When there are two opposing interests and one party acts against the interests of the other and

that action supersedes the rights of the other party, that action is said to be an "adverse act."

17. "Competent" legislation is that legislation passed by a government which, according to the division of powers between the federal and provincial governments in the constitution, has the jurisdictional authority to pass legislation in that substantive area.

18. See: The Queen vs. Isaac (1975), 13 Nova Scotia Reporter (2d) 460 (Nova Scotia Supreme Court Appeals Division); Re Paulette *et al.* and Registrar of Land Titles (1976), 63 Dominion Law Reporter (3d) 1, affirmed by the Supreme Court of Canada (1977), 2 Supreme Court Reporter, 628; Kanatewat *et al.* vs. The James Bay Development Corporation and Attorney General (Quebec) (1974), R.P. 38 (C.S.), Reversed (1975), Quebec Court of Appeal 166; and Hamlet of Baker Lake *et al.* vs. Minister of Indian Affairs and Northern Development (1980), 107 Dominion Law Reporter (3d) 513 (Federal Court Trials Division).

19. Specifically, these were "treaty commonwealth by treaties of protection."

20. Francis vs. The Queen (1956), Supreme Court Reporter 618.

21. Attorney General for Canada vs. Attorney General for Ontario (1867), Appellate Cases 199 (Privy Council).

22. The Queen vs. Wesley (1932), 4 Dominion Law Reporter at p. 788, Western Weekly Reporter at p. 351.

23. Henderson, "Canadian Legal and Judicial Philosophies."

Chapter Ten

Education and the Reclaiming of Identity: Rights and Claims of Canadian Indians, Norwegian Sami, and Australian Aborigines

by Deirdre F. Jordan

History shows that it has been not only economic development pressures that have acted to destroy indigenous culture and substitute for a positive identity the negative traits with which indigenous people have come to be stereotyped. In addition to economic forces, *one of the crucial destructive forces has been that of schooling*. In this regard, it is worth restating here a theme developed in the introductory chapter of this book. In the words of Diane Longboat:

> The education provided to Indians by the Government of Canada and its colonial predecessor governments has been an important element of an overall policy of assimilation. It has been a means of seeking to . . . modify the values of the Indian nations through those who are weakest and can offer least resistance . . . the children. Education has worked with the long-term objective of weakening Indian nations through causing the children to lose sight of their identities, history and spiritual knowledge.[1]

A similar claim has been made by Thomas Berger on the basis of testimony heard at his Mackenzie Valley Pipeline Inquiry. Said Berger: "The schools and what was taught in them offered a challenge to the culture of the Dene and the Inuit, to their very identity as a people."[2]

In the past, the identities offered to indigenous people by the dominant society have been negative; assimilationist policies carried out through schooling *made* the people dependent economically and culturally and that was reflected in their identity. Their claims today are not to new rights; they re-claim prior rights of a positive identity, rights to be ethnically distinct from (but not necessarily separate from) mainstream society, and the right to the same degree of self-determination enjoyed by members of the majority group.

Dominant groups speak of "the Sami problem," the "Indian problem," the "Aboriginal problem," but this way of looking at the situation reflects the ethnocentrism of people who have *caused* problems by breaking the bond of the indigenous people with their spirituality, their culture, their language, their land, and their means of livelihood. Yet the "problem" is actually a "white" problem. The real problem of the indigenous people is one of reconstructing an ethnic identity. They cannot return to the past, but they must establish whether there are aspects of the lifestyle from the past that can still be credibly integrated into their contemporary "theorizing" about identity in order to give coherence to the group.

The schools have been seen to destroy identity; in contemporary society, indigenous people see educational institutions as the sites for constructing or reconstructing their identity. Thus, *indigenous peoples' claims to control education are claims to control the construction of identity.* This chapter will probe indigenous education in terms of several questions. They are:

- What historical threads led the dominant group to use schooling to try to assimilate indigenous people and led the indigenous people to take on a negative identity in their own mind?
- What solutions are indigenous people developing to recreate identity?
- What place does education or schooling play in these solutions?
- What problems do indigenous people face in creating a new reality?
- What, if any, are the common threads across the groups?

The Past: Schooling and Assimilation

The missionaries established schools and brought literacy to all three peoples under consideration – the Canadian Indians, the Australian Aborigines, and the Sami. While early missionaries in many cases preserved the language of the indigenous people, they actively set out to destroy their "pagan" religious practices, and hence their culture, which in practice also meant the breaking down of the authority structures of the family and the group. The destruction was hastened by the establishment of residential schools during the period 1850-1950. In Canada, these schools were instituted to centralize educational activities. The Sami school was "reformed" in 1913 to be a school that would migrate with the people. The Sami children were accommodated in tent-like structures intended to replicate the typical Sami nomadic dwellings, but in practice these were unsanitary hovels condemned by the people. The school was deliberately of a lower standard than that of the majority population.[3] In the case of Australian Aborigines, residential schools were unashamedly seen as the best means of removing children from the influence of their parents. Many children, taken from their parents, completely lost touch with them and in later years set out on a traumatic search for their families.

For many if not most of these people, schooling away from home is remembered as a cruel experience. This is often remembered as physical cruelty, for the striking of children as a disciplinary measure is not part of the indigenous peoples' cultures. However, the psychological cruelty of removing children from their families and immersing them in an alien way of life was perceived as equally destructive, and generations of indigenous people formed negative attitudes to the "whitening" processes employed in the schools. This is illustrated in the following statement:

> In 1905 . . . someone convinced us to let some children go to residential school, and we sent ten students out. Maybe they weren't looked after, or maybe they could not get used to the environment, but anyway, they only ever sent back one of them, and nobody really knows what happened to the rest of them.[4]

As assimilation became official policy in Canadian and Australian classrooms, especially between 1950 and 1970, the attack on the culture of the indigenous peoples focused on language. In the words of one student:

> Every Friday evening . . . it was time for us to report whether we spoke our language, Cree, during the week. If we confessed to using our own language, we were denied the visit with our parents and younger brothers and sisters which was the only privilege we had. In other words, we had to lie to the ministry in order to visit with our parents and relatives.[5]

Similarly, in the case of the Sami, a "rigorous Norwegianization policy" was adopted from about 1880.[6] The term "fornorskings-politikk" (Norwegianization) was primarily associated with language and school policy. Eidheim[7] states that the school aims exclusively at communicating those values current in an idealized Norwegian society, and for generations it has had the implicit goal (at times explicit) to Norwegianize the Lappish communities. The policy of assimilation forbade the children to speak their language at school, and it was assumed that everyone was able to speak the dominant language. Thus, the children were not taught Norwegian. Yet the students were expected to understand that language and the content of the curricula – all presented in a foreign language. One person attested that a teacher friendly to the Sami, who had some understanding of their language, was forbidden to speak to them in Sami.

Adults, today in their forties, describe the humiliation of being treated as unteachable in school, when in fact they had no understanding of the content presented in another language. In general the school created negative stereotypes, so that, for the Sami people, schools were places where their lack of knowledge of the majority tongue was used to create typifications of "stupidity," and the lower level of education required expressed clearly Norwegians' categorization of the Sami as second-class citizens.

Co-existent with but contradicting the "theorizing" and practices directed toward assimilation was the belief that indigenous people are not-quite-human and, therefore, *not able* to be assimilated and not able to benefit from the same education as "white" people. Pseudo-scientists writing in the wake of Darwin's evolutionary theory decided that Australian Aborigines were the missing link between apes and men. Ruong points out that social Darwinism legitimated the treatment of the Sami as an inferior race; similarly, Eidheim refers to the familiar northern Norwegian saying: "There is a (real) difference between people and Lapps." (Det er forskjell pa folk og finn.)

In the case of many Australians for whom history courses have been silent about Aborigines, negative stereotypes of the people were accepted. The low level of schooling of adult Aborigines, as well as the lack of achievement of students in the schooling situation, was seen in terms of a social pathology model that attributed the cause to the nature of the people, not to the nature of the teaching or to the structures of schooling. Thus, the people were deemed to be of low intelligence, unteachable, good at sports, not capable of academic work, and so on. Rowley, however, in tracing policy back to the early 1900s, saw the "native problem" as one caused by white prejudice against skin colour; mainstream society did not want aboriginal people in the towns or in the schools.

> The official fuss about a few thousand persons of unsuitable complexion and the concurrence by the West Australian government in the prejudice of country town people, which was forcing these people out of the schools and even out of the towns, is an excellent illustration of how prejudice creates its own special problems. . . . The transfer of these prejudices to all offspring of Aborigines who have the aboriginal stigma has been almost universal and automatic in the past.[8]

West Australia was not the only state ("province") to force Aboriginal people out of schools and out of towns. Rowley provides a detailed account of restrictions placed on the movement of part-Aboriginal people in all states, which in turn led to restrictions being placed on their access to education.[9] The 1936 Act of New South

Wales, the 1939 Acts of Queensland and South Australia, and the Amendment Act of 1939 in West Australia all provided for part-Aboriginal people to be removed from towns to reserves. On reserves, the highest level of education considered appropriate for Aborigines was fourth grade of primary school, often taught by untrained people. In the towns, Aboriginal children were not free to enter ordinary state schools in New South Wales until 1949.[10] Well into the 1950s, each time there was a protest by white parents concerning Aboriginal children being admitted to the school, the education authorities took heed of the complainants and sent the black children home.[11] Thus, as Anderson and Vervoorn have noted:

> Aborigines have been alienated from a system which has failed to accept the cultural heritage of Aborigines as the basis of the social life and individual identity of Aboriginal people; accordingly it has remained irrelevant to their particular needs . . . and aspirations [and] even harmful to them.[12]

Fitzgerald made a similar observation:

> . . . formal education has sometimes served to divorce a child from his group, without substituting white acceptance in its stead. From the child's viewpoint, "dropping-out" is often the most sensible thing he can do when the school is inimical to self-esteem and the development of personality.[13]

Thus, in each of the countries under consideration, though the expressed, manifest aim of schooling was assimilation, the organization of the schooling often assumed that the indigenous peoples were incapable of learning. In each case, lower standards were expected in schools and fewer years of schooling were judged appropriate. The destruction of the culture and identity of indigenous people through the structures of schooling, the low expectations of teachers, and lack of opportunity have left a legacy of memories of rejection, of internalization of negative stereotyping and negative identity. Native educational experience has also left a legacy of distrust of the "white" school system.

The Post-War Period: The Construction of Policy

The events of World War II and its aftermath caused a profound shift in the view of the place of indigenous peoples within dominant societies. Indigenous people from each of the countries discussed, who had been regarded for so long as second-class citizens and stereotyped as dependent, lazy, and lacking in initiative, fought in the war with distinction. Their contribution, and the recognition of their positive characteristics, could not be denied. Furthermore, the dominant groups had experienced the apprehension, and in some cases the reality, of loss of freedom. The Norwegians, for example, suffered the trauma of Nazi occupation, the loss of democratic procedures, the curtailment of their own freedom, and the humiliations of being a subject group. It was no longer possible for them to continue to advocate human rights in the public forum of the United Nations (as they had done forcefully within the League of Nations) without concerning themselves with the rights of the Sami.

In each country under consideration, the waves of immigration following World War II also led to the need to formulate national policies about new minority groups. Assimilation gave way to policies of pluralism and multiculturalism. As left-of-centre parties came to power in the provinces of Canada, and federally in Australia and Norway, ideologies of equality of opportunity set parameters that included social, cultural, and economic equality for minority groups; these ideologies of equality meant that the stigma associated with native identity could no longer be tolerated. Furthermore, as welfare policies were implemented, the poverty and powerlessness of the indigenous people became apparent.

The rending apart of the social fabric of the entire Western world by the upheavals of war permitted new ways of looking at reality. It permitted the construction of new sets of values, and of ideologies that differed in fundamental ways from the pre-war period. New conceptualizations concerning indigenous peoples were formulated and formalized in all three countries in the late sixties and early seventies. These took on forms, such as the Dene Declaration, that reflected the push of indigenous people toward self-determination and, in turn, led to further crystallization of their claims to rights as indigenous people.

In describing these movements, a fundamental difference must be recognized between the Sami, on one hand, and the aboriginal people of Australia and Canada, on the other. In the case of Canadian Indians, the problem was to *preserve* their status as aboriginal peoples, the first nations of Canada. The Sami, however, had been subjected to policies of assimilation for over 100 years. Their status as an *ethnic* group was not, and still is not, recognized. Their problem has been to *gain* recognition of status as aboriginal people. Furthermore, the Sami differ fundamentally from aboriginal Canadians and Australians in that they are one people with a common language separated by the boundaries of the dominant nations (Norway/Sweden; Finland/Russia), by the different orthographies (i.e., that part of the grammar of the language concerned with the lettering used and accepted ways of spelling) authorized in each country, and by different census definitions of Sami. This identification of the group by outsiders (governments) has acted to fragment the group. The Swedish government, for example, recognized the Sami not as an ethnic group but as an occupational group concerned with reindeer herding. In Canada and Australia the "identification-from-outside" acted in the opposite way, as groups (e.g., Cree and Blackfoot status Indians) not sharing the same language have been *united* by government policy that has failed in the past to recognize differences. "The Aborigines" and "the Indians" were treated in education legislation as if they were a monolithic group, which, patently, they are not.

Claims to Control of Education and of Identity

The Sami

Contemporary claims to rights of identity in all three countries have arisen from a reaction to assimilationist policies. Since many of the Sami had themselves come to accept the negative identity offered to them by the Norwegians and had actively espoused the notion of assimilation,[14] the early protests tended to be individualistic and the first Sami Association (founded in 1904) did not have a strong basis of support. However, as in the case of other indigenous peoples, the revival took on greater momentum after World War II. In 1953 Sami associations founded separately in Sweden, Finland, and Norway collaborated in calling a conference. That was a milestone, both in the crystallization of a Sami national consciousness in the three Scandinavian countries and in demonstrating to the majority populations this sense of reclaimed identity.

In 1956, as a result of the 1953 conference, the Scandinavian Lapp Council was formed. Its initial concerns were with education for a changing world – but an education that preserved identity. Its policy was for children to learn to read and write Sami as a first tongue and to be instructed in the language and history of their people. A further leap forward was made in 1963 when the Stortinget (the Norwegian parliament) approved the recommendations of a commission appointed to "arrive at economic, social and cultural policy regarding the Lapps." The decisions made on the political level set in motion a series of reforms and special investigations, from which came a number of innovations in education. With the establishment of the Sami Institut'ta in 1973 in Kautokeino, a Sami village far to the north of the

Arctic Circle, a base for formulating a framework for future planning was provided. The acceptance of the institute and its policies, as evidenced by the financial support given to it by the Nordic Council of Ministers (Denmark, Norway, Finland, Sweden, Iceland), mirrors the acceptance by the Canadian government, also in 1973, of the policy proposals of the National Indian Brotherhood.

Canadian Indians
In the late 1960s, the Hawthorn Committee (see Chapter One) summarized its findings in the following way:

> The atmosphere of the school, the routines, the rewards, and the expectations provide a critically different experience for the Indian child than for the nonIndian. Discontinuity of socialization, repeated failure, discrimination and lack of significance of the educational process in the life of the Indian child result in diminishing motivation, increased negativism. [15]

The low standards of federal schooling for Natives caused the people to push for an end to segregation in schooling: the government's white paper of 1969 sought to resolve the problems caused by the lower-status education offered by federal services by relinquishing these to the more esteemed provincial education bodies. Indian people, however, saw this as removing their claims to special status as the original people of Canada:

> Indian reaction was explosively negative. Indian leaders pointed out that, until the socio-economic status of Indian people approximated the level of other Canadians, the discriminating provision of legislation constituted a modest kind of protection which they could not afford to lose. [16]

In other words, their claim to identity was at stake. Self-determination became the "catchword" of the people, and both the Department of Indian Affairs and the Indian people saw that self-determination was inextricably allied to, and based in, education, as the following quotations attest:

> The discussion of jurisdictional matters served to raise further Indian consciousness of the need for self-determination, for active Indian participation in the remaking of an Indian education system. [17]

> The government white paper caused the reawakening of political consciousness, and the emergence of provincial and territorial Indian political organizations designed to protect the rights of the first nations. . . . Education was an issue of primary concern, a pivotal developmental issue in refuting the assimilationist policies of the Government of Canada. . . . In

1972, the National Indian Brotherhood produced a landmark policy statement: "Indian Control of Indian Education". The significant feature of all these policy statements since the white paper is the call for Indian control of, and input into, all facets of education affecting Indian people. [18]

In 1972, Minister of Indian Affairs and Northern Devleopment Jean Chrétien delivered an address to the Council of Ministers of Education that was epoch-making in that it reflected and supported the aforementioned policy paper of the National Indian Brotherhood. Chrétien propounded a new conceptualization of "Indianness." Assimilation was to give way to integration. However, said Chrétien:

> Integration interpreted as a unilateral change is unacceptable to the Indian people. Our concept of integration must be revised to recognize the unique contribution which Indian culture and language have made to the Canadian way of life. *Integration should protect and foster the Indian identity and the personal dignity of each child.* [19]

Chrétien explored the problem of drop-outs/push-outs. He identified as causes the alienating structures and features of the schools: white-centred curricula that did not recognize language differences and cultural differences; history that made no mention of the Indian; the lack of training and lack of sensitivity of teachers vis-à-vis cultures other than their own; the lack of representation and participation of Indian parents on school boards. [20] Not coincidentally, all of these concerns were also being voiced by Australian Aborigines and the Sami.

Five years after Chrétien, Justice Berger made much the same points. He summarized the solutions of the native people:

> They insist that they must control the education of their children, if it is to transmit their culture as opposed to ours. They say that the curriculum must include such subjects as native history, native skills, native lore and native rights; that they must determine the languages of instruction; and they insist that they must have the power to hire and fire teachers and to arrange the school year so that it accommodates the social and economic life of each community. [21]

The National Indian Brotherhood was equally clear in what it wanted of education:

> What we want for our children can be summarized very briefly: (i) to reinforce their Indian identity; (ii) to provide the training necessary for making a good living in modern society. *We want education to give our children a strong sense of identity with confidence in their personal worth and ability.* [22]

Australian Aborigines

Early policies concerning Australian Aborigines were those of denial (the land is unoccupied) and segregation. By the 1940s the Aboriginal "problem" was a concern about "half-castes" (i.e., part-Aborigines). The solution was one of "dispersal," the forerunner of assimilation. By the 1950s assimilation had become official policy.

In the 1960s, however, the state (province) of South Australia, following the election of a state Labor government, repudiated the legislation of earlier Liberal governments. In general, that prior legislation had merely legitimated and codified the paternalistic, restrictive practices of church groups that had controlled the missions (later taken over by the government as reservations). The 1960s legislation was introduced not to legitimate but to change practice. For instance, laws were passed regarding land rights for Aborigines. Also passed were anti-discrimination laws aimed at changing the practices, if not the attitudes, of the white population vis-à-vis Aborigines. There was a move away from policies aimed at the control and containment of the Aboriginal people and toward policies requiring consultation and negotiation. For the first time, Aboriginal people were seen as adults who had opinions worth consulting, who had a right to autonomy over their lives.

To make it possible for the Aborigines to "identify with their own people" yet remain within white society, a new policy was proposed; as in Canada, assimilation was to give way to integration, defined as "the right of the Aboriginal people to live in our community on fully equal terms but retaining, if they so desire, a separate and identifiable Aboriginal heritage and culture."[23]

The policy statement supported the politicization of Aborigines, a stance totally at variance with the policy of the Australian federal (Liberal) government. It advocated the active encouragement of a "sophisticated and articulate Aboriginal public opinion." It looked to the development of autonomous government on reserves and to the participation of Aborigines in the political community. The policy of integration provided the possibility for the recognition of *alternative* Aboriginal identity located *within* mainstream society. Thus, unlike Canada and Norway, Australia does not so much present a case of government belatedly acting in response to Aboriginal initiatives and demands, but rather one of a new social awareness and initiative on the part of legislators who themselves brought about change.

When the Labor Party came into power at the federal level in 1972, policies that had been developed in South Australia concerning Aboriginal affairs became official party policy. As part of Labor's platform, educational opportunities were to be introduced that were in no way inferior to those of the general community. Preschool and adult education were to be provided as broadly as possible. Furthermore, every Australian child was to be taught the history and culture of Aboriginal Australians as an integral part of the history of Australia.

In one sense, such a policy was integrated into the overall thrust of Labor policy, which was one of providing equality of opportunity for all those in society who were disadvantaged in one form or another. However, the policy for Aborigines went beyond this. It recognized the need for positive discrimination. For example, special provision for employment was to be made in regions where there was a concentration of Aborigines.

Aborigines seized the concepts of self-determination and self-management and used them to build new, positive meanings for themselves. The tradition-oriented people expressed this by saying "The marrngu (the people) are the boss!" This slogan, expressed in different ways in different parts of the country, was used both as a rallying cry and as a firm basis for building a new world vision in which Aborigines exert autonomy. Aboriginal people at every level in society and in every sphere of action – health care, legal rights, educational policy-making – asserted "We will do it ourselves."

In sum, while Aborigines are physically located within a multicultural society, more and more they are entering into structurally alternative situations, and within these they have greater control of their futures. The Aboriginal voice, expressing Aboriginal political, cultural, physical, and educational needs, is now heard and a simple, fledgling theory or ideology of action – "We will do it ourselves" – has been realized.

Self-determination and Education: The Contemporary Situation

Canadian Natives

The acceptance of the policy of the National Indian Brotherhood in 1973 has resulted in Indian people becoming significantly involved in the control of Indian education in Canada. Before this there were some 200 Indian school committees, with the people having some more-or-less "token" input. By 1980, over three-quarters of the bands (450 out of 573) were administering all or part of their programs; there were 137 band-operated, on-reserve schools[24] and three native or Inuit school boards (the Nishgas of British Columbia, and the Cree and Kativik school boards of northern Quebec) exercising the same control as is exercised by provincial boards created under provincial law.

The Indian Affairs publication, *Indian Education Paper, Phase I*, documents the indicators of progress in Indian involvement in education. It cites greater control, greater participation in terms of enrolments, support for the teaching of language as part of the curriculum, and the establishment of cultural/educational centres. Nevertheless, it acknowledges the deficiencies in the implementation of policy. In its words:

> Although bi-lateral agreement was achieved in the adoption of the 1973 policy, adequate policy definition, devolution, preparation and procedures were not developed. As a result, a considerable gap was formed between expectations and reality. [25]

The document goes on to make the following points, which are worth summarizing at length:

- The basic problem with local control of Indian education is that the concept has been implemented without the federal/Indian relationship involved having been defined and without the necessary structures having been developed. (p. 31)
- Perceptions differ regarding the respective rights and obligations of the Department of Indian Affairs, Indian education authorities, and provincial jurisdictions.
- A time lag exists between changes in Indian society and changes in their educational services. (p. 16)
- Disparities have developed between departmental statements of intent and actions that have, or have not, been initiated to achieve these goals. (p. 17)
- The Department of Indian Affairs lacks the ability to support adequately the curriculum function ("activities are largely unco-ordinated, and there is great duplication of effort, because the Department does not have the capacity, either at headquarters or in the regions, to support a professional curriculum development program. Budgets do not offer the alternative of having this function performed under contract.") (p. 26)
- There has been little, if any, research into the reasons for low achievement of students and the high drop-out rate.
- The construction and maintenance of buildings is a problem. (p. 22)
- Staffing is characterized by high rates of turnover, inadequate training for transcultural education, and low morale. (p. 23)

Native people provide a parallel analysis:

> Roles, relations and obligations have never been clearly defined as between the Department and the First Nations in any scheme for the implementation of Indian control of education programs. Differing concepts of

control, jurisdiction, funding requirements and standards have obstructed the movement of real Indian control from a mere idea to an implemented reality. [26]

Intractable structural problems obstruct the satisfactory implementation of local control of education for Indian people. For instance, the policy is being implemented under archaic legislation that did not foresee the possibility of Indian intervention in Indians' own affairs, as even the legal right of the band councils to employ teachers has been challenged in the courts. The Department of Indian and Northern Affairs, like the Department of Aboriginal Affairs in Australia, was never constituted to administer educational programs; the budget is out of phase with the school year, support for curriculum development is lacking, and so on.

On the Indian side there are also enormous problems to be overcome. There is the lack of experience in educational policy-making and implementation. In some cases, the urgency of the need for local control impels action at a pace greater than that which can be absorbed and consolidated by the communities. There is need for education of the people to facilitate the management of their new responsibilities and to test the long-term commitment needed to solve the burdensome practicalities of developing new structures. While the National Indian Brotherhood (now the Assembly of First Nations) exists as a policy body, the agreed policy is necessarily fragmented and given different directions at the local level where it must be implemented. Different histories, different community compositions, and different local leadership styles all act to produce different conceptualizations of Indian identity, and hence of the "Indianization" of education appropriate to a particular group. The formulation and implementation of policy suited to local conditions needs great perception and time from people whose energies are already highly committed to activities furthering the advancement of the group in a multitude of areas, of which the school (though extremely important and valued) is only one. This is one concrete manifestation of a problem raised in various chapters in this book – namely, a "shallow" pool of skilled and talented human labour. Thus, in practice, *local control may be reduced to the management of a "white" curriculum, "white" organization, and "white" methodologies*, rather than offering self-determination through the creation of new structures appropriate to the building of an Indian identity.

The Department of Indian Affairs states quite clearly that Indian local government is not a service agency for the delivery of federally conceived and planned programs. However, the reality is that without personal experience in the "world" of education, it is difficult for Indians working at the level of implementation to construct a system that is fundamentally different from "white" education.

Nevertheless, despite all the problematic issues outlined above, very real progress has been made. The Inuit and Indian school boards erected under the James Bay and Northern Quebec Agreement (1975) in Quebec and the Nishga School Board in British Columbia do, in fact, control education with the power to decide on the language of instruction, the curriculum, the hiring of teachers, and the structuring of the school year. They may well provide models for other situations, as their initiatives develop. Various schools, such as the Kahnawake Survival School mentioned in Chapter Five, are controlled by boards on reserves that are "Indianizing" their philosophy, the content and structures of courses, and staffing. Where these are successful, they in turn serve as models for other bands to adapt or adopt. At a still more individual level, other "survival" schools (often off-reserve) are aimed at both the survival of Indian culture and the "survival" of individual students who are "push-outs" from mainstream schooling.

It should be noted also that non-indigenous support has been an element in the early stirrings of independence for indigenous people in each of the countries discussed. Non-aboriginals will continue to play an important role in one particular area, that of increasing the access of native people to, and their participation in, higher education. Eventually, native people themselves will be in positions of power within educational structures. In addition, universities are developing special entry programs and programs in native studies designed for Natives and non-Natives. Native people themselves have structured and control two major institutions (the Saskatchewan Federated Indian College and the Gabriel Dumont Institute) and a research association called Mokakit. All these initiatives are making a significant contribution to furthering the higher education and preparation of people needed to formulate and implement policy for the Indianization of education.

Clearly, the one common denominator reflected in all these various activities is pride in, and concern for, an indigenous identity that will be a cornerstone for the reclaiming of their autonomy.

The Sami
In Norway, since the Sami are not officially recognized as an ethnic group but merely as "those who speak Sami," contemporary Sami ef-

forts are directed at gaining legal status. Ruong analyses the effects on Sami identity of current law:

> . . . the attitude of the society is crystallized in its laws. In my opinion, legislation on reindeer pastures and reindeer breeding creates an unfortunate dividing line between reindeer breeders and other Lapps. Indeed it cuts across the Lappish nation and complicates, and in a sense prevents, a real community of interests, i.e., a deeper communication and contact between Lapps who are reindeer breeders and Lapps who are not. [27]

Since the Sami are fragmented by artificial geographical boundaries and categorizations imposed by other governments, the reconstruction of a Sami group identity has come to rely on the common history and especially common language of the Sami people. The Sami demand that their language be given full recognition in law both in those areas where Sami comprise a majority and in areas where they have come to be a minority due to Norwegian colonization. More specifically, they demand that:

- the Sami language be established as an official language;
- the Sami language be taught in schools as both a native and foreign language, and that Sami language be used as a language of instruction and a medium of information;
- teaching materials and instruction in the schools be grounded in Sami culture and traditions, in accord with the wishes of parents;
- the Sami language be used in public instruction and official transactions.

For the language to be the preferred choice in public use, it must be given prestige in the schools and in the community, and a high proportion of the population must speak it with fluency. This is dependent on the acceptance of an education policy that *promotes* (not merely tolerates) the Sami language. To make these policies effective a preeminent degree of support is given to research, particularly as it is integrated into supporting the rights claimed and making their implementation possible. The vocabulary of the language, for example, is being extended and stabilized across the geographical borders so that it can become the medium of instruction. Also, a history of the Sami has been written.

In the school curriculum, changes are recognizing the Sami movement. The first of these occurred in Norway in the immediate postwar era. It followed a 1947 recommendation to the Minister of Education suggesting co-operation with Sweden regarding the publication of Sami textbooks. A step of crucial importance for Sami solidarity was taken when Norway and Sweden adopted a common orthography.

Following the 1963 debate in the Stortinget, a Sami upper secondary school opened at Karasjok in 1969. Small grants were allocated by the government for a library to be established in the same village and for the establishment of museums at Karasjok and Tromso. The library has the largest holdings of Sami literature in Scandinavia.

The formulation and implementation of policy with regard to schooling is carried out by the Sami Education Council, established in 1975. The two basic principles enunciated by the council are that: (1) the school must give the new generation of Sami the possibility to interact with the wider society, and (2) at the same time, and as part of this, the school must give the Sami the possibility to both conserve and further create their ethnic and cultural identity. [28]

While language was the criterion of identity emphasized above all others in policy statements to government, a scanning of issues raised at successive Lapp conferences shows that growing importance is being placed on the cultivation of objective distinguishing characteristics that mark off the Sami as an ethnic group different from Norwegians and hence, in their view, substantiate their claims to autonomy. For instance, the conferences have promoted research and study about traditional Sami handicrafts associated with activities previously essential to everyday living. Related action includes the reclaiming of a particular form of folk music (the Yoik) that is unique to the Sami and the development of Sami art, poetry, and literature.

These preoccupations of the policy-makers are reflected in the structures of educational institutions. In the vocational school at Kautokeino, for example, the study of traditional handicrafts is emphasized, as well as the "modernization" of the traditional occupations of breeding and marketing reindeer.

For the Sami (as for Norwegians) the opportunity of adapting the curriculum to their particular circumstances is dependent largely on how creative the local school board and the local school are in taking advantage of these possibilities, since government policy commits it to support, however reluctantly, [29] the establishement of bilingual, bicultural schools for the Sami.

The establishment of a Teachers' College at Alta, which provides courses in Sami language and culture for both Sami and non-Sami, should provide a pool of teachers sensitive to Sami policy and qualified to develop initiatives. (A problem endemic to all indigenous people, however, is that creative teachers are drawn away from the classroom to fill other roles in the developing organizations of the indigenous groups.) The location of Sami institutions and high schools, and of Sami individuals doing research, in Sami villages, rather than in "Norwegian" urban situations, is seen as a particularly important strategy. In the case of school location, the aim is the retention of students who would otherwise drop out; in the case of teacher-training institutions and of individuals doing research, there is an attempt to prevent a separation from the "real" village situation. In each case, however, the siting is seen as a means of building and proclaiming Sami identity and autonomy.

The major Sami thrust in terms of autonomy and control, however, has been through the Sami Institut'ta. While the University of Tromso is a stronghold for the study and preservation of Sami language and literature, the Sami Institute performs additional symbolic functions: it stands as a sign of unity for all Sami across geographical boundaries; it produces unity of policy on vital issues; it provides a single organization that puts pressure on governments to unite in their policy toward the Sami; and above all, it proclaims to the world a positive identity for the Sami people.

These changes have all taken place *within* a Norwegian framework. In 1985, however, a submission presented to the Stortinget seeking the establishment of a Sami committee to advise Parliament on Sami issues (similar to the so-called Sami Parliament in Finland) was approved. Its activities will be crucial to further developments in education.

Australian Aborigines

A major difference between the situation in Australia and in Canada and Sami-land is that there is no one body embracing all Aboriginal organizations in Australia. The National Aboriginal Education Committee (established in 1977) co-exists with other organizations, each concerned with separate issues, such as land claims, the arts, the development of economic ventures, legal aid services, and health services. As Rudnicki and Dyck note in their chapter in the self-government section of this book, the National Aboriginal Education Committee and the Aboriginal State Education Committees are policy-making bodies, *consulted* by government. They lack the power that is fundamental to self-determination. The National Committee has, therefore, as one of its objectives, the establishment of a National Aboriginal Education Commission that would be a statutory body established by an Act of Parliament. The Aboriginal people believe (and they were supported in this by the Australian Schools Commission) that self-determination in decision-making relating to Aboriginal education cannot become a reality until the responsibility for funding programs for Aborigines belongs to the Aborigines themselves.

Nevertheless, despite these qualifications, the National Aboriginal Education Committee (NAEC) has more than fulfilled the expectations held out for it. It has carried out a series of evaluations on existing projects; in 1979 it researched the need for Aboriginal teachers and the opportunity for teacher training for Aboriginal people in response to a National Inquiry into Education; and it articulated and disseminated NAEC education policy that was accepted and implemented by the government and by institutions of higher education and which in turn resulted in a significant increase in the number of Aborigines graduating as teachers. In 1985, the NAEC produced a comprehensive document[30] to guide the government in the allocation of funds for the 1985-1987 triennium. Together with the Commonwealth Tertiary Education Commission it also mounted a review of support systems for Aboriginal students in higher education.[31]

The provision of greater access to and participation in education will enable the "Aboriginalization" of these services. It will also provide a pool of people who are equipped by their own background to formulate policy and who have had experience within the academic world, the world of schooling.

Australia lags sadly behind both Canada and Sami-land in its representation in the academic world. The first Aboriginal university professor was appointed in 1985; other academic appointments of Aboriginal people number less than a dozen. If Aboriginal academics are to influence the policy-making bodies of autonomous institutions such as universities and colleges of education, and also, as in the case of the Sami and the Canadian Natives, bring about an "Aboriginalization" of research being carried out on Aboriginal issues, then the 1970s thrust into higher education must be followed in the second half of the 1980s by an emphasis on entry into graduate-level education.

At the grassroots level, differences in history and development found among the aboriginal peoples of Canada are equally evident among the Aborigines of Australia. There are urban dwellers whose language has long ceased to be used, whose mother tongue is now English; there are tradition-oriented people who speak only their own language; there are people who have had contact with the white world and are able to speak a species of English (Aboriginal English) but continue to use their own language in most social interaction. The outcome of the policy of self-determination in the sphere of education has therefore taken on different forms depending on the history, ideology, geography, economic base, and social interaction of various groups. In some cases, in the far north of Australia where the Aborigines are in the majority, the response has been the *out-station movement*. The people have moved back to their homelands, away from cattle stations, away from white contact in general, to reconstruct a tradition-oriented identity. Schooling, however, and in particular the learning of English, is highly valued, and the people make the request for white teachers to follow them as they move away into isolated areas.

For other tradition-oriented groups in much the same areas, there has been a movement toward *community schools* whose organizational patterns may, to some extent, be seen as micro-versions of the Kativik and Cree school boards of Quebec and the Nishgas of British Columbia. The (Aboriginal) boards, though, most often have only one school for which they are responsible. Alternatively, in some cases, where missionary and government activities in the past have brought about an agglomeration of groups speaking different languages, the social structure imposed from outside breaks down naturally into language groups and the people move off into separate "camps" again, although only after they have secured the services of teachers. The responsibility of the Aboriginal school boards of these community schools extends to the structuring of curriculum, the hiring of teachers (who are required to respect the philosophy of the group), the structuring of the school year, and the approval of the subjects taught, their content (carefully scrutinized for anything contrary to the philosophy of the group), and the methodologies used. In the urban situation, too, there are examples of the development of *independent schools*. While the issue that triggers the founding of such a school is often the problem of combatting the drop-out of indigenous people from white schools (the problem common to all three countries), the aim is one of fostering a positive Aboriginal identity.

The Future: The Problems To Be Faced

Financial and Legal Dependence
Canadian Indians challenge the power of the government to impose restrictive legislation on them. The assertion of identity and the issue of the control of education are thus situated in a context of legal considerations concerning the recognition of rights of indigenous groups. Before the fiscal control essential for self-determination can be a reality, legal bases for self-determination must be decided. Indeed, financial support is necessary for the initial fight for justice, since the fight will always be on the terms of the dominant group.

In the case of Australia, efforts have been made from time to time to

278

have Aboriginal law recognized by identifying crimes that are, basically, against Aboriginal tribal law and should therefore be tried by Aboriginal courts. There is no recognition of Aboriginal law, however, in any of the countries concerned when there is a clash between the interests of the dominant group and indigenous groups.

The Cree and the Inuit in the province of Quebec gained full control over education in 1975 under the conditions of the James Bay and Northern Quebec Agreement. In the terms of this agreement, the Cree School Board has special powers, unequalled in other school boards across the land and certainly beyond comparison with powers related to the administration of other Indian boards in Canada. This result would seem to have occurred partly because of the financial aid given to the Cree to assemble their legal case. Self-determination, however, even when it appears real, rests on a fragile base when communities remain dependent on funding from the dominant group, whether for preparing documentation for legal battles, appointing consultants for curriculum development, or hiring teachers. Indeed, the question must be asked whether autonomy can ever be real when the finances of the group are controlled from outside. If the group is not economically viable, then the more realistic conceptualization of its political status might be one of self-management rather than self-determination.

Size of the Group
The linkage between self-determination and identity is based in a critical way on the size of the group. Schooling, whether carried out on reserves or in cities, must lead to some employment opportunity for students if they are to continue to be motivated at upper levels of schooling. If there is no connection between schooling and employment (either within the group or within the wider society), then one may expect high drop-out rates. In each situation examined, there are continuing attempts within the local communities to identify job opportunities and structure education accordingly. Nevertheless, the size of a particular group will be of paramount importance. If it is not sufficiently large to accommodate employment opportunities for youth, then they either are forced into depending on social welfare benefits or are under pressure to leave the group, thus further reducing its viability. They are similarly forced to leave the group if it is not sufficiently large to provide for the breadth of choices in subjects in secondary schools needed to allow for occupational choices. The connection between the size and viability of the group also has implications for language. If the Aborigines, or the Sami, or Canadian Indians must emigrate to the urban situation for employment, not only is the economic

viability of the home community affected, but so too is the cultural viability, for the preferred language for employment will have to become that of the dominant group. Thus, economic and cultural viability and self-determination are interwoven threads of a total fabric; fragility in any one area relentlessly pushes individuals to assimilation.

Membership of a Pluralistic Society
The contemporary granting of positive status to indigenous people is not an issue existing in isolation; it must be seen as situated within a general theory that guides practitioners' approach to pluralistic or multicultural societies. In Canada and Australia the conceptualization of a multicultural society has largely excluded indigenous people. In all three countries, the indigenous people have also acted to exclude themselves on the grounds of their unique status – they are not immigrants; they are the original people. The reality of history, however, is that their "uniqueness" has not been recognized, or rather, it was recognized and stigmatized. All their actions took place "within the framework of the dominant majority groups' statuses and institutions where identity as a minority group gave no basis for action."[32]

If self-determination in education is to have any meaning, it is of utmost importance that indigenous people form their own educational organizations and construct their own institutions from within which they can create a status that permits positive interaction with the majority group and at the same time calls forth a positive assessment from the minority group as a whole. That is, ethnic identity must be seen in positive terms by the dominant group and the minority group alike.

If the people themselves cannot perceive their institutions, and in particular their educational institutions, as offering positive opportunities and reinforcing identity, then, where physical characteristics and command of language permit people to "pass" into the dominant society, voluntary "migration" into the dominant group will be a most compelling option. That is, "pluralism" in a society offers real choices only when parallel groups receive parallel esteem.[33] If one group is stigmatized and permanently situated in the lowest ranks of the socio-economic hierarchy, then the option of choosing the identity of that group is not attractive. Ethnic groups, then, must build societies having equality of esteem with the dominant group if they are to remain viable.

Because of the diversity of history and development already mentioned, a further problem of pluralism faces aboriginal minority groups in that they must also provide for pluralism within their theorizing. Paradoxically, it is not expected that the dominant group should have formed a consensus on any and every subject (witness the violent disagreements about abortion, nuclear power, etc.), yet the dominant group, and sometimes leaders within ethnic groups, grow impatient when ethnic groups do not share a single coherent view on a particular topic. Nevertheless, despite the unreasonableness of expecting people to have one view, ethnic groups must be able to formulate an ideology and a program of action that is sufficiently coherent for the governments of dominant groups to be able to respond to the voice of the minority group, yet broad enough to allow for different modes of interpretation in local situations.

This coherent view must be projected not only to outsiders. If the next generation is to be socialized into the customs and language of the indigenous group, then there must be projected a "world-of-meaning" which is plausible not only to contemporary adult members of the group but also to the youth. Certain cultural attributes from the past, which can still have currency today, must be selected and emphasized as distinctive of the group.

The problem, however, is to find both a *mode* of theorizing that does not mythologize the group's past in a way that prevents contemporary development and a commonly accepted *site* for theorizing. The holding of pan-Sami conferences, the assembling of the diverse groups of Canada's First Nations, and the bringing together of the members of the National Aboriginal Education Committee and of other Aboriginal organizations representing Aboriginal people differing greatly in their world views all have the latent function of providing a rationale for proclaiming "We are one people with a common history: we have a strong feeling of solidarity." This feeling has been confirmed by joining with other groups in the World Council of Indigenous People; within this organization there is a perception of the common histories of oppressed peoples, which in turn leads to a feeling of solidarity with other indigenous groups and encouragement for each group to persevere in its efforts to gain autonomy.

However, for ethnic groups, the pre-eminent site of communication of values remains educational institutions. Sociologists have held that one of the functions of the school is to reproduce society and transmit its cultural values at the same time that it concerns itself with knowledge. It is therefore inescapable that all of the indigenous groups discussed have seen schools as the major site where the battle for ethnic identity was lost and where theorizing will be implemented and cohesive values formed for the reclaiming of the identity.

Notes

1. Diane Longboat, "First Nations Jurisdiction over Education: The Path to Survival as Nations" (Ottawa: mimeo), p. 1.
2. Thomas Berger, *Northern Frontier, Northern Homeland: The Report of the Mackenzie Valley Pipeline Inquiry* (Ottawa: Supply and Services Canada, 1977), p. 90.
3. I. Ruong, "The Lapps: An Indigenous People of Fenno Scandia," in *Ethnodevelopment in the Nordic Sami Region* (Karasjok: Working papers at the UNESCO meeting on Ethnocide and Ethnodevelopment in Europe, 1983), p. 45.
4. Chief Saul Fiddler, Sandy Lake, in *Report of the Royal Commission on the Northern Environment* (Toronto: Queen's Printer of Ontario, 1978), p. 207.
5. Gilbert Faries, Moose Factory, *ibid.*
6. Knut Eriksen and Einas and Einar Niemi, *The Finnish Menace: Boundary Problems and Minority Policy in the North, 1870-1940* (Oslo: Universitetsforlaget, 1981), p. 361.
7. Harald Eidheim, *Aspects of the Lappish Minority Situation* (Oslo: Universitetsforlaget, 1971), p. 87.
8. C.D. Rowley, *Outcasts in White Australia, Aboriginal Policy and Practice*, Vol. II, *Aborigines in Australian Society* (Canberra: Australian National University Press, 1971), pp. 8, 20.
9. *Ibid.*, pp. 48ff.
10. F. Gale assisted by Alison Brookman, *Urban Aborigines* (Canberra: Australian National University Press, 1972), p. 245.
11. L. Lippmann, *Words or Blows: Racial Attitudes in Australia* (Victoria: Pelican Books, 1981), p. 139.
12. D.S. Anderson and A.E. Vervoorn, *Access to Privilege: Patterns of Participation in Australian Post-Secondary Education* (Canberra: Australian National University Press, 1983), p. 125.
13. R.T. Fitzgerald, *Poverty and Education in Australia. Fifth Main Report* (Canberra: Australian Government Printing Service, 1976), p. 185.
14. Eidheim, *Aspects*, pp. 50-67.
15. H.B. Hawthorn and M.A. Tremblay, *A Survey of the Contemporary Indians of Canada: Economic, Political, Educational Needs and Policies* (Ottawa: Queen's Printer, 1966), p. 130.
16. Education and Social Development Branch, *Indian Education Paper. Phase I* (Ottawa: Indian and Inuit Affairs Program, 1982), Annex C, pp. 7, 8.
17. *Ibid.*, p. 8.
18. Longboat, "First Nations Jurisdiction," p. 3.
19. Jean Chrétien, "Address to the Council of Ministers of Education," 1972.
20. *Ibid.*
21. Berger, *Northern Frontier, Northern Homeland*, p. 181.
22. National Indian Brotherhood, *Indian Control of Indian Education: Policy Paper Presented to the Minister of Indian Affairs and Northern Development* (Ottawa, 1973), p. 1.

23. Commonwealth Hansard, *Senate Budget Debate, 1971-72, King Debate, 1971* (Canberra: Australian Government Printing Service), p. 756.

24. Education and Social Development Branch, *Indian Education Paper*, p. 14. By 1985 the number of Indian-managed schools had increased to 219, according to: Canada, *1986-87 Estimates – Indian and Northern Affairs: Part III, Expenditure Plan* (Ottawa: Supply and Services Canada, 1986), p. 2-24.

25. *Ibid.*, p. 6.

26. Longboat, "First Nations Jurisdiction," p. 20.

27. Ruong, "The Lapps," p. 75.

28. Jan Henry Keskitalo, *Education and the Native Sami, 1985* (Kautokeino: Sami Council for Education, 1985), p. 10.

29. Eidheim, *Aspects*, p. 76.

30. National Aboriginal Education Committee, *Aborigines and Tertiary Education: A Framework for the 1985-1987 Triennium* (Canberra, 1985).

31. Deirdre F. Jordan, *Support Systems for Aboriginal People in Higher Education* (Adelaide: Tertiary Education Authority of South Australia, 1984).

32. Eidheim, *Aspects*, Preface.

33. See *ibid.*, pp. 50ff.

Chapter Eleven

Native Claims and Settlement in Yukon

By James S. Frideres

General Background

Yukon Natives have been in the process of negotiating their land claims for well over a decade. This chapter will sketch the historical background to these negotiations, identify the legal context in which the negotiations are taking place, and, finally, outline the contents of the 1985 Agreement in Principle. We shall find that the proposed land settlement is unique when compared to recent land claims, although many aspects are similar to the COPE and James Bay agreements.

Archaeological sites reveal that over 27,000 years ago people were living in the area now encompassed by Yukon. Historically, Inuit lived on the Arctic coast although today there is no Inuit community in Yukon. Today the Indians of Yukon consist of two principal groups: the Dene (or Athabaskans) in the interior and the Tlingit in the southwestern part of the territory. The Dene can be subdivided into three groups: the Loucheux are found in the Peel and Porcupine River areas (Old Crow); the Kutchin live in the Yukon River watershed; the Nahanni are found in southeast Yukon. An estimated 8,000 Indians were in Yukon in the early nineteenth century, but the population was subsequently reduced to less than 1,400 by 1912. This has now increased to nearly 3,000, most of whom live in one of twelve communities, shown in Map 2. Three communities (Old Crow, Pelly Crossing, and Upper Liard) are nearly all status Indian communities. The Carmacks and Mayo Indians are a clear majority in their communities. The populations of Carcross, Ross River, and Teslin are evenly balanced, while in Dawson City and Haines Junction Indians are a minority. Finally, 1,000 Indians live in Whitehorse, but they are a small minority, as are Indians in Watson Lake. Only Faro and Elsa lack any Indian population. In addition to the status Indians, an esti-

Map 2
Native Population Settlements, Linguistic Divisions, and Migration
Routes in Yukon

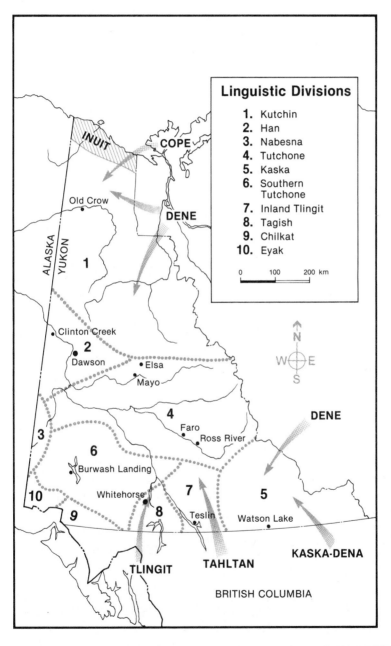

Linguistic Divisions

1. Kutchin
2. Han
3. Nabesna
4. Tutchone
5. Kaska
6. Southern Tutchone
7. Inland Tlingit
8. Tagish
9. Chilkat
10. Eyak

mated 2,500 non-status Indians also reside in Yukon. These people are not considered Indian under the terms of the Indian Act. Reserves have not been set aside for them, nor do they come under the jurisdiction of the Indian Act.

While the fur trade first brought whites into Yukon, the gold rush was not far behind. Prospectors began to enter Yukon in some numbers by 1873. By the turn of the century the world was well aware of the gold boom in the Klondike and over 30,000 people (mostly non-Natives) had entered the area. The rush brought the area into the twentieth century without any preparation or transitional period. With the collapse of the gold rush by the second decade of the twentieth century, no other economic activities took its place. Not until the early 1940s would the next economic boom occur.

The Canadian government's orientation toward native people in Yukon during the late nineteenth century could be characterized as one of salutary neglect.[1] Government policy, supported by the police, was to keep Natives in the bush, continuing their nomadic, traditional life.[2] The government's decision not to negotiate a treaty with the Indians was based on the belief that Indians were best left in their natural state. Nevertheless, "residential reserves" (land areas where Indians could live) were established. These areas were not permanent and were moved if non-Natives needed the land.[3]

With a suddenness reminiscent of the gold rush, several economic activities occurred almost simultaneously around the time of World War II. These were the Alaska Highway, the building of airstrips for the North West Staging Route, the Canol pipeline, and the building of a large oil refinery in Whitehorse. The Alaska Highway changed the traditional living patterns of Indians as the mode of transportation changed from the bush and waterways to a road system. (Today 80 per cent of the population lives along the highway.) The period 1940-43 also saw a dramatic decrease in the price of furs to the extent that many Natives stopped trapping. They still hunted in groups but now lived in settlements near the highway. This caused a strain on the renewable resources. The highway system also brought a substantial number of non-Natives into the North and Natives consequently became a minority of the population. This impact on Natives was further exacerbated by the rush to develop the mining industry pursuant to Prime Minister John Diefenbaker's "Vision of the North" and "Roads for Resources" policies.

Although the 1898 Yukon Act created Yukon as a separate territory, it would not be until 1960 that major political reforms would be implemented. At that time an Advisory Committee on Finance was established; it led to more territorial fiscal responsibility. Ten years later an Executive Committee comprising two elected council members was created to advise the Commissioner. Then in 1978 party politics were introduced. One year later the Minister of Indian Affairs and Northern Development instructed the Commissioner to follow the decision of the elected members of the Executive Committee (except for special matters of vital concern to Ottawa) and the ultimate executive responsibility was transferred from the Commissioner to the Territorial Legislative Assembly, acting through its Executive Council.

As of June, 1984, there were twelve bands in Yukon, ranging in size from seventy-three to 604 members and averaging 215. In addition, a large number of members of the British Columbia Liard River Band live in the Yukon community of Upper Liard. Going into the Yukon claims negotiations, the pattern of Indian landholdings for members of these various Yukon bands was markedly different from that in most of the rest of Canada. Virtually all land set aside for Indians in Yukon is land *other than* Indian Act reserve land. Many of these non-Indian Act units are individual lots or groups of individual lots designated for housing, settlement, or residential purposes or for village sites for individual bands. These units tend to be relatively small in area and are normally located within or near the main Yukon communities. Hence, registered Indian occupants of these lots live near non-registered Indian and nonIndian members of the community and generally share with them many of the basic facilities and services of the community.[4] On the other hand, larger tracts of land of about ten to twenty square miles (or, in the case of the Old Crow Band, 350 square miles) are also set aside for some bands, primarily for subsistence activities or grazing purposes.

Each Indian band has a band council consisting of a chief and two or more other councillors. In addition, a second tier of Indian political structure involves organizations that have been created by Indians rather than by the federal government. These are the Indian associations or brotherhoods. Prior to 1973, Yukon status Indians were represented by the Yukon Native Brotherhood (formed in 1968) and non-status Indians by the Yukon Association of Nonstatus Indians. In 1973 a new organization, the Council of Yukon Indians (CYI), emerged to negotiate a land claim settlement for Yukon Indian people. By 1980 all three organizations were integrated into a new CYI. Hence, status and non-status Indians are represented by the same organization; the remainder of this chapter will often refer to the encompassing term "Natives" (to represent the expanded constituency of CYI) rather than to Indians alone.

Legal Background

In the nineteenth century, Canada considered the North to be "terra nullius" – territory not under the sovereignty of another state – even though it held thousands of native people. Furthermore, Canada began to impose its own system of government on the indigenous peoples even though, as Cruikshank[5] points out, there is ample evidence that Yukon Indians had a system of land principles relating to the use of land and resources.

Now, as the Natives bring forth their land claims, a number of legal issues loom large. To what extent do prior statutes (such as the Royal Proclamation of 1763) bear on Yukon native claims? What role will past court decisions have on the final agreement? Furthermore, how will the negotiators deal with past political decisions related to native land claims? For example, the land cession treaties, Article 40 of the Articles of Capitulation of Quebec in 1760, and the Dominion Land Acts of 1872 to 1950 all imply recognition of pre-existing aboriginal rights. Finally, Elliott[6] suggests analogies that might be drawn between aboriginal title and the existing doctrines of English common law and international law.

Decisions made by the courts have already influenced the land claims negotiations. While there are a number of cases germane to the issue, only three recent cases will be noted here. The best known is the Nishga case (1973), in which six Supreme Court justices (out of seven) indicated that aboriginal title may exist in law on the basis of Indians having occupied the land since time immemorial. In the same year, the Kanatewat case (presided over by Mr. Justice Malouf) allowed Indians and Inuit an interim injunction to prevent the James Bay Development Corporation from continuing work on the James Bay hydroelectric project. Finally, in the 1974 Paulette case, Mr. Justice Morrow (Northwest Territories Supreme Court) ruled Indian people of the N.W.T. had aboriginal rights.

The government's subsequent successful appeals of both the Malouf and Morrow decisions, as well as the interpretation given to various statutes and political decisions, suggest that in the final analysis Canadian courts might not give legal recognition to an occupancy-based aboriginal title in Yukon. The courts have seemed reluctant to address the issue of aboriginal title, as they have shown a marked preference to limit consideration of this thorny issue to procedural or technical grounds. As one judge suggested, "these are really political issues, not legal."

Northern Land Claims

The treaty period in southern Canada ended in the 1920s and land claims remained a closed issue until after World War II, when renewed pressure by Indians forced government to deal with them. Part of that pressure came from events in nearby Alaska where, by 1968, the Tlingit and Haida Indians (related to the Yukon Indians) were awarded well over $7 million as a land settlement. That same year Atlantic Richfield struck oil and gas at Prudhoe Bay on the North Slope of Alaska. Yet, despite these events, in 1969 the Canadian government published its infamous white paper on Indian affairs, which rejected all aboriginal claims and advocated the abolition of reserves and the abolition of the legal status of Indians. This position was short-lived; by 1971 the government had conceded that this policy was not acceptable to Canadians and abandoned the policy.

The early 1970s were marked by a series of related events with seemingly cumulative effects. These were:

- 1970 – rejection of the federal government's white paper;
- 1971 – Alaska Native settlement (not Tlingit and Haida);
- 1972 – Union of B.C. Indian Chiefs' land claim;
- 1972 – Quebec Cree and Inuit injunction against James Bay Development Corporation;
- 1972 – Chiefs of Mackenzie Valley submit caveat application.

As a result of these actions, the government conceded that perhaps the Indians had more rights than they had thought and began to set in motion political structures to deal with the issue.

Origin of the Yukon Claim

Under these circumstances the Council of Yukon Indians submitted its claim, entitled *Together Today for our Children Tomorrow*, in early 1973. In response, the government formed a negotiating team that included the Commissioner of Yukon, and by late 1973 negotiations commenced. The federal government's first strategy was to make a unilateral, public offer of settlement. Rejecting the offer, the CYI was able to force the government to convert its offer into a working paper.

The federal government's initial role of negotiating with the Natives and excluding the Yukon territorial government was challenged by Yukon under Section 46 of the Yukon Act. The territory successfully argued that the federal government could not make a settlement with the Natives alone.

Yukon's formal response to the Natives' claim was made public in 1975 when a proposal (*Meaningful Government for all Yukoners*) from the office of the Commissioner was published. This document was based on a 1974 document entitled *Analysis and Position – Yukon Indian Land Claim*. The major thrust of the response included four interrelated points dealing with the native proposal and with Yukon's relationship with Ottawa. Specifically, it discussed how to integrate Natives into the Yukon government (a so-called "one-government" system), how to deliver some federal programs for Natives, how to devise a way in which Yukon resources would be brought under control of Yukoners, and how to develop a fully elected Executive Council. While technically a response to the Natives' grievances, it was really a document for Ottawa in Yukon's quest for a fully responsible government – provincehood. This stance a decade ago determined the outcome of the eventual negotiations.

Yukon's proposal was presented to CYI in 1976 for approval. The president of the National Indian Brotherhood intervened and publicly rejected the proposal. This action was supported by the CYI and by mid-year all negotiations had come to a halt.[7] Soon afterward, the three major actors in the negotiations were changed and any sense of continuity was lost. It was not until 1977 that the third round of negotiations began.

In summary, the Yukon government's proposal was first directed at maintaining a one-government structure in Yukon in which native people could participate. The proposal was also seen as a first step toward provincehood.

Procedures and Policies for Processing Indian Land Claims

For well over two centuries, Canadian Natives and various levels of government have discussed the issue of aboriginal rights. However, only in the recent past (1982) have these rights become enshrined in the Canadian constitution. Over the years a number of strategies have been used by the federal government in trying to process disputes between itself and Natives. Table 16 outlines the four most common procedures in a typology based on two factors – the use of intervenors and the terms of settlement.[8]

Until recently, coercion and adjudication were the most prevalent ways of processing disputes. The government of Canada, either through its administrative arm, DIAND, or through the courts, processed all native claims. The stronger of the disputants, i.e., the government, inevitably imposed its decision on the weaker of the parties. However, after the Nishga case it became apparent even to the federal

Table 16

Strategies of Claims Settlement Procedures

Terms of Settlement	Use of Third-Party Intervenors	
	No	Yes
Agreed by both parties	Negotiation	Mediation
Imposed on weakest party	Coercion	Adjudication

government that these procedures were not going to solve the disputes. Indeed, imposed settlements actually put Indians into a dependent status and increased their sense of alienation. New ways of trying to solve the native claims issue emerged and today negotiation and mediation are used for settling comprehensive claims.

Negotiation, as a strategy for resolving land claims, seems to have emerged in the late 1970s. As a process it deals with the problem as one of not producing winners and losers; that is, it is not to be viewed as a so-called "zero sum game" (a situation where gains by one side can be attained only at the expense of the other side). According to Rolf,[9] the assumptions underlying the government's new approach to the issue are that negotiations will: (1) lead to better decisions; (2) be more adaptable to changing conditions; (3) be fairer to all parties involved in the dispute; and (4) be better implemented than other types of decisions.

The process of negotiating has been affected by the extent to which the parties differ in power and resources. To a certain extent, moneys, information, and other technical aspects have been made available to Natives by government so that their participation in settlements has been more equal than in the past. Negotiations have also been slowed when the agenda became too narrow and thus transformed the process into a zero sum game because there was little opportunity for reciprocal concessions. On the other hand, when the negotiations have addressed multiple issues, progress in the talks has been noted. Finally, a way for parties to resolve an impasse has not been fully outlined and this poses future problems.

Today the federal government has two policies for dealing with aboriginal land claims, one for "specific" claims, the other for "comprehensive" claims.[10] Our interest is in the latter. The comprehensive policy, adopted in 1981, was embodied in a DIAND document entitled *In All Fairness: A Native Claims Policy, Comprehensive Claims*. This policy stated that the government was willing "to exchange undefined aboriginal land rights for concrete rights and benefits" (p. 19). The comprehensive claims policy set out three objectives: (1) to negotiate fair and equitable settlements to bona fide native land claims; (2) to ensure that the settlements would allow Natives to live in the way they wish; (3) in settling these claims, to respect the rights of all other people.

Some of the "concrete rights and benefits" to be acquired or recognized would be land, wildlife, and subsurface rights, as well as monetary compensation. With regard to land rights, the document stated that lands to be selected by Natives would be limited to traditional lands that they currently use and occupy. On the issue of subsurface rights, the government is prepared to give some rights in certain cases. Finally, compensation, in whatever form, is to be "specific and final."

Comprehensive claims were to be resolved by negotiation, culminating in a compromise settlement. In summary, the government's position put limits on: the scope of what native people could negotiate, their legal rights in relation to other "interests," and the type of involvement in trying to settle their claim.[11] The actors involved in the negotiations were to be the federal government, the Natives, and the territorial government.

Yukon Land Claims Negotiations

Manifest and Latent Issues
We now turn to the actual substance of the negotiations between Natives and the two levels of government. The Indians, it should be noted, are not seeking a total return to their traditional way of life; they have other priorities. One central issue is the right to use and occupy land. Related questions have been the definition of the verb "use," the duration of occupancy and use (collective versus individual), and the question of who can alienate the land (fee simple versus aboriginal rights). In addition, the extent and form of compensation, as well as the type and form of administrative structure to be created once an agreement is reached, have also become important topics in the negotiations.

Other issues have made their presence felt at the negotiating table, although rather than being openly discussed they remain like a spectre lingering in the room. One of these is the history of earlier court judgements involving aboriginal land claims. That history offers no legal precedent that could lead Natives to expect financial or other forms of compensation.[12] From this perspective, Natives are well aware of the risks of pursuing a strict legal course of action. A second shadow cast on the negotiating table is the Natives' concern that the

292

federal government could try to solve the legal issue through the strategy of proposing a treaty. While this might seem attractive to government officials, it has not been without problems. For example, if treaties are viewed as contracts, those Natives living in a treaty area but who do not sign the treaty might be exempt from the extinguishment of rights. In addition, as Morrow found with Treaties Eight and Eleven, ambiguity and misunderstandings might render some of the contents of a treaty ineffective (e.g., oral promises which are inconsistent with written provisions).

Third, in other statutes (see below) where extinguishment of aboriginal title is not explicitly stated, further complications emerge that might actually allow the federal government to return to an earlier position that claimed that aboriginal rights have already been extinguished. This issue has also been debated in American law but, as in Canada, with contradictory results. The essence of the issue in Yukon is that some non-Natives argue that government legislation, such as the Territorial Lands Act, Public Land Grants Act, and Forestry Development and Research Act, contains a number of provisions that effectively extinguished aboriginal title even though that was not its primary intent.

The land tenure system in Yukon is a fourth parameter within which the negotiations are being conducted. The system involves considerable restrictions on property ownership and has been subject – in law, at least – to considerable central government control. The Indian Act creates a protectorate or Crown trust that limits the rights of Natives. Because some Yukon Natives do not have lands regarded as Indian Act lands, some of those who do have such lands feel that the reserve system should have some bearing (in the sense of favouring them) on land settlements. Regardless, the importance of this system in Canada suggests that it may have an important bearing on the future negotiations.

The above concerns have influenced the negotiations between the three parties. However, in spite of their differences, they have managed to sign an Agreement in Principle.

The Agreement in Principle (1985)

It should be emphasized that the Agreement in Principle (AIP) has not received the assent of the constituents of the native negotiating team. About one-third of the twelve native communities strongly oppose the proposed settlement while an additional one-third are requesting major revisions. Hence, at time of writing negotiators were about to embark on a new round of negotiations. Previous comprehensive claims settlements elsewhere in Canada (e.g., COPE, James Bay) also revealed a pattern of renegotiating, although in those cases only minor changes were introduced after the Agreement in Principle was signed.

If a similar pattern is evident for Yukon, then the following discussion may provide a fairly accurate indication of what the final settlement will be. However, if Yukon Natives are successful in making changes to the AIP, the final agreement will probably change in the direction of empowerment of Natives. That is, whereas the 1985 proposed settlement gives Natives *influence* through membership on advisory boards, a future Agreement in Principle might have to give some regulatory *power* to such boards as well as increased native representation on these boards.

Until 1979 both the federal and Yukon governments took the position that land claims negotiations would include only land and monetary compensation. At the urging of the Council of Yukon Indians, in February, 1979, a Memorandum of Understanding was signed between the federal and Yukon governments. It agreed that the two governments would develop a Yukon constitutional development process to be correlated with the native claims process, although any Yukon constitutional issues would be dealt with separately. Nevertheless, the government of Yukon has taken the position that it wants to move to some form of provincial status and that it be a one-government system.[13] It argues that in order to prepare for the settlement and to make sure it operates properly and fairly, Yukoners (both Native and non-Native) need the powers of provincehood.

At that time, too, the CYI asked that the scope of negotiations be broadened to include such issues as local government, health, and education. By late 1979 the CYI formally requested that constitutional issues and the land claims settlement be negotiated as one package. Both levels of government agreed. Later that same year, the three parties agreed to certain principles for conducting native land claims negotiations. These were: (1) that special interests of beneficiaries (read Natives) would be identified; (2) that these special interests would be enshrined in the final settlement; and (3) that after the settlement, beneficiaries would be treated identically to non-beneficiaries with respect to participating in the Yukon government.

By early 1983 the federal government agreed to discuss "Yukon constitutional development" with the CYI. This suggested not only that the federal government would be making deals with one of the parties while ignoring the other and that the "land claims" discussions were progressing well beyond land claims, but also that the claims settlement might not, in fact, be final – that it might be re-opened in a later court case. The result of this change was the temporary withdrawal of the Yukon government from negotiations. However, by 1985 an overall Agreement in Principle among the Council of Yukon Indians, the territorial government, and the federal government was reached. [14] While this is not a legally binding contract, it is a declaration by all parties that they wish to reach a final settlement based on the terms and conditions set out in the February, 1979, Memorandum of Understanding.

In some important respects, Yukon native claims negotiations have been and continue to be different from both southern treaties and more recent northern settlements. The major difference is that the proposed Yukon settlement is based on a *one-government model*; that is, no reserves will be established and Natives will actively participate in the Yukon government. Any land to be granted to Yukon Natives would be held in private ownership rather than held in trust by the federal government. Hence, the notion of a land base for native government may be weakened in this instance.

The proposed settlement would replace aboriginal rights with specific guaranteed rights and special measures designed to protect the interests and culture of Natives. The special measures include such features as ownership of large blocks of land and participation on land-use and wildlife management advisory boards.

Under the one-government system *all* Yukoners would be represented by the Yukon government and *all* Yukoners would participate in the administration and control of events that affect their lives. While there would be one government representing both Natives (status and non-status) and non-Natives, beneficiaries would be given a special voice and specific settlement guarantees.

The one-government system means that Yukon native people will exchange their aboriginal claims in Yukon for specific legislatively defined rights. The alternative system, previously employed in the treaties era or more recently in the James Bay settlement, involved reserves set aside for registered Indians, various benefits and restitution (most of which are still administered under the terms of the Indian Act), and a form of municipal government. The reserve system also separates Indians residentially from other people and only status Indians could be included in such an agreement, which would pose problems for Yukoners, where Natives live in large numbers in communities with the non-Natives. Finally, small tracts of land would have to be set aside for Indians because substantially larger reserves might create a sense of injustice among Indians elsewhere in Canada. [15]

The one-government approach to a settlement tries to protect the cultural life of Natives (both status and non-status) as well as integrate them into the political and economic aspects of the larger society. This approach has recognized three general areas of concern: those of exclusive native interest, those of interest to both Natives and non-Natives, and those of common interest but with a special native interest.

A person is eligible to qualify as a beneficiary if he/she is a Canadian citizen, is one-quarter (or more) Yukon Indian, and was ordinarily a resident in Yukon between January 1, 1800, and January 1, 1940, or is a lineal descendant or adopted child of such a qualified beneficiary.

Land
One of the most important components of the AIP is the provision of lands to Yukon native beneficiaries. This aspect of the settlement is also of some concern to other Yukoners as well as other Natives who have made claims in Yukon areas. (See Map 2.) A number of constraints would be imposed to establish lands not eligible for selection by Natives. All lands privately owned, titled land, lands occupied by any agency of government, and land under lease, for example, would not be eligible for selection; nor could settlement lands be selected in a manner that would prevent the future expansion of exisiting Yukon communities.

Twenty thousand square kilometres of land would be transferred to Yukon native beneficiaries; of this, more than one-third (7,500 square kilometres) would be allocated to the Old Crow Band in order to protect its traditional lifestyle. All other bands would receive between three and fifteen rural blocks of land ranging in size from two to 650 square kilometres. In addition, fifty to 100 smaller specific land areas would be transferred to each band (e.g., for cabins, fish camps, campsites). Overall, bands in south Yukon would be provided with 2.2 square kilometres per beneficiary. Because of the lower productivity of the land in its area, the Kluane Tribal Brotherhood would receive 2.5 square kilometres per beneficiary[16] while bands in mid-Yukon would be given 2.9 square kilometres. All settlement lands would be held privately in fee simple title by band councils. Both improved rural settlement lands and community settlement lands would be taxed[17] although the government would provide financial assistance to bands for the payment of property taxes. Finally, a land-use planning process and an environmental assessment and review process would be established. These two processes would assess specific projects and attempt to minimize the negative impact of the development.

Non-resident land claims are a problem in Yukon. Both Indians from British Columbia and the Northwest Territories have potential claims. [18] As well, Inuit have put forth claims with regard to the North Slope of Yukon. This has posed a problem since the territorial government does not want to deal with several claims simultaneously. It was prepared to pay financial compensation (using federal dollars) for non-resident claims and perhaps to recognize some hunting, fishing, and trapping rights, but these would be based on current usage. The federal government agreed with this stance in 1976, but by 1978 the COPE (Committee for Original Peoples' Entitlement, representing the Inuvialuit of the western Arctic) agreement demonstrated that land on the Yukon coastline may be given to COPE and that the balance of the coastline would come under federal jurisdiction as a national wilderness park. Furthermore, the prospect was raised that COPE beneficiaries might receive employment preference over Yukoners and that the Yukon government's jurisdiction could be curtailed.

Financial Compensation

The 1985 Agreement in Principle called for the government to make a payment to beneficiary *organizations* of $130 million (1982 dollars) to be paid out annually over a twenty-year period. This money, which would not be taxed as it is paid out, is in exchange for *extinguishing* all aboriginal claims that the beneficiaries have or may have in Yukon or elsewhere in Canada. In addition, because status Indians would be relinquishing their claim on federal government programs, the federal government would pay the beneficiaries $53.69 million (1982 dollars) over a twenty-year period. Finally, annual payments (undisclosed amounts) would be made to Yukon Indian organizations.

As noted above, payments would be to native corporate structures (e.g., Yukon Indian Heritage Foundation, Yukon Indian Land Corporation, as well as one or more corporations for each band) rather than to individuals. These settlement corporations would be run and controlled by Natives who, directly or indirectly, would be equal shareholders and/or members. The specific corporations would be taxed as profit-seeking corporations. However, a central foundation (registered as a charity) would be established and would be responsible for receiving, administering, and investing settlement funds. It would also disburse income from investments. The foundation would not pay taxes on saved income as long as it maintained its charity status.

Programs

The third aspect of the Agreement in Principle centred on social and economic programs. Previously, status Indians were recipients of federal programs for which other Yukoners were not eligible. Under the terms of the 1985 Agreement in Principle, they agree to terminate those government programs in consideration of a specific sum of money. However, beneficiaries would be assured that they would be able to participate in any government program (federal or territorial) that would be established. Finally, certain programs would be created for the exclusive benefit of beneficiaries, would be administered by them, and would be financed out of settlement funds. Housing and municipal upgrading were identified as the major programs. However, other areas, such as education, health, social services, and the administration of justice, have been identified as requiring some special programs. For example, in the area of education, while the government of Yukon would continue to be responsible for educational programs, a Yukon Education Council would be established to advise the government in all educational matters. On this council beneficiaries are guaranteed at least two members or 25 per cent, whichever is greater, for a period of twenty-five years, to ensure that native cultural identity and values are taken into consideration.

Other Considerations
The area north of the Porcupine River, which contains the community of Old Crow, was singled out in the 1985 AIP as having special significance. As such, a separate land-use planning and environmental assessment and project review process would be established for this area. This planning process would have native representation and would consider the protection of the social and cultural environment of the Old Crow Band. The planning process would "take into consideration" protection of the wildlife and their habitat and the establishment of a national park within northern Yukon. Any development that might take place in the area would have to meet certain requirements respecting the above issues.

Conclusion

The 1985 proposed Yukon native land claims settlement represents a continuation of the negotiation strategy implemented by the federal government over a decade ago. It represents as well a continued effort by Canada to settle native land claims. The proposed settlement is similar to the COPE and James Bay agreements in some important respects. For example, in all cases, large areas of land were "withdrawn" in the sense of being made ineligible for selection by beneficiaries. Similarly, Natives are being asked to create corporate structures to deal with land and financial compensation. However, the Yukon AIP also differs from those earlier agreements in some equally important respects, such as the use of the one-government approach.

The proposed Yukon settlement also demonstrates that the process of negotiations that started in the Alaska settlement is still evolving. For example, in the Alaska settlement, all special rights of Natives were terminated. Later, in the James Bay and COPE agreements, there would be the creation of permanent, legislatively defined groups of beneficiaries with special rights. Today these special rights are enshrined in the Canadian constitution. In fact, some have argued that since aboriginal rights are entrenched in the Canadian constitution, they cannot be exchanged for rights under a claims settlement in Yukon unless a formal amendment is made to the constitution.

Having observed the Alaskan experience,[19] Yukon Natives are somewhat reluctant to adopt the use of native corporations as a major feature of the settlement, although they are quite aware that the sociopolitical conditions in Canada are different from those in the United States (Alaska). Nevertheless, they are well aware of the plight of the "after-born" (those Natives born after the Alaska land settlement was signed). Furthermore, the Alaska native corporations (with one or two exceptions) now find themselves deeply in debt. Poor investments, low rates of return, over-expenditures during the boom period, and decreasing prices for minerals have all combined to decrease the income of the corporations and increase the debt load. Unable to pay their debts, native corporations have used all of their "surplus" claims money. What remains today is the land. However, this cannot be alienated until 1990. Creditors are now willing to wait and then require payment in the form of collateral – land. The end result will be that Alaska Natives will have spent their claims money, given away their land, and had all their rights terminated. The "after-born" will not have benefited personally from the settlement and the generation before them will have squandered their "birthright."

It is such awareness by Yukon Natives and the general distrust that they feel toward the federal government that have made them especially wary of coming to a final settlement. The continual posturing and never-ending denouncement of both the federal and territorial governments by Natives give further evidence of their tenuous position in the bargaining process. The uncertainty of what the future holds, how the settlement will serve the goals of Yukon Natives, what new interpretations to existing statutes will emerge, and what new court resolutions will be forthcoming all prevent Natives from wholeheartedly and unanimously endorsing a final agreement.

Notes

1. Morris Zaslow (ed.), *A Century of Canada's Arctic Islands, 1880-1980*, XXIII Symposium of the Royal Society of Canada (Ottawa: Le Droit-Leclerc Printers, 1981).

2. F. Vallee, "Sociological Research in the Arctic" (Ottawa: Dept. of Northern Affairs and Natural Resources, NCRC 62-8, 1962).

3. K. Coates, "Best Left as Indians," paper presented to the Canadian Historical Association, Vancouver, 1983.

4. W.R. Morrison, "Under the Flag: Canadian Sovereignty and the Native People in Northern Canada" (Ottawa: DIAND Research Branch, 1984).

5. J. Cruikshank, "Through the Eyes of Strangers: A Preliminary Survey of Land Use History in the Yukon During the Late Nineteenth Century" (mimeo).

6. D. Elliott, "Some Constitutional Aspects of the Government of the Yukon Territory" (Whitehorse: Government of Yukon Land Claims Secretariat, 1978).

7. This stoppage would be repeated in 1978 when the Natives argued that they did not have a mandate to discuss a one-government system.

8. For a more detailed discussion of this model, see E. Colvin, "Legal Process and the Resolution of Claims" (Saskatoon: University of Saskatchewan Native Law Centre, 1981).

9. C.A. Rolf, "Negotiating a Monitoring Program," paper presented at the International Impact Assessment Conference, Calgary, 1985.

10. Editor's note: At time of writing it is unclear if or how the reorganization of DIAND announced on October 3, 1985, will affect the federal government's policies for dealing with aboriginal land claims.

11. K. Hatt, "On Hold: A Review of 'In All Fairness: A Native Claims Policy,' " *Canadian Journal of Native Studies*, 2, 2 (1982), pp. 352-55.

12. While there is no general constitutional right for compensation where property has been taken, mitigating this perspective is the view that common law is based on the assumption that the government will provide some compensation.

13. For an argument as to why these two principles are paramount, see D. Elliott, "Constitutional Change for Yukon" (Whitehorse: Government of Yukon, Land Claims Secretariat, 1982).

14. This sets out a number of general provisions respecting the final agreement and settlement legislation. It will require cabinet approval of the federal government, approval by the Yukon government, and ratification by Yukon native people.

15. Most treaties set aside one-quarter square mile per Indian. The most recent (James Bay) gave the Cree only .348 square miles.

16. The amount of land per beneficiary is determined on the basis of the availability and productivity of the land and on beneficiaries' requirements for traditional use of such lands.

17. Unimproved rural settlements will not be taxed.

18. CYI has agreed that subsistence rights granted to Indian claimants now residing outside Yukon would be taken from the CYI allotment.
19. For a description of the Alaskan experience, see Thomas R. Berger, *Village Journey: The Report of the Alaska Native Review Commission* (Toronto: Collins, 1985).

Chapter Twelve

Canadian Indians and the Canadian Constitution: A Difficult Passage Toward an Uncertain Destination

by Roger Gibbins

In June, 1969, the Liberal government of Pierre Trudeau introduced a white paper calling for far-reaching changes in the administration and principles of Indian policy in Canada.[1] The government proposed that the Indian Act be repealed and that the Department of Indian Affairs and Northern Development be abolished. Indians were to receive the same program and services as other Canadians, and those services were to be channelled through the same departments and agencies. The unique legislative responsibility of the federal government for Indians was to end. The white paper "dismissed aboriginal title claims and trivialized treaty rights."[2] In essence, the term "Indian" was to be stripped of any constitutional or legal significance; it would remain only as an ethnic or cultural designation, with no more formal weight than the terms German-Canadian or Japanese-Canadian.

Almost thirteen years later, on April 17, 1982, Prime Minister Trudeau witnessed the crowning accomplishment of his political career as Queen Elizabeth proclaimed a new constitution for Canada. The Constitution Act of 1982 patriated the British North America Act of 1867, established a formula for future constitutional amendments, and entrenched the Charter of Rights and Freedoms. The Act also provided constitutional recognition for Canada's aboriginal peoples – Indians, Inuit, and Métis – and entrenched existing aboriginal and treaty rights. At considerable length, the Act staked out a constitutional position for aboriginal peoples that was as far removed from the position envisioned in the white paper as one could imagine, even though the same government and even the same federal politicians – Pierre Trudeau and Jean Chrétien – were the principal architects of both.

This chapter, then, addresses a number of questions. First, how did we get from the constitutional vision of the 1969 white paper to the

Constitution Act of 1982? Second, what exactly does the Constitution Act say about Indian people and aboriginal rights? Third, what constitutional progress has taken place since April, 1982? Fourth, what lies on the constitutional horizon for Canadian Indians, and what is the significance of constitutional developments to date?

Indians and the Constitutional Process

At the outset of this discussion it is important to understand the role constitutions play in modern states. Rather than providing a detailed set of rules and regulations, they provide a broad set of principles upon which the practice of government is to be based and through which the wisdom and legitimacy of public policies can be assessed. Indeed, constitutions survive the passage of time to the extent that they avoid details in favour of general principles. The point to be stressed is that constitutions are best seen as political symbols rather than as detailed political blueprints. They define what, and to a degree who, merits inclusion in the basic framework of the state. Constitutional recognition can be of critical importance to groups like Canadian Indians who lack conventional political resources such as numbers, geographic concentration, wealth, or an essential role in the economy. It can be of considerable instrumental value because it provides a source of leverage within the political process and legitimizes group interests and claims. Above all else, however, constitutions are symbolic documents that spell out what is important in the political life of a country. Hence we find, for example, the intense (but unsuccessful) efforts by American feminists to secure passage of an equal rights amendment.

The Constitution Act, 1867 (formerly known as the British North America Act, 1867), which put in place the constitutional framework for the Canadian federal state, did not provide any substantive recognition for Indians, treaty rights, or aboriginal rights. Apart from assigning responsibility for "Indians and lands reserved for Indians" to the federal government, it was silent with respect to Indians and Indian issues. The Act was also silent on many other issues. It did not proclaim a set of principles, such as those found within various other countries' constitutions, but rather set forth in rather sparse and legalistic terms the nature of national institutions and, more importantly, the division of powers between the federal and provincial governments. The values embedded in the Canadian federal state are not to be found in the Constitution Act of 1867 but rather in the "unwritten" constitution, in the values and principles inherited from political practice in the United Kingdom. This unwritten constitution, which is of critical importance to an understanding of Canadian political life, is also mute on Indian and aboriginal affairs.

During the administrations of Pierre Trudeau, Canadian politicians began a long and tortuous search for new constitutional arrangements. Those put into place by the Constitution Act of 1867 were seen to be inadequate and, in some important respects, ill-shaped for the political realities of contemporary Canada. In 1971, a meeting of the first ministers – the Prime Minister of Canada and the ten premiers – in Victoria saw the formal start of an erratic constitutional process that was eventually to culminate in the Constitution Act, 1982. For their part, Indian leaders were quick to realize that a new constitution could provide the vehicle for the affirmation, entrenchment, and perhaps even expansion of aboriginal and treaty rights. Constitutional protection, they hoped, would provide an effective shield against the kinds of threats represented by the 1969 white paper. Indian leaders realized as well that the future of their people could be seriously compromised if any new constitution were silent on aboriginal and treaty rights, as silence could imply that Indian peoples and rights were not of sufficient importance to merit inclusion in the constitutional framework of the Canadian federal state. Thus, the constitutional process that stretched across the 1970s and early 1980s was of critical importance to Indians and to other aboriginal peoples.

This is not to say, however, that Indians were instrumental in the constitutional process, for they were not. The process was driven by three primary concerns: the independence movement in Quebec, intense and increasingly disruptive intergovernmental conflict, and growing alienation in the Canadian West. The search for a new constitution was not launched out of a concern for Indian issues, Indians were not direct players in a process dominated by the federal and provincial governments, and Indian issues played at best a marginal role throughout the process. Yet despite all this, Indians emerged in the end with very significant gains. Indeed, the 1982 Constitution Act has more to say about aboriginal issues than it has to say about Quebec, intergovernmental relations, or westen alienation.

In understanding this curious development, it is useful to remember that the constitutional process was largely a governmental process; it entailed ongoing negotiations among the eleven senior governments and was only reluctantly thrown open to wider public debate. Sporadic and largely unproductive negotiations in the early 1970s were almost entirely restricted to government actors. Apart from marginal participation by academics and editorial writers, the public was not engaged. Indian political organizations, which were still going through birthing pains at that time,[3] were not in a position to make any significant contribution, nor was any interest expressed in their doing so. Away from the constitutional front, however, a number of important events did take place that were to leave their mark on the constitutional process.

In 1971, after bitter protest from Indians across the country, the white paper proposals were formally withdrawn by the federal government before receiving any legislative enactment. At approximately the same time Ottawa began to provide extensive financial support for the Indian political organizations that were eventually to spearhead Indian constitutional initiatives. In the 1973 Supreme Court ruling on the Nishga land claims case, six of the seven judges acknowledged the existence of aboriginal rights beyond a "usufructuary interest" in the land.[4] That decision prompted the federal government to reverse its earlier refusal, reflected in the white paper, to negotiate Indian land claims. In 1975 the James Bay and Northern Quebec Agreement signed by Ottawa, Quebec, the James Bay Cree and the northern Quebec Inuit also provided formal recognition of aboriginal rights, even if such rights were recognized through their extinguishment under the terms of the agreement.

The constitutional process was opened up to greater public debate if not formal participation by the election of the Parti Québécois in 1976. That event caused Canadians across the land to ponder the future of their country and touched off a flood of task forces, special committees, editorial commentary, academic analyses, and public debate on both the future of Canada and the need for constitutional reform. Many of these contributions called for the constitutional recognition of Canada's aboriginal peoples and, at times, for the constitutional entrenchment of aboriginal rights.[5] As a consequence it became increasingly difficult for the federal and provincial governments to avoid aboriginal issues in their own constitutional deliberations as external lobbies and, to a greater and greater extent, aboriginal organizations themselves pushed for the inclusion of aboriginal issues on the constitutional agenda.

The constitutional process went into its most intense period following the defeat of the Quebec referendum on sovereignty-association, held in the spring of 1980. Fresh from victory in the federal election held in February of that year and committed to a "renewed federalism" by its campaign against sovereignty-association in the Quebec referendum, the Trudeau government pushed constitutional reform to the top of its and the nation's political agenda. By threatening unilateral action if necessary, the federal government was eventually able to draw nine of the ten provinces into a constitutional accord by November, 1981.

In the sixteen months between the referendum defeat and the November accord, the federal government changed its constitutional strategy in a way that worked to the direct advantage of Indians. Earlier preoccupations with Quebec, intergovernmental relations, and the West were put aside to focus on three more specific goals: patriation, agreement on an amending formula, and an entrenched Charter of Rights and Freedoms. Although Indians became entangled in the patriation issue as the only significant group to oppose this element of Trudeau's constitutional package,[6] and although they were excluded from consideration in the design of the amending formula, debate over the Charter of Rights and Freedoms provided an important strategic opening.

As discussed above, constitutions serve a symbolic role by identifying those values and principles held to be of fundamental importance to the body politic. In the Canadian case, the first ministers were unable to agree on an opening constitutional preamble that would describe, with suitable rhetorical flourishes, the values and principles upon which the Canadian state was based. Instead, these came to be expressed in Sections 1 through 34 of the Constitution Act, the parts of the Act known as the Charter of Rights and Freedoms. Through its Charter proposals the federal government tried to secure political support from a variety of groups who stood to gain from inclusion in the constitution and who might be used to pressure recalcitrant provincial governments into accepting Ottawa's constitutional package. Thus, Charter provisions embraced minority language rights, gender equality, the handicapped, equalization payments, and multiculturalism.

In that context, the exclusion of Canada's aboriginal peoples from the constitution would have seemed bizarre. Yet surprisingly, it almost happened: in the final weeks surrounding the 1981 accord, aboriginal rights bounced in and out of the constitutional package. Prior to the accord, the federal government's constitutional package had included a section stating that "the aboriginal and treaty rights of the aboriginal peoples of Canada are hereby recognized and affirmed." This provision apparently raised considerable concern among provincial governments, who felt that court action on aboriginal rights would take place largely at their expense rather than at the expense of the federal government.[7] Here, perhaps, one could argue that the premiers were acting to protect economic and, in a broader sense, class interests very much at odds with the class interests articulated by Indian organizations. In any event, the section was dropped from the accord although, as Sheppard and Valpy explain, reasons for this decision are far from clear:

> Accounts from provincial delegations vary: some say it was given up almost by accident, or by a kind of osmotic, unspoken agreement; others stick to the line that it was discarded because the native peoples themselves did not accept it. On the federal side, there are reports that the prime minister was surprised to see it missing when the proposals drawn up by the provinces were placed before him – but that he shrugged and accepted it. No one from any delegation, federal or provincial, says the issue was debated at any length in the private sessions.[8]

Whatever the reason, the section was nonetheless dropped, much to the anger and bitter frustration of Indian leaders who suddenly found years of lobbying scuttled in private by the first ministers. While provincial politicians may have been the major source of opposition to the aboriginal rights provision, federal politicians hardly emerged unscathed from the episode. As Sheppard and Valpy point out, the federal politicians were engaged

> . . . in constructing a charter of rights and freedoms that would symbolize the noblest Canada that could be. Yet to achieve this goal, Trudeau and his cabinet . . . were prepared to sacrifice recognition of the rights of Canada's original peoples. Of all the paradoxes that surfaced in the constitution jumble, this one was the most intolerable.[9]

By the end of November, however, the aboriginal rights clause had been restored, albeit with the addition of the word "existing" before the phrase "aboriginal and treaty rights." Restoration came about less as a consequence of vehement Indian and aboriginal protest than because of fortuitous and coincidental protest over the gender equality provisions of the accord, and more particularly because of the intervention of the federal New Democratic Party. The November accord had not only dropped the aboriginal rights clause but had also dropped what was to become Section 28 of the Constitution Act: "Notwithstanding anything in this Charter, the rights and freedoms referred to in it are guaranteed equally to male and female persons." Canadian women mounted a swift and powerful lobby against the exclusion of this provision,[10] a lobby that quickly forced the first ministers to "fold like omelettes"[11] and amend the November accord. With the need for amendment thus conceded, further amendment on the aboriginal front became easier. Here the key role was played by the federal New Democratic Party caucus, which declared in late November that it would not support the accord in the House of Commons unless the aboriginal rights clause was restored. In order to secure all-party support in the House for its constitutional package, the federal government gave in and, with the addition of the word "existing," was able to obtain provincial support for restoration of the clause.

It is doubtful that aboriginal protest alone would have resulted in this concession without the indirect pressure exerted by women and the direct pressure exerted by the federal New Democratic Party and the NDP government of Saskatchewan. Indeed, the events surrounding the November accord convey the impression of Indians riding the constitutional roller coaster without having any control over its direction or speed. The first ministers were quite prepared to jettison Indian interests and, in the final analysis, were prevented from doing so not by the political pressure exerted by Indians but by the pressure exerted by other actors in the constitutional process. While Indians unquestionably waged a spirited constitutional campaign, much of their effort was channelled into lost causes. There is no doubt, for example, that Indian lobbying and court action in Britain to block patriation was not only unsuccessful but wholly at odds with political and public opinion in Canada. While it would be stretching the point to argue that Indians fared well in the constitutional process despite their efforts, it would also be stretching the point to argue that they were the architects of their own good fortune.

The Constitution Act, 1982

The Constitution Act, 1982, contains sixty sections, three of which touch upon Indian affairs. All three are of considerable importance to the future of Indian affairs and Indian peoples.

Section 25 ensures that aboriginal rights and freedoms are not adversely affected by the Charter:

> The guarantee in this Charter of certain rights and freedoms shall not be construed so as to abrogate or derogate from any aboriginal, treaty or other rights or freedoms that pertain to the aboriginal peoples of Canada including (a) any rights or freedoms that have been recognized by the Royal Proclamation of October 7, 1763, and (b) any rights or freedoms that may be acquired by the aboriginal peoples of Canada by way of land claims settlement.

In one sense, Section 25 can be seen as a "stand-pat" provision designed to limit the impact of the Charter on the aboriginal status quo. However, it also knits the Royal Proclamation, a document of great symbolic value and potentially of significant legal value to Indians, into the constitutional fabric of the Canadian state.

Section 35 of the Constitution Act provides a brief but very important recognition of aboriginal and treaty rights. Section 35.1 states that "the existing aboriginal and treaty rights of the aboriginal peoples of Canada are hereby recognized and affirmed,"[12] while Section 35.2 states that the term "aboriginal peoples of Canada" includes the "Indian, Inuit and Métis peoples of Canada." Section 35.4 guarantees aboriginal and treaty rights equally to "male and female persons," notwithstanding any other provisions of the Constitution Act. (The "notwithstanding clause" is significant because it rules out the possibility that an Indian government, for example, could try to defend sex discrimination according to its traditional practices that might be recognized under Section 35.1.) Noting that it marks the first time the Canadian state has explicitly recognized aboriginal people and aboriginal rights, Asch describes Section 35 as a "singular moment in the history of this country."[13] Section 35 ends debate on the existence of aboriginal rights and shifts the terms of debate to the meaning and implementation of such rights.

The addition of the word "existing" in Section 35.1 was strongly opposed by Indians, who saw it as an attempt to limit the scope of constitutionally entrenched rights. At the time of the constitutional negotiations, and despite the Nishga case, aboriginal rights were thought by most nonIndians to extend little beyond a usufructuary interest in the land. Since that time, however, Indians have effectively turned the "existing" qualification to their advantage, arguing that since the right to self-government was never surrendered through the treaty process it remains an "existing right," and therefore that Section 35.1 constitutionally entrenches the right to self-government. While it remains to be seen if this interpretation of Section 35.1 will be sustained by the courts or through the political process, to this point it has not been strongly contested. Thus, the initial attempt by the first ministers to restrict the scope of aboriginal rights may have opened the door to the constitutional entrenchment of the broadest and most all-inclusive right of all, the right to self-government.

While Section 35.2 is of symbolic importance to Canadian Indians, it is of much greater importance to the Métis, who prior to the Constitution Act had enjoyed no form of constitutional recognition whatsoever. It is important to note, though, that Section 35.2 fails to offer any operational definition of the terms Indian, Inuit, and Métis. This is not a major problem in the case of Indians, who have already been defined in an operational sense by the Indian Act, or in the case of the

Inuit, who constitute a clearly distinct and easily delineated cultural and geographic community. In the case of the Métis, however, Section 35.2 has provided constitutional recognition of a people for whom no consensual definition exists. It remains an open question as to who might or might not be a Métis under the terms of the constitution.

Aboriginal issues were also addressed by Section 37, which stated that "a constitutional conference composed of the Prime Minister of Canada and the First Ministers of the provinces shall be convened by the Prime Minister of Canada within one year after this Part comes into force." Section 37.2 went on to state that the conference "shall have included in its agenda an item respecting constitutional matters that directly affect the aboriginal peoples of Canada, including the identification and definition of the rights of those peoples to be included in the Constitution of Canada, and the Prime Minister of Canada shall invite representatives of those peoples to participate in the discussions on that item." This conference was held in March, 1983, following which the constitution was formally amended to provide for subsequent meetings running through to 1987.

Section 37 recognizes that the Constitution Act remains incomplete in its treatment of aboriginal people and rights. Although aboriginal people have been recognized in the Act, they have not been defined in the case of the Métis. Aboriginal and treaty rights have been entrenched but not defined. At the time of the November, 1981, accord, the first ministers put off the resolution of these matters to a subsequent constitutional forum. This decision was a wise one in that the original constitutional meetings did not include aboriginal representatives and would thus have provided an inappropriate forum for the resolution of aboriginal issues. Section 37 ensured aboriginal representation at subsequent meetings while allowing the rest of the constitutional package to go forward.

It is worth stressing here that Section 37 has resulted in the formal incorporation of Indians into the constitutional process. Prior to 1982, Indians were not at the table when constitutional negotiations were taking place, even when aboriginal and treaty rights were on the agenda. Section 37, however, stipulated that aboriginal representatives were to be present at the constitutional talks required by the Act. The convention has now been clearly established that constitutional change on matters affecting aboriginal and treaty rights will not take place without the consent of aboriginal representatives. Thus, Indians have achieved an informal veto on matters directly affecting their interests. (The general amending formula contained within the Constitution Act makes no provision for aboriginal representation or consent.) At the same time, having the capacity to block constitutional change is quite different from having the capacity to achieve constitutional change, as events since 1982 have clearly demonstrated.

In summary, aboriginal people in general and Indians in particular could take a good deal of satisfaction from the Constitution Act. Aboriginal people had been constitutionally recognized, and both aboriginal and treaty rights had been entrenched. Moreover, and in the long run perhaps of equal importance, Indians had established themselves as major players in the Canadian political process.[14] An ongoing constitutional forum had been established by Section 37, one in which aboriginal peoples would be directly represented as they had not been in the intergovernmental negotiations leading up to the Constitution Act. What had initially been seen as one of the major shortcomings of the Act – the inclusion of "existing" in Section 35.1 – has been recast by Indians to imply constitutional recognition of the right to self-government. Thus, despite the fact that Indians had been able to affect the constitutional negotiations only at the margins, and despite the fact that some of their initiatives, such as the efforts to lobby the British Parliament, on one level had been notably unsuccessful, there was considerable reason to be pleased with the final constitutional product. It seemed that all that remained was to fill in the details, although this has proven to be a much more difficult and contentious undertaking than anyone could have envisaged.

Constitutional Negotiations Since 1982

The considerable gains realized by Indians in the Constitution Act cannot be solely attributed, or even largely attributed, to the efforts of Indians on their own behalf. This is not to disparage the energy that Indian organizations devoted to constitutional reform from the late 1970s until 1982, or the political skill they brought to the enterprise. The conclusion remains, however, that Indians rode the crest of the movement for constitutional reform in a manner analogous to that of a surfer. While they often, although by no means always, displayed admirable skill, the wave – the movement for constitutional reform – was generated by forces lying outside the realm of Indian affairs. Indians were successful because of the prospect of them opposing the new constitution and thereby tarnishing it or even, through New Democratic Party support, denying the constitution the political support it needed. Indians, in other words, were successful because they were players in a larger constitutional enterprise.

This conclusion is important because it helps explain the constitutional impasse that Indians have encountered since the proclamation of the Constitution Act. Prior to proclamation, the constitutional process was carried forward by other, more powerful currents within the political system than those generated by Indians alone or by Indians in conjunction with other aboriginal groups. Since 1982, however, aboriginal issues remain as virtually the only item on the nation's constitutional agenda. If governments decide not to act, other governmental interests are not threatened. There is no public pressure for constitutional matters to be resolved quickly, as there was during the early 1980s when Canada went into an economic tailspin and governments needed to move on to what were becoming more pressing economic concerns. Opposition by Indians can no longer imperil the larger constitutional process because there is no larger process. If constitutional negotiations on Indian issues come to a standstill, the rest of the political system will not be affected. Indians are therefore thrown back on their own political resources and muscle, neither of which has proven sufficient for consolidating significant constitutional progress.

Section 37 of the Constitution Act called for a First Ministers' Conference on aboriginal issues to be held within a year of proclamation, and the meeting was indeed held in March, 1983. In symbolic terms, the meeting could be seen as a success. Indian and other aboriginal representatives appeared in impressive numbers and with impressive symbolic accoutrements. For the first time the country's first ministers held a meeting for which aboriginal concerns constituted the entire agenda, and which allowed the first ministers and aboriginal leaders to bargain face-to-face while live television broadcast the meeting across the country. Through the meeting Indian leaders achieved an unprecedented stature within the political system – a stature that is unlikely to be relinquished in the years ahead; neither before nor since has a First Ministers' Conference been held with representatives from any other specific sector of the society. In this sense, the March, 1983, First Ministers' Conference was an impressive success.

In more practical terms, however, the meeting was anything but a success. Apart from agreeing to the addition of Section 35.4, which was required to bring that section into line with the gender equality provisions of Sections 15 and 28 of the Charter, the participants agreed only to meet again. No progress was made on the definition of terms, such as Indian government, or on the further constitutional entrenchment and clarification of aboriginal and treaty rights. While the meeting may have encouraged a frank and useful exchange of views between Indian and aboriginal leaders on the one hand and the first ministers on the other, that exchange did not lead to any substantive advance. Indeed, it may have done more to clarify points of disagreement than to contribute to any sense of convergence or consensus.

Two subsequent Section 37 meetings have been held, the most recent being in April, 1985. At that time a new prime minister was in the chair and Mr. Mulroney appeared determined to come out of the meeting with an agreement, if only to demonstrate that he and the new Conservative government could succeed where Trudeau and the old Liberals had failed. Indeed, at one point during the televised sessions Mr. Mulroney declared, in a not entirely jocular manner, than no one would be allowed to leave the conference site until an agreement was in hand. In the end, however, an agreement was not reached. Sharp disagreements were apparent within the Indian camp itself, among the various aboriginal camps, and between aboriginal representatives and the first ministers. There was agreement for a closed meeting of officials to take place in June, but no further progress emerged from that meeting. Thus, despite the apparent goodwill and negotiating skills that Mr. Mulroney brought to the table, and despite his party's huge parliamentary majority, nothing was accomplished apart from the agreement to meet again.

If one were to sift through the results of the Section 37 meetings with the proverbial fine-toothed comb, some evidence of forward movement might be found. Yet the general conclusion must be that little substantive progress has taken place since the proclamation of the Constitution Act in 1982. Admittedly, the issues on the agenda were difficult ones that would have defied any quick and easy solutions no matter how much goodwill and expertise were brought to the table by conference participants. It should also be stressed that the First Ministers' Conference is a clumsy mechanism in itself and becomes even more so when aboriginal representatives are grafted onto the process. [15] There are simply too many participants, playing to too many audiences in the glow of too much media coverage, to accomplish much in the way of substantive bargaining. First ministers' conferences can provide good political theatre, but their track record for policy success has not been impressive even apart from aboriginal issues. Perhaps of greatest importance, the political environment in which the Section 37 conferences took place was quite different from the climate characterizing the conferences leading up to the Constitution Act. It is this change in climate that bodes ill for future progress and to which we turn in conclusion.

The Years Ahead

There seems to be little question that Indians were well served by the reforms embodied in the 1982 Constitution Act. Indeed, if the protection of "existing" rights is interpreted to embrace the right to self-government, it can be argued that Indians fared much better than anyone, including the first ministers, expected. Since 1982, however, the wheels of constitutional change have ground much more slowly, if at all. While a number of important issues are still on the constitutional agenda of Indians, progress has been almost imperceptible. We might ask, then, what light the last decade might shed on the future of Indian affairs.

The first conclusion stems from the argument made above, that Indians were the beneficiaries of a constitutional reform process arising from sources of tension within the body politic lying outside the realm of Indian or aboriginal affairs and largely carried forward by other political actors. Since 1982, any progress on the constitutional front has had to be maintained by Indians themselves as other Canadians and, for the most part, the federal and provincial governments have withdrawn from the constitutional arena. If Section 37 first ministers' conferences held to date provide any clear guide to the future, there appears to be a strong possibility that Indians, even in conjunction with other aboriginal groups, will not be able to sustain any constitutional momentum.

If the constitutional process is not to grind to a halt, there will be a need for sustained, energetic, and focused political pressure from aboriginal organizations. Here the experience of recent years contains little ground for optimism. In the political process leading up to the 1982 Constitution Act, Indians were the least cohesive and least effective aboriginal group, the one that seemed least able to sustain a unified constitutional vision and the one least in touch with the constitutional strategies of the federal and provincial governments.[16] Fortunately, Indian interests were not seriously damaged by this. In the years ahead, when Indians themselves will have to generate pressure for further constitutional change, continued fractiousness within the Indian community could have much more serious consequences. Given an internally divided community, Canadian governments can be expected to sit back, to let constitutional change drift off their political agenda. Unfortunately, the roots of internal division within the Indian community run deep and will not easily be dislodged. For example, the 1985 meeting of the Assembly of First Nations featured a bitter struggle over the AFN leadership between treaty and non-treaty Indians, between regionally based camps, and between those committed to the AFN and representatives supporting the Prairie Treaty Nations Alliance. Following the convention, in which challenger George Erasmus defeated incumbent David Ahenakew, supporters of the Prairie Treaty Nations Alliance withdrew from AFN altogether. Unless the Indian political camp can be "put in order," and unless a more constructive working relationship can be established with other aboriginal organizations, the prognosis for significant progress on the constitutional front is bleak indeed.

If the constitutional process is brought to a standstill, this is not to say that Indian affairs will fall into a static or rigid pattern. As other chapters in this book have shown, a good deal of progress across a wide front can be accomplished without constitutional change. Indeed, it may well take decades for Indians to consolidate their 1982 gains in programs, policies, and financial support. The terms of the 1982 Constitution Act, even without further change, provide Indians with substantial leverage on the political process, leverage that, with both luck and skill, can be used to offset a continuing shortage of conventional political resources.

It should also be recognized that while further constitutional change may not be necessary for substantive progress across a broad front, neither is constitutional change a panacea for the problems afflicting so many Indian communities. The world is replete with constitutions that fail to deliver. Here we might note, for example, the constitutional protection for civil rights provided in the Soviet Union and the stillborn constitutional protections for blacks that followed the American Civil War. Thus, it cannot be assumed that Canadian governments will necessarily follow through on the aboriginal provisions of the Constitution Act with the programs, policies, and financial support that will be necessary for Indian communities. Canadian governments, for instance, could well concede the principle of Indian self-government without providing the financial support that would enable the principle to become a reality. Clearly, then, Indians cannot afford to withdraw from the larger political process but must continue to pursue their interests with all possible vigour. In this respect, continued internal fragmentation poses a threat not only to further constitutional change but to the capacity of Indians to realize fully the potential of those changes already achieved in the Constitution Act of 1982.

Notes

1. *Statement of the Government of Canada on Indian Policy*, tabled in the House of Commons on June 25, 1969, by Jean Chrétien, Minister of Indian Affairs and Northern Development. The term "white paper" is a generic one referring to a publicly released policy statement designed to encourage public discussion prior to the introduction of formal legislation. For a detailed examination of the Indian white paper, see Sally M. Weaver, *Making Canadian Indian Policy: The Hidden Agenda 1968-1970* (Toronto: University of Toronto Press, 1981).

2. Douglas Sanders, "The Indian Lobby," in Keith Banting and Richard Simeon (eds.), *And No One Cheered: Federalism, Democracy and the Constitution Act* (Toronto: Methuen, 1983), p. 302.

3. See J. Rick Ponting and Roger Gibbins, *Out Of Irrelevance: A Socio-political Introduction to Indian Affairs in Canada* (Toronto: Butterworths, 1980), Chapter Seven.

4. The term "usufructuary interest" refers to the right to *use* the land, as in hunting, fishing, and gathering berries, but does not extend to a claim to its title or ownership.

5. Robert Sheppard and Michael Valpy, *The National Deal: The Fight for a Canadian Constitution* (Toronto: Fleet Books, 1982), p. 166.

6. See Sanders, "The Indian Lobby," for a detailed account of the opposition.

7. Sheppard and Valpy, *The National Deal*, p. 163.

8. *Ibid.*, p. 170.

9. *Ibid.*, p. 164.

10. Chaviva Hosek, "Women and the Constitutional Process," in Banting and Simeon (eds.,) *And No One Cheered*, pp. 280-300.

11. Sheppard and Valpy, *The National Deal*, p. 307.

12. Section 35.3 clarifies Section 35.1 as follows: "For greater certainty, in subsection 1 'treaty rights' includes rights that now exist by way of land claims agreements or may be so acquired."

13. Michael Asch, *Home and Native Land: Aboriginal Rights and the Canadian Constitution* (Toronto: Methuen, 1984), p. 1.

14. Sanders, "The Indian Lobby," pp. 326-27.

15. See J. Rick Ponting, "Obstacles to Progress on the Aboriginal Peoples Constitutional Issue," Discussion Paper #85-1, Research Unit for Public Policy Studies, University of Calgary, 1985 (forthcoming in *Canadian Journal of Native Studies*).

16. Sheppard and Valpy, *The National Deal*, p. 166.

Part Four

Indian Self-Government

Editor's Introduction

Contemporary demands for Indian self-government are the logical culmination of an extraordinarily rapid evolution in Indian political thinking and strategizing over just one political generation. An overview of that recent history can help us to appreciate the momentum and determination with which Indians now press their demands for self-government.

In the early and mid-1970s the national Indian leadership sought to improve Indians' life situation through a combination of locally initiated community development, quiet diplomacy, and what might be called "bureaucratic interposition" or engagement.[1] National Indian Brotherhood president George Manuel promoted the idea of local Indian communities seizing the initiative to identify their own needs and priorities, mobilizing and developing their own leadership and other resources, and implementing the decisions. For various reasons, not the least of which were a scarcity of resources and a widespread sense of dependency on the government, this approach yielded sparse tangible results, although at an intangible level it marked the beginning of the gestation or revival of Indian self-government. Complementing this community development approach were Manuel's efforts at quiet diplomacy. This involved his careful cultivation of relationships with important politicians, bureaucrats (in the Department of Indian Affairs), and their advisers and speech writers. "Bureaucratic interposition" is the strategy simultaneously pursued by Manuel's vice-president, Clive Linklater. He sought and obtained Indian representation on various advisory bodies within the federal bureaucracy. The logical outgrowth of this was the federal government's 1978 Native Participation Policy[2] under which efforts were made, albeit halfheartedly in many instances, to recruit Natives into DIAND and other federal departments.

In the face of the failure of these strategies to bring dramatic progress toward improving Indian living conditions, the national Indian leadership embarked on new strategic initiatives in the mid-1970s. Having added various young and educated Indian advisers to his staff, the new NIB president, Noel Starblanket, demanded that the Indian and Inuit Affairs Program of DIAND conduct meaningful negotiations with Indian leaders while Indian policy was being formulated. A second thrust of this period involved a major emphasis on the development of a framework for socio-economic development at the band level. At the same time, Indian leaders enjoyed access to federal cabinet members and their officials due to the existence of the Joint NIB-Cabinet Committee (1974-78). That access formed the basis of a third strategy of the mid-1970s – local or regional Indian leaders pressing the particularistic needs of their constituents with cabinet members and their officials during the life of the Joint Committee.

Indians' political evolution proceeded apace in the late 1970s and early 1980s during the end of the Starblanket era, through the single term of Del Riley's presidency, and into the presidency of David Ahenakew. Earlier demands for consultation in policy-making were now replaced with demands that IIAP's policy-making role be relinquished to Indians. IIAP sought Indian participation in amending the Indian Act, but Indians spurned those overtures and instead seized the opportunity presented by the repatriation of the constitution. Indians sought to protect aboriginal rights by having them enshrined in the constitution. Out of a remarkable, yet merely partial, success at that (Constitution Act, 1982, Sections 25, 35, and 37) has come the demand of the mid-1980s for the explicit constitutional entrenchment of the right to aboriginal self-government and for the subsequent implementation of that right. On the one hand, such demands contrast sharply with quiet diplomacy and "bureaucratic interposition" as means of improving Indians' living conditions. On the other hand, though, the wheel is coming full circle back to Manuel's community development approach, for community development as espoused by Manuel is the *sine qua non* of successful Indian self-government.

Indians do not seek to be granted self-government by nonIndians, but rather to have nonIndians both recognize that viable Indian self-governments existed long before the arrival of Europeans in North America and establish the conditions that permit their revival and successful adaptation to contemporary times. Some Indian tribes had sophisticated forms of government, as the following excerpt from the *Report of the Special Parliamentary Committee on Indian Self-Government* (1983) indicates:

Witnesses gave evidence to the Committee of how these Indian political concepts had directly affected non-Indian institutions. Specifically, they described how the political philosophy of the Iroquois Confederacy had been incorporated into the Constitution of the United States. . . . "The Iroquois (as they were known by the French) or Six Nations (as the English called them) or the Haudenosaunee (People of the Longhouse, as they called themselves) have a formalized constitution, which is recited every five years by elders who have committed it to memory. It provides for a democratic system in which each extended family selects a senior female leader and a senior male leader to speak on its behalf in their respective councils. Debates on matters of common concern are held according to strict rules that allow consensus to be reached in an efficient manner, thus ensuring that the community remains unified. A code of laws, generally expressed in positive admonitions rather than negative prohibitions, governs both official and civil behaviour. Laws are passed by a bicameral legislature, made up of senior and junior houses. A council of elders oversees the general course of affairs. Since officials are chosen from each extended family, the system is called 'hereditary'. While the commonly held belief is that hereditary chiefs hold dictatorial powers, these leaders are actually subject to close control by their people and can be removed from office by them.''[3]

In various ways Indian conceptions of self-government differ from contemporary nonIndian governments. One of the key dimensions of difference is spiritual. Whereas most nonIndians in Canada would favour the separation of church and state, for many Indians self-government is profoundly spiritual and is intimately tied to Indians' relation to the Creator, to the land, and to the living creatures on the land. This fact is captured well in the following remarks by Iroquois leader and academic Oren Lyons:

> The primary law of Indian government is spiritual law. Spirituality is the highest form of politics, and our spirituality is directly involved in government. . . . We native people understand that all living things are one large extended family. . . . Central to [our] responsibility is a recognition and respect for the equality of all the elements of life on this land. . . . We believe it is equal because we are a spiritual people. . . . We are the spiritual centre and always have been. . . . We must hold on to what we have because we have 'the natural law'. . . . When a government develops laws to rule people, it must develop those laws in accordance with the natural law; otherwise the laws will fail.[4]

A major political breakthrough for aboriginal self-government in Canada came with the 1983 publication of the *Report of the Special Parliamentary Committee on Indian Self-Government*. (The committee chairman was Kenora Liberal MP Keith Penner.) The major significance of the Penner Report, as it has come to be called, was that by virtue of the all-party agreement manifested in the committee's unanimous recommendations, the concept of Indian self-government received a major boost in legitimacy among nonIndian politicians and government bureaucrats. The report identified specific directions and transitional phases and institutions for the implementation of Indian self-government.

In so doing, it reinforced aboriginal rights as a priority (temporarily) on the federal government's policy agenda, for both outgoing Prime Minister Pierre Trudeau and incoming Prime Minister Brian Mulroney sought to make their mark on aboriginal history by developing unprecedented proposals for aboriginal self-government. Said Pierre Trudeau at the 1984 First Ministers' Conference on aboriginal rights and the constitution:

> And so we are not here to consider whether there should be institutions of self-government, but how these institutions should be brought into being; what should be their jurisdictions, their powers; how should they fit into the interlocking system of jurisdictions by which Canada is governed.[5]

Similarly, a year later in the same forum Brian Mulroney approvingly quoted Inuit leader Zebedee Nungak when he said: "We're here to do constructive damage to the status quo." Prime Minister Mulroney went on to refer to Canadians' objections to excessive government intrusion in people's lives and noted that Indians, as the most over-regulated of Canada's peoples, need self-government instead of such regulation. Mulroney concluded by saying:

> I believe it is within our grasp to make this conference not just the midpoint [in the constitutionally mandated discussions due to expire in 1987], but the turning point in our efforts to identify and define the rights of aboriginal peoples. Let us decide at this conference that our constitution shall acknowledge that aboriginal peoples have a right to self-government. . . . Such an achievement would be historic in nature – the first step towards a new relationship between self-governing aboriginal communities and governments in Canada, a relationship upon which we may hope to build the mutual trust and confidence that has eluded us for so long. The Iroquois teach us that it is the obligation of chiefs and elders in councils such as this to keep in mind the unborn generations whose faces are coming towards us. Decisions are to be made, we are taught, with the well-being of the seventh generation in mind. That wisdom, that special kind of wisdom, should impress upon us the seriousness of our tasks in these discussions as we work together towards creating a Canada for the twenty-first century, for the descendants of all those who sit around this table today and unto the seventh generation.[6]

It is doubtful that such political will (however transient) to reach a new accommodation with Indians and other aboriginal peoples would have been demonstrated by these two prime ministers if there had been no Penner Report. Thus, in this part of the book we examine some of the Penner Committee's key recommendations and proposed institutions that gave such momentum to the aboriginal constitutional process and established self-government as one of the central issues around which revolve so many other Indian issues in Canada.

Although the Penner Report generated momentum and political will vis-à-vis self-government, its effects were not uniformily experienced by all of the provincial premiers. Indeed, the 1984 First Ministers' Conference, which had opened on Pierre Trudeau's upbeat note, closed in bitter frustration. By the end of the follow-up meeting to the 1985 First Ministers' Conference an impasse had been reached, and the meeting adjourned with little by way of concrete progress achieved. In fact, in some ways the gap between the participants widened. Elsewhere, I discuss differences in conceptions of aboriginal self-government by Aboriginals and non-Aboriginals and identify various other obstacles to progress at these first ministers' conferences. [7]

One of the reasons for the failure of the 1985 conference was the premiers' fear. This was both a fear of the unknown – Indian government truly is an unknown commodity to most of the premiers – and, more specifically, a fear of the political and economic costs of self-government, particularly if it were to involve the provinces providing a land base to Aboriginals who now lack one or an expanded land base to those who now have one. The chapter by William Reeves proposes a means by which a greater degree of self-determination could be attained by off-reserve Indians and by other aboriginal peoples who lack a territorial base which they control. These two categories constitute the majority of the aboriginal population in Canada. Reeves's thoughtful and well-researched proposal is rooted in the fact that for individuals who belong to ethnic groups or national minorities in independent countries like Canada, international law recognizes only individual but not collective rights of self-determination. By individual rights of self-determination is meant basic human and civil rights, especially the right to equality of access and opportunity. Reeves proposes that native people in Canada establish what he calls native *societies* and that their right to do so be constitutionally entrenched.

These associations would be modelled in part after the limited self-governments operated by such professions as physicians and lawyers. Initially, such *societies* would have the right only to *represent* their members by intervening in other institutions (e.g., government, business, education) to protect their linguistic, religious, and other cultural rights. This is not as meagre a power as it may seem, for cultural rights can be interpreted quite broadly, as Reeves points out. Furthermore, such *societies* might later enter into legal agreements with other governments whereby additional authority or powers would be transferred to them. Thus, Reeves is proposing an innovation of considerable symbolic and practical importance that is amenable to use by both territorially based and non-territorially based Indians. Over time, this can evolve in the direction of expanded powers of self-government. Such an incremental approach would presumably assuage the fears of the premiers, for they would see it in action rather than having to take "a leap of faith." Reeves's imaginative proposal warrants the careful consideration of first ministers and Natives alike.

The chapter by Ponting is distilled from a longer piece written for the Royal Commission on the Economic Union and Development Prospects for Canada (the Macdonald Royal Commission). It addresses the question: What effect will aboriginal self-government have on the attainment of aboriginal aspirations, especially at the level of local communities? One of the reasons for some premiers and their advisers being reluctant to proceed with constitutional entrenchment of aboriginal self-government is their belief that what is needed is not a constitutional solution to the problems of Indians and other Aboriginals but rather administrative (organizational) and program solutions. They are concerned that Aboriginals at the grassroots level might not share their leaders' enthusiasm for self-government. Opponents of constitutional entrenchment of self-government also exhibit a concern that the benefits of self-government might not "trickle down" past the aboriginal leadership and aboriginal bureaucracy to the grassroots of aboriginal communities. The Ponting chapter addresses those concerns using as a vehicle the concept of community social vitality. Although the concerns are not totally unfounded, and although Indian self-governments will face numerous important handicaps (e.g., in-economies of small scale that will raise the per-capita costs of delivery of services) and formidable challenges, the full benefits of self-government cannot be matched by mere administrative and programmatic tinkering. Self-government can be expected to bring numerous benefits to the grassroots aboriginal population in terms of various aspects of community social vitality. Thus, self-government is judged by the author to be both sociologically feasible and sociologically beneficial.

Gibbins's chapter is also rooted in a much longer piece done for the Macdonald Royal Commission. Gibbins offers a carefully reasoned critique that is particularly applicable to forms of self-government based on Indian sovereignty rather than on the mere delegation of federal or provincial powers to Indian governments. At the time of his writing the sovereignty model was the unyielding preference of the Assembly of First Nations. Although AFN now seems politically willing to abandon that model in return for recognition of *past* sovereignty (and other concessions), the Gibbins article remains valuable and relevant. First, it provides agenda items for concrete negotiations on the implementation of self-government. Second, vis-à-vis the Penner Report, it raises various serious implications and problems of institutional design that seem to have gone unrecognized by that report's authors. He suggests that some aspects of even that form of self-government not based on sovereign authority are virtually incompatible with Canadian federalism as we now know it. He argues that self-government could entail certain costs and dangers, such as threats to individual rights in the face of collective rights.

Some readers might not fully share the value that Gibbins, as a political scientist in a liberal democracy, places on the franchise and on individual (rather than collective) rights. Indian lawyer Roberta Jamieson, for instance, in a strongly worded critique, has taken issue with Gibbins's emphasis on the protection of individual rights offered to Indians and others by the Charter of Rights and Freedoms.[8] She points out that such protections are weakened by the ability of any province to exempt itself from certain provisions of the Charter, and that Canadian governments do not have "a shining record" of having protected Indians' individual rights in the past. Addressing Gibbins's concern about how Indian governments could be accommodated in the web of intergovernmental relations, Jamieson points to the great creativity and flexibility and numerous special provisions that Canadians have shown or devised in the past in making arrangements among governments. She stated:

> Quebec collects its own income tax and manages Canada Pension Plan funds but British Columbia does not. Constitutional provisions on French exist for New Brunswick, but not Alberta. You have overlapping or shared jurisdictions. The constitution even guarantees flexibility to the provinces on the form their governments may take. You have opting in and opting out. You delegate powers from one jurisdiction to another. You incorporate one another's laws when you find them appropriate. Your system is not rigid except where the political will to understand and work together is missing.

What she did not address, however, is the political reality underlying Gibbins's paper. In particular, she did not address the question of whether it is realistic to expect the political will, to which she refers, ever to be present on the part of nonIndian political leaders. Nor did she address the substantial complications posed by the sheer number of Indian governments that could seek to enter the federal-provincial intergovernmental negotiating forum (e.g., first ministers' conferences). She contends that "there is no reason why existing intergovernmental structures could not accommodate self-governing Indian communities across Canada" and goes on immediately to say "The question is not if, but when and how, since those communities with the right of self-government are already there." In response, the social scientist must ask "How, indeed?" for she has begged the question.

Jamieson's remarks contained an interesting passing mention that "Indian traditions are known for their tolerance of diversity, and their balance of individual rights with collective well-being." This important point warrants close scrutiny by historians, for nonIndian academics and constitutional lawyers have attached great significance to what is seen as a probable conflict between collective rights and individual rights in future Indian self-governments. If Indian history can yield lessons to be learned about the reconciliation of individual and collective rights, it would be indeed a valuable contribution to the present debate.

Just as this self-government section begins by placing contemporary self-governments in a broader context, so, too, it concludes by sketching the larger contextual background. In the final chapter of this section, by Rudnicki and Dyck, we see a variety of forms and processes of decolonization that have been tried in Australia, New Zealand, Greenland, Scandinavia, and Japan. From these various countries' experience it is possible to discern as many as five stages through which the relationship between colonizing and indigenous peoples has tended to pass. These stages are labelled by Rudnicki and Dyck as displacement, restriction, assimilation, structural accommodation, and self-determination. Canada is presently in the structural accommodation phase, during which structures previously established to impose or encourage assimilation are judged a failure. Certainly no models from abroad can be adopted holus bolus to move Canada into the fifth stage. However, policy or institutional elements can be lifted from other settings and modified to fit the Canadian situation. That is one of the great challenges of Indian affairs in Canada for the remainder of this century.

Notes

1. This "bureaucratic interposition" was one manifestation of what has also been called "the vesting of ethnic interests in the state."
2. J. Rick Ponting and Roger Gibbins, *Out Of Irrelevance: A Socio-political*

Introduction to Indian Affairs in Canada (Scarborough, Ont.: Butterworths, 1980), pp. 143-44.

3. *Report of the Special Parliamentary Committee on Indian Self-Government* (Ottawa: Supply and Services Canada, 1983), pp. 12-13.

4. Oren Lyons, "Spirituality, Equality, and Natural Law," in Leroy Little Bear, Menno Boldt, and J. Anthony Long (eds.), *Pathways to Self-Determination: Canadian Indians and the Canadian State* (Toronto: University of Toronto Press, 1984), pp. 5-13.

5. First Ministers' Conference on Aboriginal Constitutional Matters, Ottawa, March 8-9, 1984, unverified and unofficial verbatim transcript. This statement stands in marked contrast to Trudeau's remarks in the late 1960s and early 1970s when he denied the existence of aboriginal rights and sought to terminate Indian treaties.

6. From the author's tape-recording of the First Ministers' Conference on Aboriginal Constitutional Matters, Ottawa, April 2-3, 1985.

7. J. Rick Ponting, "Obstacles to Progress on the Aboriginal Peoples Constitutional Issue," Discussion Paper #85-01, Research Unit for Public Policy Studies, University of Calgary, Calgary, Alberta (forthcoming in *Canadian Journal of Native Studies*).

8. Roberta Jamieson, discussant's remarks on the Gibbins and Ponting chapters contained in this part of the book, joint session of the annual meeting of the Canadian Political Science Association and the Canadian Sociology and Anthropology Association, Montreal, 1985.

Chapter Thirteen

Proposals for Indian Self-Government

by The Special Parliamentary Committee on
Indian Self-Government

The Need for Change

Most Indian First Nations[1] have complex forms of government that go
far back into history and have evolved over time. For instance, the
Haudenosaunee (Iroquois or Six Nations) have a formalized constitution which is recited every five years by elders who have committed it
to memory. However, the Canadian government has legislatively and
administratively suppressed the Haudenosaunee and many other forms
of traditional Indian government in the process of transforming formerly free and self-sustaining First Nations into a state of dependency
and social disorganization under the nearly total control of the federal
government and its Indian Act.

There is clearly a need for a major restructuring of the relationship
between Indians and the rest of Canadian society. The present relationship has not served Indians well, for the social, economic, and
health conditions of Indian people along many dimensions are nothing
short of appalling. Of particular concern are the areas of health, education, and child welfare. For instance, despite the expenditure of large
sums of money, the grievous state of Indian health conditions persists.
These health problems are rooted in such living conditions as poverty,
poor housing, lack of clean water, inadequate disposal of sewage and
garbage, and poor diet. What is needed is an holistic approach (that
has not been forthcoming under the present legal and administrative
regime) and a system under which Indian communities would have the
power to establish priorities, to co-ordinate the overall planning, and

Abridged from *Report of the Special Parliamentary Committee on Indian Self-Government*
(Ottawa: Queen's Printer, 1983). Reproduced by permission of the Minister of
Supply and Services Canada.

to control the process of health care. This holistic approach would encompass the spiritual, social, and mental aspects of the life of the individual and the community and would view health as strength, "as togetherness, as harmony with the universe, as self-esteem, as pride in self and group, as self-reliance, as coping, and as joy in living."[2]

In the realm of child care, the imposition of nonIndian views, through the enforcement of provincial child welfare policies on Indian reserves, has had tragic effects on Indian family life. For instance, in a practice known as "the sixties scoop" provincial social workers in the 1960s scooped children from reserves on the slightest pretext in order to "save" them from what the social workers considered to be poor living conditions. Provincial child welfare officials' practice of taking Indian children into provincial "protective" custody not only had the effect of breaking up Indian nuclear and extended families, but also has been criticized for the assimilative effects it had on the apprehended children and for depriving Indian communities of some of their future leaders. The term "cultural genocide" has been used by some to describe the effect of these child welfare practices.

A restructuring of the relationship between Indians and the rest of Canada would enable Indians to exercise much greater control over health, education, welfare, and other areas and would permit the creation of sorely needed new institutional arrangements such as Indian health care commissions, Indian school boards, and Indian child welfare agencies. Such a restructuring would entail not only changes to the constitution of Canada, but also legislative changes that are fundamentally different from the Indian Act. Under the Indian Act traditional Indian governments were replaced by band councils that function largely as agents of the federal government and exercise a very limited range of delegated powers under federal supervision. The Act also fails to take into account the great diversity of Indian peoples, cultures, and needs. Witness after witness before us spoke of the Act's legacy of injustice, exploitation, bureaucratic insensitivity, and non-Indian self-interest.

A new relationship would also be beneficial to Canada; it would eliminate the tensions, the inefficient use of funds, and the unacceptable social conditons that keep Indian peoples from contributing to the country's progress. Indeed, in a democratic age it is incongruous to maintain any people in a state of dependency.

The Committee thus recommends that the federal government establish a new relationship with Indian First Nations (IFNs) and that an essential element of this relationship be recognition of Indian self-government. Many witnesses stressed that they do not wish to fragment the country through the creation of Indian self-government, but rather that the exercise of political self-determination is a necessary step toward national unity. Canada would be strengthened, not weakened, as a result.

Actually, it is quite possible that Indian governments may already have the right to self-government, for any rights or freedoms recognized by the Royal Proclamation of 1763 are now guaranteed in the Constitution Act, 1982, Section 25. Indeed, as Mr. Justice Hall of the Supreme Court of Canada wrote in the famous Nishga decision of the Court, the force of the Royal Proclamation as a statute "is analogous to the status of Magna Carta, which has always been considered to be the law throughout the Empire." Nevertheless, the Committee recommends that the right of Indian peoples to self-government be explicitly stated and entrenched in the constitution of Canada. Indian First Nation governments would form a distinct order of government in Canada, with their jurisdiction defined by constitutional amendment. Such an approach is to be preferred over the proposals advanced by the Minister of Indian Affairs in his discussion paper entitled "The Alternative of Optional Indian Band Government Legislation." Those proposals envisage Indian governments merely as municipal governments and maintain the paternalistic role of the department. The Committee rejects the minister's proposals and does not support amending the Indian Act as a route to self-government. The antiquated policy basis and structure of the Indian Act make it completely unacceptable as a blueprint for the future.

The Committee also had before it several proposals for a series of "subject acts" – for example, an Indian Education Act, an Indian Child Welfare Act, and an Indian Corporations Act – but rejects these as the basis for Indian self-government. On a national basis this approach would require passage of numerous pieces of complex legislation and the resulting framework might be too restrictive to meet the diverse needs of Indian First Nations.

The Committee recommends that the federal government demonstrate its commitment to the constitutional entrenchment of Indian self-government by introducing legislation that would lead to the maximum possible degree of self-government immediately. Such legislation should be developed jointly with Indians. The Committee is thus proposing a means through which the people of a First Nation might have their government recognized. The outlines of the proposal follow.

Structures and Powers of
Indian First Nation Governments

Witnesses were all agreed that the movement toward self-government must begin with the band. The Assembly of First Nations suggested that the Committee think, at least initially, of each individual Indian band as a "First Nation," although some bands may amalgamate and others may choose to split into two or more units. Witnesses were unanimous that each IFN government should determine its own membership, for control over membership was seen not just as a right, but as also being essential to ensure cultural, linguistic, and ethnic survival. The Committee asserts as a principle that it is the rightful jurisdiction of each IFN to determine its membership, according to its own particular criteria. There is, however, the issue of those who have been removed from band membership and the Committee recommends the adoption of procedures that will ensure that all people belonging to a particular First Nation (that is, all people who possess a common language and culture and who identify with each other as belonging to a common political entity) have the opportunity to participate in the process of forming a government, without regard to the restrictions of the Indian Act. An appeal mechanism, for those who are excluded from membership, should be established to protect individual rights. In addition, the Committee recommends that the federal government consider using a "two-tier" system under which Canada could recognize individuals as Indians (on a general list) even though they might not be recognized by an IFN as a member.[3]

Flexibility must be a central feature of arrangements for IFNs. For instance, the composition of IFNs may change as some governments choose to separate and possibly regroup (within Canada) or as several IFN governments choose to combine for various administrative, economic, or cultural purposes. Legislative authority, however, would be with Indian governments, and the primary relationship of the Indian people involved with the federal government would be through those governments.

As noted earlier, IFN governments should be recognized and protected through constitutional provisions. However, the Committee recommends that to cover the period until this can be accomplished the federal government introduce an Indian First Nations Recognition Act. Among other purposes, this Act would establish criteria to be met by any First Nation government wishing to be recognized as self-governing. These criteria might include some system of accountability by the government to the people concerned, a membership code with procedures for decision-making and appeals, and a demonstration of support for the new governmental structure by a significant majority of all the people involved in a way that left no doubt as to their desires.

The systems of accountability are particularly important and the need for them was widely supported by Indian witnesses. These systems might include provisions relating to: (a) the availability of financial and other information; (b) the reserving of certain areas of interest as ones in which officials would not have authority to act without the people's approval; (c) a system through which officials could be removed from office; (d) an appeal system for decisions felt to be unjust or improper; and (e) the protection of individual and collective rights. Each IFN should develop its own arrangements in this regard. For those IFNs thus recognized, the Indian Act would not be in effect. The particular merit of this approach is that each IFN government would assume as much jurisdiction as it wished, the scope of its jurisdiction could be changed over time, and the transition to a distinct order of government in Canada by constitutional amendment would be easier because Indian governments would already be functioning.

The Committee is also of the view that Parliament should move to occupy the field of legislation in relation to "Indians and Lands reserved for the Indians" (Section 91.24 of the Constitution Act of 1867), and then should vacate these areas of jurisdiction to individual recognized Indian governments, both to ensure that IFNs can act in all areas of competence necessary to govern themselves effectively and to ensure that provincial laws would not apply on Indian lands except by agreement of the IFN government. It is vitally important to ensure that there be no uncertainty as to the legal status of the newly recognized IFN governments. They would be governments having authority to legislate in their spheres of jurisdiction, to interact with other governments, to make contracts, to take legal action, and to own land.

The past history of the federal-Indian relationship has left a legacy of distrust and suspicion that would seriously impair the capacity of the Department of Indian Affairs and Northern Development to act as the federal vehicle for developing a new relationship with Indians. Instead, the Committee recommends that a new organization, to be called the Ministry of State for Indian First Nations Relations, be created to manage and co-ordinate the federal government's relations with Indian First Nation governments. It should deliver no services itself.

The Committee also suggests that a small panel be appointed jointly by the Minister of State for IFNR and designated representatives of

IFNs to review requests for recognition, to consider whether they meet the agreed criteria, and to forward to cabinet recommendations concerning recognition. The cabinet would in turn pass an order-in-council affirming and recording in a central register the federal government's recognition of particular IFN governments.

With respect to scope of powers, the Committee is of the view that self-government would mean that virtually the entire range of law-making, policy, program delivery, law enforcement, and adjudication powers would be available to an IFN government within its territory, including full control over the territory and resources within the boundaries of Indian lands. Chief David Ahenakew of the Assembly of First Nations put the matter very succinctly when he said:

> We expect that First Nations will retain and exercise most rights and jurisdictions which provinces now have within Canada, and some others which are the special rights of the First Nations.

Within its areas of exclusive jurisdiction, an IFN government would exercise powers over all people inside its territorial limits (including any nonIndians or members of another IFN) and would enjoy the right to raise revenues through taxation on the lands under its control and jurisdiction. Joint control will be desirable where IFN and provincial or federal jurisdictions overlap. In addition, governments must be sensitive to one another's rights and jurisdictions, as demonstrated in the following remarks from the Rainy Lake Regional Tribal Chiefs:

> [My] reserve . . . is four by four square miles, and theoretically there are certain laws which exist within that community. . . . Then you go outside of that reserve and the Ontario fish regulations apply. The Boise Cascade Corporation receives a licence and a permit to cut and remove the timbers surrounding our land. In reality, then, when there is no forest and the rivers are polluted . . . there is no way that one can practice the traditional economy.

Agreements between IFNs and the federal government would be political settlements, not air-tight legal contracts. Since the existing courts are not suited to dealing with such agreements, the Committee recommends the establishment of a specialized tribunal to decide disputes in relation to agreements between IFNs and other governments.

The Economic Foundations of Self-Government

Most Indian bands currently face many economic problems, and in many cases these are very severe. Various obstacles hinder Indian economic development. For instance, traditional aboriginal rights to hunt, fish, trap, and gather have been restricted by such legislation as the Migratory Birds Act and the Natural Resources Transfer Agreements between the federal and provincial governments. The Indian Act hinders economic development because under its provisions Indian lands cannot be used as security for a loan; Indian businesses thus have difficulty raising funds from conventional sources. Other factors are the serious infrastructural deficiencies (e.g., roads, high-voltage electricity, sewage systems) and the policies, personnel, and practices of DIAND (e.g., undercapitalization of projects, lack of business expertise, and lack of confidence in the capability of Indians). In the DIAND budget funds for assisting in Indian economic development are dwarfed by funds for "welfare."

A new relationship between IFNs and the federal government should ultimately result in the provision of an adequate land and resource base and the settlement of claims. Prospects for economic development would improve if the land base were expanded, claims were settled, and the control over resources on Indian lands were transferred to IFNs. Control of a strong economic base is essential for the effective exercise of Indian self-government. In planning for development of that economic base the people of an IFN should be able to set goals, define strategies, and then act to realize their potential. To do this will require substantial funding, and we recommend that sufficient funds be made available to IFNs to correct any serious deficiencies in community infrastructure and to begin economic development.

It will be necessary to develop innovative financing methods that will protect the IFNs' land base and at the same time permit their businesses to raise capital. If representatives of the national aboriginal organizations agree, we recommend that the $345 million Native Economic Development Program be used to found a special development bank. Additional capitalization should be sought from all sources, including Indian and nonIndian investors, unions, churches, and private investors. The federal government should provide incentives to investment and the bank's loans should be backed by federal guarantees.

Fiscal Arrangements

The federal government has developed extremely complex planning, budgeting, reporting, and financial control systems. As some bands have become responsible for the delivery of services financed by federal funds, they have been subjected to comprehensive and onerous accountability requirements that go well beyond what they need for their own local government purposes. The devolution of responsibility to Indian bands to administer DIAND programs has generated extensive negotiations each year. Said the Blackfoot Band in its submission:

[W]e are caught up in a process which requires us to negotiate annually, on a line-by-line basis, every significant individual item in our operating budget. This is a protracted and frustrating activity which absorbs great chunks of staff time and energy.

Negotiations often end by DIAND making unilateral decisions. Bands also noted that they often did not know how much money they would receive until months after the beginning of the fiscal year, and therefore sometimes had to borrow to cover initial operating expenses. Some of the other deficiencies alleged to exist in the current system included the large cost of operating the DIAND bureaucracy (estimated by our consultants to be more than 25 per cent of the Indian Affairs budget), the large amounts of "red tape" encountered in seeking funds from DIAND (such that band initiative and enthusiasm is often stifled in the process), inconsistencies by DIAND in its treatment of funds as "non-discretionary," the insufficient amount of discretionary spending authority allowed to bands, and the inadequacy and precarious status of economic development funds.

Our consultants' research revealed a long list of additional flaws, problems, and inconsistencies in the present system of fiscal accountability and fiscal administration. A wide variety of persons consulted agreed that the Committee should provide some solutions in this area. Said the Minister of DIAND, "The Committee somehow has to come up with a new set of ground rules that will be acceptable to Parliament for the handling of public moneys." The Committee agrees and is entirely convinced that Indian self-government must be supported by new funding arrangements that will enable IFN governments to decide how best to meet their peoples' needs. Self-government requires that IFN governments be free to make policies, to set their own priorities, and to allocate funds accordingly. To ensure that they exercise such powers responsibly and that the people in turn are protected against wrongful use of these powers, these governments must also be accountable to those people. Indian witnesses saw both these needs clearly.

With accountability to the members of IFNs, accountability to DIAND will have to end and the Committee would not expect a federal minister to be held accountable by Parliament for the way funds are spent by an Indian government, just as federal ministers are not held to account for the way provincial governments spend federal equalization payments.

Although claims settlements, new arrangements for resource revenue sharing, Indian control and development of their land base, and other long-term entrenched financial arrangements would, in due course, provide IFN governments with assured funding, in the interim, grants will be necessary and justified. We thus recommend the adoption of financing arrangements based on direct grants. This need not cost the Canadian government any more than is now being spent, and could be done in a manner similar to the Established Programs Financing Arrangements now used with the provinces. Under these arrangements the federal government submits legislation to Parliament to provide a statutory basis for annual payments to the provinces for these "established programs." Funds are provided on a "block funding" basis, which is to say that they are not earmarked for specific narrow purposes or for detailed budgetary line items. Special federal programs available to all Canadians as individuals should also be available to individual Indian people (e.g., grants for installing insulation in older houses, or unemployment insurance).

Under the proposed new arrangements an IFN government could provide a particular service itself, or could contract with its provincial government, a nearby municipality, a private agency, a tribal council, or even the federal government to provide the service.

With regard to the disbursement of funds, the Committee agrees with those who advocate that the funding agency should be separate from the policy and program delivery departments or agencies. We also favour arrangements that would fund IFN governments through a modified per-capita formula that could allow for adjustments to take into account the different and exceptional needs of different communities. As to the total amount to be disbursed, we recommend that this be established in negotiations between the federal government and representatives of IFNs, and that an appropriate yardstick be that sufficient funds should be made available to provide government and social services comparable to those enjoyed by nonIndian people living in neighbouring communities.

The Committee believes that this approach would reduce unnecessary administrative costs and would be the best use of scarce funds.

Lands and Resources

Indians' attachment to the land is part of a spiritual relationship with the universe, its elements, and its creatures. Land is thus a prerequisite for, and vital to, self-government. The Committee is convinced that, in order to ensure that self-government becomes a reality, each IFN must have full rights to control its own lands in the manner it sees fit.

This would include power to decide upon methods of landholding and land management on reserves. The Committee further recommends constitutional change to recognize full IFN rights to the lands, waters, and resources of all areas now classified as reserves or in future considered as Indian lands. The land base of an IFN could not be sold off and become part of another jurisdiction; it would always remain under IFN control.[4]

IFN governments not only serve their constituents in governmental matters, but also represent their members' interests in assets owned in common. In this way IFN governments are different from municipal and provincial governments. This poses a special problem for non-Indians living on Indian lands, who might feel that as residents they have a right to participate in the government of the community. Yet, as non-members, they do not share in the ownership of the assets administered by that government and thus have no right to a voice in such matters. Aboriginal rights should predominate over any claims of non-members to protection under the Charter of Rights and Freedoms, in our view.

Population growth through natural increase or from the return of members now living away from reserves will put additional pressures on existing lands. So, too, will the return to the reserves of persons who had lost their status through enfranchisement but regain it through the reinstatement provisions of Indian Act amendments. There would be a need for additional land to accommodate the increased population that could result from any of these changes, for an adequate land base is fundamental to future economic development, self-reliance, and self-government.

Canadian governments have often responded negatively to land claims made by Indians. They have claimed that there is no unsettled land available; yet they have had no trouble finding land for much larger national parks, defence bases, hydro developments, airports, and resource projects. Canada has set aside almost five times as much land for national parks as for Indian reserves. Thus, the Committee recommends that the federal government give high priority to providing a land base for those Indian communities now without a reserve and to the fulfilment of bands' land entitlements and settlement of other claims.

The settlement of claims would provide an independent economic base for IFN governments and would render them less dependent upon federal financial support. The current claims settlement arrangements involving DIAND's Office of Native Claims are the subject of much criticism (e.g., involving the lack of independence of the procedure from the federal government, the conflict of interest faced by DIAND in some claims cases, and the unilateral imposition of conditions by the federal government). The Committee recommends that a new claims settlement process, involving a neutral judge shielded from political intervention, be established through negotiations between representatives of IFN and the federal government. We are also critical of the present policy of extinguishing native rights in large-scale (so-called "comprehensive") claims settlements and recommend that the doctrine of extinguishment be eliminated from the settlement of claims.

The Trust Relationship

The special relationship between "Her Majesty the Queen" and the Indian nations of North America is often described as a trust relationship. We commissioned research into the origin, evolution, and current state of that relationship and found that Indian peoples, non-Indian governments, and the courts all have different perspectives about the nature of that trust. The issue revolves, in part, around the question of whether the existence of a trust implies that Indian people are like children or "wards" of the state, or whether the concept refers to solemn promises between nations that must be honoured. The legal aspects of the situation remain somewhat ambiguous, as recent attempts by Indian people to obtain redress in the courts for the government's alleged violations of its trust responsibilities have failed. Recently the federal government argued that it would not compensate the Musqueam Band of Vancouver for losses arising from the Department of Indian Affairs' role in the rental of band land at well below market value. The government asserted that it had no legal duty, that it was subject only to a "higher," but unenforceable, "political trust."[5]

Old, distorted, paternalistic notions about the "protection" of Indian people and nations must be discarded, to be replaced by a new relationship the elements of which have been described in this report (e.g., recognition of IFN governments, with powers and jurisdiction appropriate to a distinct order of government within the Canadian federation). The special relationship between the federal government and IFNs must be renewed and enhanced as we argued above. This will require that the duties and responsibilities of the federal government vis-à-vis IFNs be defined in the constitution and in legislation and that they be legally enforceable.

An analogy can be drawn with the situation of trusteeship under international law. Article 73 (Chapter XI) of the United Nations Charter on Non Self-Governing and Trust Territories reads as follows:

> Members of the U.N. which have or assume responsibilities for the administration of territories whose peoples have not yet attained a full measure of self-government recognize the principle that the interests of the inhabitants of these territories are paramount and accept, as a sacred trust, the obligation to promote to the utmost . . . the well-being of the inhabitants of these territories. . . .

While rejecting the view that Indian nations or peoples are "wards," the Committee agrees that the federal government has an obligation to act in the best interest of First Nations, as those interests are perceived by Indians themselves. When disputes arise the federal responsibility should be twofold. The federal government should first ensure that Indian people are able to present their own arguments in defence of their interests. Second, the federal government should be prepared to intervene on the side of Indian interests against competing claims, when called upon to do so. Thus, the Committee recommends that the responsibilities of the Minister of State for Indian First Nations Relations include the duty to promote the interests of First Nations. Where there are competing interests, it should be the specific duty of the minister to protect the rights of IFNs against encroachment by other governments or interests.

In view of the history of relations between the federal government and IFNs, a monitoring agency may also be needed. This office or commission should be separate from the Ministry of State and independent of all government departments. Its role would be to ensure that the federal government was carrying out its responsibilities toward IFNs. The office would be analogous to that of an ombudsman, and the commission should report directly to Parliament, not to a cabinet minister.

The Committee also recommends that the federal government make funds available for another office, an advocacy office, to be established under Indian auspices. Funds would be provided to enable the office to represent IFNs' interests in legal disputes affecting their rights.

Another aspect of the current trust relationship consists of the trust accounts held by DIAND for the "use and benefit" of Indian bands. The source of the deposits in these accounts is usually either proceeds from the sale or surrender of Indian lands, or oil and gas "royalties" paid by corporations extracting these resources on Indian land. There are two types of these trust funds: capital trust accounts and revenue trust accounts. As of March, 1983, the total for both types was about $366 million, $326 million of which accrued to a small number of resource-wealthy bands in Alberta. The median band has a trust fund balance of between $16,000 and $32,000 and this averages $45 per band member.

While an auditing of the present accounts is difficult, at best, the more fundamental question involves the transactions behind these trust accounts. Our consultants report that a history of DIAND's Land Management Fund "documents innumerable frauds and abuses; excessive commissions; disbursements for purposes which do not appear to relate properly to the purpose of the trust; sales with parties who were clearly involved in gross conflicts of interest; and every other form of impropriety available to an irresponsible trustee." Thus, the Committee recommends that the federal government's role of managing Indian revenue trust funds be phased out as IFNs are recognized as self-governing. Holding the minister responsible for managing Indian band moneys, as if Indian people were incapable of doing so themselves, is the antithesis of self-government. Capital trust funds should be transferred to a trust management system designated by the IFN concerned, following recognition of that IFN as having a government accountable to and supported by its membership. The trustee might be a trust company, an investment firm, or a trust organization established by a group such as the Assembly of First Nations.

Conclusion

The Committee is strongly convinced that a major change in the orientation of federal policy must occur. There is little benefit to be gained by tinkering with the Indian Act or by adjusting the present policy of devolution. In the preceding pages we have outlined a number of constitutional, legislative, and structural changes that will put Indian First Nations in a position to control their own affairs through recognized governments. The Committee strongly recommends that as IFNs exercise that control over their own affairs the programs of DIAND relating to Indian people be phased out. This process of dissolving the Indian part of DIAND should be completed within five years and should not affect the department's mandate for northern development.

In closing we address the question of how IFNs might relate to Parliament. A few countries, like New Zealand, provide for special representation of indigenous peoples or dependent territories in their national legislatures. Although a few witnesses expressed support for such special representation for Indian peoples in the House of Commons, most of those who expressed opinions were sceptical of the value of such arrangements. Our consultants concluded that the New Zealand model has a number of problems, such as the under-representation of indigenous peoples (Maoris) in Parliament, the fact that the elected Maori representatives exercise little power, and the fact that the system has weakened traditional Maori governmental structures. The Committee believes that, in the short to intermediate term at least, the best way to promote Indian rights is through Indian self-government and not by special representation for First Nations in Parliament.

In preparing this report the Committee has been cognizant of international standards. Canada is obliged to protect and promote the rights of the peoples of the Indian First Nations in accordance with international covenants to which Canada is signatory. The Committee has concluded that the implementation of the recommendations of this report in their entirety – legislatively and constitutionally – is the best means of satisfying international standards in relation to Indian First Nations.

Internationally, there is an increasing awareness that the old approaches to indigenous peoples have failed. The colonial mentality is being replaced with the recognition of fundamental human rights. Other countries with indigenous populations, such as Denmark, are seeking alternatives to assimilation. Canada now has an opportunity to develop creative mechanisms, institutional arrangements, and legislation that could give the people of the Indian First Nations a productive place in confederation without having to assimilate. Moreover, it is in Canada's best interests to do so. Throughout history, countries that have accommodated diversity have been more stable and have lasted longer. Canada can resist the evolutionary movement of Indian peoples toward greater self-determination, or it can offer international leadership. The Committee believes that the implementation of the recommendations of this report would add a new dimension to confederation and would make Canada an international leader in governmental relations with indigenous peoples.

Notes

1. We are using the term "nation" to refer to a group of people who possess a common language and culture and who identify with each other as belonging to a common political entity. It is not intended to carry separatist connotations. Throughout our report we use the term "Indian First

Nations'' (IFNs) to refer to the entities that would be exercising self-government.

2. Quoted from a report by W.G. Goldthorpe and tabled by Kwakiutl Tribal Council.

3. Editor's note: The 1985 amendments to the Indian Act adopted both this two-tier system of membership and the principle that bands be allowed to establish their own membership criteria. See the Postscript to Chapter Four for a critique of the two-tier system.

4. Editor's note: In its next paragraph the Committee's report appears to contradict this statement when it says "the Committee does not see the need for external constraints on the sale or mortgaging of these lands."

5. Editor's note: In a landmark decision the Supreme Court of Canada overturned the lower court's decision and ruled in favour of the band. This decision removes much of the ambiguity to which the Penner Committee was referring and will stimulate many other lawsuits against the Department of Indian Affairs for the way it has executed its trust responsibilities with various bands. Also, the decision will probably lead the department to pull back and allow bands to take more responsibility in their contractual dealings with external organizations.

Chapter Fourteen

Native "Societies": The Professions as a Model of Self-Determination for Urban Natives

by William J. Reeves

Introduction

The issue of aboriginal rights has recently been conceived to be a problem of self-determination. This essay considers the problem of attaining self-determination in the absence of a land-based form of self-government.[1] On the basis of a concern with the need to achieve individuals' human rights and rights of citizenship, it proposes a new organizational form, called a native *society*,[2] and argues that Natives should have the constitutional right to create such constitutionally recognized native *societies* in an attempt to remedy the stark "categoric" discrimination that has relegated them to the bottom of Canadian society.

Self-determination involves the freedom to participate in the choice of which institutions and structures of authority will shape one's life. As Robert Friedlander argues, it also involves sharing in the distribution of goods, services, and valued experiences in that society.[3] Ideally, this freedom involves full participation in the political process and the removal of all restrictions on political activity. It includes the right to adhere to the social and cultural norms of one's own group, and in so doing to participate in the political, economic, and cultural development of society.

In practice, self-determination has assumed two relatively distinct forms: one, as a "positive" right of an ethnic group to self-government, and another, as a "negative" right of an individual to equal rights of citizenship or human rights to freedom from discrimination.[4] Positive rights of self-government involve recognition of a collective interest in survival as a distinct group. By contrast, the so-called negative rights to equality and freedom are concerned with the removal of restrictions that prevent an individual's full participation in the political, economic, and social institutions of a country.[5] Constitutional recognition and implementation of a special status for Indians,

Métis, and Inuit may then take two distinct forms: (1) the establishment of self-government in territories that are occupied by Natives but are not now governed by native self-governments, and (2) the creation of special measures to promote equality and remove restrictions that have preserved inequities experienced by Natives. Each is discussed briefly below.

Self-Government

Self-determination has been recognized as a right of peoples living in non-self-governing territories – that is, for peoples in colonial territories. Such people have the collective right to establish new forms of government, authority, and social institutions to replace the colonial regime. The right to self-government is a collective right; that is, it can only be exercised by the people as a collectivity. This collective right is violated by the imposition and retention of colonial forms of domination. Indian reserves and, to a lesser extent, the administration of the Northwest Territories and Yukon are colonial forms of government that have been challenged by Natives who seek self-government for these territories.

The collective right of self-determination can be attained in several ways that fall short of separation. For instance, peoples in non-self-governing territories may be given full rights of participation (that is, equal rights of citizenship and human rights to freedom from discrimination) in the country, as is the case with some overseas territories of France. A number of countries have also undergone constitutional decentralization in which powers of government have been transferred to what until then had been non-self-governing territories, either establishing these territories as provincial governments on par with other provinces (e.g., in earlier eras of Canadian history, Quebec and the Prairie provinces) or establishing in these territories governments that give special status to certain ethnic groups residing in the territory (e.g., Roman Catholic school boards in certain provinces). Nunavut is a proposal by Inuit in the eastern Arctic for self-government with provincial status.[6] The Penner Report recommends a third order of government for status Indian bands on reserves, with a constitutional division of powers placing these governments alongside the federal and provincial governments as a third order of government.

Equality and Freedom

Many Natives do not reside where they have a land base or form the majority (or even a large minority) of the population. However, that fact does *not* deprive them of the right to self-determination. Under the liberal democratic ideology, all individuals residing in independent countries have equal rights to citizenship and human rights to freedom from discrimination.[7] Each individual – regardless of race, colour, or creed – has the right to participate fully in the country and to share in the values of society. Yet, the categoric discrimination experienced by people of aboriginal descent in Canada violates their individual rights to self-determination. Indeed, for most people of aboriginal descent, the new constitution's recognition of "existing aboriginal rights" will only be meaningful if it leads to special measures – available whether they live on reserves, in large metropolitan areas, or else-where – to redress the injustices they have long endured.

Current proposals for constitutional recognition of aboriginal self-determination hold little promise for the majority of Canadians of aboriginal descent. By equating self-determination with self-government and therefore regarding a land base as a minimum requirement for self-government, most current proposals (e.g., the Nunavut and Penner Committee proposals) are designed for native groups possessing government-recognized land bases. David Hawkes captured the inner logic of this strategy when he stated, "for aboriginal peoples eager to attain self-government but lacking a land base, such as the Métis and nonstatus Indians, the procurement of [a land base] is a necessary first step."[8] In an otherwise well-reasoned and realistic review, Hawkes's statement flies in the face of provincial and federal rejection of Métis claims, let alone non-status Indian claims, for land suitable for self-government purposes. Most commentators would agree that the number of Métis and non-status Indians is greater than the number of status Indians and Inuit with a land base. For instance, recent estimates place the number of non-status Indians, including Métis, at 280,000 to 750,000,[9] while about 30 per cent (100,000) of the approximately 350,000 status Indians live off-reserve, typically in the cities. Thus, the conclusion is inescapable: for most people of aboriginal descent, current proposals for self-government hold little promise for securing rights of self-determination.

Collective Rights and Self-Determination

The principle of self-determination has received a great deal of international attention in the twentieth century, and according to the logic of international laws since World War II, Indians, Métis, and Inuit may possess this right on two diffferent grounds: as a collective aboriginal right and as an individual right of citizenship. As noted earlier the typical meaning associated with self-determination refers to the collective right to establish new forms of government, authority, and social institutions to replace colonial forms. Now, in an attempt to avoid territorial conflicts associated with minority rights established after World War I, the United Nations has focused on individual human rights and collective rights of colonial peoples.[10] "Peoples" in territories formally designated as non-self-governing (e.g., most of Africa and much of Asia as colonies in 1945) were recognized as having collective rights to self-determination that had been denied. The carefully phrased use of the term "people" was designed to exclude immigrant ethnic groups (e.g., West Indians in Canada) *and* national minorities (e.g., Basques in Spain) residing in sovereign, independent countries. Under international law "peoples" who do *not* reside in colonial territories – that is, peoples who do not reside in territories that are the colony of another country – do *not* have a right to self-determination in the sense of a right to self-government. Individuals who belong to ethnic groups or national minorities in independent countries are recognized in international law as having individual but not collective rights of self-determination. The factors that motivate caution at the international level also account in part for former Prime Minister Trudeau's and various provincial premiers' preference for individual rights and for their resistance to constitutionally entrenching aboriginal rights as collective rights.

At the international level there is an exception to this aversion to collective rights. Article 27 of the United Nation's Covenant on Civil and Political Rights came into force in 1976 and recognizes certain collective rights of "existing" "ethnic, religious or linguistic minorities." Persons belonging to such minorities "shall not be denied the right, in community with other members of their group, to enjoy their own culture, profess and practice their own religion, or to use their own language." Significantly, proponents of minority rights have been quick to point out that persons belonging to ethnic, religious, or linguistic groups can exercise individual rights to participate in their own culture, religion, or language if and only if minorities also have the collective right to organize and maintain cultural institutions.[11]

On the face of it, Article 27 appears to establish collective rights of self-determination indirectly with regard to all matters involving culture, religion, or language. However, as worded, the government only has the duty *not to deny* individuals the right to participate in a minority culture.[12] The state has no duty to sponsor minority cultural institutions or activities. Nor, if government sponsorship is not forthcoming, do persons belonging to such minorities have a right to secede or break away in order to establish their own forms of government, authority, or social institutions. While the federal government of Canada has favoured policies of multiculturalism, receipt of government support has been merely a matter of *policy*, *not* a recognition of collective *rights* of self-determination. With the expansion of social services since World War II, provincial governments usually have been unwilling to give recognition to collective rights, as they have preferred to define their duties in terms of serving individual citizens. Recognition of "existing aboriginal rights" in the Constitution Act (1982) potentially marks a considerable shift in doctrine at both the federal and provincial levels. However, the practical significance of this recognition and of these rights is yet to be determined.

Whether aboriginal groups in independent countries have a collective right of self-determination in international law is not clear. Certainly, the fact that status Indians on reserves and Natives north of the sixtieth parallel reside in "non-self-governing" territories strengthens their claim to a collective right of self-determination. However, the reader will recall that most Natives in Canada, the Métis and non-status Indians in particular, are unable to claim this collective right of self-determination because they do not reside within "non-self-governing" territory.

Individual Rights and Self-Determination

In the years following World War II, the expectation has evolved in international law that members of ethnic groups will secure rights of self-determination through provisions for and enforcement of human rights and equal rights of citizenship.[13] For instance, the Charter of the United Nations and the Universal Declaration of Human Rights contain comprehensive nondiscrimination clauses but are silent on the collective rights of national, minority, ethnic, religious, or linguistic groups. Individuals in a state are to have equal rights "without distinction of any kind such as race, colour, sex, language, religion, political or other opinion, national or social origin, property, birth or other status."

When interpreted as an individual human right or right of citizenship, self-determination gives emphasis to *equality of access and opportunity*. Theoretically, more effective enforcement of individual human rights and of rights to equality in political participation and representation provides one possible remedy to the problems of people of aboriginal descent. The Canadian Charter of Rights and Freedoms and recent federal and provincial human rights commissions attempt to promote self-determination through enforcement of individual rights. Significantly, a recent analysis of complaints investigated by the Canadian Human Rights Commission found that the CHRC does not investigate as many complaints from Natives as one would expect given the high levels of discrimination that are reputed to exist.[14] If this pattern is indicative of Natives' experiences with human rights commissions at the provincial level, we must conclude that, in practice, this mechanism for investigating and correcting violations of human rights does not provide an effective remedy for problems of aboriginal self-determination.

The Indian Act and Self-Determination

However unsatisfactory its provisions may be, the federal Indian Act is virtually the only legislation that addresses the rights of self-determination of Canadian aboriginal peoples. (The Métis Betterment Act of Alberta is a notable exception.) The Constitution Act of 1867 (formerly known as the British North America Act) and the Indian Act have been interpreted to give, at most, very limited recognition to traditional land use as an aboriginal right, but they give no recognition to collective rights of Natives regarding culture, religion, or language. (Recall Section 27 of the Covenant on Political and Civil Rights.) Treaties concluded under the auspices of these two Acts, and before, extinguished aboriginal land rights while creating reserves to be held by the Crown in trust for registered Indians. Until 1960, the Indian Act even denied the right to vote to Indians wishing to retain their rights and privileges as registered Indians.[15] Although restrictions on marriage and the inheritance of Indian rights were lifted in 1985, the Indian Act continues to impair the credit rights of on-reserve Indians and may still limit their mobility rights by imposing residency requirements. Thus, whatever the desire to protect Indians from exploitation at the hands of settlers and land developers, the overwhelming thrust of this legislation has been to deny self-determination.[16]

Native Circumstances and Self-Determination

Two explanations have been advanced to account for the stark and persistent character of native degradation in Canada.[17] One emphasizes Natives' cultural cohesiveness and values that may motivate them to withdraw from Canadian society.[18] The other regards institutional domination and discrimination by non-Natives as the prime factors that effectively exclude Natives – especially those visibly identifying

347

with their aboriginal heritage – from access, opportunity, and success in most sectors of Canadian society.[19] However, the urban migration of Natives challenges the idea of aboriginal withdrawal and highlights the handicaps and barriers that limit the options open to Natives.

A number of service organizations now exist to address problems experienced by Natives, especially in the Prairie provinces, Ontario, and Quebec. However, the effectiveness of these organizations is questionable. Indeed, the cultural gulf that exists between Natives and non-Natives in Canada threatens the success of governmental programs and services. Often, Natives are unable to take advantage of, or unable to cope with, the public programs and services available to all citizens. The very fact that Natives constitute a sizable and visible proportion of those who are unable to "succeed" in the system calls into question the legitimacy of these public services (e.g., in education, welfare, health, and law and order). That is, if a sizable number of a particular category of people is seen to "fail" (e.g., drop out of school, end up in jail), government officials must begin to question the adequacy of program design and of the public service organization itself, instead of attributing "failure" to the personal inadequacies of individuals.[20] (It is not surprising, then, that federal, provincial, and municipal governments are becoming more willing to pass on the problem to special social service agencies oriented toward Natives.)

Unfortunately, the same cultural discontinuity that created the problem of "failure" in the first place also threatens the legitimacy and effectiveness of native organizations that attempt to tackle the problem. This is so for several reasons. First, although native organizations may attract more Natives by adapting their programs to native culture and values, they do so at the risk of violating the goals and standards of operation of federal, provincial, or municipal governments that provide essential support. Such inconsistencies in organization and program design between non-native and native organizations tend to be associated with short-term funding for limited programs.[21] The marginal status of native-oriented organizations emphasizes the fact that native-oriented programs also tend to fail to provide the skills, knowledge, and values necessary to succeed in the wider Canadian society. Second, agencies attempting to prepare Natives to meet the standards and expectations of the larger Canadian society often recruit clients who most closely meet "white" standards, thereby encouraging or reinforcing acculturation if not assimilation.[22] Both types of native organizations – those that deal with only a few well-qualified Natives and foster assimilation, and those that cater to native culture but are unable to overcome the lack of skills and social stigma that penalize Natives wishing to identify as Natives – have failed to remedy conditions that violate aboriginal rights of self-determination. No matter what their intentions toward serving native interests, existing organizations have participated in, and have for the most part been unable to change, a rather stable system of ethnic stratification that has relegated Natives to the bottom of Canadian society.

Constitutional recognition of aboriginal rights to establish native service organizations may correct this situation. Assuming that the aforementioned cultural gap persists, constitutional recognition would increase the power of native organizations to represent aboriginal interests without being compromised by that cultural discontinuity. It would thus avoid problems of legitimacy that have crippled the effectiveness of current organizations and programs serving Natives.

Native *Societies* and Self-Determination

Returning to Friedlander's notion of self-determination identified at the outset of this chapter, all evidence indicates that most Natives have not "shared in the values of Canadian society," let alone "participated in the choice of authority structures and institutions." Generally speaking, Natives have not been able to exercise their individual right to self-determination. Most observers would agree that "restrictions," notably institutionalized forms of discrimination, deny Natives their right of self-determination; it would be folly to deny that discrimination is a major problem. Furthermore, apropos of Friedlander's second point, existing governmental institutions have done more to discourage than encourage native participation in Canadian government and society. Thus, I am convinced that native participation in Canadian government and society can now be achieved only through constitutionally recognized native organizations and institutions, which I call native *societies*.

While status Indians on reserves and Inuit in the Northwest Territories may seek a form of land-based self-government, self-determination for urbanized Natives must involve effective enforcement of individual rights of citizenship and of human rights. Thus, the relationship between individual rights and aboriginal rights/status must be constitutionally defined. There needs to be some statement that existing aboriginal rights do not compromise or extinguish human rights or rights of citizenship, regardless of how self-evident such a statement may sound. This is needed because existing legislation and governmental programs (generally federal) have in the past infringed, and may continue to infringe, upon rights of citizenship or human rights. It must be made clear that such situations are unconstitutional. From another perspective, it may be necessary to state that aboriginal rights are not human rights or rights of citizenship; aboriginal rights exists over and above human rights and rights of citizenship. In this regard, aboriginal rights are akin to language rights of Anglophones and Francophones, or the educational rights of certain religious groups.

The constitutional recognition (Section 35 of the Constitution Act, 1982) of Indians, Métis, and Inuit as special ethnic groups with collective rights may provide a remedy to categoric discrimination, a remedy that would *channel aboriginal participation in Canadian government and society through constitutionally recognized ethnic institutions.* We shall turn momentarily to examples of how this could work for Natives. First, though, it is important to recognize that this remedy has already been used in Canada to ensure that certain important groups have been guaranteed rights of self-determination in Canadian government and society. For example, the constitutional status of English and French as official languages of government has been reaffirmed recently as a tool that fortifies the rights of self-determination of Francophone Canadians and encourages their participation in Canadian government.[23] The right of Roman Catholics to establish school systems at the municipal level in certain provinces is another recently reaffirmed recognition of collective rights designed to remedy potential problems of self-determination that may be experienced by distinct groups in Canada. Also, when the province of Newfoundland and Labrador was incorporated into Canada, members of the Roman Catholic Church, Anglican Church, and United Church, as well as of the Salvation Army, were each accorded the collective right to establish local school districts.

Native *societies* as envisaged here would be loosely modelled on self-government in such professions as law and medicine. Those in positions of authority within a native *society* would have the power to represent the interests of individual Natives in their dealings with institutions in the larger Canadian society. This right to representation would be analogous to the individual right to engage a lawyer to represent his or her interests.[24] Individual Natives would have the right to engage an official from a native *society* with certified competence to represent their interests vis-à-vis human/citizenship rights; and officials who were engaged would have rights of representation analogous to those of a lawyer.

Like physicians and surgeons, persons in a native *society* with certified expertise in a native culture might also occupy positions in public service organizations (or even private industry) that deal on a regular basis with Natives. Native *societies* could have a part to play in redefining such positions, like doctors in defining positions within hospitals. Job redefinition would not be unilaterally imposed by non-aboriginal regulatory agencies or employers.

Professional self-regulation is a non-territorial form of government that pertains to individuals who claim to be and are accepted as members of an occupation with jurisdiction over a distinctive type of work. Analogously, a native *society* would be composed of individuals who claim aboriginal status and are accepted as members by other Natives in the native *societies*.[25] Like professionals, Natives (where they have not done so already) "must first vest themselves with an identity that allows them to recognize each other and differentiate themselves from others."[26] Native *societies* could claim competence in activities of relevance to aboriginal culture, religion, and language, particularly where these elements of ethnic identity are relevent to restrictions that impair Natives' citizenship or human rights. The United Nations' *Study on the Rights of Persons Belonging to Ethnic, Religious and Linguistic Minorities*[27] gave some indication of the breadth of cultural, religious, and language rights. In somewhat contorted prose, Sacerdoti provides a summary of such rights:

> As to *culture*: educational policy; promotion of literature and the arts; dissemination of culture; preservation of customs and of legal traditions. As to *religion*: recognition of its juridical status; celebration of marriage; . . . observance of religious holidays; conscientious objection; taking of an oath; freedom to participate in worship and rites; rights not to be compelled to participate in the activities of other religions nor in their financing, nor to follow religious instruction in another religion; right to manage the affairs of the religious community; right to establish denominational schools and [schools] for the training of clergy. As to *language*: status of minority language; right to use such language in official and non-official matters, in communications media, in the school system; establishment of private schools . . . .[28]

As with professions, it would be expected that there would be at least several different native *societies*. Procedures, criteria, and a *constitutionally entrenched* body with heavy native representation would have to be established to determine which native organizations would be eligible to attain this constitutionally recognized status.[29] This certifying body must not be a branch of the federal or provincial governments, although these governments along with native organizations themselves might have some part to play in appointing its membership.

Depending on decisions taken with regard to both membership and the right to representation, native *societies* might assume a variety of forms. Membership might include all Natives *who wish to belong* and are accepted as members. This could include, for example, potentially all individuals in a tribe or linguistic group. In this event, only certain members ("officials") within the native *society* would be certified to represent the interests of Natives. Alternatively, strict adherence to a professional model might limit membership to those with a certified competence in the native culture, religion, or language (especially vis-à-vis human rights and rights of citizenship). A somewhat related issue concerns the types of clients that might be represented by a native *society*. A native *society* might be granted a constitutional right to represent anyone of aboriginal descent. Alternatively, a native *society* might be permitted to represent only Natives from a particular tribal, religious, or linguistic group. If the right to represent members were to be restricted so that it is held only by members who belonged to the native *society*, native *societies* would come to resemble unions more than professions – with those in positions of leadership representing the rights and interests of members. Although the form taken by native *societies* will probably be critical – inclusive versus exclusive membership, extended versus restricted rights of representation – the relative merits of the various possibilities are not clear at this time.

Besides establishing competence in areas of a particular native culture, religion, or language, native *societies* would be expected to develop expertise on the cultural, social, and economic norms that govern public service institutions having special relevance to Natives. It is the information gap, as well as the cultural gap, between Natives and various public service institutions that establishes a unique domain of competence for a native *society*. [30]

The Information Gap

Individual Natives deal with a wide variety of public service organizations – educational, health, welfare, law and order – at various levels of government. From the perspective of the individual Native, particularly the non-status Indian and Métis, the services he or she may receive are fragmented. People who provide services to Natives in one organization are generally unaware and, more importantly, not expected to be aware of the policies, programs, and requirements of other public service organizations. Specialization by function and geography may serve the interests of non-Natives, [31] but Natives often are unable to cope with or are poorly served by the conflicting expectations of different agencies. Given the marginal and often transitory status of urban Natives, many are simply unable to meet what appear to be minimal requirements, such as maintaining a stable residence.

The Cultural Gap

Even if Natives were able to surmount the problems posed by fragmented and incoherent service, they may not know or follow "the rules of the game" associated with each public service institution. Outside the realm of native affairs, the people who staff a public service organization and those who are its clients are typically from the same cultural background. Everyone has an intuitive grasp of what is expected – who qualifies, what they must do, the strategies and tactics associated with success and failure. Given the cultural gulf that separates most Natives from non-Natives, this common basis of understanding cannot be assumed to exist. Native *societies* can bridge this gap.

The Authority of Native Societies

The authority of native *societies* and their representatives must rest on two foundations: the possession of specialized knowledge of some importance to individuals and institutions in society, and the possession of a mandate from society to use that knowledge in the best interests of both Natives and non-Natives.[32] The existence of a cultural gap between Natives and non-Natives and the fragmentation of public services received by Natives suggest that native *societies* could create a knowledge base of great utility. With such information at their disposal, officials with competence certified by a native *society* could better serve the interests of individual native clients, and native clients would have reason to grant them power of attorney.

Though governments in Canada may prefer some form of direct regulation, there are reasons for favouring transferring this duty to self-regulating native *societies* on questions regarding rights of citizenship and human rights. First, native *societies* as envisaged would only have the right to represent the interests of individual Natives; *powers of adjudication and administration would remain with existing institutions unless additional powers were delegated or transferred to native societies as a result of future negotiations.* Second, the potential knowledge base of a native *society* really would be esoteric.[33] This information is currently not readily available to non-Natives and would be costly to develop. Third, the fragmented and isolated circumstances that surround problems experienced by individual Natives have not been successfully redressed to date by non-native governments. Thus, Canadian governments should look upon native *societies* as a reasonable solution to an endemic problem of native degradation in Canadian society.

The right to establish native *societies* and the rights and responsibilities of native *societies* to represent individual Natives on questions of human rights and rights of citizenship *must be entrenched in the constitution*. Without a constitutional mandate, federal and provincial governments would have the authority to ignore or undermine native *societies*. With a constitutional mandate, these *societies* are more likely to overcome the no-win situation that has crippled the effectiveness and legitimacy of public service and native organizations in the past. The Charter of Rights and Freedoms was entrenched to secure individual rights in the face of government authority. Entrenchment of native *societies* may effectively extend these rights to Natives in Canada.

Native *Societies* and Self-Government

Native *societies* should have the right to enter into negotiations with public (and private) corporations, negotiations that may augment their duties and powers. While constitutional recognition would be limited to the power to represent individual Natives in situations bearing upon rights of citizenship and human rights, native *societies* should not be prohibited from assuming other responsibilities. Specifically, they should be able to enter into administrative arrangements in which they become involved in the delivery of federal, provincial, or municipal services to Natives. Native *societies* should also be able to enter into intergovernmental agreements (i.e., accords that gain legal status enforceable in the courts). Although reserve-based status Indians reject municipal status as a meaningless form of self-government, native *societies* representing non-status Indians or Métis may wish to assume municipal status and acquire delegated powers to legislate and administer by-laws for specified governmental functions in areas coterminous with existing municipal boundaries – as for example now exists for separate school boards. The existence of native *societies*, whose rights to represent aboriginal interests will have been constitutionally recognized, would also hold open the possibility of aboriginal self-government at some future date. By transferring powers of government to native *societies*, federal and provincial governments could establish a basis for native self-government as a third order of government in Canada.

The federal and provincial governments are wary of recognizing aboriginal rights as collective rights to self-determination, and the leaders of native organizations reject government policies that reduce government obligations toward Natives. The political realities do not favour Natives;[34] the federal and provincial governments now control the means for constitutional amendment. However, these governments may be willing to endorse constitutional entrenchment of native *societies* empowered to secure individual rights. Although the powers envisaged here may pale in comparison to those proposed for self-governments on reserves and in the eastern Arctic, the creation of native *societies* would be a major step forward for urban Natives. By creating positions of authority for native leaders, the existence of constitutionally entrenched native *societies* promises real improvement in the life chances of urban Natives. The cultural and information gaps that have frustrated federal and provincial attempts to adequately serve urban Natives in the past remain as continuing incentives favouring the transfer of social services to native organizations in the future.

Once created, the potential mandate for native *societies* should be open to substantial expansion as the result of future negotiations with provincial and federal governments. At a minimum, such *societies* should start with powers to address problems of individual human and citizenship rights. As a result of future negotiation, it should be possible for them to take on powers associated with self-government, which may enable them to protect and enhance collective rights regarding self-determination of aboriginal culture, religion, and language. Certainly, more expansive powers would be required to revitalize aboriginal culture and to reverse pressures toward acculturation and assimilation.

The existence of native *societies* should not compromise negotiations for self-government by Inuit or by on-reserve status Indians. The proposal has been designed to be independent of land-based claims for aboriginal self-government. Non-territorial claims for native representation in the enforcement of citizen and human rights concern individual rights, while land-based claims of aboriginal self-government address collective rights of peoples residing in non-self-governing territories. Pursuit of one should not preclude the other. Indeed, status Indians or Inuit who succeed in establishing reserve or territorial-based governments should also be free to incorporate as native *societies*. This would allow reserve-based Indian self-government to represent the interests of status Indians who may continue to live off-reserve. Or, off-reserve status Indians might wish to form their own native *society* without reference to reserve-based Indian self-governments. Native *societies* should be able to assume powers of self-government if future negotiations produce a land base and if adequate powers are transferred from existing levels of government. This proposal recognizes the fact that status Indians and Inuit, on the one hand, and Métis and non-status Indians, on the other, are at different starting points and that they must therefore pursue different constitutional strategies. It would be unfortunate if these differences divide Natives from one another and endanger the future success of both.

Notes

1. This chapter has been written specifically for this book and for the Research Unit for Public Policy Studies, Faculty of Social Sciences, University of Calgary. A slightly longer version is available as Research Report #86-01 distributed by the Research Unit.

2. When referring to this new form of organization the word "society" will be placed in italics to differentiate it from the use of the same word (not in italics) used to refer to a much larger social unit (e.g., a people or a country).

3. Robert A. Friedlander, "Self-Determination: A Legal-Political Inquiry," in Y. Alexander and R.A. Friedlander (eds.), *Self-Determination: National, Regional, and Global Dimensions* (Boulder, Colorado: Westview Press, 1980), p. 314.

4. Robert G. Wirsing, "Dimensions of Minority Protection," in R.G. Wirsing (ed.), *Protection of Ethnic Minorities* (New York: Pergamon Press, 1981), p. 9.

5. Vernon Van Dyke, "Human Rights and the Rights of Groups," *American Journal of Political Science*, XVIII (1974), p. 741.

6. Dennis Patterson *et al., Building Nunavut* (Yellowknife: Nunavut Constitutional Forum, 1983).

7. Vernon Van Dyke, "The Individual, the State, and Ethnic Communities in Political Theory," *World Politics*, XXIX (1977), pp. 343-69.

8. David C. Hawkes, *Aboriginal Self-Government: What Does it Mean?* (Kingston, Ontario: Institute of Intergovernmental Relations, 1985), p. 25.

9. Evelyn Kallen, *Ethnicity and Human Rights in Canada* (Toronto: Gage, 1982), p. 70; *A Time To Speak Out: The Task Force on Canadian Unity* (Ottawa: Minister of Supply and Services, 1979), p. 27.

10. Friedlander, "Self-Determination," pp. 307-31; Wirsing, "Dimensions," pp. 9-11; Rita E. Hauser, "International Protection of Minorities and the Right of Self-Determination," *Israel Yearbook on Human Rights*, I (1971), pp. 92-102; Giorgio Sacerdoti, "New Developments in Group Consciousness and the Protection of the Rights of Minorities," *Israel Yearbook on Human Rights*, XIII (1984), pp. 116-24.

11. Francesco Capotorti, *Study on the Rights of Persons Belonging to Ethnic, Religious and Linguistic Minorities* (New York: United Nations Publication e.78.XIV.1, 1979), pp. 98-99; and Louis B. Sohn, "The Rights of Minorities," in L. Henkin (ed.), *The International Bill of Rights: The Covenant on Civil and Political Rights* (New York: Columbia University Press, 1981), pp. 270-89.

12. Wirsing, "Dimensions," pp. 9-11.

13. Sohn, "Rights of Minorities," pp. 271-74.

14. William J. Reeves and J.S. Frideres, "Factors Associated with the Resolution of Race, Colour, Origin, Sex, and Disability Complaints: Canadian Human Rights Commission Files – 1983-1984," The Research Unit For Public Policy Studies, Faculty of Social Sciences, University of Calgary, Calgary, Alberta, 1985 (Report submitted to the Canadian Human Rights Commission, Ottawa), pp. 54-60. While the CHRC is obliged to investigate all complaints that are formally lodged, it received thousands of inquiries in 1984 and formally investigated fewer that 500 complaints. The CHRC substantiates very few complaints that allege discrimination on the basis of race or colour or national or ethnic origin, compared to complaints of discrimination of the basis of sex.

15. Enfranchisement was regarded as the step that brought Indians into Canadian society. It established their citizenship while extinguishing their rights as status Indians.

16. Morton Weinfeld, "Canada," in Wirsing (ed.), *Protection of Ethnic Minorities*, p. 57. Green would extend this conclusion regarding the Indian Act to include the Royal Proclamation of 1763 and the common law. Leslie C. Green, "Human Rights and Canada's Indians," *Israel Yearbook on Human Rights*, I (1971), pp. 186-87.

17. For a statistical account of Indians' disadvantaged situation in Canadian society, see Chapter Two in this volume.

18. John Porter, "Melting Pot or Mosaic: Revolution or Reversion," in J. Porter (ed.), *The Measure of Canadian Society* (Toronto: Gage, 1979).

19. A.G. Darroch, "Another Look at Ethnicity, Stratification and Social Mobility in Canada," *Canadian Journal of Sociology*, IV (1979), pp. 1-25. See also Kallen, *Ethnicity*, pp. 131-36.

20. William J. Reeves and J.S. Frideres, "Government Policy and Indian Urbanization: the Alberta Case," *Canadian Public Policy*, VII (1981), pp. 592-95; James S. Frideres, "Government Policies and Programs Relating to People Of Indian Ancestry in Alberta," in Raymond Breton and Gail Grant (eds.) *The Dynamics of Government Programs for Urban Indians in the Prairie Provinces* (Montreal: Institute for Research on Public Policy, 1984), pp. 321-518. The specific reference here is to pp. 495-97.

21. Raymond Breton, "Introduction," in Breton and Grant (eds.) *Dynamics*; Reeves and Frideres, "Government Policy and Indian Urbanization," p. 591.

22. *Ibid.*; Frideres, "Government Policies and Programs," pp. 489-97.

23. Morton Weinfeld, "The Development of Affirmative Action in Canada," *Canadian Ethnic Studies*, VIII (1981), pp. 23-39.

24. Some might ask why not an ombudsman rather than representation by an official of a native *society*. The answer quite simply is that an ombudsman is an agent of the government; conversely, an official of a native *society* engaged by an individual Native represents the individual. In many cases, individual Natives may be questioning the provision of government services. Any agent of the government, even an ombudsman, attempting to represent the interests of a Native lodging a complaint would be in conflict of interest. See Douglas Sanders, "A Legal Service Program for Native Communities" (mimeographed paper, 1971), p. 2.

25. Bradford Morse, *Aboriginal Self-Government in Australia and Canada* (Kingston, Ontario: Institute of Intergovernmental Relations, 1985), p. 13. See also Hawkes, *Aboriginal Self-Government*, pp. 10-11.

26. Robert Laliberté, "The Professionalization of Occupations," in J. Dufresne, Y. Mongeau, J. Proulx, and R. Sylvestre (eds.), *The Professions: Their Growth or Decline?* (Montréal: Société de Publication Critère, 1979), p. 27.

27. Capotorti, *Study on the Rights*, pp. 57-89.

28. Sacerdoti, "New Developments," pp. 128-29. Rights to traditional use of the land (e.g., hunting and fishing), resources, and regulation of land use, while relevant to land-based forms of self-government, are of less importance to the urban situation of non-status Indians and Métis.

29. The following two sources are highly instructive on the questions and issues surrounding the establishment of professional self-regulation: *The Professions and Society*, Report of the Commission of Inquiry on Health and Social Welfare, Volume 7, Tome 1, Part 5 (Quebec City: Government of Quebec, 1970); and a commentary and review by this commission's legal counsel, René Dussault, "The Office des Professions du Québec in the Context of the Development of Professionalism," in P. Slayton and M.J. Trebilcock (eds.), *The Professions and Public Policy* (Toronto: University of Toronto Press, 1978), pp. 101-10.

30. "Because of an information gap, the interests of the client will be promoted only insofar as the [professional society] assumes . . . responsibility" for promoting the client's interests. Carolyn Tuohy and Alan D. Wolfson, "Self-regulation: Who Qualifies," in Slayton and Trebilcock (eds.), *The Professions*, p. 114. The importance of a native *society* that represents the interests of Natives becomes vital if the costs of error (in the determination of rights and interests) are high and if the necessary specialized knowledge is not generally available (especially if it is not possessed by the public service agencies).

31. Harvey Bostrum, "Recent Evolution of Canada's Indian Policy," in Breton and Grant (eds.), *Dynamics*, pp. 519-43.

32. Friedson identified these two elements as the basis of professional authority: knowledge and a mandate from society to regulate the application of that knowledge in the best interests of individual clients and society. See Eliot Friedson, *Professional Dominance* (New York: Atherton, 1970), pp. 127-45.

33. Sanders, "A Legal Service Program," p. 4.

34. Roger Gibbins, "Canadian Indian Policy: The Constitutional Trap," *Canadian Journal of Native Studies*, IV (1984), pp. 1-9.

Chapter Fifteen

The Impact of Self-Government on Indian Communities

by J. Rick Ponting

The fundamental concern of this chapter is the effect Indian self-government will have on the attainment of Indian aspirations, especially at the community level.[1] These aspirations can be summarized as: (1) greater self-determination and social justice; protection of, and control over, own destiny, rather than subordination to political and bureaucratic authorities based outside the ethnic group; (2) economic development to end dependency, poverty, and unemployment; economic justice in the sense of a fair distribution of wealth between the Indian and non-Indian populations; (3) protection and retention of Indian culture; and (4) social vitality and development that will overcome such existing social problems as ill health, the housing crisis, irrelevant and demeaning education, and alienation (including its manifest symptoms – interpersonal violence, suicide, and the abuse of drugs and other substances).

Use here of the concept "social vitality" is adapted from Matthews's work on the resettlement of outport communities in Newfoundland.[2] There Matthews demonstrated that the lack of economic viability of a community need not necessarily entail that community's demise as a sociologically viable collectivity. The work of Blishen and his colleagues among eight British Columbia Indian communities examines in more detail the concept of social vitality and the related concepts of economic viability and political efficacy.[3] Their data suggest that a threshold level of social vitality may be a prerequisite for, or a cause of, both political efficacy and economic viability. Of the three variables they tentatively attach causal primacy to social vitality. For our present purposes, though, the significance of the concept of social vitality is that it sensitizes us to many of the ways in which Indian self-government might have an impact on Indian communities.

Matthews identified three dimensions of the social vitality of a community. Each dimension refers to the presence of organizations that carry out certain types of activity for the community. These are: (1) passing on the values, norms, and skills necessary to live in the community, e.g., schools, churches, and the family; (2) communicating within the community, e.g., mass media and consultative bodies; and (3) providing opportunities for pleasurable social interaction that builds social solidarity, e.g., sports teams, service organizations, and entertainment organizations. I have extended the concept of social vitality to include several other dimensions noted below, and in so doing I explicitly equate the concept with sociological "healthiness."

First, I include the presence of meaning-conferring activities such as those which develop a sense of identity and collective pride, or those which develop integrative symbols that span cleavages within the community.[4] Second, I add the dimension of boundary-maintaining mechanisms and activities. This refers to the preservation of culture, the reproduction of the membership of the community, and the formal or informal regulation of in-migration and out-migration so that the community is neither swamped/absorbed by outsiders nor depleted by demographic haemorrhaging from within. Third, I use the term social vitality to encompass the presence of legitimacy conferred on the political regime, its incumbents, and their policy outputs. Such feelings of legitimacy will usually be accompanied by feelings of loyalty. The presence of effective mechanisms for the resolution or regulation of conflict is another feature of community social vitality. Conflict is normal in the life of any collectivity, but if it is so intense or unbounded as to immobilize the community, then the community can hardly be said to be sociologically healthy. Finally, my conception of social vitality includes the presence of leadership and organizational expertise that enables collective goals to be pursued effectively by the community as a whole or by its component groups.

The Advantageous Situation of Canadian Indians

Compared to many other cases where the attainment of indigenous self-determination is relatively recent, Canadian Indian governments will possess numerous advantages. Particularly important among these is the comparatively high level of literacy among Canadian Indians and the already increasing average level of educational attainment. A quite different advantage is that rather than having primary loyalties to particularistic groups such as one's own clan or community, many of the Indian bureaucrats who will staff Canadian Indian governments have already acquired universalistic norms of service by virtue of having worked for the federal government or for some pan-Indian organization such as a tribal council or provincial Indian political association.[5] Other advantages are the lack of deep ideological fissures within the indigenous population, the lack of major institutional interest groups (e.g., church, army, or dominant corporation) that have monopolized most political positions and impeded the growth of modern political forces independent of them (as in Central America),[6] and, of course, the advantage, as relative latecomers to the twentieth-century self-governing and nation-building phenomenon, of being able to learn from the mistakes of those who have gone before.

Immediate Contextual Changes

The advent of Indian self-government could produce relatively immediate and fundamental contextual changes in institutional structures and social relations. Those changes would constitute both problems and opportunities. Among the most important of these are the possibility of a "revolution of rising expectations"; an expansion in the size, role, and power of the Indan "state" apparatus; the exacerbation of strains between "modernism" and "traditionalism";[7] an expansion of the middle class and concomitant heightening of inter-class tensions;[8] and the development of new bases of community integration. Other problems are the delegitimation of Indian governments that fail to meet expectations; the redistribution of wealth within and among Indian communities; scarcity of highly skilled human resources; rapid obsolescence of physical plant, software, and skills; "fiscal crisis of the state"; scarcity of natural resources; ineconomies of small scale, especially vis-à-vis per-capita costs of delivering services; fiscal dependency; and remoteness from suppliers, markets, and cognate industries.

The Impact of Indian Self-Government on Community Social Vitality

The impact of self-government elsewhere around the world has been mixed. Self-government alone does not necessarily lead to democracy as we in Canada define the term. Although the most serious afflictions (e.g., militarized factionalism) of other post-colonial regimes are highly improbable in the Canadian Indian self-government situation, we know that in some countries the paternalism, dependency, and underdevelopment of colonialism have been replaced under self-government with even worse regimes. Yet we know also that the status quo can no longer be tolerated. The question remains, however, as to whether Indian self-government is likely to produce a significant improvement in the daily lives of its Indian citizens. I conclude that there are sound sociological and social psychological reasons to expect that even for those Indian self-governments that are only mildly successful *the net sociological impact of aboriginal self-government on individuals will be profoundly positive* – that their communities will experience fundamental gains in social vitality that will be reflected in positive changes in the lives of individuals.

Although the remaining discussion of the impact of Indian self-government will be organized in terms of the dimensions of community social vitality, the benefits identified below will not be uniformly experienced by all self-governing Indian communities, for the realization of those benefits is enhanced by certain contextual conditions (e.g., the presence of exploitable natural resources, a minimum-sized population base, and the presence of an economic opportunity structure) present to varying degrees in different local communities.

Impact on Institutions of Socialization
The colonial experience has subjected the family as an institution to considerable strain. For instance, a school curriculum that has denigrated Indian values has often caused the parents who espouse those values to slip in their children's esteem. That in turn has undermined parental authority. Similarly, the welfare dependency syndrome of the colonial regime has eroded the self-esteem of many adults. With such a role model, how healthy a self-concept can a child develop? Assuming that Indian self-government will have as one of its highest priorities the breaking of the welfare dependency syndrome, and assuming at least a modest degree of success at that task,[9] we can predict a strengthening of the family unit under Indian self-government.

One of the largest and most tangible positive impacts of Indian self-government will be seen in the schools. Indeed, with education having been one of the first institutions to begin to come under Indian control, the proof of the benefits of Indian control is already available in Alberta, the James Bay area, and elsewhere. The point will not be belaboured here. Suffice it to say that band-controlled schools using Indian teachers and Indian elders as resource persons have generated increased interest in school, decreased truancy and drop-out rates, and improved self-esteem.[10]

Impact on Communications Institutions
With the exception of a few radio stations and numerous newsletters issued by various programs in any given Indian government, the im-

pact of Indian self-government on Indian mass media will probably be minor. Much of the growth potential of the Indian market was probably exhausted during the 1970s when there was a flowering of various Indian newspapers and magazines and some broadcast media programs and organizations. However, the Kahnawake experience of developing its own self-sufficient radio station may be a sign of things to come in Indian communities situated close to large urban markets. Compared to television, radio programming is not costly to produce. That and the fact that it can be used to generate major gains in community identity and cohesion (as at Kahnawake) render it highly attractive as a tool of community development for various bands.[11] Notwithstanding this, the main impact on communications in Indian communities will probably be from a source quite independent of Indian governments – namely, the satellite "dish" receivers, which primarily will bring more nonIndian programming into Indian communities.

Impact on Meaning-conferring Activities
The impact of Indian self-government will probably be the greatest in this area. It is also the pivotal sphere around which so much of community social life indirectly revolves.

One of the most profound impacts of an Indian self-government that is merely modestly successful on the other dimensions is that through its accomplishments and its symbolic products it will instil in aboriginal citizens a sense of *pride* and *positive identity*; it will help restore the sense of *dignity* that derives from and contributes to people taking on greater responsibility for their collective and individual destiny. (The ideology of "Mâitres chez nous" – Masters in our own house – was an integral part of this same phenomenon in Quebec's Quiet Revolution.) Just as other Canadian governments devote considerable resources to symbol-building, so, too, will Indian self-governments, for colonialism has left disfiguring scars on the symbolic systems of Indian peoples. The need is great, and on the psycho-cultural plane the gains to be attained from symbolic politics are important.

The symbolic-psychological gains from Indian self-government derive from diverse sources: the reformed school curriculum and use of Indian teachers; displays of the majesty and power of the Indian state; displays of the physical symbols of the Indian state, such as flags and monuments; ceremonies showing respect for Indian elites (e.g., important instances of international recognition such as by the United Nations or its agencies; participation in First Ministers' Conferences;

audiences with world leaders such as the Pope and the Queen; status before world tribunals). Another source of symbolic-psychological gain under Indian self-government is the collective *control* Indians will be able to exercise over the development (including the *rate* of development) of their own community.

Admittedly, some of these crucial symbolic gains can be attained to some extent through reforms other than self-government, as is demonstrated on a large scale by the Francophone Québécois and on a smaller scale by other cases in the literature. However, the plight of some sectors of the Indian population is demonstrably worse than that of people in the aforementioned situations. Accordingly, more drastic and dramatic measures are needed.

Impact on Boundary Maintenance

The impact of Indian self-government on boundary maintenance will likely result from the kind of increased institutional completeness to which I referred in the Kahnawake case study in Chapter Five. As more needs are met within the local community, exposure to non-Indians decreases and a resultant slight decline in the rates of marrying out can be expected. Otherwise, the main impacts of self-government on boundary maintenance will likely be minimal except for cultural strengthening or revival and the lesser incidence of Indian children being placed for adoption in nonIndian homes. In addition, given the central role of the land and its living creatures in most Indian cultures, any expansion of the Indian land base of an Indian community will likely enhance the integrity of that community's Indian culture.

Impact on Legitimacy

The conferral of legitimacy on the regime, on the incumbents of that regime, and on the policies issuing therefrom is another aspect of community social vitality. Such legitimacy is derived from various sources, one of which is the traditional political order that was in place before the colonial era. Presumably, many Indian governments will restore some features of community decision-making from their political heritage. Students of public policy recognize that the processes of public policy formulation are often as important as the policy product itself; policy decisions and programs issuing from traditional decision-making structures and processes are likely to carry far more legitimacy than decisions and programs formulated by nonIndians in the distant provincial or national capital. Furthermore, the local decision-makers' familiarity with the local mores and informal power structures will likely enable them to make better decisions for implementable policies and programs.

However, if an Indian government fails to meet the legitimate expectations of its constituency, the consequence in some cases may be the delegitimation of Indian government in the minds of that electorate.

Impact on Conflict Regulation and Resolution

While the modernization that Indian self-government brings will likely entail an increased volume and scale of conflict,[12] some conflict-mediating structures (e.g., DIAND, RCMP) will no longer be present in the community. Weiner's research suggests that traditional mechanisms for releasing tension and regulating conflict will often not be viable in contemporary times. Thus, one of the more important challenges facing Indian self-governments will be to adapt old methods of conflict resolution to contemporary times and to devise new such institutions. Some models will be available in nonIndian society (e.g., ombudsmen, human rights commissions, regulatory agencies, crisis intervention teams of social workers, small claims courts, counselling agencies, arbitration boards, and conciliation boards). A large measure of success in these endeavours will be pivotal for most of the other potential benefits of Indian self-government to be realized.

Impact on Leadership and Organization

One challenge of Indian self-governments will be to retain skilled personnel. Even more difficult, though, will be the challenge of finding the right mix of public and private enterprise on the Indian territorial base and the right mix of regulation and autonomy for private-sector Indian (or nonIndian) entrepreneurs.

A not insignificant amount of the leadership and organizational potential of Indian communities has been rendered at least temporarily unavailable due to alienation, incarceration, or escapist behaviour (e.g., abuse of alcohol or other substances). Aboriginal self-government will permit the spontaneous reclaiming of some of that potential (as a result of phenomena discussed above) and the calculated reclaiming of others in that same pool by means of Indian-staffed rehabilitation programs rooted in Indian culture. However, the extent to which Indian self-governments will be able to liberate and utilize the underused leadership and organizational skills of those women who have heretofore been confined to traditional roles is difficult to predict. The question itself, though, raises interesting issues of the tensions between "traditionalism" and "modernism" and between individual rights and collective rights, which underlie so many of the decisions that will have to be made by and about Indian self-governments.

Overall Assessment of Impact

One of the main thrusts of Indian aspirations is the desire for greater self-determination and social justice. The discussion of the reclamation of lost leadership potential suggests that Indian self-government will undoubtedly give Indians greater control over their own destiny. From this, significant material and psychological benefits will flow. However, the justness of Indian governments may vary considerably from one Indian government to another. Justice is not an automatic by-product of self-government. [13]

The second main thrust of Indian aspirations was identified as economic development. It is inconceivable that this would not be a high priority on the agenda of most Indian governments. Many aspects of this discussion of community social vitality have touched indirectly on this – for instance, the breaking of the welfare dependency syndrome; the greater validity of policies based on legitimated and localized decision-making procedures; the attenuation of alienation and the increased sense of individual and collective pride; the forging of a role for the private sector; and the reclamation of temporarily unavailable leadership potential (including entrepreneurial leadership). All of these factors provide grounds for hope for the success of economic development ventures. However, there are bound to be failures. In the final analysis, though, the attainability of aspirations for economic development must depend in large part on the value of the Indian land base and on the nature of fiscal equalization arrangements reached among Indian self-governments and between Indian self-governments and other governments.

The protection and retention of Indian culture was the third general aspiration identified. The prospects for this are quite positive, as was discussed above under the rubric of institutions for socializing individuals into the values, norms, and skills of their culture. The revitalization of the schools, of course, is particularly relevant here. The discussion of the impact of Indian self-government on meaning-conferring activities also dealt with the predicted resurgence of cultural pride and individual dignity and the flow of symbolic expression in government ceremonies, honours, etc. These, too, should contribute significantly to the attainment of cultural protection and retention. Indeed, barring unrealistically high expectations, immobilizing community conflict, and colossal failure at economic development, the attainment of this aspiration seems likeliest of all.

To summarize, then, in many respects Canadian Indian self-governments are in a highly advantageous situation compared to other decolonizing peoples. They are free of many of the encumbrances and contextual difficulties with which those other peoples have had to contend. Canadian Indian self-governments will face many changes, but the prospects for at least modest success in attaining their citizens' aspirations are reasonable, although some failures are inevitable. Sociologically, aboriginal self-government is quite feasible, and in many respects it is desirable.

Notes

1. This chapter is similar to a paper, entitled "The Sociological Impact of Aboriginal Self-Government on Aboriginal Communities," presented by the author at a joint meeting of the Canadian Political Science Association and Canadian Sociology and Anthropology Association, Montreal, May, 1985. It was itself extracted from Roger Gibbins and J. Rick Ponting, "An Assessment of the Probable Impact of Aboriginal Self-Government in Canada," in Alan Cairns and Cynthia Williams (eds.), *The Politics of Gender, Ethnicity and Language in Canada*. Vol. 34, Research Studies of the Royal Commission on the Economic Union and Development Prospects for Canada (Toronto: University of Toronto Press, 1986), pp. 171-245. The present version is reprinted with the permission of the University of Toronto Press. Most of the footnotes in the original have been omitted here.

2. Ralph Matthews, *The Creation of Regional Dependency* (Toronto: University of Toronto Press, 1983).

3. Bernard Blishen *et al.*, *Socio-economic Impact Model for Northern Development*, 2 vols. (Ottawa: Department of Indian and Northern Affairs, 1979).

4. Conversely, the lack of meaning-conferring activities, or the presence of activities that produce only negative meanings, might be called alienation.

5. Compare S.N. Eisenstadt, "Problems of Emerging Bureaucracies in Developing Areas and New States," In Bert F. Hoselitz and Wilbert E. Moore (eds.), *Industrialization and Society* (New York: UNESCO – Mouton, 1963), pp. 159-74.

6. *Ibid.*, p. 166.

7. Geertz found that there "is no new state in which these two themes [traditionalism and modernism] are not present." The tension between them, he found, "pervades every aspect of national life, including the transformations of the social structures of the new state." See Clifford Geertz, "After the Revolution: The Fate of Nationalism in the New States," in Bernard Barber and Alex Inkeles (eds.), *Stability and Social*

Change (Boston: Little Brown, 1971), p. 363. The demand for change, yet the suspicion of the new – the refusal to abandon the traditional ways of doing things – has been apparent in many aspects of relations between Indians and the government of Canada and is but one concrete example of this societal tension that Indian governments will face.

8. In case after case in the social science literature, the existing middle class benefits the most from the "modernization" phenomenon. That is, "modernization" never benefits all sectors of a community evenly, nor rarely even proportionately. This is one among several sources of increased tensions between social classes in the post-colonial era.

9. Even if there is little improvement in economic conditions we can expect the administration of a welfare system to be drastically different (e.g., work-for-welfare schemes) under Indian self-government compared to under DIAND or provincial or municipal welfare agencies. Aboriginal self-government will be less likely to share with those nonIndian agencies a vested interest in keeping Indians dependent and non-productive on the welfare rolls.

10. In December, 1985, DIAND announced that it would speed up the transfer of control over education. This is to be accomplished by transferring to Indian bands and tribal councils, over a five-year period, control over the jobs of up to 1,711 teachers, principals, and their related support staff working in 253 federally operated schools across the country. DIAND will continue to fund their salaries. See Canadian Press, "Indian Affairs to Chop 1700 Jobs From Rolls," *Calgary Herald*, December 3, 1985, p. A3.

11. Rather than being a product of self-government, the creation of radio stations is perhaps just as likely to occur before self-government is formally established.

12. Myron Weiner, "Political Integration and Political Development," in Jason L. Finkle and Richard W. Gable (eds.), *Political Development and Social Change* (New York: Wiley, 1966), pp. 531-62.

13. One's assessment of that justness depends in part on whether one's standards are traditional or contemporary, collectivistic or individualistic.

Chapter Sixteen

Citizenship, Political, and Intergovernmental Problems with Indian Self-Government

by Roger Gibbins

There has been a great deal of debate on the principle of Indian self-government and on the entrenchment of Indian government within the Canadian constitution. This chapter addresses neither issue: it instead moves to a set of issues surrounding the *implementation* of Indian government.[1] I shall argue that recognition of the principle of self-government does not mean that Indian government is feasible or even, in some forms, desirable. Indeed, implementation confronts some major problems of institutional design that we are only beginning to address. These problems are related to conditions which, I suggest, should be imposed on the constitutional entrenchment of Indian government and which would significantly narrow the scope of that government.

There is no question that some of the points raised below will be contentious. To date, however, discussion of Indian government has been too narrowly confined to a debate over principles. Thus, this chapter seeks to expand that discussion. I should also stress, though, that the points raised below are no more than points for discussion; they do not masquerade as social science theory or research findings.

Proponents of Indian government generally assume that the residents of self-governing Indian communities will be *both* Indians *and* Canadians, that Indian government is compatible with Canadian citizenship, and that Indian governments can be successfully "slotted into" the Canadian federal state. To adopt the terminology of the Penner Report, Indian governments would be a distinct, third order of government *within the Canadian state*.[2] However, these assumptions impose significant constraints on the scope and implementation of Indian government.

Citizenship and Political Problems

If Canadian citizenship is to be maintained, two basic conditions must be met. First, the residents of Indian communities must retain the federal and provincial franchise. Second, residents must retain the protections provided by the Charter of Rights and Freedoms.

These points may seem self-evident. It is worth noting, however, that the first was not fully recognized in the Penner Report, which stated that "legislative authority would . . . be with Indian governments, and the primary relationship of the Indian people involved with the federal government would be through those governments."[3] One could read into this the implication that Indians would not enjoy or need the federal franchise, that they would speak to Canadian governments through Indian governments rather than through the federal or provincial ballot. (Alternatively, this passage may just reflect sloppy drafting by the Committee.) The franchise, moreover, implies other entanglements that are less commonly recognized. For instance, in democratic societies the "price" of the vote is the obligation to pay taxes, to support those expenditures approved by elected governments. Therefore the retention of the federal and provincial franchise implies that the residents of self-governing Indian communities will be subject to both federal and provincial taxation in addition to the new taxes that will have to be imposed by Indian governments themselves.[4]

It could be argued, of course, that Indians have a tax-exempt status based on the claim that taxes have already been paid in perpetuity by the surrender of aboriginal title. I suspect, however, that this argument could not be sustained in the political arena. First, the residents of self-governing Indian communities would continue to be recipients of both federal and provincial programs; national defence, old-age pensions, unemployment insurance, and provincial highways provide but a few examples. Thus, there are potential political problems with the Canadian public's reaction to a "free-rider" status. This reaction is troublesome in that it could undermine political support for fiscal transfers from the governments of Canada to Indian communities. Second, Canadian governments will insist on the power to tax non-aboriginal residents of Indian communities and are very unlikely to tolerate Indian communities serving as Canadian tax havens that shelter individual and corporate entities from federal and provincial taxation.[5] Third, existing tax exemptions may meet with little public or governmental resistance because Canadians tend to see aboriginal peoples as being relatively impoverished. However, should Indian government lead to economic success, political support for tax exemptions could be difficult to maintain. The point to stress here is that any continued dependency on fiscal transfers from the broader Canadian community gives the federal and provincial governments a very large club that can be used to force Indian compliance with conventional norms of taxation.

A related matter poses a severe design problem for Indian government. To this point, Indian communities have been spared what is perhaps the central political problem in democratic states – the redistribution of income. With self-government, Indians will face this issue on two fronts – the redistribution of income *within* and *among* Indian communities. Although substantive problems arise in both cases, it is only the second front – the redistribution of wealth among Indian communities – that I wish to address here.

There are at present a variety of mechanisms for the redistribution of wealth among Canadian provinces. The centrepiece of these is the equalization formula and the transfers that it generates from the national treasury to "have-not" provincial governments. Although one could envisage this mechanism being extended to Indian communities, there are two important problems. The first is that equalization payments are made from the national treasury; thus, access to equalization payments implies the exposure of Indian communities to federal taxation. Second, it is not clear that the existing equalization formula would come close to equalizing the fiscal revenues of Indian communities. The income range among Indian communities is far greater than that among provinces. While equalization payments could help "level up" income, they would not redistribute it from the relatively small handful of resource-rich bands. It is by no means unlikely that Canadian governments will insist on some "levelling down," some redistribution of wealth among Indian communities, as a condition for equalization payments.[6]

It might be best to leave the redistribution of income to the Indian community. Funds could be transferred from the government of Canada to Indian governments *in general*, while the distribution of such funds among Indian communities could be managed by Indians themselves rather than through existing mechanisms such as the equalization formula. This approach is envisaged in a proposal by the Federation of Saskatchewan Indians for a Canada-Saskatchewan Indian Resources Fund, "a pool of revenues to be created by statutory formula governing the Indian sharing with Canada of revenues and resources which would be controlled, managed, administered and distributed on the basis of policies established by the Chiefs of Saskatchewan."[7]

It must be recognized, however, that the redistributive problem is much greater for Indians than it is for the Canadian provinces, given the much greater variance in community wealth. It must also be stressed that any distributive mechanism would have to be *governmental* in character; the allocation of federal funds could not be carried out by a body like the Assembly of First Nations from which individual communities could withdraw if they did not agree with the decisions. Any redistributive mechanism would require the force of law, the power to divide up the federal largesse and to withstand the inevitable internal criticism over any such division.

At this point it is useful to pause to examine what is being contemplated. At the very least we are talking about a province-wide Indian government, one that would have the power to enforce its decisions with respect to its constituent bands or communities. In other words, Indian government will not simply mean an increase in power for individual bands and communities; it will also mean the transfer of a good part of that power to a larger Indian government. *The price of self-government may well be the surrender of self-government to new and larger Indian governments.*

Intergovernmental Problems

The form these larger governments might take – how they would be elected, what powers they would have vis-à-vis local communities, whether they would be federal or unitary in structure, where they would be located – is a matter that has yet to enter the debate over Indian government. And yet, I submit, the principle of Indian self-government cannot be implemented unless such larger Indian governmental units are created. Thus, bands must consider not only what powers might flow from the government of Canada into their hands in the wake of self-government, but also what powers would have to be relinquished to larger Indian governments that, like the government of Canada, would lie beyond their direct control. This matter is of particular importance for wealthier bands, who might well fear the redistributive power of larger Indian governments, and for poorer bands, who might well be dependent on those same redistributive powers.

The necessity of larger Indian governments encompassing at the very least provincial communities and potentially even the nationwide Indian community can be demonstrated from a second perspective. The existing system of government in Canada incorporates a complex array of intergovernmental relations that shape everything from the process of constitutional amendment to the delivery of social services. If self-government is to become a reality, it is imperative that Indian governments be worked into the existing structure of intergovernmental relations. This cannot be done, however, at the band level. Simply put, 578 self-governing Indian communities or even 10 per cent of that number could not be slotted into the existing inter-governmental structures. Integration will require a ''senior'' Indian government that will be able both to bargain with other governments and to enforce intergovernmental agreements within its own consti-tuent communities. Here again, then, Indian self-government will require the transfer of power from individual bands to larger govern-ments. Without such a transfer of power, Indian participation in executive federalism – the general term applied to the conduct of inter-governmental relations – would be difficult if not impossible. The present system works because the participants speak with the power of governments behind them; if deals are made, the participants know that all parties can deliver on the bargain. A situation in which the Indian representative in intergovernmental negotiations could not deliver, in which he or she could only *recommend* to one hundred or more self-governing communities, would not work.

The problem here can be illustrated by the First Ministers' Confer-ence, although the same pattern can be traced through the literally hundreds of ministerial and bureaucratic federal-provincial and inter-provincial conferences held every year. If Indian governments are to be represented in forums such as the First Ministers' Conference, and if they are to be built into such mechanisms as the amending formula, they will have to speak through a *single government*. One cannot imag-ine a situation in which individual bands or even province-wide Indian governments could be represented in some continuing and effective fashion at First Ministers' Conferences. There would have to be a single Indian representative, a *governmental* representative, to speak for an Indian constituency much more diverse than that faced by any pro-vincial premier.[8] Like the prime minister and the premiers, he or she would have to be able to deliver on intergovernmental agreements. The representative could not go back to the local bands to consult, nor could local bands have the power to resist decisions. Thus, again we find the need for large-scale Indian governments, a need that has yet to be addressed and indeed has yet to be recognized by the proponents of band-based Indian government.

It is not surprising that the format of such large-scale Indian govern-ments has yet to be worked out, although it is surprising that the need for such governments has not been more widely recognized. Certainly the problems of institutional design are complex if not intractable. It will be necessary, for example, to divide the powers of the state not just two ways, as is done within the existing federal system, but three ways among the Canadian, provincial, and Indian governments, and then again within the system of Indian government so that some appropriate balance of power is struck among band, provincial, and national Indian governments.

It is tempting to say that these problems of institutional design should be left to Indians, that they are details to be worked out once the principle of self-government is constitutionally entrenched. Unfortunately, the matter is not that simple. Given that Indian governments must "mesh" with the institutional structure of the Canadian federal state, the Canadian and provincial governments are necessarily involved. More importantly, an important constitutional principle must be worked out, and that is the application of the Charter of Rights and Freedoms to Indian governments, whatever form they might take.

Problems in Protecting Individual and Collective Rights

What is at issue here is the protection of individual rights within the jurisdictional domain of Indian governments. This is an issue to which Indian organizations are particularly sensitive, and there is a general recognition that a balance will have to be struck between collective rights, the protection of which provides the *raison d'être* for Indian government, and individual rights. There is less agreement, however, on the mechanisms through which individual rights might be protected. Indian organizations tend to prefer internal codes, tribunals, and commissions rather than the external protection provided by Canadian courts and the Charter. The Charter itself is rightly seen as an infringement on the political sovereignty of Indian communities, while the courts are seen as insufficiently sensitive to both collective rights and aboriginal traditions.

It can also be argued, however, that the residents of self-governing Indian communities should be entitled to the full protection of the Charter and of the Canadian courts, that the Charter should apply within the jurisdiction of Indian governments just as it applies within the jurisdiction of the provinces, and that residents should have access to external appeal extending beyond the boundary of the Indian community. To some, this argument may smack of paternalism: it might suggest a lack of faith that Indian communities, if left to their own devices, would adequately protect the rights of their residents. Yet if one argues that Indians must remain Canadian citizens, and that the Charter has become the definitional statement of what Canadian citizenship entails, then the argument transcends paternalism.

The Charter takes on additional importance when we realize that individual rights and freedoms are likely to come under greater threat from Indian governments than they are from other governments in Canada. This is not because Indians are particularly insensitive toward individual rights, although the desire to protect collective rights could well encourage such insensitivity. The threat to individual rights and freedoms comes from the size and homogeneity of Indian communities rather than from their "Indianness" per se. Indian communities tend to be small and characterized by extensive family and kinship ties, and it is in just such communites that individual rights and freedoms are most vulnerable.

In the debate surrounding the establishment of the American constitution in the late 1700s, American nationalists associated with James Madison developed a compelling argument that individual rights and freedoms are at greatest risk in small, relatively homogeneous communities. Where social and economic diversity is lacking, Madison argued, the "tyranny of the majority" is most likely to prevail. Therefore, the argument continued, individual rights and freedoms are best protected within larger, more heterogeneous communities where it is more difficult to articulate a majority will and where a multitude of conflicting and competing interests fragment and immobilize the majority. In short, the rights and freedoms of the individual are better protected in Toronto and Montreal than they are in Cache Creek or Glace Bay.

The Madison argument appears to be of special relevance to Indian communities that are not only small but also very homogeneous relative to the provincial or Canadian communities. Within such communities, individual rights and freedoms may come under intensified pressure from the majority community. Moreover, the small size of Indian communities coupled with extensive kinship ties may prevent any effective separation of powers and may encourage nepotism and corruption. The neutrality of government, of bureaucratic organizations, and of judicial institutions can easily be compromised under these conditions. In a trial, for example, it could well happen that the defendant and the police, the lawyers and the judge, the jury and the aggrieved are all known to one another, that many are linked by ties of kinship and clan. Whether justice would prevail in such circumstances is dependent, of course, on how one defines justice. There is a strong possibility, however, that the procedural foundations of the Canadian judicial system would not prevail. In this case, there may be a compelling need for external appeal and review.

It should be stressed again that I am not arguing that Indian communities pose a threat to individual rights and freedoms, or to democratic norms and bureaucratic neutrality, *because they are Indian*. At the same time, it would be foolish to proceed with the implementation of

Indian government on the assumption that Indian governments will necessarily be good, honest, and efficient. Indian communities can expect their fair share of crooks and thieves, of individuals who will compromise the neutrality of the state to the advantage of themselves or their kin. Indeed, if Madison is right, the nature of Indian communities may make Indian governments particularly vulnerable to the forms of abuse that afflict all political systems. One might argue, then, that the governments of Canada would be irresponsible if they were to endorse Indian government without first being assured that individual rights and freedoms will be fully protected. They would be irresponsible because Indians today enjoy those rights *as Canadian citizens.* These rights are not something that the governments of Canada can barter away in the implementation of Indian government.

Conclusion

I am left in the rather uncomfortable position of appearing to agree with opposition to aboriginal self-government expressed by some of the western premiers during the April, 1985, First Ministers' Conference. I hesitate to endorse their opposition, for by doing so I might appear to sanction the motivations that lay behind their opposition. At the same time, however, I find compelling their argument that the constitutional entrenchment of aboriginal self-government should not proceed until all parties have a clearer understanding of just what the implementation of self-government would entail. As I have tried to illustrate, the principle of self-government provides little guidance as to implementation. At this point we cannot assume that self-government can be implemented without inflicting serious damage to democratic principles, to the intergovernmental structures of the Canadian federal state, and to the citizenship rights of Canadian Indians. In short, there is more work to be done before we conclude that the only obstacle to the implementation of self-government is to be found in the intransigence of western premiers. The problems of implementation extend much further and will not be resolved easily.

Notes

1. This chapter is similar to a paper, entitled "Indian Government: Expanding the Horizons of Discussion," presented by the author at a joint meeting of the Canadian Political Science Association and Canadian Sociology and Anthropology Association, Montreal, May, 1985. That paper was adapted

from Roger Gibbins and J. Rick Ponting, "An Assessment of the Probable Impact of Aboriginal Self-Government in Canada," in Alan Cairns and Cynthia Williams (eds.), *The Politics of Gender, Ethnicity and Language in Canada*. Vol. 34, Research Studies of the Royal Commission on the Economic Union and Development Prospects for Canada (Toronto: University of Toronto Press, 1986), pp. 171-245. Most of the footnotes in the original have been omitted here.

2. *Report of the Special Committee on Indian Self-Government*, Ottawa, November, 1983.

3. *Ibid.*, p. 56.

4. Self-government, even if modelled after Canadian municipalities, implies that Indian governments will raise at least part of their revenue by taxing their residents. This aspect of Indian government has understandably received much less attention than has been received by the increased power and control that self-government would bring.

5. Here the Federation of Saskatchewan Indians has suggested to the contrary that only Indian governments should be able to tax nonIndians living and working on a reserve and nonIndian corporations located on a reserve. Federation of Saskatchewan Indians, "Revenue and Resource Sharing and Indian Economic Development," undated draft, p. 26.

6. The equalization formula is based on revenues derived from close to thirty provincial tax sources. It would thus have to be determined which of these sources fall within the powers of Indian governments. Indian governments would then be under pressure to impose those taxes falling within their domain.

7. Chief Sol Sanderson, President of the Federation of Saskatchewan Indians, "Submission to the Parliamentary Task Force on Federal-Provincial Fiscal Arrangements," Ottawa, May 12, 1981, p. 34.

8. One could imagine that in some forums there would have to be a single aboriginal representative who could speak with authority not only for Indians but also for the Métis and Inuit.

Chapter Seventeen

The Government of Aboriginal Peoples in Other Countries

by Walter Rudnicki and Harold Dyck

This chapter is based on an examination of the literature pertaining to the structures of government that selected countries have used to relate to and deal with aboriginal peoples; it also assesses the relevance of these structures to the Indian situation in Canada. The peoples and countries considered are: the Ainu in Japan; the Samis (formerly known as Lapps) in Norway, Sweden, and Finland; the Maori in New Zealand; the Aboriginals in Australia; and the Inuit in Greenland. Unfortunately, the literature describing these situations is rather uneven from country to country and this must be recognized as a limitation of this chapter.

There exists a plethora of formal political and administrative arrangements for the governing of aboriginal peoples. There are almost as many organizational arrangements as there are countries with enclave or territorially associated aboriginal populations. Each set of arrangements reflects the basic policy orientation of the government of the respective colonizing or formerly colonizing society. Indeed, in none of the countries studied have aboriginal political systems of authority been recognized or allowed to evolve free of direct structural impositions from the colonizing society.

Case Studies

The Ainu of Japan (1799-1899)

It is generally believed that the relationship between the Japanese and the Ainu dates back to mythological times. However, in the middle

From Policy Development Group, *The Government of Aboriginal Peoples*, Report prepared for the Special Parliamentary Committee on Indian Self-Government (Ottawa, 1983). Reproduced by permission of the Minister of Supply and Services Canada.

ages the control of the Japanese government began to disintegrate and Hokkaido was left in the hands of the Abe family. During the 1400s immigration from mainland Japan to Hokkaido became substantial and during the latter half of that century and throughout the sixteenth century a series of armed conflicts took place between the Ainu and the recently arrived immigrants. The immigrants gained the upper hand and peace was made with the various Ainu tribes. Having made peace, the Japanese governing authorities began to impose restrictions (e.g., on trade and movement). In 1669 the Ainu engaged in a revolt, which was doomed to failure due to Japanese military superiority. Early in the nineteenth century, when it was recognized that Russian colonization was a threat to Japan, Japanese authorities adopted a formal and concerted policy of assimilating the Ainu. It was exceedingly successful, as can be seen in the fact that the 300,000 ''full-blooded'' Ainu estimated to exist in 1800 have been reduced to approximately 300.

Until 1799 Japanese-Ainu relationships had been primarily commercial and the government of Ainu territories had been left almost entirely to the Otona, the chiefs of Ainu villages and territories. With the perceived threat of Russian colonization the Japanese increasingly came to view the Ainu as a potential labour pool to be trained and exploited for national objectives, such as defence. To accomplish the intended transformation of the Ainu, it was deemed necessary to assume direct control over them. A welfare system (to prevent the pool of labour from being depleted by illness and starvation) and a commission form of government were established. Under the commissioners and magistrates a considerable bureaucracy developed. Administration rested with the commissioner or the magistrate. At strategically important locations local offices were established and administered by resident officers who oversaw the administration of justice, trade and commerce, and the education of the Natives. In most places the Ainu system of authority was left unchanged, but it was neither recognized nor reinforced by the colonizers. Ainu members were appointed to certain specially created positions to serve as communications intermediaries and to conduct symbolic functions.

The bureaucrats were responsible for implementing a very comprehensive native policy involving Japanization in the spheres of language, family relations (abolition of polygamy), religion, and daily life in general. The policy also involved such elements as a comprehensive relief program for times of natural calamity, the imposition of a new legal system, enforcement of fairness in matters of trade and commerce, and the conduct of elaborate ceremonies to remind the Ainu of the power and generosity of the Japanese authorities. Despite later efforts to "protect" the Ainu, the process of assimilation had taken such a hold in the nineteenth century that it could not be reversed. Insufficient vestiges of aboriginal authority remained to stem the tide.

From our specific case studies, certain more generalized models of governance can be identified. The case of the Ainu gives rise to what we have called the *hierarchical model* – a model also operative in Canada's relations with its Indian peoples. In this model, central governments take on responsibility for aboriginal affairs constitutionally, by statute, or by edict. Aboriginal governments and authorities are not recognized as having any degree of sovereignty and are integrated with the central administrative apparatus used by the government to deal with aboriginal affairs. Authority from the central government is therefore hierarchical; it flows downward to indigenous communities. Traditional aboriginal political authority may be allowed to remain, but its functions are limited to those areas of no interest to the central government and aboriginal authority is not recognized formally. The central government assumes a trustee and protectorate role in relation to its aboriginal subjects.

The Canadian experience with Indian band governments suggests three major problems with the hierarchical model of government. First, in limiting the functions and regulating the activities of the aboriginal authority (e.g., the band council in Canada), this model is unable to deal with the holistic nature of aboriginal community life. That is, state-established aboriginal administrative institutions at the community level do not fit the cultural requirements of the community. Second, such state-established aboriginal authorities must respond to priorities and procedures established by a central administrative agency, rather than by the local Aboriginals themselves, and thus find it difficult to represent the interests of their communities. In other words, these councils tend to be oriented to the central administrative agency rather than to the needs of their communities. Third, and finally, in a system where community priorities and programs are established outside the community, that community lacks a great deal of latitude in self-government.

The Samis of Northern Fennoscandia

The Sami settlements in northern Fennoscandia extend from the Kola Peninsula in the northwestern corner of the U.S.S.R. across the northern parts of Finland, Sweden, and Norway to the Norwegian Sea. The Samis have had a long history of contact with outsiders. For instance, as the Finns entered present-day Finland from the south around the time of the birth of Christ and extended their colonization to the north, the Samis either retreated further north or were absorbed.

In the nineteenth century the state began to intervene explicitly in the matter of the rights of ownership over land and water in the north, as administrative officials were allowed to make territorial grants to settlers out of lands occupied by the Samis. When the courts of the day recognized the historic property rights of the Samis, the state transferred the responsibility for decisions concerning Sami landholdings to provincial administrations, and in so doing apparently freed central government of any responsibility for the Sami people.

Today the Samis are a divided people. They are divided between four different governments – Finland, Sweden, Norway, and the U.S.S.R.; they are divided into at least four major linguistic groups, the dialects of which are mutually unintelligible; and they are divided occupationally between the reindeer-breeding Samis and those who make their living in other ways. They are also dispersed over an enormous area in very small groups or bands. Given this situation, one would expect a high degree of susceptibility to assimilative influences. Indeed, in Norway their population has decreased by more than 50 per cent, according to official census data, and a large proportion of those not engaged in reindeer-breeding have increasingly adopted the Norwegian lifestyle.

In both Norway and Sweden the Sami people have no special status, but those who breed reindeer are directly regulated by the central government, not as an ethnic group but as an occupational group. The state seeks to protect the occupation rather than the ethnic culture. In all respects the Samis in Norway have been extended the rights of ordinary citizenship. By putting the Sami villages under the same local and regional administrative arrangements as the rest of Norway, the state at least undermined, if not emasculated, many of the traditional Sami community functions. Similarly, in the eighteenth century in Finnmark the Sami system of collective ownership of land was undermined by the state's refusal to recognize collective rights to land and property; the state owned all common land. This paved the way for the institutions of the larger Norwegian society to exert their influence on the Samis.

Essentially, little difference exists between the Norwegian and the Swedish approaches to the Samis. Culturally, the Samis have from the outset been quite alien in Swedish society. As in Norway, the Samis in Sweden differ from the majority population in most major respects, including language, type of domicile, means of livelihood, family structure, political structure, customs and mores, and clothing. As in Norway, the Samis in Sweden have not been accorded any special status. Their cultural uniqueness is not recognized in policy, and state control over them and their economy was entrenched in the Reindeer Pasturage Law of 1886 (and subsequent amendments). This law regulated the way the Samis were to pursue their livelihood in reindeer breeding and set out how it would be administered. The Samis were assigned to Sami villages, for which the county administration drew up by-laws. (These villages extended over wide areas following the migratory routes of the herds.) Every village was given its village prefect, who was responsible under the law for supervising reindeer breeding. The powers of the annual assembly of the Sami village were severely limited, and the Sami villages were even obliged to accept anyone who migrated to the community under official sanction.

Under this regime the fate of the reindeer economy was to be the fate of the Sami people. However, it is estimated that only about 25 per cent of the Samis in Sweden are reindeer herders (in Norway, the figure is only about 5 to 10 per cent). Thus, the vast majority of Samis are not acknowledged even as an occupational group in Swedish policy and receive no protection whatever as an aboriginal group. The administrative structures established for the Sami people under the statutes of both Norway and Sweden are occupational management units, not governments in any sense.

In Finland Sami affairs have taken a rather different course, in part because Finland is already a bilingual and bicultural nation. A state committee on Sami affairs examined the Sami situation during the period 1971-73 and recommended a legal framework to safeguard the rights of the Samis to economic and political development in their home region and a mechanism for Sami political representation. The result was the establishment of the Sami Parliament, a body consisting of twenty representatives elected by Sami voters. However, the Sami Parliament does not have the power to make decisions binding on either state or local administrations. It is merely empowered to take initiatives, make proposals, and present statements to authorities concerning various matters in the Sami home area. It does name representatives to a number of public boards at the county, provincial, and national levels of government, but otherwise it is linked with the national government only on the basis of negotiation.

The Norwegian and Swedish cases are illustrative of what we have called the *equality model*. Under this model the central government has no constitutional responsibility for its aboriginal peoples and assumes no statutory authority for dealing with them as a special aboriginal group. Aboriginal peoples have no special status and so are treated in the same way using the same programs as the non-indigenous citizenry – at least officially. They are accorded ordinary rights of citizenship – no more and no less. The same institutions of government that serve the majority society serve these minority aboriginal groups, as no historic obligations toward the aboriginal peoples have been recognized in treaties and no trust relationship has been established between the aboriginal people and the central government.

This model does not in any way accommodate the principles of self-determination. It instead contributes greatly to the process of assimilation, as it has in both Norway and Sweden, where the Sami children are being educated in the curriculum established by the central governments, the Sami language has been gradually giving way to the Scandinavian languages, and the occupational structure of the Samis increasingly approaches that of the larger society. This model is thus unacceptable to most aboriginal peoples, including some Sami spokesmen.

The Maori of New Zealand

In 1840 the Maori population of New Zealand was 100,000 people; a century earlier it had been closer to 500,000. A century of destructive contact with European culture and a prolonged period of intense intertribal warfare using European weaponry reduced the Maori population drastically. Today the Maori population stands at about 280,000 people who are of half or more Maori descent. A wider definition, including all those who specify some degree of Maori origin, brings that population figure up to 385,000 in 1981.

Throughout the 1860s wars over land issues were waged between settlers and Maori. These wars occurred despite the signing of the Treaty of Waitangi (1840), under which the Maori chiefs ceded sovereignty to the British Queen and her colonial administrators. According to the treaty, the Maori had all the rights and privileges of British subjects. In addition, four Maori parliamentary seats were created in 1867 (in a Parliament that has numbered between 83 and 91 seats since then), each to be filled by open ballot by Maori electors. This was envisioned as a temporary measure that would last only until the Maori were properly assimilated.

Although the treaty guaranteed that the Maori would be ruled by their own chiefs, the fact of having four Maori members in the colonial legislature undermined the Maori system of authority, for the New Zealand Parliament did pass laws affecting the Maori. Land legislation, for instance, was a key factor in restricting traditional Maori activities. The Native Land Court, established by Parliament in 1865, undermined the traditional Maori land tenure system in which land was held by the whole tribe and land tenure and use could be altered only with the consent of all the land users in the tribe. The Native Land Court was mandated to issue legal Crown grants to replace the traditional title. Ten names were designated on each Crown grant as the owners who could henceforth sell the land. Communal tribal titles were converted into individual Crown titles and private purchasers could then deal with individual Maori instead of having to deal with the whole tribe or a portion of it. In this way the court knocked away one of the main pillars of Maori organization and authority, opened the way for the separation of the Maori from their land in the legalized land grabbing of the 1870s and 1880s, and contributed directly to the breakdown of Maori government.

The Maori have undergone a significant transformation during the last half century, as evidenced in their rate of urbanization. In 1926 the urban Maori population was 10,000 or approximately 16 per cent of the total Maori population. By the 1981 census urban Maori numbered 219,000, or 78 per cent of the Maori population.

The establishment of special seats in Parliament for the Maori was not unusual for New Zealand at that time, as other types of "special representation" (e.g., for gold diggers) already existed. Until 1967 Maoris were required by law to enrol in the Maori electoral rolls and were disqualified from offering themselves as candidates in any non-Maori constituency. The Maori electorate enrolment system continues to this day, and the four seats are still reserved for Maori representatitives.

The New Zealand form of structural integration has been attended by many problems. For instance, not until 1937 were the Maori elections held by secret ballot. Maori elections were characterized by bribery and corruption and the Maori electors themselves sometimes considered the electoral arrangements more or less a joke. The Maori level of voting participation is low (e.g., in the 1972 election only about one-third of the voting-age Maori population actually voted), the non-Maori legislators and the general public have largely ignored the Maori voting system, and the Maori people are under-represented in the Parliament compared to their proportion of the population (5 per cent versus 8 per cent). Rather than assisting the Maori to be full and integrated partners in New Zealand society, separate representation has in fact contributed to a considerable amount of Maori withdrawal from the political process.

Another method used to draw the Maori into the policy-making process is the Maori Council, established under the Maori Welfare Act of 1962. It is a hierarchical administrative structure consisting of the council itself, ten district councils, executive committees, and 367 Maori committees. Some would view this council system in its entirety as a form of Maori government. However, it has no real powers other than recommending courses of action. It also can be criticized for cutting across tribal boundaries, ignoring other Maori organizations such as tribal trust boards, and being unrepresentative of all Maoris. Communication through the rather deep hierarchy is slow, the system does not effectively articulate the interests of the urban Maori majority, and its financing is usually inadequate because it depends on levies on the lower tiers. Furthermore, the fact that it was set up by the government makes it suspect among many Maoris.

The New Zealand case suggests a third general model, which we have called the *integration model*. Unlike the equality model, in this model aboriginal peoples are recognized as a unique group. They are accorded a special status and some arrangements and structures are formally created to ensure their authoritative participation in policymaking. However, traditional political authority of the aboriginal peoples is not recognized and sovereignty is not accorded them by the larger society. Aboriginal administrative structures are not necessarily used to deliver services.

Apart from numerical under-representation, probably the main drawback of parliamentary representation as it has been developed in New Zealand is that the aboriginal representatives were not accorded positions of power in Parliament and were therefore unable to bring about the changes demanded by Maori communities. Their credibility in the eyes of their constituents suffered accordingly and this served to further undermine the effectiveness of the system. Thus far the numerous calls for reform of this system of representation remain unheeded.

A second major approach for bringing aboriginal peoples into the policy and decision-making processes of government is a statutory mechanism for allowing the articulation of aboriginal interests directly to the political levels of government. The Maori Council is designed to do this, as is the Sami Parliament in Finland and the National Aboriginal Conference in Australia (see below). Yet, each of these has encountered three major problems. First, because they are prescribed by government, problems of legitimacy for these bodies exist in the eyes of their aboriginal constituents. Frequently they cannot function effectively because of inadequate resources; if they are ineffective, their credibility is dismissed by the aboriginal community. Second, none of these agencies has appropriate or adequate administrative structures for the conduct of its work and each is thus rendered rather inefficient. Third, with the exception of the Sami Parliament, these structures have very deep hierarchies that also militate against efficiency.

The Australian Aboriginals

With the establishment of European settlements in Australia from 1788 onward, the equilibrium between Australian Aboriginals and nature was catastrophically upset. The settlers appropriated the more productive lands and thereby greatly restricted the food-gathering and certain ritualistic activities of the Aboriginals. The Aboriginals found themselves increasingly pauperized and numerous clashes occurred in the nineteenth century between them and the European settlers. Inevitably, the Aboriginals lost and were displaced; in Tasmania they were exterminated.

The aboriginal population has been estimated to have been as great as 300,000 in 1788. By 1976 those identifying themselves as Aboriginals in the census numbered 161,000.

No treaties were signed, and not until the 1920s did the white community begin to feel any need for aboriginal policies and programs. The federal government of Australia had no constitutional authority to deal with aboriginal affairs, so this matter was left entirely to the states, whose policies amounted to some form of welfare and community services, plus assimilation. By the 1950s the federal government was becoming increasingly concerned to hasten aboriginal development, with the object of their eventual assimilation, and in 1959 it initiated a program whereby all Aboriginals would come under the provisions of federal social welfare laws. In 1960 a state-federal conference resolved to abandon quickly the practice of isolating Aboriginals on reservations and to take measures to assist their assimilation. In 1962 Aboriginals were given the federal vote.

Pressures for a greater federal presence in aboriginal affairs grew in the 1960s, especially with the growing recognition that the Aborigines were not doomed to extinction and that the "protectionist" policies did not meet the developing criteria of international human rights conventions. Thus, in 1967 Australians overwhelmingly approved a referendum proposal to give the federal government shared responsibility for aboriginal affairs with the states. Since then the federal government has established a number of different bodies to deliver myriad services to the aboriginal communities. It has established a Department of Aboriginal Affairs, a Council for Aboriginal Affairs, and an Aboriginal Development Commission (somewhat similar to a

Canadian Crown corporation in status). In addition, a number of district land councils, elected and run by Aboriginals, have been established under both state and federal statutes.

Australian Aboriginals had been absolutely dispossessed of their lands without compensation or acknowledgement, and only since 1972 have aboriginal land rights been recognized in Australian policy. Two approaches were taken. First, an Aboriginal Land Commission was established to purchase alienated lands to which justified claim was made. Second, a commissioner was appointed to give inalienable free hold title of unalienated Crown lands to aboriginal communities where the existence of traditional ownership rights could be established. However, progress on this front has been slow.

After the constitutional changes of 1967, which gave the federal government some responsibility for aboriginal affairs, it was necessary to establish a new paradigm for aboriginal policy development and implementation; successive governments engaged in much organizational experimentation to this end. This first Minister of Aboriginal Affairs established the National Aboriginal Consultative Committee as an elected statutory body mandated to advise the minister. It soon found itself in conflict with the minister over its role and lasted only three years. The new government elected in 1976 created two new bodies, the National Aboriginal Conference and the Council for Aboriginal Development. The former was an elected body intended to serve as a forum for articulating aboriginal policy positions, while the latter was a small advisory committee to the minister. The former spawned various other organizations (e.g., the Committee for Aboriginal Development, the National Aboriginal Executive, the National Aboriginal Annual Meeting, and the National Aboriginal Conference state branches), but was really merely a consultancy body consulted by the minister when and if he so chose. The Council for Aboriginal Development was an advisory body with the right to provide advice directly to the minister whether he asked for it or not.

Not only has Australia attempted to bring the articulation of aboriginal interests close to the centre of policy-making, it has also created a variety of agencies for the development and management of aboriginal communities and land. Under the provisions of the Aboriginal Land Rights Act (1977), two territorial aboriginal land councils were created to manage extensive tracts of aboriginal lands. These elected councils (and a comparable one established at the state level in South Australia in 1980) are obliged to protect the interests of traditional land owners and are empowered to grant leases or licences, to enter contracts, to acquire or dispose of lands, and to organize their operations. They are the first manifestation of an aboriginal form of territorial government in Australia.

In 1980 the federal government passed the Aboriginal Development Commission Act, which established a central agency to further the economic and social development of Aboriginals. It is administered by an all-Aboriginal board of commissioners appointed by the government and with its staff of over 100 persons it operates much like a Crown corporation.

The Australian case is an example of what we have called a *multi-level model*. It entails a considerable variety of agencies that deal with aboriginal matters – a mix of elected and appointed agencies, state and federal bodies, territorially based and centrally based organizations, and statutory organizations run by aboriginal peoples. Responsibility for aboriginal peoples is constitutionally divided between the federal and the state levels of government, and while some states have transferred their responsibility for aboriginal affairs to the federal government, others have not due to their fear of losing control over their lands in the light of recognized aboriginal land rights.

This mixed, multi-level system has been in effect in Australia for only about fifteen years; it is therefore much too early to speculate on its longer-term performance. However, there have already been major problems between the states and the federal government in dealing with the land issue and very different relationships have evolved with aboriginal peoples from state to state. For many years to come there will continue to be a variety of policy contexts under which Aboriginals in Australia will live.

The Greenlanders

The relationship between aboriginal Greenlanders and Europeans extends back to the Middle Ages, when some 3,000 Norse occupied various parts of Greenland. However, they died out in the fifteenth century and there is no record of any further contact until the early 1700s, when Danish missionaries and trade monopolists arrived.

In the 1860s the Danes established democratic government in the form of councils on a local, regional, and provincial basis. It was highly Danized and distinctly colonial, and neither the local nor the provincial councils were utilized by Greenlanders for the expression of their interests and demands. The colony itself was rather rigidly ethnically stratified, with the higher occupational positions occupied by whites and the lower positions occupied by the Inuit. The great distance between the two ethnic groups has been narrowed only slightly since the so-called post-colonial period was initiated in 1953, and the Inuit have been diligent in restricting the kinds of contacts that may be had with non-Greenlanders. Hence, and also because of Greenland's geographic isolation, the Inuit of Greenland have not undergone as rapid a process of assimilation as have aboriginal peoples elsewhere.

In 1953 the constitution of Denmark was changed to allow Greenland to become a full-fledged county of Denmark. However, the promise of the ensuing reforms and development programs was not met and the rigid ethnic stratification persisted and gave rise to the formation of the Sakak political party and its demands for ''normalization'' or the abolition of arrangements that were different from the rest of Denmark. Of particular concern here was the abolition of the Ministry of Greenland in Copenhagen and the unravelling of the almost total control of Greenlandic trade and commerce by the Royal Greenlandic Trade Department, a non-profit Danish organization. Home rule was established in Greenland in 1979, after Greenlanders had attacked the overwhelming influence of Danish authorities in the design of the Greenlandic school system. However, home rule for Greenland was qualified in some important ways. For instance, Denmark's constitution in its entirety continues in force for Greenland and sovereignty continues to rest with Danish authorities. Greenland does have a popularly elected legislative assembly and a Greenland administration chosen by that assembly, but Denmark reserves unto itself absolute jurisdiction in the fields of the constitution, foreign affairs, national finances, and defence. A carefully developed plan has been formulated for the phased transfer of authority over Greenland's domestic affairs (e.g., taxes, fisheries, conservation, trade planning, social welfare, education, culture, health, housing, in-land transport, etc.) throughout the 1980s.

The most controversial aspect of the agreement pertains to the management and ownership of mineral resources. It gives both governments decision-making authority and veto power in the field of natural resources and uses mineral resource revenues to replace grants from Denmark to Greenland. In other words, the intent of the government of Denmark was to ensure that the benefits of Greenlandic mineral resources accrue to the country as a whole. This agreement has been highly controversial in Greenland.

Finally, it should be noted also that the home rule act provided that Greenlandic would be the principal language of Greenland, though it is required that instruction be provided in the Danish language as well.

The Greenland case is an example of what may be called the *territorial self-government model*. This model is used by governments as an instrument of decolonization. It consists of a grant, by constitution or statute, of some measure of home rule and involves the establishment (or, if they already exist, the recognition) of governmental bodies to exercise political, administrative, and some judicial powers on territories occupied by or reserved for the aboriginal peoples. These aboriginal governments are empowered to levy taxes and may have a limited form of sovereignty recognized by the former colonial government. This is the only model in which the full range of functions (legislative, administrative, and judicial) necessary to govern are brought together under aboriginal control. It has been applauded by aboriginal leaders in a variety of countries as being a step in the right direction and shows the most promise for self-determination of aboriginal peoples.

Conclusion

Around the world the relationship between colonizing and indigenous peoples has tended to proceed through as many as five stages – stages for which beginnings and endings are often difficult to discern and which often overlap with each other as vestiges of an earlier stage persist through later stages. These five stages might be described as: (1) displacement; (2) restriction; (3) assimilation; (4) structural accommodation; and (5) self-determination. The reader will recognize these phases more readily in some of the preceding case studies than in others and will note that Canada and most of the other countries included in this study are in the stage of structural accommodation. This is the stage where structures previously established to impose or encourage assimilation are judged a failure, which leads governments to try to adjust those institutional structures to try to accommodate new priorities such as health services delivery, education, and clan government. During this phase aboriginal peoples tend to become mobilized as forceful lobby groups pressing for change, as we have seen in Canada since the late 1970s.

Self-government is a necessary, but not sufficient, condition that must be present if a people is to move into the fifth stage, self-determination. Adequate resources are also necessary if self-rule is to be effective and have any chance of surviving. Contrary to popular wisdom that self-government should be granted only after an aboriginal people's economic development has reached a certain point, we submit the reverse. That is, during the period of transition to self-government, substantial financial assistance will be needed by aboriginal peoples, and only after the rights to self-determination are extended to the aboriginal political realm will economic development proceed on a sure footing.

We recommend that the government of Canada reject its current approach of merely modifying the colonial framework and devolving responsibilities to Indian bands. In place of that approach we recommend that over the next decade or so a constitutionally entrenched order of Indian government be developed in the Canadian polity. That would transform profoundly the present relations between Indians and the government of Canada – relations that are strongly coloured by being situated in the evolutionary phase of structural accommodation with its remnants of the assimilative era. What we are calling for is the development of Indian government as a distinct and unique order of government in the Canadian polity, with some form of "home rule" involving limited sovereignty. A number of different approaches could be taken to achieve this major transformation. One suggestion is that the relationship could move through a transition period involving three interim phases prior to Indian governments being recognized as almost like provinces. These phases might be: (1) protectorate status; (2) territorial administration; and (3) responsible territorial government.

As can be seen, we are opting for the territorial model, which was described earlier as the only model that brings together the full range of functions necessary to govern. It offers the added advantages of bringing Indian nations into the Canadian polity authoritatively rather than as interest groups and of making Indian governments accountable to an Indian electorate. In the final phase, which would involve a status approximating but not identical to that of a province, the Indian government would be responsible to an Indian legislature elected by Indians. Like Quebec, an Indian province would enjoy special status under the Constitution. Authoritative Indian participation in broader Canadian affairs, and particularly in matters of special concern to them, would almost certainly accelerate the process of dealing with a long unfinished agenda between Indians and Canada.

Part Five

Conclusion

Chapter Eighteen

Assessing a Generation of Change

by J. Rick Ponting

Since the release of the federal government's 1969 white paper on Indian affairs, Indians in Canada have been experiencing profound social change. At first the change was manifested more in the philosophical outlook and political orientation of individual Indian leaders. However, in the intervening years the change has acquired considerably greater breadth and depth and has begun to erode significantly the colonial regime that dominated Indian life in Canada for generations. It has, though, been an arduous journey and promises to continue as such for the next generation, for the vested interests buttressing colonialism are tenacious. This chapter will pull together and assess the disparate strands of change identified in the preceding chapters and then look ahead toward the end of this century.

If change is to be assessed in terms of progress toward decolonization, it is useful to reiterate what is meant by that term. The following are defining characteristics of internal colonialism as it has been experienced in Canada: (1) the forced integration of Indians into the larger society; (2) major power differentials structured into the relationship between Indians and the larger society, so that a dominant group controls and administers Indians and makes decisions for Indians; (3) a system of "indirect rule" whereby local Indian leaders act as agents for implementing the policies and decisions of nonIndian power-holders outside the community; (4) racially based barriers to Indians' upward socio-economic mobility; (5) exploitation of Indians for their labour; (6) cultural destruction; and (7) a racist ideology.

We now come to a consideration of the major changes in the situation of Indians in Canada since the release of the 1969 white paper. The most important changes have been: (1) demographic changes in the Indian population; (2) the 1985 amendments to the Indian Act; (3) the recognition of aboriginal rights; and (4) the politicization of Indians.

Demographic Changes

The demographic changes in the Indian populations have been numerous and profound. Some are indicative of decolonization, while others are cited here because they constitute important features of context for the remainder of the discussion.

Perhaps the most general demographic indicator of decolonization is to be found in the significant decline exhibited by the Indian death rate. For instance, in the decade after 1971, the Indian infant mortality rate declined from the lofty levels characteristic of dependent Third World nations to less than half that level. It is, though, still slightly higher than the rate for the total Canadian population. In that fact, and in the enormous discrepancy between Indians and nonIndians in the rates of death by accidents, poisoning, violence, and suicide, we have a measure of the length and toll of the remainder of the decolonization journey. Similarly, improvements in life expectancy at birth have been dramatic, yet a wide gap (ten years) still remains.

The sixfold increase (1971 to 1981) in the proportion of the Indian out-of-school population having attained at least some post-secondary education is another indicator of decolonization, or at least of the potential for decolonization. That is, it reflects Indians' increased capacity for carrying out the technical, managerial, and other information-gathering and decision-making tasks needed to take over the management of their own affairs from the federal government. Accompanying this change in the pool of skilled labour are changes in the occupational composition of the Indian labour force. The proportion of the Indian labour force in service occupations exceeds the corresponding proportion for the nonIndian Canadian labour force, and the proportion of the Indian labour force in "managerial, technical, or professional" occupations approaches the corresponding figure for Canadians as a whole. Many of these highly skilled Indians are working on reserves or for Indian organizations where they are tackling responsibilities formerly handled by the Department of Indian Affairs.

Another indication of a progression toward decolonization is to be found in the increased wealth of the Indian population. The income disparity between Indians and other Canadians, while still large, narrowed significantly between the 1971 and 1981 censuses. In addition, a small number of bands acquired substantial wealth through resource extraction or claims settlement. This has given some Indians a degree of economic power not only unusual among colonized peoples but also convertible into other resources (e.g., legal expertise, publicity, public opinion poll data, etc.).

Various other changes in the Indian population are not indicators of decolonization. Rather, they constitute parameters that must be taken into account as policy-planners seek to further the decolonization objective. Perhaps the most important of these is the increase in the size of the labour force age group and the corresponding decline in the young dependent population (aged 0-15 years). This increase in the labour force age group translates into a heightening of demand for meaningful employment opportunities. To the extent that these are not provided on-reserve, the constellation of forces will be such as to continue to draw scarce human talent off-reserve and often out of service to Indians. The decline in the young dependent population, however, translates into a larger disposable income for those who do have income.

Another important population change is in its size, which will amount to about one-half million people by the turn of the century. This will provide a significant impetus toward decolonization, for along with the increase in the Indian population will come an increase in the costs of retaining the present system and an increase in non-Indian politicians' awareness of the long-term financial savings to be realized through decolonization. However, whether the population will continue to grow at its present rate beyond the turn of the century is open to question, for the present rate of growth is attributable not to high birth rates but rather to the sheer size of the cohort of Indian baby-boom children of the 1960s who are now in the child-bearing ages. By the turn of the century they will have largely passed out of the child-bearing years. Regardless, the present rate of population growth is placing strong pressure on existing housing stocks and is a contributing factor behind the increase (to 30 per cent) in the proportion of the Indian population that now resides off-reserve.

Finally, although the on-reserve housing stock has improved considerably over the last ten years, the highly unsatisfactory housing situation on most reserves remains an important political factor influencing decolonization. That is, while the housing crisis persists the pressures from the grassroots for decolonization will likely also persist, for the reality of colonization is literally brought home to large numbers of Indians on a daily basis in the form of their own overcrowded or otherwise substandard housing. (For example, in a 1985 study almost one-half of Indian housing was found to fall below basic standards of physical condition.) On the other side of the coin, though, is the possibility that to the extent the housing crisis and the unemployment crisis are attenuated, the grassroots Indian support for decolonization could wane. Although other socio-political forces might sustain the drive toward decolonization, the aforementioned possibility should not be overlooked. Nor should analysts overlook the possibility of the federal government attempting to blunt the thrust for self-government by structuring incentives to attract Indians away from reserves, thereby shrinking the "critical mass" of on-reserve population. Although this would constitute a new policy departure, it is significant that senior federal government policy-makers, as represented in the deputy prime minister's 1985 task force report on native programs, are thinking in terms of "eliminating any incentive through housing assistance to remain in areas of high unemployment."[1]

Amendments to the Indian Act

As we saw in Kathleen Jamieson's chapter, the sex discrimination in the Indian Act prior to 1985 took a considerable toll on Indian women and their families when those women married nonIndians. After strenuous lobbying by women[2] and years of broken promises by the federal government, the Act was finally amended to remove the provisions that discriminated on the basis of sex and to give bands control over their own band membership. The legislation clearly qualifies as being of a decolonizing nature in that by eliminating involuntary enfranchisement it removes one of the instruments that forced Indian women's integration into the larger society. Similarly, inasmuch as the expulsion of these women from their reserves, where enforced, cut them off from their own cultural roots and thereby undermined Indian culture for them and their children, the repeal of these provisions can also be seen as an act of decolonization. However, it is inordinately difficult to predict how great will be the consequences of this act of decolonization, for we do not know how many will seek reinstatement, what their characteristics will be, how soon they will apply, how many will be admitted to band membership, or what their distribution will be across bands.

The legislative change will have both "positive" and "negative" ramifications, and any given ramifaction may be evaluated differently by persons with different vested interests. For instance, the reinclusion of these women onto band electoral rolls or their involvement in running for elected office could be a destabilizing influence in Indian politics at the band level or at "higher" levels. They might disrupt delicate accommodations that have been made; they might press for a restructuring of the political agenda; they might challenge Indian male political dominance. Any one of these changes could be seen as highly desirable by some and as an anathema by others.[3] Similarly, if one band admits a disproportionately large number of members it may produce a proportionate reallocation of government funds among bands when those allocations are based on per-capita funding formulas.

Various other arguments against the legislation have been made by Indian organizations. Many point to the unlikelihood that the Indian land base and government funding will be expanded in proportion with the increase in band populations arising from the amendments. Others point to the likely exacerbation of the on-reserve housing crisis, while the primary concern of yet others is that a fixed sum of natural resource revenues will have to be divided among a larger number of people, thereby lowering the per-capita share of those revenues.

On the sociological plane the potential ramifications are numerous. First, as Kathleen Jamieson noted in her postscript, the legislation creates new varieties of "second-class citizens," such as Indians who are reinstated on the general register but are denied band membership under the terms of the membership code adopted by their band. There might always be a need for a Department of Indian Affairs to serve this sector of the Indian population. Second, by creating a category of persons who are band members but not enrollees on DIAND's official Indian Register (e.g., Aboriginals from another country who are fugitives from "justice" abroad), the legislation sets the stage for a confrontation in the courts between bands and the federal government on the issue of Canadian citizenship and the sovereignty of Indian governments in Canada.

In cases where they have been living off-reserve, reinstated women and their children are also likely, on average, to be more assimilated than Indians who have lived all or most of their lives on-reserve. Upon returning to the reserve the reinstatees might challenge the male dominance that prevails in many Indian cultures or might simply provide new and different role models that exert a more subtle influence on reserve life. Some observers have predicted a heightening of the tensions already found between the sexes or the races on many reserves (e.g., women's resentment toward Indian men who succeeded in blocking reinstatement for so long, or Indian men's resentment of Indian women for marrying out, or Indian men's resentment of reinstated women introducing their husbands into the reserve community).

On a more positive note, the amendments have the potential of creating many benefits. One of the greatest of these is family reunification, as some women expelled from their home reserve will now be able to return to parents, siblings, etc. Their children will also no longer be deprived of frequent interaction with their grandparents and other members of their extended family. This, then, is an integrative effect that will partially counteract the disintegrative effects cited above. A related benefit is that this family reunification will strengthen the family support systems that are often so tenuous in the city. Indian culture should also be strengthened through the more frequent exposure of the returnees to it (e.g., exposure to grandparents who can pass on traditional Indian legends, skills, and language). In a similar vein, the ability to return to their home reserves will reduce the sense of marginality felt by many of the exiles and strengthen in them a positive sense of identity and self-worth. Another benefit is related to the fact that the demands of Indian government and Indian political organizations (e.g., for skilled labour and skilled leaders) are so great as to exceed the capability of the Indian male labour force alone to meet them. To the extent that the reinstatees participate in the collective endeavours of Indian communities and organizations, the pool of talent will be deepened, the burden on Indian males may be somewhat lightened, and the "burnout" rate among Indian males could conceivably decline.

For the individual returnees there are other important benefits to be reaped from the amendments, including tax exemption for income earned while residing on the reserve, financial support for their children's post-secondary education, and access to other entitlements enjoyed by registered Indians. In leaving the city to live on the reserve, returnees and their children will also reduce their exposure to non-Indian police and may reduce their likelihood of coming into conflict with nonIndian law. In addition, the removal of penalties for marrying out will likely result in more of these women marrying their non-Indian partners rather than living common-law with them. This may have both positive and negative consequences.

Finally, two additional benefits for reserve-based Indian communities should be mentioned. These are the larger tax base that will result for Indian governments as a result of the incorporation of returnees into the jurisdiction of those Indian governments, and the deepening of the pool of human talents within Indian communities as a result of the incorporation of these women and their spouses and children.

These are just a few of the plausible consequences of the 1985 amendments to the Indian Act. The extent to which they will become manifest will vary from community to community. As a process without parallel in the history of immigration and ethnic relations in

Canada, the reinstatement phenomenon warrants the close scrutiny of sociologists and policy-planners interested in the broader field of social impact assessment.

Recognition of Aboriginal Rights

In 1969 Prime Minister Pierre Trudeau, in defending the white paper, said:

> It's inconceivable, I think, that in a given society one section of the society have a treaty with the other section of the society. We must all be equal under the laws and we must not sign treaties amongst ourselves. . . . Our answer is no. We can't recognize aboriginal rights because no society can be built on historical "might-have-beens."[4]

In a letter to Indian leader Dave Courchene, Trudeau wrote around that same time:

> If the Indian character can survive only by the protection of special legislation, then it will disappear on its own account. . . . But our diversity must continue on its own merits, not artificially through special legislation or by seeking the protection of history.[5]

Significantly, less than fifteen years later that ahistorical, "survival of the fittest" orientation had been replaced by a fundamentally different world view. As noted in the introduction to Part Four of this book, at the 1984 First Ministers' Conference on Aboriginal Constitutional Matters Trudeau's opening remarks included the following:

> [W]e are not here to consider whether there should be institutions of self-government, but how those institutions should be brought into being; what should be their jurisdictions, their powers; how they should be fit into the interlocking system of jurisdiction by which Canada is governed.

Obviously, much had changed in the interim. Foremost among those changes was the 1973 Supreme Court of Canada decision on the Nishga land claim. The fact that three out of seven eminent jurists – intellectual peers of Trudeau – could rule in favour of aboriginal rights led him to reconsider his government's policy of refusing to recognize what he had contemptuously called "historical 'might-have-beens.' " The ensuing policy reversal, announced publicly seven months after the Supreme Court handed down its decision, marked a turning point in Indian affairs in Canada. Whether they recognized it or not (and subsequent documents suggest that they did not), by agreeing to compensate Indians for aboriginal title never extinguished

400

by treaty or superseded by law, government officials were sounding the death knell to assimilationist policy. Indians through their treaties or their aboriginal rights in effect had been given the special status of "citizens plus," which the Hawthorn Report had recommended in the 1960s. Rather than aboriginal rights being able to be "bought out" through financial compensation and then assimilation proceeding apace, the recognition of aboriginal rights would be used by Indians as a wedge in the door and as a foundation on which to build the institutions that would affirm their difference. Contrary to the liberal ideology's emphasis on equal rights for *individuals*, Indians would seize upon the Supreme Court decision and the federal policy reversal to make the case for *collective* rights, including the right to reinstate Indian laws and Indian governments with jurisdiction over a long list of fields. Indeed, by 1978 even the federal government's own policy statements on aboriginal claims had abandoned their assimilationist tenor and contained provisions, such as economic development by Indian-controlled corporations, that were collectivistic in orientation.

Thus, probably more than any other prior event in Canadian history, the Supreme Court's decision on the Nishga case stands as an important watershed in the decolonization of Indians. It set in motion a series of changes that have acquired a momentum – a sense of what has been called "cumulative directionality" – that, sociologically and politically, is probably irreversible. It led, for instance, to a land claims settlement policy that provides substantial sums of money (and hence the capacity for a degree of economic self-determination) and varying forms of input on many of the key decisions that will affect the claimants' daily lives in the future. Even more importantly, it led eventually to the *constitutional* recognition of, and to a certain degree of constitutional protection for, aboriginal rights.

The entrenchment of aboriginal rights in the constitution in 1982 is another watershed in the decolonization of Indians in Canada. Of paramount importance in this regard is the realization, by all parties concerned, that the constitution's recognition of "existing aboriginal rights" could conceivably be interpreted by the courts to mean the right to aboriginal governments with sovereignty over a broad range of jurisdictions. This prospect, and the uncertainty involved in not knowing for sure how the courts would rule if the issue were ever put to them in a test case of Indians' choosing, provides the incentive for the federal and provincial governments to negotiate with Indians, albeit probably toward the nonIndian governments' goal of some limited range of jurisdiction for Indian governments. The outcome of these negotiations will strike at two of the central pillars of colonialism – the system of indirect rule whereby local Indian leaders act as agents for implementing the policies and decisions of nonIndian power-holders, and the control exercised by those external authorities over the daily lives and decision-making of Indians.

The recognition of aboriginal rights in the constitution was also instrumental in bringing about the creation of the Special Parliamentary Committee on Indian Self-Government (the Penner Committee). This Committee's report marked such a fundamental change in world view on the part of Parliament as to constitute what social scientists call a "paradigm shift." That is, it reconceptualized Indian government so profoundly as to yield new insights, new problems, new relationships, and new possibilities for development.[6] Furthermore, it provided a major boost in legitimacy for the concept of Indian self-government and, in recommending the dissolution of the Department of Indian Affairs and Northern Development, inflicted a severe blow on the vehicle of implementation of the government's past colonial policy. Although DIAND by no means can be pronounced dead just yet, and may in one form or another remain an important actor in the lives of some Indians (e.g., those with only a rudimentary form of self-government), it now appears likely that before the decade expires DIAND will have undergone some profound changes severely limiting its mandate and capacity to be an instrument of colonialism.

The Nishga decision, the Penner Report, and certain policy changes that evolved between them have contributed to the institutionalization of another important development. I refer here to the recognition of governments based on ethnicity rather than on territoriality. The liberal ideology, to which both leading federal political parties subscribe, regards individual rights as paramount and collective rights as an anathema, particularly in the sense of special rights being granted on the basis of racial criteria. To the liberal, government ("the state") is first and foremost an instrument for maintaining law and order, achieving economic and social progress, and creating the conditions of individual liberty. Based on reason and rationality, it is the antithesis of the emotionalism that underlies the notion of the "nation-state." For the liberal, the state also has social obligations, such as ensuring that material goods and rights are distributed in a rational and just fashion among its citizens. On the other hand, the nation-state, which is to say the governing body of a political unit whose boundaries are coterminous with those of the ethnic group, distinguishes certain types of individuals – calling them "nationals" – and in pursuing its primary obligation of protecting their best interests is bound to discriminate against non-nationals. The liberal is particularly concerned that that discrimination by the nation-state will be of an authoritarian character. Furthermore, the liberal points out that the individual in the nation-state has other interests (e.g., those stemming from his/her occupation, education, social position, etc.) than those which stem from his/her ethnicity. The nation-state is thus seen by the liberal as being unrealistic in expecting to be able to exact from the individual full devotion to the ethnic cause. Finally, liberal philosophers believe that the nation-state is bound to destroy itself because minorities will continually be discovered within a majority and those minority groups will then develop a sense of ethnicity and will seek to secede to form their own new nation-state. Yet, as events have unfolded, federal politicians have thoroughly compromised the liberal ideology's important tenet of opposition to group rights and have even gone so far as to entrench group rights in various places in the constitution.[7]

Two other important changes flowing from the recognition of aboriginal rights should also be mentioned. By entrenching aboriginal rights in a constitution that can only be amended with the consent of the provincial governments, politicians have given to provincial governments a new prominence in Indian affairs. So far the provinces have given more indication that they will be a conservative rather than an innovative force in the move toward decolonization. They and their constituents have a vested interest (particularly in terms of resource revenues, land, and keeping their jurisdictions intact) in the status quo, which will not be relinquished easily. The final point to be made is that a new dimension has been added to status Indians' aboriginal rights by the 1985 Supreme Court of Canada decision in the Musqueam case. As part of the federal government's exploitative colonial orientation, the Indian Affairs Branch down through the years had often acted ostensibly on Indians' behalf but actually against Indians' best interests, particularly in selling or leasing Indian lands to non-Indians. The decision in the Musqueam case affirmed the Indian Affairs Branch's trust responsibility to status Indians. In so doing, it paved the way for numerous other bands also to claim substantial damages from the federal government for the Indian Affairs Branch's failure to live up to its trust responsibilities. This has already had an observable effect on the behaviour of DIAND staff and will likely become institutionalized in government directives, the main thrust of which will be non-colonial or anti-colonial in nature.[8] For instance, in relations between bands and third parties (e.g., persons wishing to lease band land), DIAND is now likely to pull back to let bands do more for themselves, thus minimizing the department's vulnerability to other lawsuits claiming that DIAND did not act in Indians' best interests.

The Politicization of Indians and Indian Affairs

A final major characteristic of the period since the release of the 1969 white paper is the politicization of Indians and Indian affairs. This period was by no means the beginning of Indians' politicization, for various political efforts had been undertaken earlier in the twentieth century, particularly after World Wars I and II.[9] However, during the 1970s and 1980s Indians' political skills within the Canadian political system were refined and the whole issue of aboriginal peoples and their concerns became implanted on governments' political agendas. During this period, too, Indian politics became "nationalized." With the formation of the National Indian Brotherhood, political cleavages and rivalries previously played out in other forums (e.g., provincial associations) now were raised at the national level along with the new and old interregional and intertribal rivalries. Indian leaders thus found themselves confronted with the task of articulating Indian needs in the context of a very heterogeneous constituency.

Two early changes of particular significance occurred as a direct result of the politicization of Indians. One was the Trudeau government's decision, at least formally, to abandon the 1969 white paper and its individualistic orientation designed to assimilate Indians. The other was the federal government's adoption of the policy of Indian control of Indian education. Both were a direct result of a concerted lobbying effort by Indian political leaders. The first was a necessary prerequisite for the subsequent policy reversal on aboriginal rights (discussed above). The second, although hindered for many years by implementation problems rooted in the federal government, is an important milepost on the road to decolonization. Its significance lies in the fact that under this policy the schools are being turned from an instrument of colonization (in the sense of destroying Indian culture and identity and propagating a racist ideology) into an instrument of decolonization. That is, in Indian-controlled schools Indian languages and cultures are being taught, Indian identity is being reaffirmed, and Indian students are no longer being alienated and pushed out of the system into the ranks of the unemployed where they serve as a potential pool of cheap labour in the larger Canadian economy. Instead, in increasing numbers those students are proceeding to post-secondary education where they are acquiring the skills to take on responsibilities from the federal government. Indian control of Indian education is thus of pivotal importance in the evolution of Indian self-determination.

The politicization of Indians and "nationalization" of Indian politics has also meant that Indian politicians can make important political gains with their own constituency by denouncing the federal government in general and DIAND in particular. The behaviours of these latter two actors have provided no shortage of grist for this Indian political mill. One outcome has been that Indian leaders have often succeeded in their demands to replace the arbitrary discretionary decision-making, which characterized the Indian Affairs Branch at the height of the colonial era, with meaningful Indian participation in resource allocation decisions, even if less so in the development of the actual broader policies themselves. Through a generation of harangue that culminated in testimony before the Penner Committee, Indian politicians have succeeded in so effectively undermining DIAND as to lead to its likely emasculation. Although that will constitute perhaps the first nail in the coffin of the colonial regime, it is by no means to be assumed that Indians will be free of the enormous bureaucratic encumbrances the federal government is fully capable of imposing by design or by default.

In the Northwest Territories the combination of the demographic composition of the population and the politicization of Indians and other Natives has resulted in the choice of a Native as government leader during each of the last two legislative sittings. There, Natives are acquiring invaluable experience at governing, although the colonial relationship the Northwest Territories, as a *region*, has with the federal government imposes a ceiling on the range of experience they can acquire.

In the 1980s the great heterogeneity of the national Indian constituency is posing major problems for the aggregation and articulation of Indian interests to the federal and provincial governments. Building and maintaining a national Indian consensus is proving impossible beyond the level of the most abstract of first principles. However, the grassroots Indian constituency may be becoming restless both with first principles and with the stalemate that has emerged on the implementation of constitutionally entrenched principles of self-government. Symbolic victories can sustain them only so long in the face of daily adversity. Perhaps partly as a consequence of this we are experiencing in the mid-1980s a "denationalization" of Indian politics. The Assembly of First Nations, for instance, has become a shifting coalition into and out of which members move at will, sometimes turning their "guns" on each other in the process. This and DIAND's new emphasis on community-level initiatives raise the likelihood that the next generation of Indian politicians (through to the turn of the century) may achieve the greatest progress toward further decolonization at the level of individual communities or district-level "supra" governments. There the problems of consensus-building, demand aggregation, and accountability are reduced to manageable proportions that do not convulse the entire Indian body politic. This is one reason why, in the introduction to Part Three, I suggested that it is time for Indian leaders at least to consider a new constitutional strategy involving building up Indian institutions at the community level and using them to test the degree of elasticity of the present constitution. This we observed being done with some degree of success in the chapter on Kahnawake. Such a change of strategy involves turning away from efforts to vest Indian interests in the nonIndian state and embracing instead a commitment to the maximum feasible degree of institutional completeness of local-level Indian states and Indian communities. [10]

Finally, it is worth mentioning that the mobilization of Indian political energies has occurred under an ideology of self-determination. The larger Canadian political community has not been unresponsive to that manner of casting the issue. Through intensive political lobbying on constitutional matters native organizations have made significant progress in educating provincial and federal bureaucrats and political leaders as to the present need for that self-determination, the historical precedents for it, and the prospective benefits it offers for the future. Resistance is softening and with the turnover in the ranks of the provincial premiers in the mid-1980s, we possibly shall see an extension of the scheduled constitutional conferences (due to expire in 1987) to the end of the decade. How productive that would be, though, is an entirely different matter.

The Road Ahead

In the early 1980s self-government appeared to be the central issue around which all other Indian issues revolved. The road ahead, it appeared, would be mapped almost entirely in terms of the landmarks of self-government. Over a relatively short period of time, though, that view of the future has been called into question on many fronts, some of which are discussed in detail in the preceding pages. The constitutional express train has practically ground to a halt. Practical problems, such as those identified in Gibbins's chapters, loom large in any thorough assessment of the "implementability" of self-government. The very notions of sovereignty being promoted by Indian political leaders have come under attack as a betrayal of fundamental Indian values. Some Indian communities are losing interest in self-government and constitutional pursuits, due in part to their members' perceptions that the future portends more bureaucracy and more external elites, albeit Indian, directing their lives and absorbing funds that they feel could be put to better use at the grassroots level in the community. Indians themselves point to problems in overcoming the dependency mentality, to problems in delegating and distributing responsibility, and to the security (although not necessarily comfort) of the present accommodations that some Indian individuals have reached with the status quo. Said one interviewee at Kahnawake, a community that can boast of considerable accomplishments:

> Its's hard to overcome the dependency mentality. We've come a long way, but we need to overcome the fear of taking that next big step. It seems that each step is a very painful process of self-doubt and fear, and before taking it we have to make sure there are safeguards in place. We are almost afraid to take the risk, for fear of losing. Yet what have we got to lose?

Even a majority of a sample of Indian "leaders-in-training" (status Indian university students in native studies programs in the Prairie provinces) in a survey in 1981 expressed reservations about whether Indians are ready for self-government. [11] Finally, it has even been suggested (by an Indian) to the author that some Indian political organizations pursuing self-government and constitutional reform not only operate without a mandate from the grassroots of Indian communities, but also are so far out ahead of their constituents that they dare not seek a mandate now.

In short, from the vantage point of the mid-1980s, self-government appears to be far off on the horizon for most Indian communities. However, Indian communities are unlikely to play the role of passive victims of the status quo. On the contrary, members of Indian communities across the country are asserting themselves with increasing frequency and effectiveness to develop the local institutions which, in small but tangible ways, give them increased control over their own life. Particularly noteworthy here are band efforts in the fields of language training and child welfare. [12] Both of these fields are fundamental building blocks, or first steps, for fortifying culture and retrieving or protecting an Indian identity, and as such they are likely to take on increased prominence during the last half of the 1980s. Indeed, in some respects it is surprising that language preservation has not received a higher priority from Indian communities. Furthermore, it is a field in which Indian governments can make important symbolic accomplishments without having to rely too heavily on external funding. Economic development also will take on increased importance during the remainder of the 1980s and may be linked with the more sociological side of community development.

As the above remarks of the Kahnawake resident attest, the decolonization journey has been an arduous one to this point. It is likely to continue to be just as taxing. It is entirely conceivable, though, that out of the struggle will emerge models of decolonization that will be emulated not only elsewhere in Canada but also elsewhere around the world.

Notes

1. The present example is a good illustration of the "damned if you do, damned if you don't" predicament in which federal policy-makers frequently find themselves in grappling with Indian issues. The passage quoted in the text was extracted from a larger passage recommending that housing programs apply equally on-reserve and off-reserve. While this policy is subject to the criticism that it seeks to undermine self-government by attracting Indians away from reserves, a policy of housing assistance for reserves only is subject to the criticism that the federal government is failing to live up to its constitutional responsibilities to all Indians.

2. For a discussion of the native women's movements, see Caroline Lachappelle, "Beyond Barriers: Native Women and the Women's Movement," in Maureen Fitzgerald *et al.* (eds.), *Still Ain't Satisfied: Canadian Feminism Today* (Toronto: The Women's Press, 1982). For a useful bibliography on the broader topic of native women, see Kathleen Jamieson, *Native Women in Canada: A Selected Bibliography* (Ottawa: Supply and Services Canada, Catalogue #CR22-17/1983E, 1983).

3. It should be noted that the provision empowering bands to determine their own membership codes could have somewhat of a mitigating impact on these changes.

4. Quoted in Sally M. Weaver, *Making Canadian Indian Policy* (Toronto: University of Toronto Press, 1981), p. 179.

5. *Ibid.*, p. 180.

6. The reconceptualization was not original to the Penner Committee, for Indian leaders had been advocating a comparable approach for years. Rather, this was the first time that a parliamentary body had adopted this reconceptualization and fleshed out many of the institutional ramifications of the conceptualization.

7. Reference here is not only to aboriginal, treaty, and land claim rights, but also to the rights of official language minorities (English and French) and, in what may yet prove to be a "sleeper" clause with far greater ramifications than the framers of the constitution envisaged, the affirmation of the multicultural character of Canada.

8. However, there is also the likelihood that the Musqueam decision will lead to greater secrecy within DIAND.

9. For a discussion of the history of Indian political organizations, see J. Rick Ponting and Roger Gibbins, *Out Of Irrelevance* (Scarborough, Ont.: Butterworths, 1980), pp. 196-98, and the references cited there.

10. The term "vesting Indian interests in the nonIndian state" is based on Raymond Breton, "The Vesting of Ethnic Interests in State Institutions," paper presented to the Calgary Sociology Colloquium, University of Calgary, March, 1984. If the interests of some group or category of people are "vested" in state institutions, they are routinely taken into account by public authorities in the handling of state affairs. Examples of Indians' attempts to get Indian interests vested in the institutions of the Canadian state are the constitutional revision process, the Joint National Indian Brotherhood/Cabinet Committee (1974-78), and the National Indian Brotherhood's strategy described in Chapter One as "engagement."

11. J. Anthony Long and Menno Boldt, "Concepts of Indian Government Among Prairie Native Indian University Students," *Journal of Canadian Studies*, XX, 1 (1984), pp. 166-77.

12. By 1985 about one band in every five was operating its own child welfare program, while almost three-quarters of all bands administered the DIAND social services program. See Canada, *1986-87 Estimates – Indian and Northern Affairs Canada: Part III, Expenditure Plan* (Ottawa: Supply and Services Canada, 1986), p. 2-50.

Glossary

Block funding: A form of government financing given to organizations or to other governments, whereby the funds are designated for certain very broad substantive areas (e.g., criminal justice) rather than for narrow programs (e.g., a courtworker program) and the accountability requirements are minimal. This stands in contrast to another form of financing, conditional grants-in-aid, in which the funds provided can be used only for certain narrow purposes and in accounting for the manner in which the funds were spent the recipient government or organization must demonstrate that the conditions under which the grant was made have indeed been met.

Boundary maintenance: The preservation of social and/or physical boundaries between a people (typically an ethnic group) and the larger society in which they live. This is accomplished by various mechanisms, such as the prohibition of mixed marriages, the regulation of entry to and exit from the ranks of the ethnic community, and the establishment of institutions operated by members of the ethnic community to meet the needs of other members of that ethnic community.

Categoric discrimination: Unjust treatment suffered by individuals because others have classified them as belonging to a stigmatized (usually visible) category of people. The categories may exist in the popular culture of a society or in the norms, regulations, and form of organization of the government, such as in the apartheid system of South Africa.

Caveat: A statement of legal interest in a parcel of land; a warning to others who might be considering undertaking some activity on, or purchase of, that parcel of land that the title to that land might carry a legal encumbrance.

Comprehensive claims: A type of aboriginal claim which, as defined by the federal government, meets the following criteria: treaties were never signed with the claimants; the territory in question was traditionally used and occupied by the aboriginal people involved in the claim; and aboriginal rights were never extinguished. An example is the claim of the James Bay Crees that was settled in the James Bay and Northern Quebec Agreement.

De facto: In fact, whether by right of law (*de jure*) or not.

Defeasible estates: A property interest capable of annulment or liable to forfeiture.

Ethnocentrism: A belief in the inherent superiority of one's own group or that group's way of doing things.

Experienced labour force: The total labour force minus unemployed persons fifteen years of age and older who have never worked or who have worked only prior to a certain date (January 1, 1980, as the term is used in Chapter Two).

Fee simple absolute title: The most encompassing (least encumbered) type of property ownership under British law. Fee simple absolute title is of infinite duration, freely alienable, and without any other person's interests impinging upon it. This term is sometimes shortened to "fee simple title."

Ideology: A set of interrelated attitudes, opinions, beliefs, perceptions, and ideas that shape our understanding of the world and guide our actions.

Infant mortality rate: The number of deaths to children before they reach the age of one year per 1,000 live births in a given year. Stillborn births are not included in the calculation of births or deaths.

Institution: The belief systems and the organizational structures that characterize relatively distinct sectors, segments, or industries in society.

Internalization: Acceptance, in one's own mind, of the validity of the views and assessments (often pejorative) of others, and the basing of subsequent behaviour on those views.

Kahnawakeronon: The people of Kahnawake.

Latent function: Underlying (often unintended) purpose, use, or contribution.

Liberal democracy: A political system of majority rule, universal adult suffrage, and secret ballot, where the major value is placed on the rights and freedoms of individuals and the role of the state is envisaged as primarily that of maintaining law and order impartially, achieving social and economic progress, and creating the conditions of individual liberty.

Liberal democratic ideology: Belief in the justness and desirability of liberal democracy.

Loan/loss ratio: The ratio of the total value of loans extended (by a financial institution) to the total value of loans defaulted.

Matrifocal: A term describing a social system where social relations are centred on the mother, often due to the absence of the father.

Matrilineal: A term describing a kinship system in which descent is traced through the mother.

Matrilocal: A term describing a social system in which the married children live in the community, or the household, of the wife's family.

Orthography: That part of the grammar of a language that is concerned with the lettering used and the accepted ways of spelling.

Particularistic: Having reference to the idiosyncratic characteristics of a certain individual, group, organization, or situation; often associated with favouritism shown toward relatives or others known personally by a social actor.

Primary-sector occupations: Such occupations as hunting, fishing, trapping, farming, forestry, logging, and mining.

Secondary-sector occupations: Mainly manufacturing, processing, and machine production occupations.

Stratification: A system of unequal allocation of power, prestige, privilege, and wealth.

Tertiary-sector occupations: Managerial, professional, technical, service, sales, and clerical occupations ("white-collar" jobs).

Total institution: An institution, such as a convent, prison, mental hospital, or ship, in which all of the daily needs of the residents (inmates) are met by the authorities in control of the institution. The relationship between the authorities and the inmates is often characterized by coercion exercised by the authorities and dependency on the part of the inmates.

Transfer payments (government): Includes family allowances, old age security pension, guaranteed income supplement, Canada or Quebec pension plan benefits, unemployment insurance benefits, social assistance payments, and other cash payments to individuals from any level of government; excludes salaries and wages of public servants and moneys paid for services rendered under contract to a government.

Trust obligations (relationship): The obligations of the federal government to act in the best interests of Indians when acting on their behalf in a trusteeship capacity. These obligations, which are rooted in the treaties and the Indian Act, are akin to those exercised by one country vis-à-vis another that has been made a protectorate of the first.

Usufructuary right: The right to use a certain parcel of land, as in hunting, fishing, trapping, and gathering, but without full ownership (fee simple title) over that land.

Universalistic: Having reference to one common standard applied equally to all without favouritism toward any.

Zero sum game: A situation, often in negotiations, where gains made by one of the parties to the relationship can be made only at the expense of the other party to the relationship.